Competitive Strategies in the Pharmaceutical Industry

Competitive Strategies in the Pharmaceutical Industry

Edited by Robert B. Helms

The AEI Press

Publisher for the American Enterprise Institute
WASHINGTON, D.C.

1996

Available in the United States from the AEI Press, c/o Publisher Resources Inc., 1224 Heil Quaker Blvd., P.O. Box 7001, La Vergne, TN
37086-7001. Distributed outside the United States by arrangement with
Eurospan, 3 Henrietta Street, London WC2E 8LU England.

Library of Congress Cataloging-in-Publication Data

Competitive strategies in the pharmaceutical industry / edited by
    Robert B. Helms.
        p.   cm.
    Includes bibliographical references.
    ISBN 0-8447-3882-4 (cloth : alk. paper)
    1. Pharmaceutical industry.   2. Drugs—Prices.   3. Competition,
International.   I. Helms, Robert B.
    HD9665.5.C66   1995
    338.4'76151—dc20   95-18401
                                                                      CIP

ISBN 0-8447-3882-4 (alk. paper)

THE AEI PRESS
Publisher for the American Enterprise Institute
1150 17th Street, N.W., Washington, D.C. 20036

Printed in the United States of America

Contents

v

LIST OF FIGURES

Contributors

DONALD L. ALEXANDER is associate professor of economics at Western Michigan University. Mr. Alexander has held faculty positions at the College of William and Mary and Penn State University and positions with the Federal Trade Commission, Capital Economics, and the International Trade Commission. His current research interests include: R&D productivity in the pharmaceutical industry, the demand for ethical pharmaceutical drugs, telecommunication bypasses of the local exchange network, and the effects of motor carrier deregulation on highway safety in the interstate trucking industry.

CLAUDE E. BARFIELD is director of science and technology policy studies and coordinator of trade policy studies at the American Enterprise Institute. He has served as a consultant to the Office of the U.S. Trade Representative and is the author of the Reagan administration's "Statement of Trade Policy." Before joining AEI, he was a staff member for the Senate Committee on Governmental Affairs, a deputy assistant secretary for research and development at the Office of Policy Development and Research at the Department of Housing and Urban Development, and the science and technology reporter for the *National Journal*.

J. HOWARD BEALES III is associate professor of strategic management and public policy at the George Washington University School of Business and Public Management. In 1987 and 1988 Professor Beales served as a branch chief in the Office of Management and Budget's Office of Information and Regulatory Affairs. From 1983 to 1987 he was associate director for policy and evaluation in the Bureau of Consumer Protection at the Federal Trade Commission. Professor Beales has published numerous articles on the economics of information and its application to consumer protection problems, including *State and Federal Regulation of National Advertising* (1993).

ERNST R. BERNDT is professor of applied economics at the Massachusetts Institute of Technology's Alfred P. Sloan School of Management and research associate at the National Bureau of Economic Research. He serves as head of the economics, finance, and accounting faculties at Sloan. Before joining MIT, he was on the economics faculty at the University of British Columbia and was an economist in the Executive Office of the President, where he helped administer President Nixon's wage and price controls. At MIT, Mr. Berndt has published extensively on issues surrounding the measurement of productivity growth and more recently has focused on factors affecting the U.S. pharmaceutical industry.

JOHN E. CALFEE is a resident scholar at the American Enterprise Institute and was a visiting senior fellow at the Brookings Institution. He spent seven years as a member of the marketing faculties of the University of Maryland and, later, the Graduate School of Management at Boston University. He served in the Bureau of Economics at the Federal Trade Commission, where he focused on consumer protection policy including regulation of food and drug advertising. He is a frequent contributor to *Advertising Age* and the *Wall Street Journal*, and he is the author of scholarly articles on topics including advertising regulation by the FDA and the FTC.

KENNETH W. CLARKSON is professor of law and economics and director of the Law and Economics Center at the University of Miami, a research and educational institute focusing on economic analysis of public policy issues and providing economics education to professional audiences. In addition to serving as consultant to various public and private organizations, he was the associate director for human resources, veterans, and labor at the Office of Management and Budget. Mr. Clarkson's Ph.D. dissertation examined economic aspects of hospital management.

IAIN M. COCKBURN is assistant professor of policy analysis and strategy in the Faculty of Commerce at the University of British Columbia. He teaches courses on technology strategy, industry analysis, and public policy. His research focuses on the economics of technological change and problems of productivity measurement, with a particular focus on the pharmaceutical industry.

WILLIAM S. COMANOR is professor of economics at the University of California, Santa Barbara, and also professor of health services at the School of Public Health at the University of California, Los Angeles. At UCLA, he is director of the Research Program in Pharmaceutical Economics and Policy. He published "The Political Economy of the

Pharmaceutical Industry," in the *Journal of Economic Literature*, and his doctoral dissertation was entitled "The Economics of Research and Development in the Pharmaceutical Industry." He has also served as chief economist and director of the Bureau of Economics at the Federal Trade Commission. He has written widely on antitrust economics and other topics in industrial organization.

PATRICIA M. DANZON is Celia Moh Professor at the University of Pennsylvania's Wharton School, where she is chair and professor of the Health Care Management Department, and professor of insurance and risk management. Before joining Wharton, she held positions at the University of Chicago, Duke University, and the RAND Corporation. She has been widely published in the fields of health care, insurance, and liability systems. She has been elected to the Institute of Medicine of the National Academy of Sciences. She has served as a consultant on international health care issues to the World Bank, the New Zealand government, the Asian Development Bank, and the U.S. Agency for International Development.

HENRY G. GRABOWSKI is professor of economics and director of the Program in Pharmaceuticals and Health Economics at Duke University. Before joining Duke in 1976, he was a visiting scholar in the Office of Research at the Health Care Financing Administration. He was also a research associate at the National Bureau of Economic Research and an assistant professor at Yale University. He has written extensively on the economics of innovation and government regulation of business. His works include *The Regulation of Pharmaceuticals: Balancing the Benefits and Risks* (coauthored with John Vernon), and "Pharmaceuticals and Health Care Costs," in *Proceedings of the International Health Care Forum, Health Care Policy and the Pharmaceutical Industry*.

PAUL E. GREENBERG, a vice president of Analysis Group, specializes in the application of industrial organization economics and finance theory to complex business problems in health economics. Mr. Greenberg's research and analysis in this area include pharmacoeconomic investigation in clinical trials, development of simulation models of treatment strategies, cost-of-illness research relating to clinical depression, and public policy analysis of the antitrust implications of consolidation in the health care sector. He is a member of the American Economic Association, the American Bar Association, and the National Association of Business Economists.

ZVI GRILICHES is Paul M. Warburg Professor of Economics at Harvard University and program director of productivity and technical change at the National Bureau of Economic Research. He was the Taussig Research Professor at Harvard University and the Einstein Visiting Fellow at the Hebrew University, Jerusalem. He also taught at the University of Chicago. He is a member of the National Academy of Sciences and past president of the Econometric Society and the American Economic Association. His major fields of interest are econometrics, productivity and technical change, the economics of education, and agricultural economics. His current research focuses on estimating the returns to research and development, the analysis of patent statistics, and the measurement of prices and quality change.

RONALD W. HANSEN is associate dean for academic affairs at the William E. Simon Graduate School of Business Administration at the University of Rochester. He is responsible for academic programs and faculty development at the Simon School. His primary research is in drug-development policy and the regulation of the pharmaceutical industry. He served on the study committee on the "Children's Vaccine Initiative" at the Institute of Medicine. His teaching interests include public economics, particularly cost-benefit and cost-effectiveness analysis.

W. BRIAN HEALY is executive director of economic and industrial policy at Merck & Company, Inc. He is responsible for the development of Merck's Human Health Division policy and strategic initiatives in the key areas of health care financing and reform cost containment. Mr. Healy headed the economic affairs department and developed Merck's international pricing function into a model for the industry and established Merck's Centre for European Government Affairs in Brussels. Before joining Merck in 1976, he was an assistant professor of international political economy at the University of Pennsylvania.

ROBERT B. HELMS is a resident scholar and director of health policy studies at the American Enterprise Institute. He has written and lectured extensively on health policy, health economics, and pharmaceutical economic issues. He has recently edited three of AEI's publications on health policy, *American Health Policy: Critical Issues for Reform*, *Health Policy Reform: Competition and Controls*, and *Health Care Policy and Politics: Lessons from Four Countries*. From 1981 to 1989 Mr. Helms served as assistant secretary for planning and evaluation and deputy assistant secretary for health policy in the Department of Health and Human Services.

REBECCA HENDERSON is associate professor of strategic management at the Massachusetts Institute of Technology, where she specializes in technology strategy and problems of product and process management. Her current research focuses on the pharmaceutical industry. Before joining MIT, she worked for the London office of McKinsey and Company. Her publications include "Underinvestment and Incompetence as Responses to Radical Innovation: Evidence for the Photolithographic Industry," in the *RAND Journal of Economics*, and "Scale, Scope and Spillovers: The Determinants of Research Productivity in the Pharmaceutical Industry," in the *RAND Journal of Economics*.

PETER BARTON HUTT is a partner in the law office of Covington & Burling, where he specializes in food and drug law. From 1971 to 1975 he served as chief counsel for the Food and Drug Administration. Mr. Hutt has been a lecturer on the history of government regulation of the pharmaceutical industry for the postgraduate course in clinical pharmacology, drug development, and regulation at Tufts University and teaches a course on food and drug law at Harvard Law School. He has published numerous books and articles, including *Food and Drug Law: Cases and Materials* (coauthored with Richard A. Merrill).

PAULINE M. IPPOLITO is an economist with the Bureau of Economics at the Federal Trade Commission. She has held a variety of management and staff positions since joining the FTC staff in 1979. Her research interests include the economics of information and advertising in consumer product markets and the design of public policy governing advertising and labeling claims. In recent years she has focused on the role of advertising in food markets and has been active in assessing the current debate about the best policy toward diet-disease claims for food products.

JOSEPH M. JADLOW is professor and head of the Department of Economics at Oklahoma State University, where he has taught courses in industrial organization since 1968. His doctoral dissertation analyzed the economic effects of the 1962 Drug Amendments on innovation and market structure in the pharmaceutical industry. He has since studied the effects of market structure on rates of innovation in therapeutic drug markets and the implications of prescribing generic drugs. His research also examines rent-seeking behavior and the implications of alternative property rights structures on the technical efficiency of hospitals.

DAVID I. KASS is coordinator for health statistics at the Bureau of Economic Analysis of the U.S. Department of Commerce. Before joining the bureau, Mr. Kass was director of resource analysis and management systems for the assistant secretary for health at the Department of Defense, as well as senior health economist at both the Federal Trade Commission and the General Accounting Office. He has published numerous articles in the fields of health economics, industrial organization, and corporate finance. His recent research has focused on the measurement of health care prices and expenditures within the national economic accounts.

WILLIAM C. MACLEOD is a partner in the law firm of Collier, Shannon, Rill & Scott. From 1986 until 1990 he was director of the Bureau of Consumer Protection of the Federal Trade Commission, the chief enforcement agency governing advertising, franchising, and credit practices. Before coming to Washington, Mr. MacLeod headed the FTC's Chicago Regional Office. Mr. MacLeod has also served as adviser to the chief of the antitrust division and the chairman of the FTC.

JEFFREY S. MCCOMBS is associate professor of pharmaceutical economics and policy in the School of Pharmacy at the University of Southern California. He joined the faculty in 1987 and holds joint appointments in the Schools of Gerontology and Public Administration at USC. His previous positions include assistant professor at Johns Hopkins University and social science research analyst with the Health Care Financing Administration. Mr. McCombs is the author of numerous articles in professional journals, such as the *Journal of Health Economics* and *Medical Care*. He has served as a consultant to the Health Care Financing Administration and several pharmaceutical companies.

STEWART C. MYERS is Gordon Y. Billard Professor of Finance at the Massachusetts Institute of Technology's Sloan School of Management and director of MIT's International Financial Services Research Center. He is past president and director of the American Finance Association and coauthor of the leading graduate-level textbook on corporate finance. His research is primarily concerned with the valuation of real and financial assets, corporate financial policy, and financial aspects of government regulation of business. He is a research associate of the National Bureau of Economic Research and is active as a financial consultant.

JONATHAN RATNER is Associate Director for Health Financing Issues at the U.S. General Accounting Office. He is responsible for research studies on health financing topics such as international comparisons of pharmaceutical prices, the factors driving U.S. hospital costs, and evaluation of Medicare's methodology for paying health maintenance organizations. Before joining the GAO in 1984, he taught at Wellesley College and the State University of New York at Albany. He is the author of professional articles on macroeconomics, forecasting, and defense economics and is a contributor to GAO reports on the federal budget deficit, the defense budget, and the social security trust fund.

ROBERT ROGOWSKY is director of operations at the U.S. International Trade Commission. Previously, he was director of the ITC's Office of Industries, and he also served as the executive assistant to a previous chairman. He was deputy director of the Bureau of Consumer Protection at the Federal Trade Commission, acting executive director of the Consumer Product Safety Commission, economics adviser to commissioners at the CPSC, and a research economist at the FTC. He has published a number of studies on antitrust and regulation, including *Relevant Markets in Antitrust* and *Political Economy of Regulation*.

FREDERIC M. SCHERER is Larsen Professor of Public Policy and Management at the John F. Kennedy School of Government at Harvard University. He also taught at the University of Michigan, Northwestern University, and Swarthmore College. His research specialties are industrial economics and the economics of technological change. He is the author of *Mergers, Sell-Offs, and Economic Efficiency, Industrial Market Structure and Economic Performance*, and *International High-Technology Competition*. His research as a U.S. Census Bureau fellow centered on how the R&D spending of U.S. companies reacts to import competition.

LAKSHMI SHYAM-SUNDER is an analyst at the World Bank. She was previously a visiting professor at the Massachusetts Institute of Technology's Sloan School of Management and assistant professor of business administration at the Tuck School at Dartmouth College. Professor Shyam-Sunder conducts research on the interaction of corporations with capital markets, and her primary interests are the relationship between capital structure and real investments and the motivation for firms' financing choices.

JAMES H. SINCLAIR is branch chief of the nondurable goods section of the Producer Price Index Program that develops price indexes in the foods, chemicals, pharmaceuticals, fuels, and construction industries. He first joined the Bureau of Labor Statistics to work on the Consumer Price Index Revision team in 1974 after having been an assistant professor of economics at Dunbarton College of Holy Cross. Mr. Sinclair served one year as an economic consultant for Ruttenberg, Friedman,

Kilgallon, Gutchess and Associates. He recently published "An Experimental Price Index for the Computer Industry," in the *Monthly Labor Review*.

VALERIE Y. SUSLOW is associate professor of business economics and public policy at the School of Business Administration at the University of Michigan. She is also a faculty research fellow at the National Bureau of Economic Research. Professor Suslow's teaching and research interests are in the field of industrial organization. In the course of her research she has performed empirical analyses of problems that are of strategic interest to firms in concentrated industries. She has written on the issues of recycling, pricing of durable goods, pricing over the business cycle, and cartel contract duration. Currently, she is studying pricing of brand-name pharmaceutical goods.

LACY GLENN THOMAS III is associate professor of organization and management at Emory Business School, Emory University. Before joining the Emory faculty, he held positions at the Brookings Institution, the University of Illinois, the Graduate School of Business at Columbia University, and the Stern School of Business at New York University. His research focuses on the overlap between strategic management and government industrial policy. He is writing a book contrasting the industrial policies of ten nations toward the pharmaceutical industry and the impact such policies have on the global competitiveness of firms based in these nations.

JOHN M. VERNON is professor of economics at Duke University. He also served on the faculties of the University of Bristol and Harvard University. Professor Vernon was project director at Marketing Science Institute in Cambridge, Massachusetts. His research interests include industrial organization and public policy, the economics of innovation and regulation, and applied microeconomics. He has published numerous books and articles in those areas, including *Economics of Regulation and Antitrust*, coauthored with W. K. Viscusi and J. Harrington.

1
Introduction

Robert B. Helms

This volume is a continuation of a series on pharmaceutical economics and policy that I edited for AEI from 1975 through 1981 (Helms 1975, 1980, 1981). Two decades have now elapsed since the first volume and fourteen years since the last. After such a passage of time, one might expect a substantial difference in the topics addressed in the present volume because of major changes in the industry and the health care marketplace. There are differences, but they are mostly in data, methodology, and emphasis. In reviewing those earlier volumes, I am struck by the similarity of the issues this volume explores to issues the earlier volumes addressed. The competitive performance of the industry, for example, and the effects of Food and Drug Administration regulation continue to be the focus of the economists studying the pharmaceutical industry.

The similarity of the issues does not mean that the industry has not encountered economic changes. Indeed, changes have occurred both on the demand side in terms of how pharmaceuticals are marketed and on the supply side with respect to research and development. The growth of government programs in the United States and other developed countries and managed care in the United States have altered how pharmaceuticals are marketed and sold. Such change has shortened the expected revenue stream from most products at the same time that new technologies have increased both the cost and the medical attractiveness of those products.

Both pharmaceutical company managers responsible to their stockholders and policy makers responsible for managing the budgets of medical benefit programs have thus experienced new pressures. While the concerns of the 1970s about industry and FDA performance are still with us, the changing market has increased the intensity of those concerns. Managers of government and private health care programs are looking for new ways to reduce the cost of drug benefits, while company R&D managers are seeking ways to speed the regulatory process and develop new domestic and international markets to cover the increasing cost of research.

The simultaneous pursuit of those objectives has created some obvious conflicts driving public policy disputes in most developed countries. Both public and private buyers are attempting to purchase products on more favorable terms by demanding discounts or, as in the case of governments, by legislating some form of price controls. To the extent such policies reduce buyer costs, they threaten the industry's traditional source of funding for research and development of new products. When managers expect smaller future revenue for a successful product, they must reduce R&D expenditures and make more careful decisions (guesses) about which potential new products to pursue. To the extent that they guess correctly and concentrate their scarce research funds on the most promising products, they will improve the cost-effectiveness of the R&D process. But given the uncertainty in predicting the outcome of medical research, pharmaceutical companies may invest less in R&D and thus produce less new information.

Conflicts in public policy are intensified because the savings from lower prices seem real to consumers and health program administrators, while the potential losses are hypothetical. Those losses are more real to the scientists seeking specific information about scientific relationships and potential products. Both economic markets and political policy making attempt to balance those conflicting goals. But the balance reached by the two approaches is not the same—economic markets emphasize the long run while politics focus on the short run. Thus, we have the continuing dispute in economics and medicine about what is in the best interest of consumers. Contributors to this volume explore that debate.

This volume comprises five parts, four of which present recent research on various aspects of the continuing policy dispute. To summarize the research and look ahead, the fifth part offers several views on the future of the pharmaceutical industry. A synopsis of each of those parts follows.

Pricing and Competitive Dynamics

Armen A. Alchian, professor of economics at the University of California, Los Angeles, once told his graduate students that some of the biggest disputes in economics are about "what is on the horizonal axis." He was, of course, referring to the common practice of economists to explain changes in economic activity by using supply and demand graphs with price on the vertical axis and quantity on the horizontal axis. His point reminds us that the price we observe in any market is for a well-defined product of a given quality in a specific geographical market at a specific time. These are all real-world differences that may be "assumed away" in the often misunderstood, but extremely useful, process of making simplifying assumptions to build powerful economic models.

Nowhere is the dispute about the definition of a product more evident than in the measurement and comparison of pharmaceutical prices, the subject of the three chapters in this part. Each deals with some aspect of attempts to measure prices over time and between countries. Those analyses emphasize our need for a firm grasp of "what is on the horizontal axis" if we are to use price comparisons in discussions of industry performance or predictions about policy changes.

The chapter by Zvi Griliches and Iain Cockburn is part of a series of studies they have conducted on how the producer price index measures pharmaceutical prices. The authors use case studies of two products to assess the potential overstatement of pharmaceutical price increases that may result from the Bureau of Labor Statistics's practice of excluding the prices of new generic versions of a drug from the PPI. After recalculating the indexes, they show that the increases in prices measured by the BLS may actually have declined substantially when the prices of generic substitutes are included in the calculations.

The chapter by Ernst Berndt and Paul Greenberg takes a more aggregate look at the measurement of pharmaceutical industry prices by the BLS. They investigate two sources of potential bias in the BLS index: the effect of the limited sample of drugs the BLS uses and the effect of the BLS procedure that does not immediately include new products in the sample. They conclude that the BLS calculation and sampling procedures overstate industry price increases because they oversample old products and undersample new products. Since newer product prices rise more slowly than older product prices, those procedures substantially overestimate actual industry performance.

The chapter by Valerie Suslow tackles a problem that has always been a major issue in the economic interpretation of price indexes: the effects of changes in the quality of the products whose prices the index measures. The most straightforward interpretation of a change in a price index is that it measures a pure price effect of a standardized product that does not change over time. But that is hardly the case with technologically advanced products like pharmaceuticals, which are typically being improved.

Suslow uses a hedonic methodology to measure a quality-adjusted price index that she then compares with the unadjusted price indexes calculated by the BLS. She uses a large data base of prices

3

of anti-ulcer drugs for the years 1977 through 1989 as a basis for her comparisons. She finds that prices for those products did not increase as much as indicated by the BLS index as a result of changes in dosing regimes, the number of drug interactions, and information on side effects. She concludes that unadjusted price indexes do not account for quality improvements that are valued by physicians and patients.

James Sinclair of the Bureau of Labor Statistics, Joseph Jadlow of Oklahoma State University, and David Kass of the Bureau of Economic Analysis discuss those three chapters. Each discussant addresses the biases in the BLS's measurement of pharmaceutical prices and what can be done to correct them. Sinclair reports on several activities by the BLS to reduce those biases through more frequent and larger samples of products. While the BLS uses hedonic methodologies in some technologically changing industries, he is skeptical that the bureau will have the resources to apply such methods to pharmaceutical price measurements.

The International Market for Pharmaceuticals

There can be little doubt that the volume of international trade in pharmaceuticals has grown in recent years.[1] Such growth presents new issues and challenges to those who attempt to measure and compare the performance of the industry. Three chapters in this part of the book explore various aspects of the international behavior and performance of the industry.

Patricia Danzon offers a detailed discussion of the "uses and abuses" of international price comparisons, a topic that has received increasing attention in recent years in the United States and in Europe. She points out the theoretical and practical data problems inherent in attempts to provide meaningful comparisons. Not only are existing price indexes inappropriate for such calculations, but regulatory policies in many countries make it impossible to conclude that observed price differences represent the actual pricing strategies of producing companies. She illustrates how U.S. prices can be higher or lower than foreign countries' prices depending on the sample of products chosen,

---

1. While difficult to measure, the two following statistics illustrate that growth. Data from the Organization for Economic Cooperation and Development in 1980 constant dollars show that exports of drugs and medicines (SIC 3255) for all OECD countries increased from 23.5 percent of total production in 1982 to 28.5 percent in 1992 (National Science Board 1993). Annual surveys of U.S. member firms by the Pharmaceutical Research and Manufacturers of America (PhRMA) indicate that sales abroad as a percentage of total sales increased from 31 percent in 1970 to 34 percent in 1994 (PhRMA 1995).

the way they are matched up with competing products, the methods for measuring prices, and the units used. The illustrations are based on a comparison of price and sales data from the United States and eight other large producing countries. She concludes:

• Past studies of international drug price comparisons have over-stated the relative price of drugs in the United States.

• Both detailed price regulation and rate-of-return regulation create inefficiencies in the production of drugs and in the comparison of drug prices.

• Attempts to allocate joint costs and to measure the cost of produc-ing drugs as a guide for price comparisons are futile.

• No economic rationale can justify a single world price, and at-tempts to establish equal prices would not be in the best interests of consumers.

• The process of competition among rival health plans that attempt to attract consumers by providing and managing their drug benefits is a more efficient means of controlling costs than European regulatory schemes because consumers are given more choices about the types of benefits and services they desire.

Lacy Glenn Thomas analyzes the way that various countries' in-dustrial policies have affected competitive performance in interna-tional markets. Reviewing several measures of competitive performance, he finds two distinct groups of performers among the nine major producing countries. The United States, by far the most successful in international markets, leads Switzerland, Great Britain, and Germany, the group that he calls "strong competitive perform-ers." "Weak competitive performers" include France, Italy, Sweden, the Netherlands, and Japan. He looks at the industrial policies of coun-tries and the competitive strategies of major companies to identify the causes of the superior performance of the strong performers.

In defining industrial policy, Thomas includes a broad range of implicit and explicit government policies that determine the competi-tive environment in which the firm operates. He discusses three fac-tors—safety regulation, government funding of R&D, and price levels—that have been the driving forces behind the success of U.S. firms in global markets. Those policies combined to reward technologi-cally advanced firms that could capture the advantages of early intro-duction of innovative products. He contrasts U.S. policies with those of Japan and France to illustrate how the United States encouraged innovation and global success, while Japan and France developed in-dustries that concentrated on duplicative products for their domestic markets. His explanation of U.S. success illustrates how various ap-

5

proaches to health reform could either continue the successful performance of the U.S. industry or turn it into a relatively unsuccessful industry of the type found in other countries. Reform policies that help create more competitive health markets with their emphasis on cost-effective new technologies could lead to continuing success, while regulatory strategies with a narrow emphasis on cost containment could substantially change the performance of the U.S. pharmaceutical industry.

Donald Alexander examines the determinants of R&D productivity and the role that they play in the ability of a pharmaceutical firm to succeed in global markets. He uses data from twenty-six international firms for the years 1987 through 1989 to study the relationship between firm size and productivity. His results reveal three major conclusions:

- Firm size is an important determinant of R&D productivity.
- Firms with higher productivity do have higher market share in global markets.
- There is a positive relationship between the number of marketing employees and a firm's global market share.

Robert Rogowsky of the International Trade Commission, Jonathan Ratner of the General Accounting Office, and Brian Healy of Merck and Company discuss the chapters in part two. Rogowsky compares the findings of those studies with the studies of the International Trade Commission. He stresses the importance of uncertainty in affecting the decisions of pharmaceutical company managers and notes the considerable variation in the performance of any one company over time. Such uncertainty and variation are not always evident in studies that rely on industry averages. Ratner focuses primarily on the international price comparisons by Patricia Danzon. He points out several differences between Danzon's comparisons and those made by the General Accounting Office and makes several observations about the proper interpretation of differences in prices in different countries.

Healy discusses the three chapters in light of his experience of negotiating prices with several European governments or health authorities. In his view, the United States can learn from the European experience. As he points out, the Europeans have curtailed their provision of free health and social services and now stress cost containment and consumer cost sharing. In addition to price controls, companies in European markets also face the effects of individual countries' industrial policies that attempt to promote domestic industry. Such policies often conflict with the stated goals of the European Common Market. Such an atmosphere undermines the productivity of the pharmaceutical industry and reduces the number of new products available in Europe and in global markets.

The Risks of and Returns to Pharmaceutical Investment in Research

In this part, four studies explore the measurement of the pharmaceutical industry's performance. To the outsider, this may seem like a highly technical debate among economists. But this long-running controversy has important policy implications evident in congressional hearings from the 1950s until the present. The policy rationale for those who want more extensive economic regulation of the industry and those who want a more laissez-faire approach depends on arguments about the competitive performance of the industry. Those arguments involve such topics as the productivity of the industry, the profitability of the competing firms, and the way capital investors view the risks of pharmaceutical R&D. As the chapters illustrate, the long life cycle of pharmaceutical products and the process of competition through R&D and marketing strategies present challenges to the simple application of economic and accounting models as a guide to policy. The stakes in this debate are high, since a regulatory policy based on a misdiagnosis of the nature of competition among R&D-intensive firms could impose substantial costs on the industry and markedly reduce its productivity.

The study by Rebecca Henderson and Iain Cockburn looks at the determinants of research productivity in the industry. They use a detailed set of data based on the internal records of ten major pharmaceutical firms to study the reasons behind the industry's decline in research productivity. They document the decline over the past twenty years, as evidenced by the increase in the real costs of both research and development expenditures and the decline in important patents. They conclude that the diminution most likely cannot be explained by a shift of research to more difficult areas or by an increase in so-called racing behavior among competing firms. Instead of pointing to wasteful duplicative investment among firms racing to market, their results are more consistent with a hypothesis of significant spillover effects from investment in projects within the same firm and among competing firms. Henderson and Cockburn conclude that the presence of several competing firms in a single therapeutic area may increase social welfare. If spillover effects among competing firms are important, they caution against concentrating on the average cost of a single product. Such a practice, they assert, could substantially understate the resources required to discover a new drug.

Henry Grabowski and John Vernon use actual data on the costs of research and development and sales revenues over the life cycle of a sample of products introduced during the years 1980 through 1984 to calculate the returns to pharmaceutical R&D. They find that the mean internal rate of return is within one percentage point of the industry's cost of capital. Thus, they find no evidence of large excess returns from that sample of products. They also find that the distribution of returns is highly skewed, with only the top decile of products in the sample earning very high returns. They use data on that sample to simulate the effects of regulatory policies designed to reduce industry rates of return. They find that a policy of limiting the net present value of the top decile of drugs to the average of industry R&D costs would have reduced the net present value of the average new drug introduced in the 1980 through 1984 period by $82 million. When only a small proportion of new products achieves above-average returns, regulating the returns of only the successful products would have a substantial negative effect on the incentives to undertake the investments necessary to achieve successful new products.

To contrast the probable effects of regulation with the effects of more competitive pharmaceutical markets, they simulate the effect on average rates of return under the assumption that generic drugs achieve substantial market domination following the expiration of the patent for products in the sample. They find a negative effect of about $30 million on the average product's net present value, a much smaller effect than the $82 million they simulate for a regulatory policy aimed primarily at successful products.

A major issue in the measurement of industry performance is the cost of capital faced by the investing firm, a cost that all analysts agree is affected in capital markets by the risks associated with each investment. As evidenced by the Office of Technology Assessment's major study of pharmaceutical R&D, the cost of capital has been used as the standard for judging the reasonableness of industry rates of return (U.S. Congress 1993).[2] The chapter by Stewart Myers and Lakshmi Shyam-Sunder assesses what modern financial analysis can contribute to the measurement of the cost of capital for the pharmaceutical industry. They provide a detailed discussion of both the conceptual problems of measuring the cost of capital and the practical problems of using publicly available financial data to measure the various components of those calculations. They emphasize the difficulties in measuring the risk of pharmaceutical investment projects. Their measurements of the nominal and real cost of capital for seventeen major

---

2. See especially appendix C, pp. 276–83, which is based substantially on a background paper prepared for OTA by Lakshmi Shyam-Sunder and Stewart Myers.

U.S. research-intensive firms for the years 1980, 1985, and 1990 show, for example, that the average cost of capital for those firms in 1990 was about 15 percent in nominal terms and about 10 percent in real terms. They also find that smaller pharmaceutical firms face higher costs of capital. In conclusion, they assert that all their calculations are lower-bound estimates of the cost of capital, since the sequential investments involved in pharmaceutical R&D involve higher risks than established products that face only the risks of production and selling.

Kenneth Clarkson examines the effect of intangible capital, specifically investment in R&D and promotion, on accounting rates of return. Since standard accounting practices do not include investments in intangible capital in measurements of profitability, accounting rates of return among industries have systematic biases. Industries with high investments in intangible capital will have high accounting rates of return when compared with industries with less of those investments. Clarkson illustrates the magnitude of those measure biases in two ways: the recalculation of rates of return for one pharmaceutical firm and the calculation of economic and accounting rates of returns for fourteen industries.

In the first illustration, he finds that one large pharmaceutical firm's average rate of return on equity from 1980 through 1993 declined from 30.4 percent to 14.6 percent when intangible expenditures are treated as capital investments. In the second illustration, he calculates economic and accounting rates of return for ninety-nine firms in fourteen industries. Comparing average industry rates of return, he finds that uncorrected accounting rates of return for the pharmaceutical industry are twelve percentage points greater than the average for all fourteen industries. When corrections are made for intangible capital investments in R&D and promotion for all of the ninety-nine firms, the pharmaceutical industry's above average rate of return is reduced to only 3.1 percentage points. On the basis of those comparisons, Clarkson concludes that the high profitability measures of the pharmaceutical industry used in public policy debates are, in large part, an accounting illusion. The result has been an overemphasis of the monopoly explanation of firm behavior in congressional hearings and in the economics literature. He calls for a more careful study of the measurement of firm and industry profit rates to eliminate those systematic (and correctable) measurement errors.

Frederic M. Scherer of Harvard University and William Comanor of the University of California, Los Angeles, both economists with many years of experience researching the pharmaceutical industry, discuss those four chapters. Both attempt to bring out the common themes they see in the studies to explain the economic performance of

9

the industry in the past two decades. Scherer uses the findings of the authors to discuss his views about what is really guiding the behavior of firms. He discusses several competitive strategies that might explain industry performance and concludes that monopoly rents are almost completely dissipated as a result of competition, even though the firms adopt a wide variety of strategies. Comanor focuses on the long-standing political concern about the profitability of the industry. Since there is no question that firms in the pharmaceutical industry possess market power, the political question focuses on the legitimacy of the profits. He discusses the studies' findings regarding the role of profits and raises several questions about the assumptions used in each study. In conclusion, he asserts that attention should be paid to the differences in the firms in the pharmaceutical industry because they are not homogeneous.

Cost-Effective Information and Promotion

Lester Telser (1981) provided an extremely informative explanation of the economic behavior of both producers and users of pharmaceutical products. An integral part of his explanation is the role of information: how it is produced and how it is used. He pointed out:

> The product of a drug company is not merely the physical drug. It is a joint product consisting of a number of attributes, all of which the physician has come to recognize and appraise (186).

By concentrating on the role of information, Telser provides a logical explanation of how the production of information adds value to the physical product and allows the producing company to capture a return on an intangible capital investment with many of the attributes of a public good.

Part four of the volume continues the Telser tradition of concentrating on the role of information as a key ingredient of competitive strategy in the industry. The three chapters look at different aspects of the production, use, and regulation of information in the pharmaceutical industry, an industry that has undergone some important changes since Telser's explanation of industry behavior. In particular, since the late 1970s, the industry has been characterized by increased entry of branded products in most therapeutic markets, increased competition from generic products, and the growth of the managed care segment of the health care market, which has placed more emphasis on the cost-effectiveness of pharmaceutical products. At the same time, the FDA has changed the way it regulates the use of information. Those changes have raised questions about the value of various types of information to physicians and consumers and the effects of such regulation on the competitive behavior of the industry.

Advertising has played a contentious role in policy debates about the performance of the pharmaceutical industry. To critics of the industry, advertising is a wasteful activity that misleads physicians and enhances the profits of the industry. But to most economists and business analysts, advertising is a cost-effective way of educating physicians and promotes both competitive entry into new markets and lower prices. Indeed, a series of empirical studies attempts to shed light on the actual effects of producer-provided information.[3] In "New Uses for Old Drugs," J. Howard Beales provides the latest in that series of serious empirical studies.

To measure the effects of various types of promotional activities, Beales compares the characteristics of a large sample of therapeutic markets before and after FDA approval of additional uses for existing drugs. Such approval allows a company to advertise the new uses of the product to physicians. Before those additional uses are advertised, physicians may use a drug for any purpose they choose, but they have to rely on word of mouth or medical journals to learn about additional uses. Beales uses that change in the legal ability of companies to promote additional uses of their products to measure the effects of their promotional activities. His sample consists of 201 observations on seventeen drug and indication combinations that received FDA approval for an additional indication between 1984 and 1987. He focuses primarily on the effects of journal advertising and direct promotion to physicians (detailing) on changes in therapeutic market share and competitive prices.

Beales finds that before the new approval, physicians do respond to the information they receive from journal articles. But he finds a much greater effect on physician use once the company is allowed to tell physicians about the new use in its journal advertising and detailing activities. Therefore, consumers benefit from the greater use of the more appropriate therapy, the company benefits from the faster growth in market share, and prices are lower than they would have been without the increased competition from the new product. Beales concludes that the FDA's regulatory policy of insisting on prior approval before producer-provided information can be disseminated imposes significant costs on consumers. To enhance consumer welfare, he calls on the FDA to relax its efforts to tighten such regulation and to

---

3. J. Howard Beales provides an extensive list of references to that literature.

do what it can to shorten the time it takes to approve new uses for old drugs.

John Calfee looks at how the FDA regulates pharmaceutical information. He compares FDA regulation of advertising claims for products for which the agency does not regulate market approval with its regulation of products for which it does have power over market approval. He finds a difference in the behavior of both the FDA and the regulated industries in those two situations. Firms whose products do not require FDA approval for marketing have been more aggressive and successful in challenging the FDA's attempts to extend control over advertising claims and practices arbitrarily. But firms whose products must be approved by the FDA before marketing have been extremely reluctant to challenge the FDA's gradual extension of regulatory control over advertising claims. Calfee refers to that result as "the leverage principle," whereby the FDA uses its power over the approval process to extend its regulation over product information far beyond any basis found in legislation.

In the process of describing his comparison of industry responses to regulatory power, Calfee reviews the literature on the economic effects of commercial advertising. He predicts that the FDA's "information lag" will likely increase because the effects of suppressed information are not always obvious in the marketplace. He finds substantial evidence that the FDA has suppressed the dissemination of information that would benefit consumers. He discusses several legal and regulatory changes that could help correct the FDA's overregulation of pharmaceutical information by eliminating the agency's ability to use the leverage principle.

Ronald Hansen provides a third perspective on the role of information in pharmaceutical markets by examining the emerging field of pharmacoeconomics or cost-effectiveness studies of pharmaceutical products. After presenting a brief history of that new field of study, he explains why various changes in the market for pharmaceuticals have increased the demand for such studies. He compares the advantages of studies that emphasize economic costs and benefits with those of studies that emphasize medical outcomes or quality-of-life measures. Each has its own use depending on the importance of the physician, the patient, or the third-party payer in selecting products.

While Hansen points out the marketing and medical advantages of cost-effectiveness studies, he also reviews the potential biases and misuses of such studies. Although such studies could provide useful information in pharmaceutical markets that are placing increasing emphasis on economic competition and comparative economic costs, whether those studies will be cost-effective themselves depends on whether researchers can develop methodologies for this field that users can trust to yield unbiased and dependable information. Hansen believes that professional peer review is more likely than government regulation to create such acceptance.

William MacLeod of Collier, Shannon, Rill & Scott, Pauline Ippolito of the Federal Trade Commission, and Jeffrey McCombs of the University of Southern California discuss the chapters on information and promotion. MacLeod and Ippolito both point out the reluctance of politicians and public health officials to consider the role of commercial advertising in health-related markets. Ippolito focuses mostly on the study of advertising by Howard Beales. She raises several questions about his methodology, especially whether he can distinguish between the effect of FDA certification and the effect of promotion. But she strongly supports his and other empirical studies that provide evidence of the effects of advertising on consumers and on the incentives of producers. McCombs, perhaps reflecting his experiences in California, discusses each of those studies in light of the growth of managed care in health markets. Among other things, he points out that the increased purchase of drugs by managed care organizations should reduce the political concern about prices since those large buyers have strong incentives to negotiate for lower prices. Managed care incentives also increase the demand for cost-effectiveness studies but at the same time should reduce any need for those studies to be included in the FDA approval process. He also points out that the growth of managed care may decrease the effectiveness of physician-focused advertising relative to direct-to-consumer advertising. Thus, Beales's findings on the effectiveness of advertising may not hold in future markets.

The Future of the Pharmaceutical Industry

In this part of the volume four short essays speculate about the future of the pharmaceutical industry. None of the four individuals, including the editor, has ever been employed in the industry. But three of us, Frederic M. Scherer, Peter Barton Hutt, and I, have been students of the industry for most of our careers. While not a specialist on the industry, Claude Barfield, a student of the economic and political factors affecting international trade, brings a different view on the prospects for the industry in world markets.

My own essay, which introduces this discussion, presents concerns about the effects of direct government regulation of the process of innovation and discovery. Although the expectations of managers in any industry are always important, they play a crucial role when the life cycle of products involves long periods of time, large up-front

13

investment costs, delayed revenues, and great uncertainty. In such situations government controls can have strong and immediate effects on investment decisions. Competitive markets can also affect managers' expectations, but unlike government controls, the expectation of future competition does not remove the incentive to develop new and cost-effective products that can benefit future consumers. I believe that the best way to achieve an efficient rate of innovation is to avoid both government price controls and any action that will protect firms from the effects of market competition.

Frederic M. Scherer points out that recent advances in science could create another golden age of pharmaceutical discovery, if we do not adopt bad public policy to hinder that potential. Bad policy could evolve from U.S. adoption of either price controls or British-style rate-of-return regulation. He points out that either direct government regulation or the increased power of purchasers could reduce industry margins, but between the two he would prefer to let the power of buyers control the market. Market competition would create the right incentives to search for and develop new and beneficial therapies. Government does not know how to bring about the right results through direct economic regulation.

Peter Barton Hutt provides "ten easy lessons" on how to destroy the pharmaceutical industry. Among the ten, he discusses how our present policies raise the costs of clinical investigation, delay the approval of new products, impose taxes on producers, discourage exports, and prohibit public education about drug use. He contends that the United States practices all ten now. To achieve the potential of the industry, those public policies must be reformed.

Claude Barfield looks at the future of trade and industrial policy and notes that the economics profession does not know how to tell the government which industries and technologies should be selected for special treatment. He reviews a number of trade and industrial policy ideas being promoted by the Clinton administration and asserts that it is far from certain that such interventions in the market will succeed in achieving the stated objectives. He warns the pharmaceutical industry that the growing competitiveness of international markets makes the success of government industrial and trade policies highly unlikely.

References

Helms, Robert B., ed. *Drug Development and Marketing.* Washington, D.C.: AEI Press, 1975.

———. *The International Supply of Medicines: Implications of U.S. Regulatory Policy.* Washington, D.C.: AEI Press, 1980.

————. *Drugs and Health: Economic Issues and Policy Objectives.* Washington, D.C.: AEI Press, 1981.

National Science Board. *Science and Engineering Indicators*, 1993.

Pharmaceutical Research and Manufacturers of America. *U.S. Pharmaceutical R&D and Sales.* Washington, D.C.: Pharmaceutical Research and Manufacturers of America, January 1995.

Telser, Lester G. "The Market for Research and Development: Physician Demand and Drug Company Supply." In *Drugs and Health*, edited by Robert B. Helms. Washington, D.C.: AEI Press, 1981, pp. 183–221.

U.S. Congress, Office of Technology Assessment. *Pharmaceutical R&D: Costs, Risks, and Rewards*, OTA-H-522. Washington, D.C.: Government Printing Office, February 1993.

PART ONE
Pricing and Competitive Dynamics

2
Generics and the Producer Price Index for Pharmaceuticals

Zvi Griliches and Iain M. Cockburn

Drug prices and their rate of inflation are matters of central concern to the health care reform debate. This chapter addresses an important issue in measuring movements in drug prices: how to account for the effect of patent expirations and generic entry. Loss of patent protection often brings about dramatic changes in the market for a prescription drug. Typically, generic versions quickly become available, selling at discounts of 30 percent to 50 percent below the price of the branded product, and large numbers of consumers switch away from the brand. It is not uncommon for generic producers to reach a 50 percent quantity share of the market within a year after the patent expires. These movements in prices and quantities imply substantial welfare gains for those consumers who (like the Food and Drug Administration) regard the branded and generic products as being more or less perfect substitutes, which are not captured by the current methods used by the statistical agencies to compute price indexes such as the producer price index. This chapter applies some alternative procedures that allow for this effect to detailed data on the wholesale drug prices, with quite startling results. For one of the drugs examined, a price index calculated using the standard methodology *rose* by 7 percent over the forty-five months following patent expiration, while our preferred alternative fell by 48 percent. We conclude that the currently calculated PPI for pharmaceuticals may be a rather poor indicator of actual prices paid for drugs and concomitant changes in consumer welfare.

This chapter is a summary and an extension of Griliches and Cockburn (1993). We acknowledge financial support from the Bradley Foundation, the Sloan Foundation, and the National Science Foundation. We are indebted to E. Berndt, J. Hellerstein, J. Rosett, and S. Ellison for work done on the IMS data.

19

New Goods and Price Indexes

The appearance of generic versions of an existing drug is but one instance of the pervasive and difficult problem presented by new goods and quality change in constructing price indexes. Price indexes compare prices and quantities of a bundle of goods in period 1 to prices and quantities in some base period 0, and the problem presented by the appearance of a new good in period 1 is that p^0 and q^0 are undefined. The statistical agencies address this problem by periodically revising the consumption bundle and "linking in" new commodities to the existing index (Early and Sinclair 1983). The difficulty with this procedure is that it rules out making any comparison between new goods and existing goods: only changes in the prices of new goods after their appearance in the marketplace contribute to the overall index. Price differentials between the new commodity and comparable existing commodities, interpretable as reflecting differences in quality, are ignored. This may be appropriate for some commodities, which are truly "new," but surely not for all. Furthermore, as a matter of policy, the statistical agencies define commodities very narrowly—treating almost every variation in characteristics such as packaging, color, sales outlet, or manufacturer as the appearance of a new, distinct, different commodity. While this approach may be defensible in some circumstances, it can lead to some serious difficulties. For example, the rise of discount and self-service retail outlets has left almost no trace in the official statistics of prices and production (Reinsdorf 1993). Arguably, in attempting to solve the quality-change problem, the statistical agencies have aggravated it.

The theoretical answer to this problem is well known (Fisher and Shell 1971, 1972): set $q^0 = 0$ and estimate p^0 as the reservation price of the new commodity in the base period, that is, the price at which the demand for this particular commodity (or version) would be zero. To implement this in practice requires estimating demand models that may have burdensome data requirements or entail making heroic assumptions about functional form. For example, for new goods that differ from existing goods along measurable characteristics, the hedonic price index approach could be used to infer the reservation price.[1] Alternatively, the recent literature on preferences for variety and differentiated product markets (Dixit and Stiglitz 1977; Spence 1976; Grossman and Helpman 1991; Feenstra 1994) suggests assuming a constant elasticity of substitution form for the utility function over varie-

---

1. See Griliches (1971, 1990) and Suslow (1992) for an application to pharmaceuticals.

ties, which implies a reservation price of infinity for a new commodity. Here we take advantage of the very close similarity between branded and generic versions of a drug to construct price indexes based on a much simpler linear random-utility demand model: consumers buy the branded version when their valuation of "brandedness" exceeds the price premium paid over the generic version, and the reservation price of the representative consumer is just the mean valuation of brandedness.

Generic Drugs as New Goods

Generic drugs present a particularly simple case of the new-goods problem because they are a variety of a previously existing good that is identical in almost all respects to the previously available version. Unlike many other commodities, in this case a government agency, the Food and Drug Administration, certifies generic drugs as being therapeutically equivalent to the branded version in their "Orange Book" publication, *Approved Drug Products with Therapeutic Equivalence Evaluations*. The generic version differs only in packaging (including the inert matter enclosing the active ingredients), in labeling, and in provenance. In all but a few cases, the products sold by generic entrants to the market are certified by the FDA to be perfect substitutes for the incumbent's branded product in that their active ingredient is chemically identical and that they are "bioequivalent" in the sense of being statistically indistinguishable from the incumbent's product in key aspects of therapeutic use, such as blood concentration profiles.

Equivalence between branded and generic drugs is a hotly debated topic. Products certified as "therapeutically equivalent" by the FDA are: (1) pharmaceutically equivalent, in that they contain the same active ingredient(s), are of the same dosage form, are identical in strength and route of administration, and meet applicable standards of purity and quality; (2) bioequivalent, in that *in vivo* or *in vitro* tests show that a product meets statistical criteria for equivalence to the reference drug in the rate and extent of absorption of the active ingredient and its availability at the site of action; (3) adequately labeled; and (4) manufactured in compliance with Current Good Manufacturing Practice regulations. Therapeutically equivalent products may nonetheless vary in characteristics such as shape, color, flavor, scoring, packaging, labeling, and shelf life. Those apparently trivial factors may still influence the clinical effectiveness of the drug insofar as they affect patients' ability to distinguish between different tablets and dosages, or their readiness to take the medicine at the times and in the amounts prescribed. Therapeutic equivalence ratings also do not take into account

21

differences in stability under adverse storage conditions, or possible reactions by patients to coloring or preservative ingredients.

Taking the FDA at its word—"a pill is a pill is a pill"—the correct price index is straightforward to calculate, being just the average price of a drug across all suppliers. Taking the opposite extreme position, that of the statistical agencies such as the Bureau of Labor Statistics, implies treating generic versions of the drug as entirely distinct commodities. The fact that not all consumers treat branded and generic versions as being fully equivalent lends some support for this second position. But many consumers do switch to the cheaper generic versions once they become available, either because they perceive no difference between brand and generic varieties or because they take the price differential as more than sufficient compensation for any difference in quality. Thus, excluding the gains that they experience from the appearance of generics in the marketplace renders movements in official indexes of drug prices potentially rather badly biased indicators of changes in consumer welfare. We present below some alternatives to those two extreme positions, which we believe more accurately reflect changes in welfare.

Two Case Studies

Figures 2–1 through 2–4 illustrate developments in the market following expiration of patents for two quite different drugs, cephalexin and prazosin. Cephalexin, an antibiotic developed and marketed by Eli Lilly under the brand name Keflex, is widely prescribed for conditions such as ear or respiratory tract infections. Prazosin is an antihypertensive developed and sold by Pfizer under the brand name Minipress. In the year preceding patent expiration, wholesale sales of Keflex were $270 million in 1986, while wholesale sales of Minipress were $118 million.[2]

Several interesting features are apparent in those figures. For several years before patent expiration, both incumbent producers raised

---

2. The data series are computed from wholesale invoices sampled by a market research firm, IMS America. While revenues are simply the total monthly sales of the drug, the price series are a significant summary of the raw data. Each drug is sold in as many as thirty distinct "presentations"—variations in formulation (capsules, tablets, syrups), packaging, and quantity per package. The incumbents' price series are a monthly Tornqvist-Divisia Index computed from monthly revenues and quantities of each presentation of the branded product. The generics' price series are computed similarly, but with information from a changing number of manufacturers. Quantity shares are the ratios of "quantities" calculated by deflating total revenues by those price indexes.

FIGURE 2–1
BRAND VERSUS GENERIC PRICE OF CEPHALEXIN

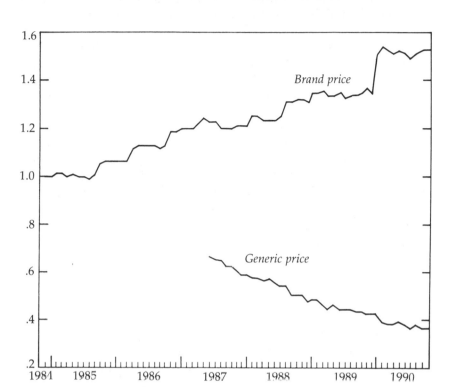

prices steadily at roughly the general rate of price inflation. In both cases generics enter at a very substantial price discount, which slowly widens over time as the incumbent continues to raise its price roughly at the rate of inflation and competition between generic manufacturers pushes down their prices. When the patent on Keflex expired in April 1987, generics entered at an average discount of 46 percent, which widened to over 66 percent over the next two years. The price gap is somewhat wider for Minipress: the generic price discount was 42 percent at entry, which widened to 85 percent after two years. Several years after patent expiration, generics had gained a significant quantity share in both markets, although the incumbent retained a respectable share of revenues.

Interestingly, generics were much more successful at penetrating the market for cephalexin than for prazosin: in the two years after patent expiration, their share of quantities rose from 34 percent to 80

23

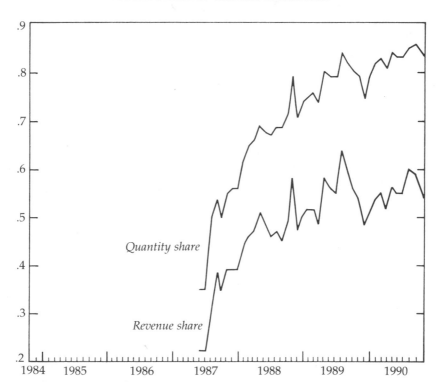

FIGURE 2–2
MARKET SHARE OF GENERIC CEPHALEXIN

percent, while their revenue share went from 22 percent to just over 50 percent. In contrast, generic entrants achieved only a 52 percent share of quantities in the prazosin market that they won by offering much deeper price discounts. Generics had only a 17 percent share of prazosin sales two years after patent expiration. We speculate that this reflects a greater degree of risk aversion on the part of consumers and physicians confronted with a more serious medical condition requiring a much more precise dosage of the drug.

Those changes in market share and relative prices in our data are consistent with the results of a number of previous studies, which report on larger numbers of drugs.[3] We note that quantities respond rather slowly to movements in relative prices, reflecting "diffusion" of

3. For richer detail and analysis, see Masson and Steiner (1985), Grabowski and Vernon (1992), Hurwitz and Caves (1989), and Caves, Whinston, and Hurwitz (1991).

FIGURE 2–3
BRAND VERSUS GENERIC PRICE OF PRAZOSIN

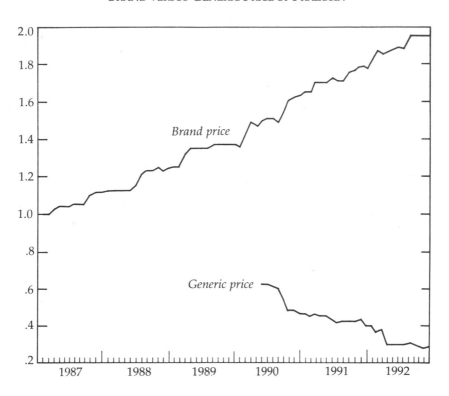

generics through distribution channels, and gradual accumulation of information about the availability, relative price, and quality of generics.

Given the rather large price differentials, it is striking that not all consumers switch to the new, cheaper variety. For this to make sense, consumers must differ in their expectations about the efficacy and quality of generics, despite what the FDA says, and some of them prefer to pay much higher prices for the branded version. This implies significant heterogeneity of tastes, but standard consumer theory is rather uneasy with this fact. We invent the concept of the representative consumer who consumes a bit of every variety, taking one branded and two generic pills every day!

Alternative Indexes

Tables 2–1 and 2–2 present results from computing price indexes for cephalexin and prazosin using a number of different approaches. The

FIGURE 2–4
MARKET SHARE OF GENERIC PRAZOSIN

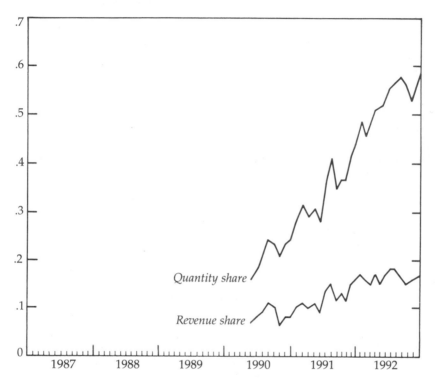

first of these, labeled "BLS," attempts to approximate the outcome of the official PPI procedures, had they been applied to those data. Besides the "linking in" issue, which has been our focus up to this point, these procedures have a number of well-known problems. First, the official market baskets are changed rather slowly. The four-to-five-year rolling sampling basis used in constructing the market baskets that make up the PPI and CPI does not pick up the appearance of new goods fast enough. Like many other "new goods," generics tend to experience significant price declines in the earlier part of their life cycle.[4] Second, because the official indexes have fixed weights, which are revised rather infrequently, the growing market share of generics means that they are underweighted even once they make it into the index.

---

4. For additional evidence and discussion of this, see Triplett's discussion in Foss et al. (1993).

TABLE 2–1
ALTERNATIVE PRICE INDEXES FOR CEPHALEXIN

Cephalexin (87.04 = 1.00)	Time after Entry				
	First month	Six months	One year	Two years	Three years
Monthly					
BLS	.99	.97	1.00	1.00	1.07
Tornqvist-Divisia	.99	.95	.94	.88	.86
Paasche (u)	.91	.87	.86	.80	.78
Fisher Ideal, $p^r = p_b$	.93	.89	.88	.82	.80
Tornqvist-Divisia, $p^r = p_b$	.91	.88	.87	.79	.79
Paasche (u), diffusion adj.	.91	.82	.77	.66	.62
Average price	.83	.71	.63	.51	.47
Yearly					
Paasche (u)			.81		
Tornqvist-Divisia, $p^r = p_b$			.82		

NOTE: (u) signifies adjustment for uniform distribution of brand preference.

TABLE 2–2
ALTERNATIVE PRICE INDEXES FOR PRAZOSIN

Prazosin (90.05 = 1.00)	Time after Entry				
	First month	Six months	One year	Two years	Three years
Monthly					
BLS	1.01	1.08	1.13	1.21	N/A
Tornqvist-Divisia	1.01	1.07	1.11	1.12	N/A
Paasche (u)	.97	1.02	1.06	1.07	N/A
Fisher Ideal, $p^r = p_b$	1.01	1.03	1.08	1.09	N/A
Tornqvist-Divisia, $p^r = p_b$	1.00	1.06	1.10	1.11	N/A
Paasche (u), diffusion adj.	.97	1.01	1.02	.97	N/A
Average Price	.92	.92	.92	.71	N/A
Yearly					
Paasche (u)			.99	.83	N/A
Tornqvist-Divisia, $p^r = p_b$			1.01	.84	N/A

N/A = not applicable.
NOTE: (u) signifies adjustment for uniform distribution of brand preference.

The official PPI was based on a basket of drugs chosen in 1981. It was rebased in January 1988, using information collected in 1987 (and earlier) on value shares to sample individual products.[5] Thus, for cephalexin, for example, we "link-in" generics at 88.01 into a Laspeyres type index, with a relative weight of 0.27, their revenue share during the first quarter of their availability in mid-1987.[6] The resulting index dramatically illustrates the problems of slow introduction of new goods and using fixed weights: three years after generics entered the market, with well over half of the quantity sold being purchased at a generic discount of over 50 percent, the BLS index is *up* by 7 percent.

We can easily solve those two problems by collecting more timely and more detailed data and by switching to a chain-weighted index formula such as Tornqvist-Divisia. Following the spirit of the BLS, treating generics as new commodities with no direct price comparisons to existing goods, we computed a standard Tornqvist-Divisia index (so labeled in the tables) that introduces generics quickly—in the second month following their entry—and continually revises their weights in the overall index as they gain market share. This index falls quite rapidly for cephalexin and implies a much lower general inflation rate than our BLS index for prazosin. Taking the opposite approach, we also calculated Tornqvist-Divisia and Fisher's Ideal indexes, in which consumers switching to generics are assumed to have done so from a reservation price of $p_r = p_b$, the price of the branded product in the month of entry, but have a base-period share of zero.

We also computed an average price index, taking the FDA at its word and treating all sources of the drug as equivalent. These fall very rapidly: two years after patent expiration, the average price of cephalexin fell by about 50 percent, with prazosin falling by 30 percent. Comparing this index with the Tornqvist-Divisia index gives a measure of how serious the "pure" generics problem is. Faster introduction of generics and quickly changing weights account for only about half the distance between the BLS and FDA extremes.

Clearly, some adjustment for the introduction of generics is indicated. This requires taking account of two phenomena that stand out in the data: the heterogeneity of tastes for "brandedness," or equiva-

---

5. See Berndt, Griliches, and Rosett (1993) for details.

6. This is probably already an overestimate of what the BLS might have been able to do at the time, both because actual lags in the availability of information are likely to be longer and because the establishments sampled were most likely based on lists collected in 1986 or earlier and may not have contained generics-producing plants, to the extent that they were new, rather than a redirection of the output of an existing plant.

lently in reservation prices, and the relatively slow diffusion of generics.

Taking account of heterogeneity of tastes requires some reformulation of price index theory. Fisher and Griliches (1992) argue that despite the underlying fact of consumer heterogeneity, aggregate Paasche and Laspeyres computations are useful in providing bounds for the social planner's ideal index (which gives the minimum amount needed to keep each individual on his base utility level when prices change). In Griliches and Cockburn (1993) we present formulas for such aggregate indexes in a world in which consumers purchase one of two goods: the branded or generic version of a particular drug. The choice is modeled in a simple, linear, random-utility framework: generics are chosen by individual h if $p_b > p_g + b_h$, where b_h is the premium required by individual h when purchasing generics to compensate him for the putative loss in security or quality associated with this switch.

If we assume that we know the reservation price $p_h{}^r$ for every consumer, then the aggregate Paasche price index is

$$P_a{}^1 = \frac{Q_b{}^1 p_b{}^1 + Q_g{}^1 p_g{}^1}{Q_b{}^1 p_b{}^0 + Q_g{}^1 \bar{p}^r},$$

where the subscripts b and g refer to brand and generic respectively, and $\bar{p}^r = \dfrac{\sum_h q_{gh}{}^1 p_h{}^r}{Q_g{}^1}$ is the average reservation price of those individuals who bought generics in period 1, weighted by the size of their purchases, with capital Q denoting aggregate quantities. Other price indexes can be defined in a similar fashion.

The main problem with implementing this approach is where these reservation prices are to come from. The hedonic price index approach would allow us to estimate the supply price of the new variety using yesterday's technology, but for generics all the relevant measurable characteristics are the same as the branded version, except for "provenance." It is not the case that the two commodities differ, but that consumers differ in their perceptions of their relative values. In the linear, random-utility framework, the probability of any consumer's switching from brand to generic depends on $p_b - p_g > b_h$, and the share of generic users in the total is thus $s_g = F(b_h)$, where $F(\ )$ is the cumulative distribution of reservation prices (for a fixed p_b). Assuming that $b_h \geq 0$, that is, that b_h is a nonnegative random variable, no consumer being willing to pay more for a generic version than for a branded one if the branded one is available, the average reservation price for the switchers is bounded between p_b and p_g and depends on the shape of $F(\ )$. Here we assume that unobserved tastes for brandedness are uniformly distributed, which allows for considerable computational simplification, and appears to be reasonably consistent with the data.[7] The implied average reservation price is halfway between p_b and p_g, "splitting the difference" between the two extremes of the BLS approach, which assigns all of the brand-generic price differential to quality differences, and the FDA approach, which sets it to zero. In the figures and tables we refer to that index as Paasche (u).

We can account for diffusion in two ways: either by waiting for sufficient time to pass for the diffusion to be largely completed (here between six months and a year) before linking them into the overall index, or by modifying the index number formulas discussed above to reflect the assumption that consumers who switch to the generic do so at an average reservation price that is half of the previous period's brand-generic price differential. These indexes are denoted (d) in the figures and tables. For both drugs, the diffusion adjustment pushes the indexes down even further.

Conclusions

This is an interim report from a continuing study, and it would be premature to generalize from the limited number of cases of patent expiration and generic entry that we have examined so far, but it is clear that the potential exists for indexes such as the PPI for pharmaceuticals to be quite badly biased upward. Where generics quickly gain a large share of the market for a drug, as they did for cephalexin, the standard official procedures used in computing price indexes are likely to seriously overestimate actual prices paid. Here the BLS approach gives an *increase* in the wholesale price index of about 7 percent over the forty-five months observed in our data; the opposite extreme, assuming that branded and generic versions are perfect substitutes, gives a price decline of 53 percent; and our preferred "adjusted Paasche" index falls by 48 percent. These are very substantial differences. Where generics are less successful, like the case of prazosin, the different approaches to price index construction give less dramatic, but still quite significant, results.

Table 2–3 reports results from computing the BLS, FDA, and Paasche (u) indexes for ten major drugs that went off patent in the 1980s and that were the subject of the Grabowski and Vernon (1992) study. The data are somewhat less comprehensive than those used by

---

7. We are currently trying to estimate, rather than to assume, the shape of $F(\ )$ from the observed relationship between prices and market share.

TABLE 2–3
MARKET TRENDS AND ALTERNATIVE PRICE INDEXES
TWO YEARS AFTER GENERIC ENTRY

Drug	Generic Quantity Share	Generic Revenue Share	P_g/P_b	BLS	FDA	Paasche (u)
Thioridazine	.408	.28	.57	1.064	.909	1.004
Indomethacin	.497	.29	.41	1.194	.874	1.019
Methyldopa	.372	.24	.53	1.152	.973	1.057
Chlorpropamide	.387	.09	.15	1.039	.768	.902
Ibuprofen	.553	.36	.46	.995	.697	.843
Lorazepam	.465	.22	.33	1.151	.813	.959
Diazepam	.513	.14	.16	1.074	.755	.908
Flurazepam	.310	.16	.41	1.170	1.016	1.083
Haldoperidol	.621	.44	.47	.925	.636	.732
Clondine	.566	.20	.19	1.236	.731	1.016

Mean Difference	After One Year	After Two Years
BLS − FDA	.149	.283
BLS − Paasche (u)	.097	.148

SOURCE: Data kindly provided by Henry G. Grabowski and John M. Vernon.

us in computing the results reported above, since they cover only the most popular presentation of each drug, and the sample is somewhat selective, but the results are again quite striking. On average, the BLS and FDA indexes were 28 percent apart after two years, while our "Paasche (u)" index was almost 15 percent lower.

Official agencies are hampered by resource constraints, but we believe that they could substantially improve the accuracy of their price measures by moving toward a more current sampling of new products, faster introduction, and more current weighting. Where new goods are an important phenomenon, as they are in many sectors other than pharmaceuticals, we suggest that new "gaining" varieties and outlets can and should be introduced with a direct comparison with incumbent products, with at least half of the apparent price difference being taken as real.

Appendix 2-A

Data Sources. The primary source of data for this study is audits of wholesale transactions conducted by IMS America Inc., a market research firm. Sales revenues and quantities are derived from two sources: invoices of a panel of purchasers and information provided by wholesalers. We examine only "systemic anti-infective" drugs for which the incumbent firm's patent expired in the period of time covered by the machine-readable file.

Individual items in the file are identified by: (a) "manufacturer," which may be the actual producer of the drug or a firm specializing in distribution; (b) "product name," either the brand name or the generic name of the drug; (c) "description," a brief summary of the dosage, formulation, and packaging of the item. Correspondences between brand names and generic names were checked using *Drug Facts and Comparisons*, a standard reference source used by pharmacists.

For each drug, all items were classified by using this information into a "product" code, within which items are identical in terms of active ingredient, formulation, dosage, and packaging. For cephalexin, there were thirty-eight distinct "products," for example "250mg tablets, 100 count," or "Suspension, 125mg/5ml, 250ml, × 6." In a small number of cases, there appear to be errors and ambiguities in labeling, making it difficult to classify these items. For the two drugs examined here, this was not a serious problem, and we are confident that our classification is accurate. For other drugs, particularly those administered parenterally, there are serious problems in assigning items in the IMS file to homogeneous "product" codes.

Within each product, we classified manufacturers as "incumbent" or "entrant" and were careful to recognize that some "firms" are in fact subsidiaries or divisions of a parent company. We also computed the total amount of the active ingredient in each package, which, when multiplied by the number of packages on the invoice, gives an alternate measure of quantities.

References

Berndt, Ernst R., Zvi Griliches, and Joshua G. Rosett. "Auditing the Producer Price Index: Micro Evidence from Prescription Pharmaceutical Preparations." *Journal of Economics and Business Statistics* 11 (1993): 251–64.

Caves, Richard E., Michael D. Whinston, and Mark A. Hurwitz. "Patent Expiration, Entry and Competition in the U.S. Pharmaceutical Industry." *Brookings Papers on Economic Activity: Microeconomics* (1991): 1–66.

Dixit, Avinash, and Joseph Stiglitz. "Monopolistic Competition and Optimum Product Diversity." *American Economic Review* 67 (1977): 297–308.

Early, John F., and James H. Sinclair. "Quality Adjustment in the Producer Price Indexes." In *The U.S. National Income and Product Ac-*

counts: Selected Topics, NBER Studies in Income and Wealth, vol. 47, edited by Murray F. Foss. Chicago: University of Chicago Press, 1983, 107–46.

Feenstra, Robert C. "New Product Varieties and the Measurement of International Prices." *American Economic Review* 84 (1994): 157–77.

Fisher, Franklin M., and Zvi Griliches. "Aggregate Price Indexes, New Goods, and Generics: A Note." Mimeo, 1992.

Fisher, Franklin M., and Karl Shell. *The Economic Theory of Price Indices.* New York: Academic Press, 1972.

Fisher, Franklin M., and Karl Shell. "Taste and Quality Change in the Pure Theory of the True-Cost-of-Living Index." In *Price Indexes and Quality Change,* edited by Zvi Griliches. Cambridge: Harvard University Press, 1971, 16–54.

Foss, Murray F., Marilyn E. Manser, and Allan H. Young, eds. *Price Measurements and Their Uses,* NBER Studies in Income and Wealth, vol. 57. Chicago: University of Chicago Press, 1993.

Grabowski, Henry G., and John H. Vernon. "Brand Loyalty, Entry and Price Competition in Pharmaceuticals after the 1984 Drug Act." *Journal of Law and Economics* 35 (1992): 331–50.

Griliches, Zvi. "Hedonic Price Indexes and the Measurement of Capital and Productivity: Some Historical Reflections." In *Fifty Years of Economic Measurement,* edited by E. Berndt and J. Triplett, NBER Studies in Income and Wealth, vol. 54. Chicago: University of Chicago Press, 1990, 185–205.

Griliches, Zvi, ed. *Price Indexes and Quality Change.* Cambridge: Harvard University Press, 1971.

Griliches, Zvi, and Iain Cockburn. "Generics and New Goods in Pharmaceutical Price Indexes." NBER Working Paper no. 4272, February 1993.

Grossman, Gene M., and Elhanan Helpman. *Innovation and Growth in the Global Economy.* Cambridge: MIT Press, 1991.

Hurwitz, Mark A., and Richard E. Caves. "Persuasion or Information? Promotion and the Shares of Brand Name and Generic Pharmaceuticals." *Journal of Law and Economics* 31 (1989): 299–320.

Masson, Alison, and Robert L. Steiner. *Generic Substitution and Prescription Prices: The Economic Effects of State Drug Laws.* Bureau of Economics, Federal Trade Commission, Washington, D.C.: 1985.

Reinsdorf, Marshall. "The Effect of Outlet Price Differentials on the U.S. Consumer Price Index." In *Price Measurements and Their Uses,* NBER Studies in Income and Wealth, vol. 57, edited by M. F. Foss, M. E. Manser, and A. H. Young. Chicago: University of Chicago Press, 1993, 227–54.

33

Spence, A. Michael. "Product Differentiation and Welfare." *American Economic Review, Papers and Proceedings* 66 (1976): 407–14.

Suslow, Valerie Y. "Are There Better Ways to Spell Relief: A Hedonic Pricing Analysis of Ulcer Drugs." University of Michigan, School of Business Administration Working Paper No. 696, 1992.

3
An Updated and Extended Study of the Price Growth of Prescription Pharmaceutical Preparations

Ernst R. Berndt and Paul E. Greenberg

The current health care reform initiative has focused considerable attention on the pharmaceutical industry. Some observers have argued that pharmaceutical manufacturers have sustained high levels of profitability by raising prices at a very rapid pace. To support that argument, observers have generally pointed to growth in the producer price index for prescription pharmaceutical preparations. For example, from 1987 through 1991, the PPI for prescription drugs rose at a compound average annual rate of 8.3 percent, while the PPI for finished goods grew at a rate of 2.9 percent per year.

Price indexes published by the Bureau of Labor Statistics are blended averages based on the price changes of a basket of relevant products. Because manufacturers of prescription pharmaceuticals sell thousands of different products at any point in time, it can be difficult to develop and maintain a representative basket of goods. The rapid pace of new product introductions results in substantial flux not only in the composition of a representative basket of goods from year to year, but also in the importance of any particular item in that basket

The authors thank Almudena Arcelus, Leslie Finch, and William Heslam of Analysis Group, Inc., for their substantial research assistance. In addition, Joshua Rosett and Zvi Griliches provided thoughtful input in designing and implementing the analysis and in interpreting the results. Finally, we gratefully acknowledge the assistance of Gary Persinger of the Pharmaceutical Research and Manufacturers of America, who was instrumental in coordinating the project among all of the participating firms. The opinions expressed in this chapter are those of the authors and do not necessarily reflect the views of the participating companies or the PhRMA. Any remaining errors are the sole responsibility of the authors.

over time. Thus, when evaluating changes in a price index such as this, it is important to analyze the representativeness of the products in the basket at any moment in time, as well as the appropriateness of the weights assigned to each of the components of that basket.

This study examines those two issues with respect to the basket the BLS compiles in developing its price index for prescription pharmaceutical preparations. We use the same methodology as the BLS and thereby isolate the effects of expanding the sample of products contained in the basket so that it is more representative of the industry as a whole. In addition, we use a different methodology that more appropriately weights all products, including new product introductions, in proportion to their changing sales revenue.

This research analyzes the price changes in the prescription pharmaceutical industry from 1987 to 1991. We use two index methodologies to analyze price increases. First, using the Laspeyres approach adopted by the BLS, we compute a fixed-weight price index. A fixed-weight price index does not allow new products to be introduced after the base year has been chosen. This index simulates the BLS index for the sample and time period we consider. Second, using the Divisia approach, we employ a moving-average weight index that incorporates new products as they enter the market. That index provides a method to account for the rapid rate of new product introductions in the prescription drug industry.

The Laspeyres index developed by the BLS for prescription pharmaceuticals is based on prices for a fixed basket of products drawn from selected manufacturing establishments that report on a voluntary basis each month. Several points are worth noting to understand why such an approach may not be the best procedure to measure price increases in the pharmaceutical industry.

First, until January 1994, the fixed basket of products was chosen through a sampling procedure implemented at irregular intervals across industries; that sampling frequency depended in part on the perceived stability of the industry. The BLS conducted detailed surveys of pharmaceutical manufacturers in 1980 and 1987. Such a sampling frequency was not sufficient for an industry characterized by frequent product introductions.[1]

Second, in principle, the sample is drawn from the universe of all products from domestic establishments, whose main production is in standard industry classification 28341. In practice, the choice of products sampled may depart significantly from the probability sampling

---

1. Starting in January 1994, the BLS began sampling prices in the pharmaceutical industry every two years.

procedure. BLS field representatives visit selected establishments during the survey year and use a procedure called disaggregation to settle on which products to sample. The number of products taken from an establishment depends on industry concentration, price variations within and across establishments, establishment size, and the number of products manufactured at each establishment. BLS representatives use substantial judgment to overcome problems caused by the voluntary nature of the process, such as reluctance to provide certain information.

Finally, although the BLS clearly requests transactions rather than list prices, it often receives net list prices that may follow different growth paths compared with net transaction prices.

Audit of PPI for Prescription Pharmaceutical Preparations

Previous Price Index Research. In an earlier study Berndt, Griliches, and Rosett (1993) reported results of a detailed audit of the PPI for prescription pharmaceutical preparations from 1984 to 1989. In that study the authors used monthly product net revenue and unit shipment data from four large pharmaceutical manufacturers to create a comprehensive database containing all their prescription pharmaceutical products. A fixed-weight Laspeyres index generated from that sample of products grew at substantially lower rates than the government's reported PPI. Whereas the BLS reported average annual price increases of 9.09 percent from January 1984 through December 1989, Berndt, Griliches, and Rosett computed a price index that grew at a rate of 6.68 percent per year over that period. Furthermore, when they used a smoothed-weight Divisia approach that incorporated new goods immediately, they found that the resulting four-firm price index grew at a rate of only 6.03 percent per year.

In examining why the official BLS price index grew approximately 50 percent faster than the Divisia price index (9.09 percent versus 6.03 percent), the authors investigated whether the difference could be attributed to the representativeness of their four-firm sample with respect to the entire industry. They rejected that explanation after comparing the growth rates of prices among items sampled by the BLS at the four firms (8.94 percent) with the official PPI (9.09 percent) and after comparing a Divisia index of the four companies with a Divisia index computed using a comprehensive prescription pharmaceutical database for a particular therapeutic class of drugs.[2]

---

2. The IMS database that was used in making this comparison contains information based on prescription purchases made by hospitals and by retailers.

TABLE 3–1
COMPARISON OF DATA CHARACTERISTICS IN THE PREVIOUS
AND EXTENDED STUDIES

	Previous Research	Extended Research
Time period	January 1984 to December 1989	January 1987 to December 1991
Number of products	2,090	6,150
Number of firms reporting	4	17
Percent coverage of domestic industry shipments (in 1989)	24	80

Berndt, Griliches, and Rosett showed that a substantial proportion of the difference in the price indexes can be attributed to the fact that the BLS tends to undersample younger products, which experience below-average price increases, and to oversample medium-age drugs, which demonstrate above-average price growth. Since the role of newer products was significant in the pharmaceutical industry over the 1984 to 1989 period, failure to incorporate new goods promptly and with appropriate weights into the price index calculations appears to have resulted in the upward-biased price-growth rates the BLS reported.

Data Used in Extended Price Index Research. This study extends the earlier research by incorporating comparable data from an additional thirteen drug companies and by considering the more recent period from 1987 to 1991. Our analysis includes all prescription pharmaceutical preparations, as defined by SIC 28341. To calculate prices we divided net revenue for a particular month by total units sold in that period.

The data set comprises all products sold by the seventeen firms, including old and new prescription drugs. Many new products represent extensions or modifications of existing brands, such as a new format of an existing product with modified packaging or larger size presentation. Other products constitute more important milestones for the specific company, such as the first presentation of a newly approved drug, or for the industry, such as a breakthrough drug. This extended analysis includes a sample of 6,150 products from the seventeen pharmaceutical companies, which represents about 80 percent of U.S. sales in the industry. Table 3–1 compares the characteristics of the data assembled for the two different studies.

Methodology Used in Extended Price Index Analysis. Following the research of Berndt, Griliches, and Rosett (1993), the extended study uses two specific methodologies to calculate price indexes with the expanded product sample: a Laspeyres methodology, which approximates the methodology employed for the PPI, and a Divisia methodology, which incorporates new products as soon as they are released into the market.

The Laspeyres price index is a "fixed weight" index calculated on a monthly basis from January 1988 through December 1991. The weight, or the denominator of the index, is fixed to reflect the relative net revenues of products during 1987. All products that were introduced after 1987 are not included in the index, while products sold during any part of 1987 are included with base-period sales revenues adjusted to approximate full-year sales. When a product that was available in 1987 is not sold in subsequent years, it is dropped from the index.

The formula we used to develop the Laspeyres price index is:

$$
I_t = \frac{\sum_{j=1}^{n_t} (P_{j,t} \times Q_{j,a})}{\sum_{j=1}^{n_t} (P_{j,0} \times Q_{j,a})} \times 100,
$$

where

I_t = the Laspeyres price index in month t;

$P_{j,0}$ = the transaction price of product j in January 1988;[3]

$P_{j,t}$ = the transaction price of product j in month t;

$Q_{j,a}$ = the quantity of product j shipped during 1987, the weight-base period; and

n_t = the number of products included in the index in month t.

The Divisia—or "chained"—price index is calculated monthly from January 1988 through December 1991. Unlike in a Laspeyres index methodology, the products and revenue weights used when computing a Divisia index vary over time. This has two clear advantages. First, new products can be added to the index as they are introduced in the market. Second, the product weights reflect current product sales more accurately than product sales in the "weight-base" period.

The Divisia index is calculated in two basic steps. First, for each

---

3. The transaction price of each drug is calculated by using net revenue and quantity data provided by the individual pharmaceutical companies. Net revenue is gross revenue adjusted to reflect returns, rebates, charge-backs, cash discounts, and other adjustments reported by each manufacturer.

period t, the difference in the natural logarithm of prices at times t and t-1 is calculated as:

$$\ln(P_t) - \ln(P_{t-1}) = \sum_{i=1}^{n_t} \bar{s}_{i,t} \times (\ln P_{i,t} - \ln P_{i,t-1}),$$

where

$$s_{i,t} = \frac{P_{i,t} \times Q_{i,t}}{\sum_{i=1}^{n_t} P_{i,t} \times Q_{i,t}} \text{ and } \bar{s}_{i,t} = .25 \times (s_{i,t-2} + s_{i,t-1} + s_{i,t} + s_{i,t+1})$$

and
$P_{i,t}$ = the transaction price of product i in month t,
$P_{i,t-1}$ = the transaction price of product i in month t-1,
$Q_{i,t}$ = the quantity of product i shipped during month t,
n_t = the number of products included in the index during month t,
$s_{i,t}$ = the revenue share of product i in month t, and
$\bar{s}_{i,t}$ = the four-month weighted revenue share for product i in month t.

Then the value of the difference in log prices is set to 0 in January 1988 (the first month for this index), accumulating the monthly differences in log prices and exponentiating the cumulative differences. This exponentiated value is the monthly Divisia index.

Results of Extended Price Index Research. For the period from 1988 through 1991, the monthly Laspeyres and Divisia price indexes calculated using the seventeen-firm sample are compared with the PPI, as shown in table 3–2. Figure 3–1 shows that the Divisia index is generally lower than the Laspeyres index and that both are below the PPI throughout the period of analysis. The compound average annual growth rate of the PPI over the 1988 through 1991 period is 8.42 percent, while the compound average annual growth rates for the Laspeyres and Divisia indexes over that time are 6.86 percent and 5.97 percent, respectively. As shown in table 3–3, the average growth rates for those indexes are always below the PPI, when examined on an annual basis. In some years, however, the Divisia index grows more rapidly than the Laspeyres index.

There are several years of overlap between the two price index analyses described here. Figure 3–2 shows the Laspeyres indexes calculated in the previous research and the results of the current study for 1988 and 1989. Figure 3–3 shows a similar comparison for the Divisia indexes. Each figure shows two indexes that tend to follow similar patterns over time. The differences between the indexes are quite small in

TABLE 3–2
COMPARISON OF PRESCRIPTION DRUG PRICE INDEXES, 1988–1991

Month	PPI, SIC 28341	Laspeyres Index	Divisia Index
Jan-88	100.0	100.0	100.0
Feb-88	100.5	101.0	100.8
Mar-88	102.2	100.6	100.5
Apr-88	102.9	102.3	101.1
May-88	103.5	102.4	101.6
Jun-88	103.2	102.4	101.3
Jul-88	103.9	103.1	101.6
Aug-88	104.5	103.0	102.1
Sep-88	105.8	104.2	103.2
Oct-88	106.2	104.7	103.5
Nov-88	107.8	105.5	104.3
Dec-88	107.4	106.6	105.2
Jan-89	109.2	105.4	104.5
Feb-89	109.4	105.5	104.7
Mar-89	111.0	107.5	107.2
Apr-89	112.1	108.0	107.4
May-89	112.1	110.7	109.5
Jun-89	112.9	111.0	109.8
Jul-89	113.8	110.6	109.0
Aug-89	115.5	111.6	109.8
Sep-89	115.7	113.2	111.7
Oct-89	116.4	113.0	111.3
Nov-89	117.0	114.5	113.4
Dec-89	117.7	115.9	114.6
Jan-90	118.9	116.0	113.5
Feb-90	121.0	116.7	114.3
Mar-90	121.6	117.8	115.3
Apr-90	122.8	117.9	115.3
May-90	123.9	119.9	117.5
Jun-90	122.8	120.1	118.8
Jul-90	123.8	119.4	117.3
Aug-90	124.6	120.0	117.5
Sep-90	124.7	122.6	119.5
Oct-90	125.9	125.6	119.7
Nov-90	126.5	125.6	121.6
Dec-90	127.3	124.7	123.3
Jan-91	128.5	122.2	119.3
Feb-91	130.1	123.2	119.7
Mar-91	130.5	124.5	121.1
Apr-91	133.3	125.6	122.5

(Table continues)

41

TABLE 3–2 (continued)

Month	PPI, SIC 28341	Laspeyres Index	Divisia Index
May-91	133.3	127.6	123.6
Jun-91	133.5	128.2	124.4
Jul-91	135.1	128.1	125.1
Aug-91	135.9	128.1	123.3
Sep-91	135.2	129.0	124.2
Oct-91	137.6	127.6	124.4
Nov-91	137.1	129.8	124.6
Dec-91	137.2	129.7	125.5

SOURCES: PPI–U.S. Department of Labor, Bureau of Labor Statistics, Producer Price Indexes, 1988, 1989, 1990, 1991. Laspeyres and Divisia indexes–proprietary data based on sample of seventeen PhRMA-member firms compiled by Analysis Group, Inc.

FIGURE 3–1
COMPARISON OF PRESCRIPTION DRUG PRICE INDEXES, 1988–1991
(January 1988 = 100)

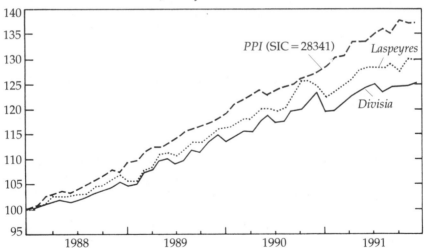

SOURCES: PPI–U.S. Department of Labor, Bureau of Labor Statistics, Producer Price Indexes, 1988, 1989, 1990, 1991. Laspeyres and Divisia–proprietary data based on sample of seventeen PhRMA-member firms compiled by Analysis Group, Inc.

TABLE 3–3
COMPARISON OF ANNUAL PRICE INDEX GROWTH RATES

Compound Annual Growth Rates
January 1988–December 1991

PPI	8.42%
Laspeyres	6.86%
Divisia	5.97%

Compound Annual Growth Rates
December–December

Year	PPI*	Laspeyres	Divisia
1988	8.07%	7.25%	5.71%
1989	9.61%	8.74%	8.95%
1990	8.12%	7.51%	7.58%
1991	7.85%	4.02%	1.77%

NOTE: Compound annual growth rate (CAGR): $(\text{index}_{end}/\text{index}_{begin})^{(12/\text{number of months})} - 1$, where index_{end} refers to the index value at the end of the growth period, index_{begin} refers to the index value at the beginning of the growth period, and number of months refers to the duration, in months, of the growth period. In computing the CAGR for January 1988 through December 1991, the growth period is forty-seven months. In computing the CAGR for 1989, 1990, and 1991, the growth period is twelve months (December to December). In 1988 the growth period is eleven months (January to December).
SOURCES: PPI–U.S. Department of Labor, Bureau of Labor Statistics, Producer Price Indexes, 1988, 1989, 1990, 1991. Laspeyres and Divisia indexes–proprietary database on sample of seventeen PhRMA-member firms compiled by Analysis Group, Inc.

month-by-month comparisons. Since the findings from the previous research generally indicated smaller price growth than what is shown here, the four companies included in both studies may have had somewhat below-average price growth over that period.

It is important to note that the Laspeyres index is calculated without attention to new product introductions between 1988 and 1991. Since many products that were sold in the 1987 base year dropped out in subsequent years, the Laspeyres methodology leads to a consistently declining share of industry sales following 1987. In contrast, the Divisia index incorporates the effects of new products as soon as they are introduced. Thus, although the percentage of industry revenue reflected in the Laspeyres index is only slightly lower than that represented by products in the Divisia index during 1988, the differential

FIGURE 3–2
COMPARISON OF LASPEYRES INDEXES FOR PRESCRIPTION DRUGS, 1988–1989
(January 1988 = 100)

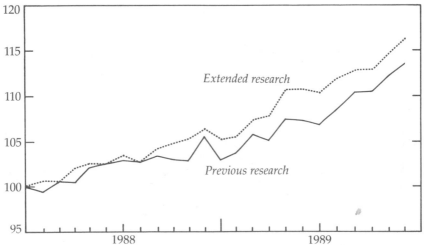

SOURCES: Previous research data are based on four-firm sample compiled in NBER research, March 1992. Extended research data come from proprietary data based on sample of seventeen PhRMA-member firms compiled by Analysis Group, Inc.

grows significantly each year through 1991.[4] As table 3–4 shows, the percentage of industry revenue represented by the Laspeyres index falls from 65 percent in 1988 to 48 percent in 1991, while the percentage represented by the Divisia index grows from 68 percent to 83 percent during the same period.[5]

The difference in percentage of industry revenues included in the

4. Of the seventeen companies included in the sample, two firms did not report data for 1987 and 1988, and one company did not report data for 1991. Therefore, we must interpret year-to-year changes in the average number of products and percent of industry sales included in the Laspeyres and Divisia indexes (summarized in table 3–4) with caution.

5. To analyze the representativeness of the sample used in the current research, we performed chi-square tests to compare on an annual basis the distribution of revenues by therapeutic class within our sample relative to that of the industry as a whole. Our analysis defined therapeutic classes on the basis of the Bureau of the Census product codes. In each year we were unable to reject the hypothesis that the distribution of revenues in the sample was equivalent to that of the industry generally. We concluded, therefore, that our analysis was based on a representative sample in each year.

44

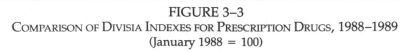

FIGURE 3–3
COMPARISON OF DIVISIA INDEXES FOR PRESCRIPTION DRUGS, 1988–1989
(January 1988 = 100)

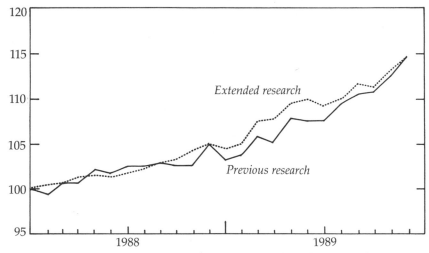

SOURCES: Previous research data are based on four-firm sample compiled in NBER research, March 1992. Extended research data come from proprietary data based on sample of seventeen PhRMA-member firms compiled by Analysis Group, Inc.

Laspeyres and Divisia indexes is likely a result of the rapid rate of product introductions that characterizes the pharmaceutical industry and the fact that the Laspeyres methodology does not include attention to those changes. This difference underscores the importance of new and relatively young products in the industry. In addition, since new and young products are generally associated with slower price growth, this lends credence to the hypothesis that failing to incorporate new goods promptly and with appropriate weights into the price index calculations results in an upward bias in estimated price growth rates.

Conclusion and Further Extensions of Price Index Research

Because prices in the pharmaceutical industry tend to rise more rapidly at later stages of the product life cycle, if the age distribution of the basket of goods used to compute a price index is not representative of the industry as a whole, aggregate price growth estimates will be biased. Earlier research demonstrated that the PPI for prescription pharmaceutical preparations consistently overstated actual price growth in the industry. Using a sample of four drug companies,

45

TABLE 3–4
Comparison of Drug Industry Revenues Underlying Price Indexes, 1987–1991

Year	Total Industry (a) Value of shipments ($000)	Seventeen-Firm Sample (b) Net revenue ($000)	(c) Percent of industry (b)/(a)	Included in Laspeyres Index (d) Average number of products[a]	(e) Net revenue[b] ($000)	(f) Percent of industry (e)/(a)	Included in Divisia Index (g) Average number of products[a]	(h) Net revenue[b] ($000)	(i) Percent of industry (h)/(a)
1987	17,756,409	11,709,091	65.94						
1988	20,014,618	13,718,760	68.54	3,894	12,983,424	64.87	4,045	13,718,760	68.54
1989	22,171,284	17,814,127	80.35	3,654	13,757,480	62.05	4,591	17,814,127	80.35
1990	24,136,209	20,022,659	82.96	3,347	13,342,547	55.28	4,806	20,022,659	82.96
1991	26,618,350	22,209,372	83.44	2,799	12,798,304	48.08	4,370	22,209,372	83.44

a. "Average number of products" refers to an annual average of the products reported that were used in the computation of the index.

b. "Net revenue" refers to the annual net revenue of the products that were used in the computation of the index.

Source: Total industry—U.S. Department of Commerce, Bureau of the Census. "Pharmaceutical Preparations, Except Biologicals," *Current Industrial Reports*, 1988, 1989, 1990, 1991. Seventeen-firm sample proprietary data based on sample of seventeen PhRMA-member firms compiled by Analysis Group, Inc.

Berndt, Griliches, and Rosett (1993) closely examined 2,090 products that accounted for 24 percent of industry sales in 1989 over the period 1984 to 1989. They found that the PPI overstated price growth by 50 percent; the PPI reported an annual average of 9.09 percent compared with the 6.03 percent they estimated. This overstatement results from the fact that the BLS tends to undersample younger products and to oversample mature drugs. Furthermore, because the BLS relies on the Laspeyres methodology in computing price changes for prescription drugs, it does not routinely incorporate new products into its published index.

The current analysis updates and extends those results. We analyze price growth of prescription drugs from 1987 to 1991 and expand the sample beyond the original four firms to include thirteen additional manufacturers. Collectively, those seventeen firms accounted for 80 percent of industry sales in 1989. Using the same Laspeyres methodology as the BLS, but with a representative sample of 6,150 products, we continue to find that the PPI consistently overstated price growth for prescription drugs. We then use that expanded sample and a Divisia methodology to incorporate the effects of new products immediately as they are introduced to the market. Whereas the official PPI rose by 8.42 percent from 1987 to 1991, we find an annual increase of 5.97 percent. That implies that on average, the PPI overstates price growth by 41 percent over that time period.

Further extensions of our research focus on alternative specifications of "price" that incorporate the effects of important trends in the prescription drug industry. For example, although price per day of presentation typically falls when larger package sizes containing the same chemical entity are introduced to the market, the BLS methodology does not link similar products of that sort in constructing its price index. Therefore, the BLS index fails to capture the effects of package size changes on price within a given brand. Investigation is currently underway concerning the appropriate method to link explicitly various presentational forms of the products included in the price index. Using a type of hedonic analysis, researchers are evaluating a quantitative relationship between price and package size. Preliminary results indicate that there is an inverse relationship between package size and unit price. A modified Divisia price index to account for that effect would likely further reduce reported rates of price growth in the industry.

There are other important industry trends that official price indexes for prescription drugs do not capture that may tend to exacerbate the overstatement of the industry's price growth. New drugs often confer huge benefits on consumers by improving quality of life. Further hedonic analysis can be undertaken to evaluate the relationship

47

between price and a variety of quality measures, such as the side effects of a particular medication, the effects of a specific drug on the patient's productivity at work, and the extent to which a pharmaceutical product therapy replaces an invasive surgical procedure.[6] On a quality-adjusted basis, price growth in the prescription pharmaceutical industry is likely far different from that reported by the BLS. In fact, it is possible that quality-adjusted prices of drugs in certain therapeutic classes have *declined* over time, with substantial improvements in their characteristics from one generation of products to the next.

Another direction for refining the results published by the BLS involves making explicit adjustments for the effects of generic entry over time. Price indexes that link a generic product with its patented antecedent would capture the immediate average price decline that usually follows patent expiration. Since that effect is not now captured by the BLS, its PPI for prescription pharmaceuticals likely overstates price growth for yet another reason.[7]

References

Berndt, Ernst, and Stan Finkelstein. "Price Indexes for Antihypertensive Drugs That Incorporate Quality Change." MIT Working Paper no. 6-92, 1992.

Berndt, Ernst, Zvi Griliches, and Joshua G. Rosett. "Auditing the Producer Price Index: Micro Evidence from Prescription Pharmaceutical Preparations." *Journal of Business and Economic Statistics* 11 (1993): 251–64.

Griliches, Zvi, and Iain Cockburn. "Generics and New Goods in Pharmaceutical Price Indexes." In *Competitive Strategies in the Pharmaceutical Industry*, edited by Robert B. Helms. Washington, D.C.: AEI Press, 1995.

---

6. An example of the application of hedonic techniques to a specific therapeutic class of drugs is contained in Berndt and Finkelstein (1992).

7. For an analysis of the effects of generic drugs on price index calculations, see Griliches and Cockburn (1995).

4
Measuring Quality Change in the Market for Anti-Ulcer Drugs

Valerie Y. Suslow

The General Accounting Office released a study in August 1992 of twenty-nine sampled prescription drugs that reported an average increase in price of approximately 138 percent between 1985 and 1991 (GAO 1992, 4, table 1).[1] Those and other published price indexes are increasingly being used in the public policy arena to focus the debate on the potential regulation of pharmaceutical prices and the coverage of health insurance. In an industry where products are multidimensional and the rate of technological progress is brisk, misinterpretation of unadjusted indexes of drug prices can easily arise. This in turn can lead to mistaken conclusions regarding appropriate policy for the pharmaceutical industry.

Researchers have addressed numerous general theoretical issues concerning the construction and interpretation of price indexes (Fisher and Shell 1983). Two issues of particular interest for pharmaceutical markets are the new goods problem, which deals with the introduction of generic drugs into a drug price index, and the quality problem, which recognizes that newer versions of drugs with the same basic chemical action may be superior in certain dimensions to drugs already on the market. Specific to pharmaceutical markets, Berndt et al.

This research was funded by Warner Lambert Company and the University of Michigan Business School. Special thanks to workshop participants at NBER, UCLA, Chicago, and the Ad Hoc Working Group on the Economics of the Pharmaceutical Industry. Thanks also go to Ernst Berndt, Zvi Griliches, Bill Comanor, Craig Pirrong, and Tim Bresnahan. Research assistance was provided by Scott Woosley, Eric Alf, Mike Hoff, and Martin Betancourt. Any errors are my own. An earlier version of this chapter was circulated under the working paper title, "Are There Better Ways to Spell Relief? A Hedonic Pricing Analysis of Anti-Ulcer Drugs."

1. The average price increase figure reported above is a simple average of the price increases reported by the GAO.

(1993) have also argued that the sampling procedure used by the Bureau of Labor Statistics to calculate pharmaceutical price indexes is flawed. Each of those problems deserves careful analysis. This chapter focuses on the issue of product quality measurement and quality change.

Following Rosen (1974), one can envision differentiated products comprising various characteristics that are valued by both buyers and sellers. We can view each good in a differentiated products market as a tied bundle of characteristics. For example, pharmaceutical products differ along therapeutically important dimensions, such as convenience and side-effect profiles. Those product specifications change as new technologies become available and as consumers express their preferences for particular product attributes. Although individual characteristics are not priced explicitly in the market, the price of a given product represents the valuation of all its characteristics.

We can therefore speak of each characteristic as having an "implicit" price. In equilibrium the marginal implicit prices represent the joint envelope of the consumers' value functions and the firms' offer functions. The implicit characteristics prices can be revealed by regression of prices of different models (or in this case, brands of drugs) on the model characteristics. The hedonic methodology, although widely used for adjusting price indexes in automobile and computer markets, is just starting to be used for pharmaceutical markets (Afuah 1992; Berndt and Finkelstein 1992).

In this chapter I use data from the antispasmodic ("anti-ulcer") market, one of the largest prescription drug markets in the United States, to estimate a hedonic price function that will account for the quality changes in brand-name products over time. Employing this approach, I calculate a quality-adjusted price index for antispasmodic drugs between 1977 and 1989 and then use the results to compare quality-adjusted with unadjusted price indexes. I find a small but significant decrease in the rate of inflation in ulcer drug prices after accounting for nonprice characteristics. In particular, I find that both the dosing regime and certain more serious elements of the side-effect profile have a significant influence on the daily dose prices in the market.

In the remaining sections of the chapter, I provide a brief history and description of the antispasmodic market, discuss the measurement of drug characteristics and its problems, describe the data, comment on the empirical results, and offer a brief set of concluding remarks.

Overview of the Market for Antispasmodic Drugs

Traditionally, nonsurgical treatments of peptic ulcer disease have been directed at reducing acid secretion or neutralizing gastric acidity (Bayless 1990, 66). Before 1977 the market for anti-ulcer drugs was minimal, and the two major pharmacotherapeutic approaches to reducing gastric acidity were antacids and anticholinergics. The only other alternative was surgery.

Antacids work by making acid less damaging to the stomach; they relieve the symptoms but do not heal the ulcer. Anticholinergics, which reduce acid secretion, were first prescribed in the 1950s. A leader in this class of drugs is Searle's Pro-Banthine, which was first marketed in 1953. Because anticholinergics have many side effects (including blurred vision) at the dosage levels necessary to decrease gastric secretions significantly, anticholinergics have enjoyed only limited use, and they are not recommended for use as the sole basis of therapy.

A revolutionary class of ulcer treatments known as histamine H_2-receptor antagonists, which act by blocking the action of histamine, a biochemical produced at an early stage of the process of acid secretion, entered the market in 1977. A four- to six-week treatment period is associated with a healing rate of 70 to 80 percent in patients with duodenal ulcer. Best known of the H_2-antagonists are cimetidine (Tagamet), introduced by SmithKline Beecham in late 1977, and ranitidine (Zantac), a Glaxo product that came on the market in 1983. Two other drugs in that class are famotidine (Pepcid), which arrived on the market in 1986, and nizatidine (Axid), introduced in 1988.

The original dosage of Tagamet was 300 mg, four times daily. More potent than Tagamet, Zantac's dosage is 150 mg, twice daily.[2] Physicians see this quality as an advantage for Zantac: "A twice-daily or once-at-bedtime regimen will increase patient compliance" (Ohning and Soll 1989, 266). Pepcid and Axid are also long-acting drugs and can be given just once a day. A single daily dose form of Tagamet became available in 1987.

An alternative therapy is sucralfate (Carafate), which Marion Labs introduced into the U.S. market in 1981. Carafate promotes healing by forming a protective coating over the ulcer. While Carafate is relatively free from side effects, the dosage regime is inconvenient for many patients.[3] Throughout the 1980s Carafate held roughly 6 percent of the anti-ulcer market.

---

2. Those dosages are for treatment of an active ulcer. While short-term treatment often results in healing, discontinuance of therapy is frequently followed by recurrence of the ulcer. For patients in a high-risk group, maintenance therapy with a reduced nighttime dose may be instituted (Ohning and Soll 1989, 268–69).

3. Although Carafate has been shown to be as effective in healing as Tagamet or Zantac, it has a few disadvantages. First, it does not relieve pain as quickly as the acid inhibitors (*Chicago Tribune*, June 4, 1986). Second, it has

51

Research into a new generation of anti-ulcer drugs continued throughout the late 1980s. In 1989 the Food and Drug Administration approved Cytotec for the prevention of gastric ulcers caused by nonsteroidal anti-inflammatory drugs (such as ibuprofen). The active ingredient in Cytotec is a synthetic prostaglandin, which is believed to have a protective effect on the lining of the stomach ("Agitation" 1989, 9). Other drugs have entered the market since 1990, but are beyond the sample period of this study.

Zantac and Tagamet are the clear leaders in the market consisting of the "new" anti-ulcer drugs, and a fierce battle between the two was waged throughout the mid to late 1980s. Because of its different molecular structure, Zantac binds more efficiently to the H_2-antagonists than Tagamet and thus results in a greater inhibition of acid secretion and a reportedly decreased incidence of side effects. Glaxo made early claims about the better side-effect profile of Zantac when it launched a massive marketing campaign to introduce its product and thus sparked a heated debate over the side-effect profiles of Tagamet and Zantac (Dreyfus 1983; "Agitation" 1989).

Following its heavily promoted U.S. introduction in 1983, Zantac generated the largest first-year sales for a new prescription drug in the history of the U.S. pharmaceutical industry (*Chemical Marketing Reporter* 1986). Not all of Zantac's sales came at the expense of Tagamet sales however. Total H_2-antagonist sales grew from $417 million to $537 million during Zantac's first full year on the market (December 1983 through December 1984). Over that period Zantac sales shot up 290 percent (from $41 million to $159 million), while Tagamet sales stayed roughly constant at $358 million.[4]

Tagamet, which controlled 86 percent of the market before Zantac's arrival on the scene, rapidly lost market share to the newer drug. By 1987, Tagamet had ceded more than half of the market to Zantac, and by the end of 1989, Zantac's market share had grown to roughly 60 percent, while Tagamet's had fallen to about 15 percent. That rapid shift in market share between those two drugs occurred despite the fact that Zantac's average price was consistently higher than that of Tagamet by 20 to 30 percent.

Some might argue that the market growth in ulcer treatments in general and Zantac's status as leader in particular were due to a suc-

---

problems of convenience and compliance, given that it should be taken on an empty stomach one hour before meals. Its main advantage is its limited side effects, which makes it the ideal treatment for older patients and patients in intensive care.

4. These figures are calculated from IMS data described below.

cessful advertising campaign by Zantac's promoters. I shall argue that while that is likely to be true in part, it is also true that the bundle of product attributes that Zantac offered was of therapeutic value to both physicians and patients.

Measuring Drug Characteristics

The first step in estimating a hedonic price function is to decide what attributes to include. A drug is a complex combination of active and inactive ingredients. Users do not value the ingredients for their own sake, but for the result they deliver—perhaps a cure, perhaps some relief of symptoms. There have been numerous surveys conducted to investigate which individual factors appear to be important in drug selection or prescription. In 1988 SmithKline Beecham funded a study specifically focusing on ulcer treatments (Yankelovich et al. 1988). In a telephone survey 800 heads-of-household were asked what they look for in a drug to treat ulcer-related symptoms. Those surveyed rated four attributes on a six-point scale, where six was "very important" and one was "not very important." The most highly rated attribute according to those potential patients was that the drug "be safe." This was followed in order by "make you feel better quickly," "be convenient to take," and "be affordable in cost."

In a more general price sensitivity survey of European physicians, Dajda and Owen (1987) found a similar list of attributes to be important. The physicians sampled listed the following characteristics in order of importance for prescription decisions: effectiveness, freedom from side effects, reliability, convenient dosage, ease of use, and price (Dajda and Owen 1987, 105, table 1).[5] McCann (1987, 140) chose the asthma market to investigate price awareness on the part of physicians. The five factors ranked by doctors were: dose regime, side effects, price, efficacy, and speed of action.

Those studies indicate that there are several standard attributes, in addition to price, that physicians and potential patients consider important in choosing which brand of drug to use for treatment. In general, the efficacy of a drug, its safety, and its convenience are the three major categories of attributes that affect demand. For specific drugs those characteristics can be measured by using medical tests, reference books, and clinical study results. For cholesterol drugs, efficacy is measured by the change in LDL and HDL cholesterol that comes from taking the drugs (Afuah 1992, 23, table 1). For antihyper-

---

5. Unfortunately, neither this study nor McCann (1987) defines how the nonprice attributes are measured.

tensive drugs, efficacy might be measured by the reduction in blood pressure.

There are, however, innumerable complications that arise in this measurement exercise. For example, is quality based on the number of side effects, the number of most serious side effects, the number of life-threatening side effects, or the number of side effects shown in clinical trials to occur more than x percent of the time? There is no theoretical answer. In this study I categorize side effects by seriousness but not by frequency of occurrence. I discuss this in more detail below, after giving an overview of the market.

Market Data for Anti-Ulcer Drugs

Market Selection. The main data source for this chapter is the database held by IMS International, a market research firm that collects data on a variety of dimensions relating to medical care and medical products. The database is organized by therapeutic category (for example, analgesics, cardiovascular therapy, and psychotherapeutic drugs), and categories are disaggregated further by IMS America's "Uniform System of Classification" or USC codes. In this classification system, products are grouped into five-digit USC classes within each therapeutic category. For example, psychotherapeutic drugs are disaggregated into tranquilizers, antidepressant/tranquilizers, antidepressants, and lithium products. The tranquilizer category is further broken down into major tranquilizers and minor tranquilizers, which are in turn broken down further into benzodiazepines, and so on.

The classification system IMS America used is not always consistent with the grouping of products that an economist would choose to analyze a market. As an example, consider the category of minor tranquilizers, which is subdivided into four five-digit USC classes. Valium falls within the five-digit USC class of minor tranquilizers and benzodiazepines, but it clearly competes with selected products in the other three five-digit categories of minor tranquilizers. In addition, Valium can be used as a muscle relaxant, a group of drugs classified under a separate IMS therapeutic category. Thus, an economic study of pricing in the minor tranquilizer market would have to include data on products in each of those separate USC classifications.

Fortunately, the antispasmodic category as defined by IMS fits fairly closely with the definition of the economic market. Since antispasmodic drugs are used for little else, keeping a narrow focus is unlikely to cause a significant bias in the empirical estimates.[6] There

---

6. Some of the anticholinergic drugs can be used as preanesthetic medication and appear to have a few other possible miscellaneous uses (*Drug Facts and Comparisons* 1990, 1374).

are six five-digit USC categories within the IMS America therapeutic class 23000, antispasmodic/antisecretory agents:

23100 antispasmodic, synthetic
23200 antispasmodic, belladonna
23300 antispasmodic, with tranquilizers
23400 antispasmodic/antisecretory, other
23500 urinary tract antispasmodics
23900 other gastrointestinal agents.

The data used in this study consist of monthly observations for the 23100–23400 classes from January 1975 through December 1989. The products in the 23100–23300 classes are the anticholinergic drugs. All of the H_2-antagonist ulcer drugs fall within the 23400 category. In 1984, for example, there were fifty-three products in the 23000 category as a whole. While only three of those fifty-three products that year were classified in the 23400 category, they accounted for 79 percent of total 23000 market sales.

Class 23500 is excluded on the grounds that urinary tract drugs do not compete with the gastrointestinal anti-ulcer drugs because they are not used for the same indications. Class 23900, the "all other" category, was first created in June 1981. The major brand-name drug in 23900 is Reglan (metoclopramide)—an anti-emetic drug used to help prevent or relieve nausea (during chemotherapy treatment, for example). It is a gastrointestinal stimulant, not an anti-ulcer treatment, and is therefore excluded from the sample.

I obtained the unit and sales data for specific ulcer drugs from the IMS U.S. Drugstores Audit, which provides a monthly report on the volume, in dollars and in physical units, of ethical and proprietary pharmaceuticals products purchased for resale by retail outlets in the continental United States. That audit represents the movement of drugs into drugstores and is gathered at the product-pack level (for example, 100 mg tablets in bottles of 30, 60, or 100). The national estimates are based on the purchases of a panel of independent pharmacies, chain operations, and wholesalers. IMS does not sample mail order purchases or purchases made by pharmacies in department stores and food stores (IMS 1990). Prices that are calculated from those data represent prices manufacturers or wholesalers charge to the pharmacies.

Product Selection. The IMS audits present information at a highly disaggregated level. Unit and sales data are given for each different presentation of the drug, be it in capsule form, tablet, or injection. For

55

TABLE 4–1
REAL DAILY DOSE PRICES
(1982 $)

Classification	Number of Observations	Mean	Standard Deviation
23400			
Tagamet-300mg	149	1.27	.36
Tagamet-400mg	72	1.43	.24
Tagamet-800mg	44	1.55	.08
Zantac-150mg	78	1.75	.27
Zantac-300mg	47	1.76	.12
Pepcid-40mg	38	1.65	.13
Pepcid-20mg	38	1.70	.15
Carafate	98	1.29	.26
Axid	20	1.69	.07
Cytotec	11	1.79	.04
23100			
Bentyl	180	.32	.12
Pro-Banthine	180	.87	.50
23200			
Bellergal	159	.93	.45
23300			
Librax	180	1.06	.63

example, in December 1983 the Tagamet presentations and their associ-ated market shares are as follows:

tablets	300 mg	100 tabs/bottle	78.9%
tablets	200 mg	100 tabs/bottle	5.4%
tablets	300 mg	100 s.u.p.*	.5%
liquid	300 mg/5 ml	8 oz.	.8%
vial	300 mg/2 ml	2 ml	.1%
vial	300mg/2 ml	8 ml	.1%

*s.u.p. = drug is suspended in liquid.

Table 4–1 presents the means of the IMS America price data for each of the drugs in the 23400 category and the market leaders in the 23100–23300 categories. I calculated average prices for each drug in each month by dividing retail dollar purchases by the number of units. The prices listed in table 4–1 are daily dose prices (in 1982 dollars).[7]

---

7. There are some compromises that had to be made in calculating the daily dosages. See the data appendix for details.

For example, the recommended dosage for Zantac is 300 mg per day. Therefore, to calculate the price that the patient would pay per day for 150 mg tablets of Zantac, I doubled the 150 mg price. Table 4–1 shows that the average daily dose price of Zantac, whether presented as 150 mg tablets or 300 mg tablets, is approximately $1.75 per day. Prices for different presentations of Tagamet range from $1.27 to $1.55. The older generation of drugs is priced significantly lower on average.

Many empirical studies of pharmaceutical pricing use data only on the leading presentation of the leading products. A leading presentation is the form of the drug that has the highest market share. Although I include all of the *products* in the 23400 category, I follow the normal practice and use only the leading presentations (for example, Tagamet presented in the 300 mg form in 100 tablet bottles).

To check the reasonableness of the underlying assumption, that prices for different presentations of the same product behave similarly, I compared the raw price correlations for various presentations of the 23400 products over the sample period. As expected, the price correlations are extremely high (over .90) across presentations of a given product.

For the remaining three categories (23100, 23200, and 23300), I use the leading presentation of the leading product. From 1975 through 1989 the leaders in market share for the 23200 and 23300 classes were Sandoz's Bellergal-S and Roche's Librax, respectively. In contrast, there was no clear-cut market share leader for 23100 over the 1975 through 1989 time period. Therefore, I chose two products: Merrell-Dow's Bentyl and Searle's Pro-Banthine.

The result of this sampling procedure is a panel of ten brand-name products (four leading products in the 23100–23300 classes, and by the end of the sample, 1989, a total of six products in the 23400 class).[8]

The extent to which medical insurance programs cover expenditures for prescription drugs obviously affects the validity and interpretation of the price data. Unfortunately, systematic data on actual insurance coverage for specific anti-ulcer drugs from 1975 through 1989 are unavailable on a nationwide level, but the year dummies that are used in the hedonic regression may capture at least some of the changes in coverage over time.

Anti-Ulcer Drug Characteristics. The specific attributes that I have measured for the ulcer market are: dose regime, number of drug inter-

---

8. Of those ten leading products, there is only one company producing more than one antispasmodic drug: Searle manufactures both Pro-Banthine, introduced in 1953, and Cytotec, introduced in the United States in 1989.

actions, side-effect profile, and average efficacy.[9] I also include two pharmacological actions. The first is the absorption rate, which, by capturing how quickly a fraction of a dose reaches the plasma site of measurement, reflects the speed with which the drug enters the bloodstream. The second is the half-life, an indicator of how long the drug remains in the body, measured as the time required for the blood drug concentration to decrease by half. The half-life of a drug is an important characteristic in that it helps to establish a drug's dosing interval.

The variable acronyms and definitions and the range of each variable for the full sample appear in table 4–2. I report the mean both for all drugs (including the anticholinergics) and for new drugs only. I measured the characteristics over time for each of the ten brand-name drugs in the sample.

Drug attribute information was compiled primarily from the 1980 through 1990 volumes of the *U.S. Pharmacopeial Convention, Dispensing Information*, or *USP DI*. Prescribing information is full disclosure information. In contrast, dispensing information is written under the assumption that the decision to prescribe has already been made: "*USP DI* is not intended to be 'full disclosure' information . . . [instead, the] *USP DI* contains selected information. Selection is based on what is considered practical, clinically significant information needed to assist in the monitoring of drug use and to help assure that a drug is being safely and effectively used" (*USP DI* 1993, viii).

Time-series information on attributes from the *USP DI* was available for the 1980 through 1989 period only. Characteristics for 1977 through 1989 were taken from the 1980 edition of the *USP DI*. Details on the methodology, definitions, and assumptions for the attributes data appear in the data appendix to this chapter.

Table 4–3 gives selected information, as compiled from the *USP DI*, on the characteristics for individual drugs in the cross-section for 1989. The first column in panel A of the table lists the typical dosage of each drug (for example, in 1989 Tagamet was administered as a 400 mg tablet, twice daily). The second through the seventh columns give the side-effect profile of each drug. The *USP DI* has two categories of side effects: those indicating need for medical attention and those indicating need for medical attention only if they continue or are bothersome. In table 4–3 I label those side-effect categories *SE1* and *SE2*,

---

9. There are two other characteristics that are important, but the appropriate data are lacking. Those two attributes are "flexibility of dosing regime," for example, whether the drug must be taken with meals or an hour before meals, and "relief of pain."

TABLE 4–2
VARIABLE DEFINITIONS FOR DRUG CHARACTERISTICS

			Mean	
Name	Description	Range	All	New
DDP	Daily dose price ($/day)	.22–2.16	1.06	1.43
FREQ	Frequency of dosage per day	1–5	3.78	3.11
DI	Number of significant drug interactions	0–9	4.11	1.56
SE1M	Number of more frequently occurring side effects requiring immediate attention	0–7	1.73	0
SE1L	Number of less frequently occurring side effects requiring immediate attention	0–4	.61	0
SE1R	Number of rarely occurring side effects requiring immediate attention	0–9	3.15	2.94
SE2M	Number of more frequently occurring side effects needing attention if they continue or are bothersome	0–6	3.23	.31
SE2LR	Number of less frequently or rarely occurring side effects needing attention if they continue or are bothersome	2–17	3.24	7.08
ABS	Absorption rate (percent)	5–94	46.16	48.92
HALF	Half-life (hours)	0–3	1.93	1.64
HEAL	Average healing rate for six-week treatment (percent)	40–84	54.33	75.03

respectively. Within each category I group the side effects according to reported incidence: more frequent (M), less frequent (L), and rare (R). In the SE2 category the USP DI often groups the L and R categories together, and that is reflected in the heading of column seven (SE2-L& R). Two noteworthy aspects of the product comparison reflected in panel A are the significant reduction in the number of serious side effects (SE1M) in the newer drugs and the markedly higher average healing rates of that same newer generation of drugs (HEAL in panel A).

Although panel A shows only the 1989 values for the product attributes, the absorption rate, half-life, and average healing rate are, in

TABLE 4–3
DRUG ATTRIBUTES

Panel A. 1989 Cross-Section

Drug	DOSE	DI	SE1			SE2		HEAL	ABS	HALF
			M	L	R	M	L&R			
Tagamet	400; 2	7	0	0	6	0	7	72	70	2.0
Zantac	150; 2	7	0	0	6	0	7	70	50	2.5
Pepcid	40; 1	1	0	0	6	0	4	72	45	3.0
Axid	300; 1	1	0	0	1	0	2	77	5	0.0
Cytotec	.2; 4	0	0	0	0	2	6	77	94	1.5
Carafate	1000; 4	0	0	0	0	1	9	84	88	0.5
Bentyl	20; 3	6	1	1	1	3	9	40	67	1.8
Pro-Banthine	15; 5	7	1	1	2	6	10	40	50	1.6
Bellergal	n.a.; 3	3	7	— 4 —		6	8	40	50	2.7
Librax	n.a.; 2	7	0	— 9 —		6	5	40	10	2.4

Panel B. Tagamet, 1980–1989

Year	DOSE	DI	SE1			SE2	
			M	L	R	M	L&R
1980	300; 4	1	0	0	1	0	5
1981	300; 4	1	0	0	4	0	5
1982	300; 4	1	0	0	4	0	5
1983	300; 4	2	0	0	5	0	8
1984	300; 4	2	0	0	5	0	6
1985	300; 4	2	0	0	5	0	6
1986	400; 2	7	0	0	5	0	6
1987	400; 2	7	0	0	5	0	6
1988	400; 2	7	0	0	5	0	6
1989	400; 2	7	0	0	5	0	7

NOTE: *DOSE* = mg; frequency per day. *DI* = number of drug interactions. *SE1* = number of side effects requiring immediate attention (*M* = more frequent, *L* = less frequent, *R* = rare). *SE2* = number of side effects needing attention if they continue or are bothersome. *HEAL* = average healing rate (percent). *ABS* = absorption rate (percent). *HALF* = half-life (hours).

fact, constants over time.[10] The dosing interval, number of drug interactions, and side effects are not. Of the drugs listed in panel A, Tagamet had the most recorded changes in its measured attributes over the 1980 through 1989 period. Panel B therefore shows Tagamet's entire time series of attributes.

Looking at the first column of panel B, we can see how Tagamet's dosage frequency declined over time. That change was a direct response to Zantac's lower daily dosage. On the other hand, the number of drug interactions and less frequent or rare side effects have increased over time. Although not reported in the tables, the values of SE1R and SE2-L&R for Zantac also increased from three to six and from five to seven, respectively, between 1984 and 1989. Those increases in the number of side effects reflect the growth in information accumulated about Zantac as physicians prescribed it to thousands of patients over a number of years. Thus, while our initial assumption may be that increased side effects are "bad" and should have a negative correlation with price, closer examination reveals that this assumption can only be true if knowledge about the drug is held constant. Therefore, the sign on the side-effect coefficient could go either way.[11]

Hedonic Regression Results

Model Specification. The hedonic price function for product i in year t is specified in general as:

$$p_{it} = p(z_{it}) + r_{it},$$

where z_i represents product attributes, $p(z_i)$ is the systematic component, and r is the residual price (an independently and identically distributed error term). Shifts in the hedonic function over time are accommodated by adding a dummy variable for each year t.

As Trajtenberg (1990, 109) writes, there are "virtually no theoretical guidelines to follow" for choosing a functional form for the hedonic equation. It is common to compare the fit of several functional forms. Since most of the drug attribute variables I use have zero as a meaningful value (for example, zero recorded side effects), I have restricted my

---

10. Note that not all of these attributes are literally constants. It is difficult, however, to find a consistent data source that would show time-series variations in these variables.

11. An interesting issue for further research, beyond the scope of this study, is the rate at which this kind of information on changes in the side-effect profile is disseminated to physicians. Scouler (1993) presents evidence that physicians' perceptions of drug "safety" can be at odds with published data and that those perceptions are slowly updated, if at all.

consideration of functional form to linear and log-linear, which perform roughly equally. I report the log-linear results here:

$$\ln p_i = \beta_0 + \sum_j \beta_j z_{ij} + e_i \text{, for } i = 1, \ldots, 10,$$

where i indexes products and j indexes attributes (with the t subscript suppressed). There are a total of 130 possible observations for the regression—thirteen years, from 1977 through 1989 and ten products. Since not all of the products were on the market for all years, however, the actual number of observations for this unbalanced panel is eighty-eight.

I add a series of annual time dummies to capture inflationary effects. I can then construct a hedonic price index directly from the regression coefficients. This estimated quality-adjusted price index will isolate pure price changes, unrelated to quality variations.

Two additional econometric issues arise. The first is heteroscedasticity of the error term. The anti-ulcer drugs sampled differ markedly in terms of sales. To correct for this scale effect, I use weighted least squares where the weights are the annual sales of each brand. In the results below I present both weighted and unweighted estimates. The second issue concerns brand-name effects (or manufacturer effects). Drug safety can be measured statistically to some degree, but physicians (and, to a lesser extent, patients) form expectations that may be based in part on past experience. We can potentially capture such elusive characteristics by including dummy variables for each manufacturer or "make."

I expect a positive sign for the coefficients on healing rate, absorption level, and half-life. I expect a negative correlation between price and drug interactions, side effects, and frequency of medication. (As mentioned above, this is true holding constant the state of knowledge about a particular drug. Here I do not separate the two effects.)

Empirical Results

I summarize the regression estimates for the pooled 1977 through 1989 sample period in table 4–4. I report both weighted and unweighted results for the full sample and for the subsample of "new"—class 23400—drugs only. All regressions include the fixed ("manufacturer" or "make") effects discussed above. In the new drug subsample I had to drop selected characteristics because of singularity problems. Finally, although it would have been instructive to run separate regressions for pairs of adjacent years, particularly for the new drugs, there were not enough observations to have confidence in the results. In all

TABLE 4–4
PARAMETER ESTIMATES OF HEDONIC PRICE FUNCTION

	All Drugs		New Drugs	
	Unweighted	Weighted	Unweighted	Weighed
FREQ	−.276	−.277	−.48	−.023
	(.128)	(.083)	(.017)	(.013)
DI	−.007	−.002	.007	.002
	(.012)	(.002)	(.005)	(.003)
SE1M	−.104	−.098		
	(.014)	(.010)		
SE1L	−.030	−.037		
	(.027)	(.012)		
SE1R	−.063	−.057	−.017	−.025
	(.020)	(.007)	(.014)	(.010)
SE2M	.536	.542	−.035	−.061
	(.074)	(.061)	(.033)	(.037)
SE2LR	.006	.004	.002	.005
	(.009)	(.002)	(.003)	(.002)
ABS	−.004	−.003	−.003	−.003
	(.002)	(.001)	(.0004)	(.0004)
HL	.358	.326	−.210	−.178
	(.175)	(.095)	(.067)	(.043)
HEAL	.059	.060	−.059	−.059
	(.004)	(.002)	(.008)	(.005)
D77	−5.036	−5.058	4.925	4.825
D78	−4.994	−5.000	4.914	4.815
D79	−4.942	−4.983	4.909	4.809
D80	−4.854	−4.942	4.940	4.841
D81	−4.656	−4.703	5.095	5.004
D82	−4.544	−4.645	5.109	5.049
D83	−4.437	−4.542	5.196	5.131
D84	−4.385	−4.489	5.256	5.190
D85	−4.240	−4.327	5.375	5.329
D86	−4.124	−4.211	5.482	5.431
D87	−4.044	−4.139	5.519	5.501
D88	−3.925	−4.058	5.612	5.579
D89	−3.781	−3.919	5.693	5.678
Observations	88	88	36	36
R^2	.98	.98	.99	.99

NOTE: Dependent variable is logarithm of daily dose price. Standard errors in parentheses. Note that the standard errors on the time dummies are approximately .7 for unweighted regression and .4 for weighted.

of the regressions reported here, both the time and make effects are jointly significant.

Most of the coefficients have the expected sign. For example, an increase in the frequency of dosage decreases the price. This result fits well with the statements of consumers and physicians, who purport to value convenience in a drug. An increase in the number of most frequently observed side effects (SE1M, SE1L, SE1R) also is associated with a lower price and therefore carries a negative value to users.

Those variables not having the expected sign are the "less dangerous" side-effect variables (SE2M and SE2LR). The positive coefficients imply that the higher the number of these side-effects, the higher the price, which is contrary to intuition.[12] Note that including an age variable (time since introduction) has no effect on the results. The coefficient on the age variable is positive, but insignificantly different from zero, and is not reported.

Turning to the regressions for the new drug subsample, I find a high degree of multicollinearity among the five side-effects variables, and among the side-effects variables, the measure of drug interactions, and the average healing rate. Therefore, for the new drug subsample I drop SE1M and SE1L.

Several changes in sign occur for the new drug subsample. The drug interaction coefficient becomes positive (it continues to be insignificant), and the half-life and healing rate coefficients change sign as well. The magnitude of the frequency and side-effects coefficients declines as well. Two explanations for the changes in the magnitude of the coefficients are possible. First, there is less variation in some of the side-effects and drug interaction variables over the new drug sample, which suggests a closer clustering of products in terms of their therapeutic profiles. For example, the variance of DI falls from 9 to 5.3 when the sample is restricted to class 23400 drugs, and the variance of SE2M falls from 7.1 to .27. Second, the firms producing the new drugs may be exerting their market power by setting prices more independently of product characteristics. Since the hedonic equation reflects both demand and supply forces, it is possible that, while the general direction of the correlation is the same between attributes and price, the magnitude of the effect is being dampened by supply-side effects.

---

12. In an earlier draft of this study, the side-effects measure was a single variable derived as a simple sum of the number of side effects reported. The sign on this variable was positive. It was suggested that this might be due to measurement error. Although the problem has not disappeared with the addition of the disaggregate side-effects variables, it is somewhat comforting that the expected negative sign now appears for the more important side-effects variables.

Many would argue that promotional expenditures should be included as a product "attribute." I have data on annual promotional expenditures for drugs in the 23400 category from 1977 through 1989.[13] Those data are IMS's "combined media" data, which are aggregated from separate audits covering promotions by mail, advertising in magazines and professional journals, and detailing—direct sales calls by company representatives to physicians and hospitals. According to a pharmaceutical company representative, the IMS estimates of detailing expenditures are an underestimate of actual promotional expenditures.[14] For example, IMS does not capture expenditures on promotional displays put on by drug companies at medical conventions. The bias in the data is reportedly thought to occur across the board and is not particular to any product or manufacturer. Compared with Smith-Kline's initial promotional expenditures on Tagamet, the data show that Glaxo promoted Zantac heavily upon its introduction in 1983. Cytotec's promotional campaign was also aggressive in its introductory year on the market. When added to the hedonic regressions, the coefficient on the promotional variable is positive, as expected, but insignificantly different from zero, and I do not report it.

Using the estimates in table 4–4, I report a quality-adjusted price index for anti-ulcer drugs over the 1977 through 1989 period in table 4–5, where I normalize the 1977 index level to 100. I give both unweighted and sales-weighted indexes. The rate of increase was fairly flat or decreasing at the beginning of the sample, but then begins to increase in 1981.

We can make several interesting comparisons. For example, the last column of table 4–5 gives a simple, unweighted, index that might be constructed quickly from data on prices (although still converting to daily dose prices). A comparison of this raw data index with the "new drugs" index (either weighted or unweighted) shows the effect of quality adjustment on the interpretation of drug price inflation. The raw data index increased roughly 270 percent from 1977 through 1989, while the quality-adjusted index increased slightly more than 100 percent over the same period. The magnitude of the difference between the unadjusted and adjusted indexes obviously depends on the baseline index used for comparison. One might want to compare these indexes with a fixed-basket Laspeyres price index, similar to what the Bureau of Labor Statistics might use. As an example, the annual average growth rate in the Laspeyres index calculated from 1984 through

---

13. Because of budgetary constraints, I do not have promotional data for the 23100–23300 series.

14. Telephone conversation with a Glaxo, Inc., representative.

TABLE 4-5
Quality-adjusted Price Index for Anti-Ulcer Drugs, 1977–1989

Year	All Drugs, Unweighted		All Drugs, Weighted		New Drugs, Unweighted		New Drugs, Weighted		Raw Data Unweighted
	Index	%Δ	Index	%Δ	Index	%Δ	Index	%Δ	Index
1977	100	—	100	—	100	—	100	—	100
1978	104	4.2	106	5.6	99	−1.1	99	−1.1	103
1979	110	5.1	108	1.7	98	−0.5	98	−0.5	107
1980	120	8.4	112	4.0	102	3.1	102	3.1	117
1981	146	18.0	143	21.2	119	14.4	120	15.0	143
1982	164	10.6	151	5.7	120	1.4	125	4.4	158
1983	182	10.1	167	9.7	131	8.3	136	7.9	191
1984	192	5.1	176	5.2	139	5.8	144	5.7	208
1985	221	13.5	208	14.9	157	11.2	165	13.0	237
1986	249	11.0	233	11.0	175	10.1	183	9.7	273
1987	270	7.6	251	6.9	181	3.6	196	6.7	292
1988	304	11.3	272	7.8	199	8.9	213	7.7	328
1989	351	13.4	312	13.0	216	7.8	235	9.4	370

1989 for the fixed basket for Tagamet, Zantac, and Carafate is 9.5 percent. A similar quality-adjusted index for those same products grows at the rate of 8.7 percent.

Finally, one can observe from table 4–5 that the largest price increases come in 1981, 1985, and 1989. Coincidentally, those increases lead the entry of Zantac, Pepcid, and Cytotec into the field. Such a pattern may be due to a segmenting of the market. In continuing work Perloff, Suslow, and Seguin (1995) develop a model of a spatially differentiated market where entry may cause an incumbent's price to rise. Future research on pharmaceutical pricing must address strategic issues, as well as the problems of quality measurement.

Concluding Remarks

Measuring the characteristics important in drug demand is a difficult task. Even something as apparently straightforward as the dosing interval is dependent upon the particular therapy, the patient profile, and the physician's discretion. This chapter takes an initial step toward quantifying the important characteristics for pharmaceutical products to estimate a quality-adjusted price index. I find that increases in the dosage frequency, number of drug interactions, and the more serious elements of the side-effect profile all are correlated with a lower daily dose price. The estimates show a small but significant upward bias in the price index based on the raw data because of a failure to control for product innovation in anti-ulcer drugs over the sample period. A large portion of these price increases reflects quality improvements along dimensions that doctors and patients value.

I conducted my analysis with data from IMS International. The data set includes information on shipments and sales of individual drugs, at a highly disaggregated level. It would be relatively straightforward to use this type of data set to analyze other pharmaceutical markets to obtain a better estimate of the importance of this issue across a broad spectrum of products, so that we may better advise policy makers of the magnitude of the bias when using unadjusted prices to formulate policy. The analysis presented here is a first step toward evaluating the applicability of hedonic price estimates for general use in pharmaceutical markets, as well as for highlighting some of the technical issues that need further research.

Appendix 4-A

Data for Drug Attributes. The drug attribute information was compiled primarily from the 1980 through 1990 volumes of the *U.S. Pharmacopeial Convention, Dispensing Information*, or *USP DI*.[15]

---

15. Note that the 1982 volume of the *USP DI* was not published, due to a format change. Therefore, 1981 data are used for 1982.

The dosage information is for the "usual adult oral dosage" (tablet form) for an active duodenal or benign gastric ulcer. Various complications arose in using the dosage information. As one example, table 4–3, panel B shows the usual dosage for Tagamet changing from 300 mg, four times daily, to 400 mg, two times daily. The *USP DI* does not actually state which is the preferred dosing regime. It merely shows that, as of 1986, Tagamet was available in a 400 mg strength, along with the recommended dosage for 400 mg tablets. In 1987 Tagamet could also be taken as an 800 mg tablet once per day. I have used the 400 mg, two times daily, figure as an average. Other drugs cause different problems. Pro-Banthine, for example, has a usual dosage of 15 mg, three times daily, *and* 30 mg, once a day. Still other dosages may be listed as "1 or 2 tablets, 3 or 4 times daily." In such cases I use a simple average to calculate daily prices.

I selected drug interactions on the basis of their potential clinical significance. The *USP DI* identifies certain drug interactions as "significant." For example, taking antacids at the same time as H_2-receptor antagonist drugs may help the pain, but taking too many simultaneously will decrease the absorption of the H_2-antagonist and therefore decrease its effectiveness. This drug interaction would not be counted. An H_2-antagonist taken at the same time as anticoagulants or antidepressants could heighten the actions of the latter drugs to the point where a medically dangerous reaction could result, however. The latter drug interaction was marked as significant in the *USP DI*.

Selected side effects are also listed in the *USP DI*. Selection is based on seriousness, frequency of occurrence, the effect on lifestyle, and the likelihood that a nonthreatening side effect might cause concern in the patient if he or she were not aware that the effect might occur (*USP DI* 1983, ix).

The average healing rate is measured as the average rate at which the ulcer is expected to be healed over a four-week period. I obtained information from the medical sources listed in the references. I used earlier editions of those sources for the 23100–23300 drugs. Documentation on the 23400 drugs is much more detailed, both because those drugs are newer and because they are used much more frequently than the drugs in the 23100–23300 categories.

The absorption and half-life data come from a variety of sources: *USP DI*, Medex and Genmed files on Lexis, and clinical pharmacology books listed in the references.

References

Afuah, Allan N. "Technical Progress and Product Market Success in Pharmaceuticals: The Case of Cholesterol Ethical Drugs." Sloan

School of Management Working Paper #3495–92 BPS, November 1992.

"Agitation in a Crowded Anti-ulcer Drug Market." *Chemical Week* (January 25, 1989): 9.

Bayless, Theodore M. *Current Therapy in Gastroenterology and Liver Disease—3*. Toronto: B. C. Decker, 1990.

Berndt, Ernst R., and Stan Finkelstein. "Price Indexes for Antihypertensive Drugs That Incorporate Quality Change: A Progress Report on a Feasibility Study." MIT Program on the Pharmaceutical Industry, December 1992.

Berndt, Ernst R., Zvi Griliches, and Joshua Rosett. "Auditing the Producer Price Index: Micro Evidence from Prescription Pharmaceutical Preparations." *Journal of Business and Economic Statistics* 11 (1993): 251–64.

Bochner, Felix, et al. *Handbook of Clinical Pharmacology*, 2nd ed. Toronto: Little, Brown and Company, 1983.

Caves, Richard E., Michael D. Whinston, and Mark A. Hurwitz. "Patent Expiration, Entry, and Competition in the U.S. Pharmaceutical Industry." *Brookings Papers: Microeconomics* (1991): 1–48.

Chemical Marketing Reporter (August 25, 1986): 18.

Cocks, Douglas L. "Product Innovation and the Dynamic Elements of Competition in the Ethical Pharmaceutical Industry." In *Drug Development and Marketing*, edited by Robert B. Helms. Washington, D.C.: AEI Press, 1975.

————, and John R. Virts. "Pricing Behavior of the Ethical Pharmaceutical Industry." *Journal of Business* 47 (1974): 349–62.

Court, A. "Hedonic Price Indexes with Automotive Examples." In *The Dynamics of Automobile Demand*. Detroit: General Motors Corporation, 1939, 98–119.

Dajda, Richard, and David Owen. "Price Sensitivity Analysis in the U.K. Pharmaceutical Market." In *EPHMRA/ESOMAR Seminar on Pricing and Forecasting in the Pharmaceutical Industry*. United Kingdom: EPHMRA, 1987.

Dao, T. "Drug Innovation and Price Competition." In *Pharmaceutical Economics*, edited by B. Lundgren. Lund: Swedish Institute for Health Economics, 1984.

Dell'Osso, Filippo. "When Leaders Become Followers: The Market for Anti-ulcer Drugs." London Business School Case Series, no. 12, February 1990.

Dranove, David. "Medicaid Drug Formulary Restrictions." *Journal of Law and Economics* 33 (1989): 143–62.

Dreyfuss, Joel. "SmithKline's Ulcer Medicine 'Holy War.'" *Fortune* (September 19, 1983): 129–36.

Drug Facts and Comparisons, 44th ed. St. Louis: Facts and Comparisons, 1990.

Fisher, Frankin M., and Karl Shell. *The Economic Theory of Price Indexes: Two Essays on the Effects of Taste, Quality and Technological Change.* Cambridge: MIT Press, 1983.

General Accounting Office. *Prescription Drugs: Changes in Prices for Selected Drugs.* Washington, D.C.: Government Printing Office, August 1992.

Gilman, A.G., et al. *Goodman and Gilman's: The Pharmacological Basis of Therapeutics*, 6th ed. New York: Macmillan, 1980.

Griliches, Zvi, ed. *Price Indexes and Quality Change.* Cambridge: Harvard University Press, 1971.

Hurwitz, Mark A., and Richard E. Caves. "Persuasion or Information? Promotion and the Shares of Brand Name and Generic Pharmaceuticals." *Journal of Law and Economics* 31 (1988): 299–320.

IMS. *IMS Pharmaceutical Database Manual.* Plymouth Meeting, Penn.: IMS America Ltd., 1990.

Katzung, Bertram, et al. *Clinical Pharmacology '88/'89.* Norwalk, Conn.: Appleton & Lange, 1988.

McCann, Christine. "General Practitioners' Price Awareness in the Asthma Market." In *EPHMRA/ESOMAR Seminar on Pricing in the Pharmaceutical Industry.* Sale, England: EPHMRA, 1987.

McFadden, Daniel. "Econometric Models of Probabilistic Choice." In *Structural Analysis of Discrete Data with Econometric Applications*, edited by Charles Manski and Daniel McFadden. Cambridge: MIT Press 1981.

Maddala, G.S. *Limited-Dependent and Qualitative Variables in Econometrics.* Cambridge: Cambridge University Press, 1983.

Merck Manual of Diagnosis and Therapy, 15th ed. Rahway, N.J.: Merck Sharp & Dohme Research Laboratories, 1987.

Ohning, Gordon, and Andrew Soll. "Medical Treatment of Peptic Ulcer Disease." *American Family Physician* 39 (1989): 257–70.

Perloff, Jeff, Valerie Suslow, and Paul Seguin. "Higher Prices from Entry: Pricing of Brand-Name Drugs." University of Michigan Business School, August 1995.

Physician's Desk Reference, various years.

Reekie, W. D. "Price and Quality Competition in the United States Drug Industry." *Journal of Industrial Economics* 26 (1978): 223–37.

Rosen, Sherwin. Hedonic Prices and Implicit Markets: Product Differentiation in Pure Competition. *Journal of Political Economy* 82 (1974): 34–55.

Scouler, Bonnie. "A Segmentation Analysis of the Ulcer Drug Market." Master's thesis, Massachusetts Institute of Technology, May 1993.

Sleisenger, Marvin H., and John S. Fordtran. *Gastrointestinal Disease*, 2nd ed. Philadelphia: W. B. Saunders Company, 1978.

Sourcebook of Health Insurance Data. Washington, D.C.: Health Insurance Association of America, various issues.

Trajtenberg, Manuel. *Economic Analysis of Product Innovation*. Cambridge: Harvard University Press, 1990.

Triplett, J. "The Economic Interpretation of Hedonic Methods." *Survey of Current Business* 66 (1986): 36–40.

U.S. Pharmacopeial Convention, Dispensing Information (USP DI): Drug Information for the Health Care Provider. Rockville, Md.: various years.

Yankelovich, Skelly and White/Shulman Clancy. "Consumer Concerns with Ulcer Symptoms and Experience with Antacid Usage." Report for SmithKline Beecham. Westport, Conn.: March 1, 1988.

Commentary on Part One

James H. Sinclair

There has been a lot of press lately on producer price indexes in the pharmaceutical area. I am responsible for calculating the PPI for pharmaceutical prescriptions at the Bureau of Labor Statistics. The studies by Zvi Griliches and Iain Cockburn, by Ernst Berndt and Paul E. Greenberg, and by Valerie Suslow are important research efforts that allow a continuing dialogue on major issues important to both index calculators and index users. We must meet those issues head on.

I shall discuss the three studies in terms of the issues the authors raise regarding the PPI methodology. The goals of the research price indexes presented and the official PPI are the same: to search for an accurate deflator for prescription drugs.

The issues Griliches and Cockburn, Berndt and Greenberg, and Suslow raise concern the development of constant quality price indexes, the inclusion of new goods in the official producer price indexes, and the treatment of generics in the official deflators.

Suslow addresses quality-adjusted price indexes by examining one particular drug class—antispasmodic or anti-ulcer drugs. I applaud her efforts in attempting to quantify nonprice characteristics as they pertain to prescription drugs. The PPI uses a resource cost—fixed and variable costs with some sort of return for the entrepreneur marked up to wholesale—estimate to measure product changes. Many times, the quality-adjustment data are unavailable from the respondents. Therefore, we miss any quality improvements. For example, the efficacy of the drug may increase, but no cost information is available to reflect properly the true price change for the product. Assuming that the old drug is no longer manufactured or shipped—a PPI program requirement—we substitute the new product for the old and ask the respondent for a value of the improvement expressed in terms of resource costs. In many cases pharmaceutical manufacturers cannot give us that value. We therefore treat the difference in the prices either as all quality improvements or as all price changes. The former cause no change in the index level; the latter allow a direct comparison that causes the index to go up by the amount of the price differential. It is conceivable that the amount of the quality improvement that a hedonic function estimates is equal to or greater than the price change so that the actual quality-adjusted price declines. In the absence of company information or regression estimates to measure those quality changes, our price indexes will not reflect constant quality. We need more research to assist us in evaluating embodied technological changes. Hedonic estimates such as those Suslow used to quantify in dollar terms the improvements related to dose regime, number of drug interactions, the side-effect profile, average efficacy, and even the influence of brand-name identification would be of great assistance in developing constant quality price indexes. The Bureau of Labor Statistics currently uses hedonic estimates in other high-technology industries, such as computers and mass storage devices, but we have not applied the approach to the pharmaceutical industry. Given the current budget constraints and the possibility of staff reductions, adding this project on top of our current responsibilities would be ambitious, indeed. Second, the new-goods issue raised by Griliches, Berndt, and Rosett (1993) is real, and I am happy to report to you today that something is being done about it. We traditionally sample industries on a five- to seven-year cycle because it takes a great deal of time to analyze 500 industries in the mining and manufacturing sectors. We are currently budgeted to analyze forty-three additional industries in the service sector. As a result of that effort, we publish approximately 10,000 price indexes monthly from about 100,000 price quotations.

Obviously, there are certain industries that require a more rapid evaluation because of the increased exit and entry of firms and, more important, the advent of tremendous technological changes in the products manufactured. The pharmaceutical industry is a candidate for our new policy of sampling a few high-tech industries more frequently. We shall analyze the pharmaceutical prescription industry for the most recent recycling period every four years and augment our sample of new products and companies every two years. We have substantially increased the number of companies participating in our program, have almost tripled the number of quotations collected, and have used new procedures to ensure that we cover important product categories. Specifically, we have selected products by therapeutic class broken down into their Uniform System of Classification codes first and then have visited companies to collect pricing and product information. Following those measures, we have included products in our 1988 through 1993 market basket that should significantly reduce the age bias Griliches and Cockburn described. Thus, we may close the gap of a 50 percent differential between the PPI series and the Divisia calculations of Griliches, Berndt, and Rosett and the 41 percent differential calculated by using Berndt and Greenberg's methodology. Again, with the availability of more resources, we hope to continue our "fast-track" resampling effort.

Finally, the issue of how we treat generics in the PPI is a special case of the new-goods problem and is not so easy to remedy from both a methodological and an operational viewpoint. As Griliches and Cockburn indicated, the PPI treats the introduction of those goods as "new" and therefore links them into the indexes. That was the procedure for the 1988 through 1993 market basket, and it will *generally* be true for the new market basket for the 1994 through 1998 period. Assuming that the pioneer and generic drugs are equivalent (according to the Food and Drug Administration, they are), we shall include them in the index and directly compare the two goods, that is, show the price reduction at the introduction period. We understand, however, that there is some controversy between bioequivalence and therapeutic equivalence, but we shall assume that the FDA's definition is correct. We directly compare the two goods *only* if the same manufacturer produces them. The exact time period for inclusion in our index will be a function of the $N-4$ correction policy period of the BLS—we do not consider price indexes final until the fifth month after publication, to allow for any possible corrections caused by late reporting—and the estimated weight of the new generic vis-à-vis company projections or secondary-source information. The operational procedures we plan to use for properly weighting the generic introduction directly address the "diffusion" principle Griliches and Cockburn describe. If new companies introduce the generic drug into the market, however, we shall treat the drug as we treat all products of new companies and link it into the index showing no index level change for the introduction month.

The PPI methodology is based on the neoclassical model of the theory of the firm, where we assume fixed technology for a given revenue stream. Archibald (1977) best describes how that model is applied to the PPI program. If the production functions differ between companies (the experience through "learning by doing" that the pioneer accumulates during the patent protection period gives the pioneer a different production technology from that of the generic counterpart), we cannot directly compare the generics with the pioneer drug and be consistent with our PPI methodology. This issue is somewhat different when compared with the consumer price index quality adjustment, in which such a comparison (as inputs to consumers) seems simply a matter of whether the products are therapeutically equivalent. An example might help to clarify this point in the context of our Laspeyres fixed input-output price index methodology. Assume that a dominant computer manufacturer that has enjoyed a patent on its architecture produces a 32-bit computer with an 80386DX microprocessor that crunches data at a 33 megahertz speed and has an expanded keyboard and a VGA color monitor. That company has a unique production function and sells the product at a certain price. After the patent expires, new firms enter the market and offer clones with the same features. The entrants' production functions for manufacturing the personal computers are different for producing essentially the same good that the dominant firm manufactured. If those companies reported to the BLS, we would treat their products as new goods and link them into the index without directly comparing the prices between dominant product and the clone in the introduction month. If we treated those goods as having the same production functions, we would be violating the economic model on which we based our producer price index. The same principle holds true for generic drugs: we shall not compare prices between the pioneer and generic drugs across companies during the introduction month because of differences in the manufacturing process—different production functions.

In a Laspeyres framework we do not have the luxury of changing quantity weights every month or every year. Such "restrictions" of a methodology using a Laspeyres index do tend to cause a lag for including a product and therefore support the idea of the Laspeyres index as an "upper bound" to price index methodologies that incorporate constantly changing quantities. We believe, however, that collecting data from manufacturers directly, adjusting for modifications or substitutions as they occur to maintain index continuity, and obtaining net transaction prices help us meet the BLS's mission of developing accurate and timely price indexes for the general public.

References

Archibald, Robert B. "On the Theory of Industrial Price Measurement: Output Price Indexes." *Annals of Economic and Social Measurement* 6 (1977): 57–72.

Berndt, Ernst R., Zvi Griliches, and Joshua G. Rosett. "Auditing the Producer Price Index: Micro Evidence from Prescription Pharmaceutical Preparations." *Journal of Economics and Business Statistics* 11 (1993): 251–64.

Joseph M. Jadlow

The excellent studies of Griliches and Cockburn, Berndt and Greenberg, and Suslow reveal various shortcomings of the government's producer price indexes for the U.S. pharmaceutical industry. It seems likely that the same weaknesses exist for price indexes reported for any industry that has a continuing flow of new products to the market. Therefore, the potential benefits from continuing this research go far beyond the drug industry.

These studies generally show that the picture official government statistics provide about patterns of pharmaceutical prices is very misleading. Thus, any inclination to allow such statistics to influence public policy toward that industry would be a gross mistake as long as the government continues to use current methodology to generate those numbers.

The three studies have some common themes. These studies, as well as recent related work by these and other researchers, identify various built-in biases in the procedures used to compute producer price indexes for the pharmaceutical industry. The Bureau of Labor Statistics employs a Laspeyres-type index with fixed weights that it revises only every few years. In an industry in which new products are the rule rather than the exception, new drug products are given too little weight in the calculations. This problem is evidently made worse by BLS sampling procedures that cause younger products, which have less than average rates of price increase, to be underrepresented (Berndt, Griliches, and Rosett 1993, 258–59). Berndt and Greenberg find that if alterations in methodology are made to correct for those problems, the annual rate of increase in pharmaceutical prices is substantially lower—in fact almost one-third lower—than what the BLS methodology suggests. Similarly, using hedonic prices to study certain therapeutic drug categories, Suslow finds that the rate of increase in drug prices is significantly lower when she calculates a "quality-adjusted" price index as compared with unadjusted price indexes.

The most serious problem incorporated in the BLS's methodology, however, would seem to be the treatment of generic versions of a brand-name product as completely *new* goods. When a generic is introduced on the market, the price of its progenitor often remains constant at first and later may rise somewhat; although no price relief occurs for consumers of the brand-name product, many consumers switch to the generic version, which frequently will be priced 50 percent to 75 percent lower than the brand-name drug. The BLS price indexes reflect none of the direct price relief enjoyed by the consumers who substitute the generic for the branded version. Thus, the official statistics may indicate that prices are going up, when, in fact, they have declined substantially. For example, Griliches and Cockburn's study showed this for one product, cephalexin, whose price rose 14 percent during a given period of time according to the BLS approach but declined by 53 percent when the branded and generic versions were treated as perfect substitutes.

There is a certain amount of irony in this latter paradox. Given the recent criticism of high prices in the pharmaceutical industry (Rosenbaum 1993),[1] drug firms have an interest in seeing the BLS treat branded drug products and their generics as identical goods so that the official indexes more accurately reflect the reduced price benefits that generics provide to consumers, and thereby relieve some of the public pressure on drug companies to restrain their prices. At the same time, we all know that the major pharmaceutical companies have expended considerable resources over the past several decades to convince physicians, pharmacists, and the public that brand-name drug products and their generic counterparts are *not* perfect substitutes and that generic prescribing and generic substitution should not occur. No doubt, some of this has been a legitimate attempt to provide information on real differences between goods, while some of it has merely been rent-seeking behavior designed to differentiate products or to convince the government to erect barriers to the competition from generics. In any case, if the official statistics reflect more of the competition between branded and generic products, the pharmaceutical industry will be less likely to have the government impose direct price controls on drugs.

This raises substantial challenges for the Bureau of Labor Statistics, whose leadership up to now, according to James H. Sinclair, has been convinced that brand-name drugs and their generics have different production functions and therefore are different goods. The BLS must, or should, come up with a methodology that will allow the official indexes to reflect the price competition between branded and generic products without necessarily making the extreme assumption that the two are perfect substitutes. It would be unfortunate if the BLS's own limited resources—a major constraint according to Dr. Sinclair— kept it from doing this. At the same time, it seems imperative that the sampling procedures employed in the future give more weight to new and young products than is now the case and that the market baskets used be revised much more frequently than they currently are. Perhaps an index along the lines of the adjusted Paasche index, which Griliches and Cockburn seem to prefer, may be feasible.

In any regard, research such as that reported in these three studies

---

1. In a sense, Rosenbaum makes the same mistake as the BLS. He chooses to emphasize the fact that the prices of brand-name drugs are often raised when their patents expire. What he fails to appreciate is that the concurrent growth in market share of generics selling at much lower prices helps ensure that consumers as a group have substantial welfare gains.

provides useful guides as to the types of improvements that should be made in the official indexes. In the meantime, it seems clear that anyone making public policy proposals who relies on the official producer price indexes as evidence of substantial inflation of pharmaceutical prices is misleading the public and possibly himself.

References

Berndt, Ernst R., Zvi Griliches, and Joshua G. Rosett. "Auditing the Producer Price Index: Micro Evidence from Prescription Pharmaceutical Preparations." *Journal of Business & Statistics* 11 (1993): 251–64.

Rosenbaum, David E. "America's Economic Outlaw: The U.S. Health Care System." *New York Times*, October 26, 1993, pp. A1 and A11.

David I. Kass

Before discussing the studies of Griliches and Cockburn, of Berndt and Greenberg, and of Suslow and showing how they may relate to reforming health care and the pricing of pharmaceuticals in a competitive market, I shall provide a brief perspective on the size of the pharmaceutical industry. For 1993 total expenditures at retail outlets in the United States on prescription drugs were $38 billion. Nonprescription drug sales at retail outlets equaled $20 billion. The total expenditures on prescription and nonprescription drugs at retail outlets, $58 billion, represented approximately 7 percent of national health expenditures.[1]

In 1991 third parties paid for 45 percent of the total expenditures for prescription drugs (Letsch et al. 1992, table 2). That is a substantially smaller percentage than the 97 percent share that third parties reimbursed for hospital services and the 82 percent they paid for physicians' services (Letsch et al. 1992, table 15). The third parties that do pay for prescription drugs are primarily private insurers and Medicaid.

Griliches and Cockburn, Berndt and Greenberg, and Suslow focus on the producer price index for prescription drugs. For background, I would like to contrast briefly the consumer price index, which is the

---

The views expressed in this discussion are those of the author and do not represent an official position of the Bureau of Economic Analysis or the Department of Commerce.

1. Bureau of Economic Analysis detail underlying line 45: "Drug preparations and sundries" of table 2.4, Personal Consumption Expenditures by Type of Expenditure. Those expenditures exclude prescription and nonprescription drugs dispensed by hospitals, nursing homes, physicians, and other health professionals as well as government purchases.

most frequently cited measure of inflation, with the producer price index. To do that I shall present a brief overview of the medical component of the consumer price index. That component has several difficult measurement problems.

Over the past ten years, the medical component of the CPI has grown at twice the rate of the overall CPI. It is important to note that the medical component is not intended to measure medical price inflation throughout the economy. It is designed to measure a component of a cost-of-living index, which in turn measures the consumer expenditures needed to maintain a constant living standard. The medical component of the CPI prices only medical goods and services paid for out-of-pocket by consumers or by insurance policies purchased by consumers. Goods and services paid for by employer-purchased health insurance or by federal programs are out of the scope of the medical component of the CPI. Since most medical care is not paid for by consumers out-of-pocket or by consumer-purchased insurance, the medical component of the CPI should not be used as a deflator for total medical care spending. The weights of the medical component of the CPI are appropriate for a price index defined, as is the CPI, on consumer expenditures. For example, since the weights for the medical component of the CPI are based on out-of-pocket costs and consumer-purchased insurance, hospital prices get about the same weight as physicians' prices because actual consumer outlays for hospitals and for physicians are approximately equal. Total national hospital expenditures are twice physicians' expenditures, however. Similarly, although the medical component of the CPI has a weight of 6.9 percent in the calculation of the CPI, total national health expenditures equal approximately 14 percent of gross domestic product.

With respect to the prescription drug component of the CPI, which has been growing slightly faster than both the medical component of the CPI and the PPI for prescription drugs, the Bureau of Labor Statistics measures price changes in the same item at the same outlet. Therefore, the BLS does not capture changes due to consumers' switching to different outlets. For example, if a consumer last year was purchasing pharmaceuticals from a local drug store and this year through a mail-order operation at a much lower price, the current CPI would not capture that price difference. In addition, the BLS captures price changes from brand to generic drugs *only* when the particular outlet where the BLS collects prices no longer carries the brand-name drug but does carry a generic equivalent (Knudsen 1993).

With respect to the PPI, it is important to note that the goal of that index is to measure changes in selling prices that domestic producers receive for their outputs. Both the study by Griliches and Cockburn and the study by Berndt and Greenberg discuss the desirability of having the BLS sample pharmaceutical prices more frequently, since new drug prices generally increase at lower rates than older drugs. The BLS is beginning to address that problem by sampling pharmaceuticals every two years instead of every five to seven years, as it previously did. Although more frequent sampling would certainly ameliorate that problem, it does not eliminate it.

This is true for any industry in which firms rapidly introduce new products and change prices for new products differently from the way they do for old products. In this regard, I would like to quote from a paper by Jack Triplett, the chief economist at the Bureau of Economic Analysis. Triplett (1993, 200–201) says:

> We want the PPI to be based on a probability sample of *current* price *changes*. The present PPI sampling methodology approximates a probability sample of *sales* in the *initiation* period. [This] may be adequate when little change occurs in the range of products that are for sale, when yesterday's products are pretty much the same as today's. Or . . . when the prices of any new products that are introduced move more or less consistently with those of established products. [The sampling mechanism, however,] is inadequate in the PPI for prescription drugs, where new introductions show price movements that differ substantially from those for established drugs. . . . A price index that records only price movements in established products misses much of the price change that occurs in the industry.

Triplett (1993, 201) asserts that "new introductions bias is a sampling problem, a case where rapid technological change creates a sample that is not representative of current price change in the industry."

Suslow's study uses hedonic regressions. The BLS is studying that technique so that it can remove from its reported prices a measure of price change associated with quality. In that regard I would like to suggest a potential application of quality-adjusted price measures relating to proposals for health care reform, such as those offered by the Clinton administration and, by extension, also relevant to the pricing and marketing of drugs to third-party buyers. Specifically, an integral part of the administration's proposal is the formation of a national health board. Within the national health board, the administration proposes a breakthrough drug committee with the stated purpose of encouraging reasonable pricing of breakthrough drugs and of making public declarations regarding the reasonableness of new drug prices.

If Congress enacts legislation containing proposals such as the national health board with its proposed role on breakthrough drug

81

prices, some important questions will be raised about what the improvements offered by the new drugs are worth. It may create some very interesting applications for hedonic pricing techniques. It seems to me that one application of Professor Suslow's work, and that of others working in this area, would be for pharmaceutical companies to perform, either in-house or outside, a hedonic pricing analysis of new drugs to estimate the value of additional attributes or "quality" so that they could estimate "reasonable" prices for new drugs. Simultaneously, one might expect the national health board to do their own analysis in-house or outside to see whether they get similar results. The same approach could be useful in marketing to formulary committees in large health maintenance organizations.

To conclude, the work being performed by Professors Griliches and Cockburn, Berndt and Greenberg, and Suslow is extremely important in the measurement of price change. Clearly, we are in a very early stage of research in that area, and much additional research needs to be done. Finally, in the general context of health care reform, it is important for policy makers to be able to explain as accurately as possible the extent that increases in health care expenditures result from price increases versus increases in the quantity and quality of services provided. The work of Griliches and Cockburn, Berndt and Greenberg, and Suslow makes important contributions in that area.

References

Knudsen, David. Bureau of Labor Statistics. Personal communication. October 21, 1993.

Letsch, Suzanne W., Helen C. Lazenby, Katharine R. Levit, and Cathy Cowan. "National Health Expenditures, 1991." *Health Care Financing Review* (Winter 1992): 1–30.

Triplett, Jack E. "Comment." In *Price Measurements and Their Uses*, edited by Murray F. Foss, Marilyn E. Manser, and Allan H. Young. Chicago: University of Chicago Press, 1993.

PART TWO

The International Market for Pharmaceuticals

5

The Uses and Abuses of International Price Comparisons

Patricia M. Danzon

Governments are increasingly using cross-national comparisons of pharmaceutical prices to justify regulatory strategies to control health care costs. Price regulation schemes in Italy, France, and Canada routinely compare specific prices. The German government considered broader comparisons to justify the reference price system introduced in 1989. Such studies are receiving increasing attention in the United States. In 1992, in response to congressional concern over the rising cost of prescription drugs, the General Accounting Office (1992) published a comparison of drug prices in Canada and the United States, followed in 1994 by a comparison of drug prices in the United Kingdom and the United States (GAO 1994). Previous studies had found that some prescription drug prices were substantially higher in the United States than in other countries, but these studies were said to be inadequate to support strong conclusions about the pricing practices of manufacturers, either because they measured prices at the retail or wholesale level rather than at the manufacturer level, or because of the "relatively small drug samples, which might give a misleading impression of the average price of a broad array of prescription drugs" (GAO 1992). The GAO's comparisons of drug prices in Canada and the United Kingdom with those in the United States suffer from severe methodological flaws that again make the studies inadequate as a basis for broad conclusions about pricing by manufacturers, costs to consumers, or appropriate public policy.[1]

There are formidable obstacles to constructing valid international comparisons of drug prices—some are unavoidable, given the available data, but others are avoidable. In any case, a comparison of prices

---

1. The GAO implicitly recognized some of the flaws in its U.S.-Canada study by substantially revising its methodology for the comparison of drug prices in the United States and the United Kingdom.

alone, even if undertaken with the best feasible methods, does not provide a valid basis for policy prescriptions about pharmaceutical regulation because of other effects on costs, product availability, and consumption patterns.

This chapter lays out some of the intrinsic problems in comparing international drug prices and some of the avoidable errors of omission and commission in existing studies. I illustrate those points with evidence from my continuing study that uses more robust methods and more comprehensive data. I conclude that even with the best available data, it is not possible to construct price indexes that are truly representative or that could form a valid basis for welfare conclusions. Moreover, cross-national price comparisons implicitly or explicitly presuppose that prices should be uniform. But economic theory indicates that, given the importance of joint costs that are largely invariant regardless of the number of consumers worldwide, prices optimally should differ across countries. Attempts to achieve uniform prices could make all consumers worse off.

Purposes of International Drug Price Comparisons

The appropriate design of a study comparing drug prices cross-nationally depends on the question being addressed. Prior studies often have not clearly articulated their planned objectives, and this has led to a mismatch between methods and policy conclusions. The apparent purpose of the GAO's studies is to draw conclusions about the pricing practices of manufacturers that would be valid for a broad array of prescription drugs. Those studies set out to compare manufacturer prices for the 200 most frequently prescribed branded prescription drugs in the United States in May 1991. The GAO required that products match on brand name, manufacturer, dosage form, and strength. That resulted in a sample of 121 drugs for the Canadian comparison.[2] The study compared the (unweighted) cost of that sample of

---

2. The U.S. prices are the wholesale acquisition cost (as listed in the Medi-Span Master Drug Data Base-Select) for a single common dosage form, strength, and pack size. For Canada, that was compared with an imputed price for a similar pack, based on the best available price listed in the Ontario Drug Benefit formulary. Drugs with different brand names were considered equivalent if they had the same generic name and either were sold by the same manufacturer or the Canadian firm was a subsidiary of or was operating under a marketing or licensing agreement from the U.S. firm. Since most of the Ontario formulary prices were per unit (tablet or capsule), a price per pack was imputed by multiplying the per unit price by the number of units per pack. This linear imputation is likely to understate the price per pack in Canada, since

drugs in the United States relative to the cost in Canada and concluded that drug prices in the United States are 32 percent higher than in Canada. The median of the price relatives, with Canada as the base, showed the United States 43 percent higher than Canada. U.S. prices were reported to be higher for 81 percent of the drugs in the sample. The GAO's study has been used to support policy recommendations for price regulatory schemes in the United States.[3]

What questions can such a study validly answer? The study design suggests several possible objectives.

Comparison of Pricing Policies of Drug Manufacturers. The explicit concern of the 1992 GAO study is the "pricing practices of drug manufacturers." The focus on branded products marketed by the same manufacturer suggests that the objective is to compare prices charged voluntarily by the research drug industry in different countries.[4] But voluntary pricing strategies simply cannot be observed because prices are regulated, directly or indirectly, in most countries, including Canada and the United Kingdom. Even in the United States, although prices to private sector purchasers are unregulated, they are heavily influenced by the federal requirement for Medicaid best price and cost-of-living rebates.[5] Thus, a cross-national comparison reveals at most a confused and partial picture of manufacturers' pricing policies that are constrained by complex and sometimes obscure details of diverse price regulatory regimes and health care reimbursement systems.

Effects of Regulation. If the goal is to compare the general effects of competitive versus alternative regulatory regimes for purposes of making policy decisions, this requires a comprehensive cost-benefit analy-

---

the best available price is "almost always" based on the largest pack size for a given drug and the per unit price is typically lower in larger packs. The GAO reports that using the largest U.S. pack size reduced the median U.S.-Canadian price differential from 43 to 35 percent. The GAO did not report effects for a more valid index of price difference.

3. The GAO (1992, 3) cites this view without endorsing it. The study notes the uncertainty about the adverse effects of price regulation on R&D and the availability of new drugs.

4. If this is the objective, the GAO's inclusion of products that were operating with a marketing or licensing agreement from a U.S. company is inappropriate, since such agreements typically do not specify a price.

5. The Omnibus Budget Reconciliation Act of 1990 requires that manufacturers give rebates to Medicaid equal to the greater of the best discount offered to any private payer or 15.7 percent, in addition to a rebate for excess inflation above the consumer price index.

sis to capture all ramifications—hidden as well obvious—of drug price regulation. A single point-in-time comparison of branded drug prices—even if accurately done—would be only one component of a complete analysis of the costs and benefits of alternative regulatory regimes. A full analysis should also include how regulation affects the price and availability of generics, the choice of therapies and consumption patterns of consumers, the costs to manufacturers, and the incentives to develop innovative new drugs. Moreover, regulatory influences span national boundaries. In the European Union, for example, parallel importing can export regulatory influences in one country to prices charged in other countries and make it very difficult to assign effects observed in one country solely to its regulatory system.

Costs of Drug Therapy to Consumers. If the objective is to compare the cost of drug therapy to consumers in two countries, then standard index number theory should be applied to a fully representative sample of products in those countries. In practice there are serious intrinsic obstacles to constructing such indexes for drugs. Those intrinsic problems have been exacerbated by inappropriate methods adopted by earlier studies, including the use of a small and nonrandom sample of products that excludes generics and compares prices for only one of the many dosage forms, strengths, and pack sizes that are available. I discuss and illustrate those limitations in the following sections.

Problems in Performing Cross-National Price Comparisons

Assumptions Necessary for Welfare Conclusions. The literature on price indexes has addressed the problems of constructing a price index that provides a meaningful summary measure of price differences between two situations.[6] An ideal consumer price index would measure the change in expenditure required to maintain the consumer at a given level of utility if prices change. Since we cannot observe utility or the hypothetical quantities that a particular consumer would buy if faced with different prices, we have to choose from several possible indexes that can be constructed with the available data. All those indexes have limitations, however, and we can draw welfare conclusions only under very specific assumptions. Those assumptions include: identical consumer preference structures in the two circumstances under comparison; identical range of products and product qualities available; control for all relevant substitutes and complements; and informed consumer choice in competitive markets.

---

6. Diewert (1981) provides a survey of this literature.

For international drug price comparisons, all the assumptions necessary for welfare conclusions are violated. Consumer preferences probably differ cross-nationally, and the range of available products certainly differs. Actual drug consumption patterns do not reflect the choices of informed consumers in competitive markets; rather, they reflect medical norms, subject to the incentives and constraints of insurance and reimbursement systems and regulatory regimes. Indexes that focus only on drug prices fail to control for prices or quantities of other medical services that are important substitutes and complements for drugs, such as patient time and the price of a physician office visit. These violations of standard assumptions imply that index numbers cannot be used to justify conclusions about consumer welfare.

Weighting. Since a cost-of-living index is intended as a summary measure of the differences in prices for many goods and services between two situations, prices of more frequently used products should receive greater weight. The 1992 GAO study used the unweighted ratio of the sum of prices in the United States to the sum of the prices in Canada. That index assigns each product an equal weight, regardless of whether it is rarely or very frequently used, so it does not represent expected cost to consumers. Moreover, the index is sensitive to the individual pack sizes used, so it is not a widely accepted index.

The most commonly used indexes are the Laspeyres index (using U.S. quantity weights) and the Paasche index (using foreign quantity weights). The Fisher index, which is the geometric mean of the Laspeyres and Paasche indexes, has several advantages. In particular, it meets the country-reversal test; that is, the conclusions are the same regardless of whether the United States or the other country is used as the base, after taking inverses. The Laspeyres and Paasche indexes fail this test, so conclusions vary, depending on which country is used as the base.

If cross-national differences in consumption patterns reflect differences in consumer preference structures, medical norms, and regulatory factors, then the Fisher index becomes a less reliable indicator. For example, if consumption patterns in the United States would be unlikely to adjust to patterns in the United Kingdom, even if the United States faced U.K. prices, then the Laspeyres index that uses current U.S. quantity weights may be more appropriate than either the Paasche or the Fisher index, which both include foreign quantity weights. Because consumption patterns would surely respond somewhat to price changes, however, the Laspeyres index probably also overstates the change in drug expenditures that U.S. consumers would incur if they faced U.K. prices.

Unavoidable Sample Selection Bias from Nonmatching Products. A significant fraction of drugs that are available in one country are not marketed in other countries. Thus, even with data on the full universe of drug sales, the sample of matching products is not fully representative of drug therapy in the two countries under comparison. This leads to bias if the matching drugs are systematically different from the nonmatching drugs or if they are differently priced. Economic theory and anecdotal evidence suggest that such gaps are not random. Products that have high therapeutic value are more likely to be globalized because they are more likely to generate sufficient revenue to cover the fixed costs of entering a foreign market, including registration and marketing costs. Thus, a significant fraction of the "domestic" products that are consumed in some foreign countries but that are not marketed in the United States are likely to be of relatively low therapeutic value.

Moreover, the structure of regulatory systems in several countries is likely to be biased against global or foreign products. If so, indexes based solely on matching products give a biased measure of the relative cost of drug therapy. Although multilateral index number methods offer techniques for imputing prices for the missing products, such imputations would lead to systematic bias if the available products were atypical of the missing products.

A more subtle variant of the problem of nonmatching products is that standard dosages, strengths, and even therapeutic use of the same product may differ across countries. For cardiovascular drugs, for example, requiring that products match on dosage and strength form, broadly defined, excludes roughly 20 percent of U.S. sales from the comparison that is possible if matching dosage form is not required. Such cross-national differences in consumption patterns reflect different preferences and medical practice as well as the response to the incentives and constraints of different health care and price regulatory regimes. If the same drug is used to treat different conditions in two countries or a given condition is treated by different drugs because of differing medical norms or preferences, then comparing the price of the drug in the two countries does not compare the cost of the same course of therapy. What looks like an "apples-to-apples" comparison is actually not. A fundamental proposition of index number theory is that if tastes or the product mix differs across countries, so that comparing consumption patterns does not simply reflect adjustment to different relative prices, then welfare conclusions based on the comparisons are invalid.

Avoidable Sample Selection Bias from Exclusion of Generics. The intrinsic problem of nonmatching products is exacerbated by studies that intentionally select only the leading products and require matching on manufacturer, brand name, dosage form, and strength. Such a restrictive sample would be appropriate if the objective were to measure pricing strategies of manufacturers, but as we have noted, that is impossible. More important, an unrepresentative sample cannot support valid inferences about the cost of drug therapy to consumers. By construction, a sample that focuses on matching branded products excludes all products sold under license by foreign manufacturers and most generics, which offer consumers a cheaper alternative to branded products.

Excluding generics tends to bias inferences about the efficacy of competition relative to regulation as a mechanism for controlling the cost of drug therapy to consumers because generic market share is generally larger and prices are lower, relative to branded products, in competitive regimes. The generic share of the U.S. market is already considerable and is certain to expand rapidly in the near future, with projected patent expiration for many of the leading branded drugs and rapid growth in managed drug benefit programs that aggressively substitute generic for branded drugs. Generics also have a significant market share in some other countries, including Canada, Germany, and the United Kingdom. But even if market shares of generics were equal in the two countries under comparison, this would not eliminate bias, because the brand-generic price differential is typically larger in the United States than in other countries. Thus, comparisons that exclude generics are likely to overstate relative prices in the United States.

Nonrepresentative Packs. The sample becomes even less representative when confined to a single-dosage form, strength, and (possibly different) pack size. The mix of dosage forms, strengths, and pack sizes differs significantly across countries—a reflection of medical norms and responses to regulation. Price indexes can be very sensitive to the particular unit that is analyzed. For example, when we compare the prices of single-molecule cardiovascular products, those products appear to be 32 percent cheaper in Japan than in the United States if we base the comparison on the average price per standard unit. If we base the comparison on the average price per gram of active ingredient, however, Japanese prices are 2 percent higher than American prices. This discrepancy reflects the fact that strength per dose is typically lower in Japan. Similarly, Canadian cardiovascular drugs are 7 percent cheaper than the American drugs on a price per standard unit basis and 9 percent more expensive on the basis of the price per gram of active ingredient.

Pack size may also matter. For example, some countries require unit pack dispensing, whereas in others, including the United States, pharmacists commonly purchase large-volume packs that are subsequently split to fill multiple prescriptions. The requirement of matching or nearly matching pack size means that we must eliminate those larger-volume packs from the analysis. This leads to a bias if the price per pill decreases with pack size.

List Prices Overstate Net Transactions Prices. The GAO's measure of prices in the United States is based on listed wholesale prices as reported in the Medi-Span Master Drug Data Base-Select. These list prices are intended to approximate prices charged to the retail pharmacy sector, but they overstate the manufacturer's true average price in the United States because of rebates, chargebacks, and other forms of discount. Discounts are the norm in managed care plans, mail order, and managed drug benefit programs that are increasingly being adopted even by indemnity insurers. Medicaid and other federal programs receive rebates and other forms of discount that are not reflected in list prices.

Status Quo Prices Yield a Biased Forecast for the Future. Even if it were possible to construct an index based on the weighted average of current transaction prices in the United States with a weighted average discount for all market segments, such a comparison would still overstate a reasonable forecast of future drug price levels. Managed drug benefit programs that demand discounts and generic substitution are likely to become the norm, with or without health care reform, as developing information systems make such programs more cost-effective. The leading health care reform proposals provided for universal coverage, including an outpatient drug benefit, and relied heavily on managed care to control costs. If the future U.S. health care system will look more like managed care than the current mix of managed, unmanaged, and no drug benefits, then the appropriate basis for comparison for forward-looking policy is the managed care sector, not the weighted average of all market segments and still less the uncontrolled retail sector.

Results

I shall illustrate the problems in performing cross-national price comparisons with some evidence from a continuing study of international prices.[7] The study uses IMS data on the universe of drug sales, includ-

---

7. Results for cardiovasculars are reported in Danzon and Kim (1993).

ing all dosage forms and strengths, reported separately for pharmacy and hospital sales.[8] The analysis here focuses on pharmacy sales of single-molecule products. The sample of matching products consists largely of prescription products but includes some over-the-counter products. On theoretical grounds there is little reason to exclude over-the-counter products because they are substitutes for prescription products from the consumer's perspective. In comparing our results with those of other studies, however, we must remember that we have included over-the-counter products. We shall report results excluding over-the-counter products in later work.

Prices are at the manufacturers' price levels. Because U.S. prices do not reflect discounts, rebates, and chargebacks to managed care, mail order, Medicaid, and other large buyers, however, the U.S. price levels we report overstate true net manufacturer prices in the United States. We average prices over all dosage forms and strengths to yield two measures: price per kilogram of active ingredient and price per standard unit—a rough measure of price per dose.[9] Price per kilogram may more closely approximate the ideal but unobservable measure of price for a quality-constant course of therapy, whereas price per standard unit is affected by cross-national differences in average strength per dose.

We use two strategies to match products internationally: matching on the international product name and matching on the molecular content and therapeutic category. Matching on the international product name matches products if they share two of three conditions: the same chemical composition, the same brand name, or the same manufacturer. This matching strategy includes some unbranded generics, so it is broader than the same-manufacturer requirement used in other studies, but it excludes branded generics and licensed originator products that are sold under different brand names in different countries. Matching on molecular content and therapeutic category compares the weighted average price over all products with the same chemical composition in the same therapeutic category, regardless of manufacturer or brand. Our results focus on the latter matching because it permits a larger and more representative sample.

---

8. The IMS collects data at wholesale price levels. IMS adjusts these data to ex-manufacturer levels by netting out the average wholesale markup and, where relevant, VAT and other taxes. Foreign currencies are converted to U.S. dollars quarterly at current exchange rates. We exclude from the full sample products that had less than 1,000 packs or 1 kilogram of active ingredient, to reduce the possibility of sampling error.

9. IMS defines a "standard unit" as one tablet, one capsule, or 5 ml of a liquid as a rough proxy for a single dose.

Table 5–1 reports summary data and illustrates the extent to which alternative matching criteria represent the market in each country. In panel A we show the number of local products, international product names, and molecules, by country.[10] Although the United States has more than twice as many local products as any other country, it ranks fifth in terms of number of molecules, after Germany, France, Italy, and Japan. The United States has on average 5.7 different manufacturers of each molecule, compared with 2.02 in Canada and 1.68 in the United Kingdom. That difference reflects the larger number of generics in the United States.

Panel B shows the percentage of products that can be included with international product name and molecule matching, respectively. For the United States, less than 20 percent of all international product names are included if matching is by international product name, whereas over 40 percent of all molecules are included if matching is on the basis of molecular content and therapeutic category. For Canada, 45 percent of international product names and 74 percent of molecules match; for the United Kingdom 33 percent of international product names and 59 percent of molecules match. The percentage of total sales represented is much greater (panel C), because products that are marketed internationally have above-average sales, as expected under the hypothesis that international products are not a random subset of all products. When we match by international product name, the U.S.-Canada comparison includes 74 percent of the U.S. market and 70 percent of the Canadian market; those results increase to 90 percent of the U.S. market and 88 percent of the Canadian market for the molecule-matched indexes. In comparing matching sales in the United States and the United Kingdom, we find that the international product name indexes represent 59 percent of U.S. sales and 63 percent of U.K. sales; those increase to 86 percent of U.S. sales and 89 percent of U.K. sales when we match on molecular content and therapeutic category. Thus, there is a trade-off: by dropping the requirement of same brand or manufacturer and matching all products in the same molecule and therapeutic category, we can include licensed products and generics, which increases the extent to which the indexes are representative. That gain is even greater for other European countries and Japan.

Table 5–2 shows price indexes for the eight countries in the study where we match by molecular content and therapeutic category. We express prices in other countries relative to the United States as a base. Thus, a value of .9 means that prices are 10 percent lower than in the United States. The Laspeyres indexes weight by U.S. volumes, the

---

10. Multiple products with the same IPN are combined.

Paasche indexes weight by foreign volumes, and the Fisher indexes are the geometric average of the two. The discussion here focuses on the indexes by molecule, since they provide a more representative measure of the cost of therapy, averaging over branded and generic products.

The main point that emerges from those indexes is that the measure of price difference varies widely, depending on the unit of measurement, the weighting, and the sample. For example, drugs in Japan are 8 percent less expensive than in the United States on a price per dose basis, but 28 percent more expensive than in the United States on a price per gram of active ingredient basis. The difference reflects the fact that doses are weaker on average in Japan than in the United States. In general, the Paasche indexes using foreign quantity weights are much lower than the Laspeyres indexes using U.S. quantity weights. Those large differences imply that foreign countries consume relatively higher quantities of products that are relatively inexpensive in that country. This is consistent with some price sensitivity in the demand for pharmaceuticals.

When we use U.S. quantity weights, the indexes based on the price per kilogram of active ingredient show that drugs in Japan and Switzerland are more expensive than in the United States and are less expensive in the other countries. Germany is only 3 percent lower, and the United Kingdom is second lowest, at 32 percent less than the United States. When we use the indexes based on the price per standard unit, drug prices in Canada, Germany, Switzerland, and Sweden are more expensive than in the United States, and the United Kingdom has the lowest prices—24 percent less than those in the United States. Recall that those indexes overstate prices in the United States relative to other countries because of the omission of discounts and rebates. They also include some over-the-counter products, so they are not strictly comparable to studies that focus exclusively on prescription products. Because the Paasche indexes are much lower than the Laspeyres indexes, the Fisher indexes show that drug prices in all countries are less expensive than in the United States. Which index is preferred depends on whether U.S. medical norms and consumption patterns would become more like those in other countries if we adopted their regulatory regimes.

Discussion and Conclusions

Limitations of Cross-National Price Comparisons. This analysis has shown that measures of international drug price differentials can differ dramatically, depending on the sample selected, the inclusion of ge-

TABLE 5–1
EFFECTS OF ALTERNATIVE MATCHING
(single molecule, all categories, pharmacy, 1992)

	United States	Canada	Germany	France	Italy	Japan	United Kingdom	Switzerland	Sweden
Panel A. Number of Products									
Local products	5269	1255					1288		
IPN[a]	2616	1074	2769	1595	1892	2561	1137	868	618
Molecules	922	621	1249	1136	1042	1019	766	675	464
Products per molecule	5.71	2.02					1.66		
Panel B. Percentage of Matching Products									
U.S. IPN match		19	10	9	10	7	15	8	8
Foreign IPN match		45	9	14	13	7	33	25	34

Percentage of Matching Molecules

U.S. molecules match	50	51	45	44	43	49	33	28
Foreign molecules match	74	38	36	39	39	59	46	56

Panel C. Matching Sales

U.S. sales IPN match	74	59
U.S. sales MOL/ATC match	90	86
Foreign sales IPN match	70	63
Foreign sales MOL/ATC match	88	89

a. IPN = international product name.

TABLE 5-2
PRICE INDEXES FOR SINGLE-MOLECULE PHARMACEUTICALS IN ALL CATEGORIES, 1992

Panel A. Matched by IPN

Index	United States	Canada	Germany	France	Italy	Japan	Switzerland	Sweden	United Kingdom
Laspeyres-KG	1.000	.971	.840	.481	.601	1.678	.791	.674	.688
Laspeyres-SU	1.000	.826	1.092	.581	1.001	1.222	1.303	.863	.697
Paasche-KG	1.000	.637	.525	.291	.460	.656	.457	.472	.475
Paasche-SU	1.000	.458	.410	.271	.452	.442	.492	.274	.494
Fisher-KG	1.000	.787	.664	.374	.526	1.049	.601	.564	.571
Fisher-SU	1.000	.616	.669	.397	.672	.734	.800	.486	.586
N	2616	484	252	229	249	187	219	208	380

Panel B. Matched by MOL/ATC

Index	United States	Canada	Germany	France	Italy	Japan	Switzerland	Sweden	United Kingdom
Laspeyres-KG	1.000	.870	.972	.570	.739	1.282	1.049	.811	.678
Laspeyres-SU	1.000	1.030	1.273	.701	.907	.923	1.444	1.089	.761
Paasche-KG	1.000	.664	.521	.416	.331	.486	.657	.566	.479
Paasche-SU	1.000	.447	.368	.326	.465	.448	.465	.370	.465
Fisher-KG	1.000	.760	.711	.487	.494	.789	.830	.677	.570
Fisher-SU	1.000	.678	.684	.478	.649	.643	.819	.635	.595
N	922	458	471	412	406	396	308	261	453

nerics, the measure of price, and the weighting scheme. More fundamentally, even with appropriate methodology applied to the full universe of data, it is not possible to construct truly representative indexes of the cost of drug therapy to consumers because many products are available in one country but not the others. If prices for the global products that can be included in the indexes are atypical of prices for more minor products in most regulatory regimes, for example, because regulation tends to constrain most the highest priced products, then those price indexes that are necessarily based on global products provide a biased measure of the true cost of drug therapy in regulated markets relative to the so far largely unregulated U.S. market.

Earlier studies have overstated the relative price of drugs in the United States for several reasons. Contributing factors include the use of small nonrandom samples, excluding generics, and focus on list prices. Even the results reported here overstate relative prices in the United States because data on discounts are not available.

Other Effects of Price Regulation. Even an accurate comparison of prices would be only one component of an assessment of the full effects of price regulatory schemes. The evidence suggests that price regulatory regimes in France and Italy have significantly affected not only the incentives for innovation but also consumption patterns in those countries (Thomas 1993; Danzon and Kim 1993). The pharmaceutical price regulatory system in the United Kingdom forgoes the futile attempt to set "appropriate" prices for every individual dosage form and strength of all drugs on the market—several thousand individual prices. Rather, the United Kingdom regulates the rate of return on capital and leaves manufacturers free to set prices, subject to the constraint that their overall rate of return on capital not exceed some benchmark (currently 17 percent). That system avoids the most perverse incentives created by microregulation of individual prices.

The United Kingdom's pharmaceutical price regulatory system is likely to create distortions of its own, however. By basing the allowed return on capital, the system creates incentives for inefficient capital expenditures, inefficient substitution of capital for other inputs, and substitution of capital in the United Kingdom for capital in other countries. France and Italy compete in the inefficiency game by also offering price premiums if plants are located in those countries, and Ireland offers generous tax incentives. Other regulatory distortions include influences on mix of dosage forms and pack sizes and incentives to introduce marginally "new" products to qualify for a price increase. The Japanese engage in this practice. Thus, a full cost-benefit accounting of the costs of those regulatory regimes should include the excess costs

99

that result from such input distortions and the indirect effects on con-sumer well-being due to the consumption of a distorted mix of prod-ucts.

Invalid Inferences about Price-Cost Markups. Even if a fully repre-sentative and accurately constructed index showed that prices in the United Kingdom are lower than in competitive managed care systems in the United States, we cannot use price differences to infer differences in price-cost markups. Costs related to obtaining regulatory approval, postlaunch monitoring, and compliance with manufacturing stan-dards are generally recognized to be higher in the United States than in most other countries, but precise measures are unavailable. Those costs include the time value of money due to delay in launch that com-pounds the higher out-of-pocket costs associated with more extensive and more costly clinical trial requirements (DiMasi, Hansen, Grabow-ski, and Lasagna 1991).

But attempting to measure the contribution of cost differences to price differences is ultimately a futile exercise—as is the attempt to use costs as a guide to price regulation. The cost structure of the research-based pharmaceutical industry is markedly different from that of most other industries because of the significance of joint costs, some of which cannot meaningfully be attributed to any single product, and certainly not to a specific dosage form sold to a specific market seg-ment in a particular country. Most of the costs of research and develop-ment, including the cost of the many compounds that never make it to market, are joint costs to all users. Those costs of obtaining information are a pure public good: they are the same whether one patient or mil-lions of patients use the drug. We cannot rationally attribute most of those costs to particular users, except to the extent that some users require more extensive trials. Other costs—including some fixed costs of registration, marketing, and production—are country-specific but joint to all dosage forms and strength of a particular product in that country, and some are joint across products. The only safe conclusion is that costs that can be attributed to the use of a specific product in a specific country are a small fraction of total costs. Thus, regulatory at-tempts to assess the reasonableness of price by examining costs—as is nominally done in Italy and is proposed for the United States—is a futile exercise. This applies all the more to specific dosage forms and strengths of specific products.

Because joint costs not only constitute a large fraction of the total cost of bringing drugs to market but also are sunk by the time the product is launched, regulators and large buyers in all countries face a strong temptation to try to force down prices. How low can prices go?

In the very short run, products that have obtained marketing approval, that have established manufacturing and distribution systems, and that are at the stage of price negotiation, have very low marginal cost. Hence the price that can be set without adversely affecting supply is very low. In the medium run, to continue to attract products that have been developed for other markets, each country must offer a price-volume combination that at least covers the marginal costs of obtaining marketing authorization, production, and distribution for that particular country. But even some country-specific costs are joint across products and cannot be rigorously allocated to specific dosage forms and strengths. Note that for purposes of covering joint costs, what matters is price times volume, so countries that have relatively low prices but relatively high volume may nevertheless contribute more to joint costs than do countries that have higher prices but lower volume. We cannot precisely allocate to any country the globally joint costs of R&D. Nevertheless, those joint costs must be covered if the product is to break even on worldwide sales.

Given such a cost structure, all buyers—but particularly those that constitute a small fraction of global sales—face an irresistible temptation to try to avoid paying any contribution to joint costs. It would thus not be surprising to find that drug prices in heavily regulated countries are lower than in less regulated countries, including the United States, although large buyers in the United States have similar incentives. Small countries that make trivial contributions to global sales can indefinitely take a free ride without affecting the supply of new drugs. But if the United States and buyers in other large markets also try to take a free ride, then there is no one left to pay for the gas. The supply of innovative products that is critically dependent on R&D expenditures must in the long run be adversely affected.

Should Prices Be Uniform? There is no economic principle that says that joint costs should be equally allocated to all users. Even if regulation or competition could force a single price worldwide (or for some subset of users), that would not serve the best interests of consumers in general and would probably not even benefit the majority of consumers in the United States. Such a single world price would probably lie somewhere within the current range of prices paid by the most affluent and the least developed markets, depending on the mix of regulatory and competitive strategies adopted in different countries. If the single price lies close to the upper end of the range, that would price out of the market many developing and low-income countries, whose current low prices cover their country-specific marginal costs although they contribute little to joint costs. Such a strategy would inflict a tragic loss on poorer countries that could no longer afford innovative therapies, with no gain to the richer countries that must still cover the joint costs in addition to their marginal costs. In fact, to the extent that some users who made some but not a pro rata contribution to joint costs cut their consumption at the higher price, their dropping out of the market would increase the joint cost burden on those consumers remaining in the market.

Alternatively, the single price could be closer to levels that poorer countries can afford. In the very short run wealthy consumers would enjoy lower prices. But in the longer run the flow of innovative products must fall, although revealed preference suggests that those consumers would be willing to pay prices sufficient to cover the joint costs in addition to their marginal, user-specific costs. In that case wealthy consumers lose by this sour grapes policy. And since poorer countries also lose, everyone loses. Yet that is the predictable outcome if all countries engage in international price comparisons and each tries to pay no more than the lowest—or even the mean. Thus, in the long run, when different consumer groups differ in their ability or willingness to pay for a product that entails significant joint costs, no one gains in the long run from a uniform price policy and everyone may lose.

The problem of pricing to cover joint costs is not unique to the research-based pharmaceutical industry. But it is particularly acute because joint costs are a relatively large share of total costs and are harder to measure, because of unsuccessful ventures, long lags, and time costs between research initiation and product launch.

Economists have extensively analyzed the problem of pricing to cover joint costs in the context of electricity generation, telephone systems, and other traditional public utilities. The theoretically optimal Ramsey-pricing solution—and one that is also implemented to varying degrees in some regulated utilities in practice—is to charge higher prices to those users who more highly value the product. Of course, in practice willingness to pay is often difficult to measure, but there may be rough empirical guides. For example, the costs of electricity-generating capacity are charged disproportionately to peak period users because their higher demand necessitates the additional capacity. Similarly, airlines charge divergent prices to different users, and that practice is widely accepted (albeit with some grumbling) as a necessary price to pay to cover the fixed costs of maintaining hubs, aircraft fleets, and a frequency of service that is designed primarily to serve the demand of business travelers.[11] Despite this prima facie evidence of

---

11. Some price differences may reflect differences in marginal cost across users, associated with maintaining the capacity necessary to offer flexible

market power, the rash of recent airline consolidations and bankrupt-cies indicates that limited ability to impose price discrimination is no guarantee that the firm will cover joint costs and that the enterprise will break even overall.

Applying those lessons to pharmaceuticals, price differentials across user groups or across countries may be the socially optimal way to recoup joint costs. Those consumers whose demand is more inelas-tic, who have a higher real willingness to pay for innovative therapies, or who demand higher standards of safety and efficacy (and therefore more extensive clinical trials that entail higher out-of-pocket costs and greater delay in launch) should appropriately pay more than consum-ers who, for reasons of lower income, tastes, or other factors, are will-ing to make do with older or less effective therapies or to tolerate less extensive trials and possibly higher risks. Similarly, within the United States, charging different prices to different user groups may be a so-cially optimal way of recouping joint costs. Consumers who choose managed care plans that use restrictive formularies presumably place a lower value on free choice of drugs than do consumers who choose indemnity plans with unrestricted choice. If so, the common practice of giving discounted prices to managed care buyers may be consistent with the efficient recovery of joint costs.[12]

In practice, of course, pricing according to willingness to pay is very difficult because each purchaser or group will try to conceal its true valuation, in the hope of taking a free ride and leaving someone else to pay a larger share of the joint costs. The difficulty of observing true willingness to pay is exacerbated in medical care, because third-party payment makes consumers insensitive to full prices and imper-fect information forces consumers to rely on physicians as agents. Phy-sicians may sometimes reflect consumers' interests as best they can, but they certainly also have their own incentives when they face reim-bursement controls, utilization review, and other forms of regulation.

Nevertheless, a casual review of the evidence suggests that, com-pared with citizens of virtually all other countries, Americans place a relatively high value on medical care in general and, in particular, a

---

booking, last minute schedule changes, etc. But other discounts—for example, for staying over a Saturday night—suggest pricing differences primarily to cover fixed costs, given customer differences in demand elasticity or willing-ness to pay.

12. Another reason for discounts to managed care is that manufacturers incur lower costs of marketing to managed care, where marketing efforts focus on the centralized decision-maker, with less investment in providing informa-tion to each individual physician.

high value on prompt and unrestricted access to advanced medical technologies. The per capita use of most high-technology therapies is higher in the United States than in most other countries at comparable income levels. If that is a rough indicator of true willingness to pay for advanced health technologies, it would be appropriate that American consumers should pay more than a pro rata share of the joint costs of developing those technologies. That principle applies to pharmaceuticals as well as to other technologies that entail significant research and development costs.

Given comparisons such as those by the GAO, however, Americans may take the sour grapes stand and refuse to pay higher prices than do other countries that have lower incomes and more moderate demand for medical care. But if Americans adopt such a position, they will be the greatest losers. If their relatively high valuation makes it appropriate for them to pay higher prices, their loss will be greatest from a reduction in the supply of innovations that will surely result from a significant cut in pharmaceutical revenues.

On this point it would be erroneous to point to the U.K. pharmaceutical industry, which flourishes despite a regulatory scheme that results on average in lower prices than those in the United States and despite regulation-induced production inefficiencies. The U.K. market is a small share of global pharmaceutical sales of the U.K. research-based drug industry. By contrast, the U.S. market is the largest single market and provides a disproportionately large share of revenues for U.S.-based pharmaceutical firms. Because total pharmaceutical sales in the United States are eight times larger than total pharmaceutical sales in the United Kingdom and the share of total sales spent on innovative products is probably greater in the United States, a cut in prices in the U.S. market would have at least an eight-fold larger effect on revenues and R&D incentives than a similar cut in the U.K. market. The impact would disproportionately hit U.S.-based firms, which receive a larger share of their revenue in the United States, but U.K. firms and the global research-based industry would all be adversely affected.

Managed Care as a Substitute for Regulation. The current interest in international price comparisons, including the two GAO studies, grew in part out of congressional concern over the cost of outpatient drugs to Medicare beneficiaries. Although many Medicare beneficiaries have some drug coverage through Medicaid, Medigap supplementary policies, or enrollment in a health maintenance organization, out-of-pocket drug costs can be a significant expense for those with chronic conditions. Medicare beneficiaries typically buy drugs from retail pharmacies that pay list prices, which was presumably one reason for GAO studies to focus on list prices paid by retail pharmacies.

If that is the concern, however, regulating drug prices is an inappropriate solution to what is fundamentally an insurance problem. The risk of high drug costs for some of the elderly and others who cannot afford health insurance is an insurance problem that should be addressed through appropriate insurance coverage, which is likely to involve management of the drug benefit.[13] The managed care sector has demonstrated strong competitive incentives to develop strategies to control drug costs through the use of formularies, negotiated discounts, product bundling, and utilization review. Some of those strategies are structurally very similar to some of the regulatory strategies foreign governments use to control their drug bills.

But the critical difference is that when the government applies controls as a monopsony purchaser and monopoly provider of health care, consumers have nowhere else to go if they do not like the government package. By contrast, competing managed care organizations must design their drug benefits to trade off costs against consumer satisfaction. If one plan focuses solely on cost, for example, by offering only the cheapest products, consumers who prefer a more comprehensive choice, even if it costs a little more, can switch to another plan that accommodates their willingness to pay by offering a wider range of products and services, including some more costly therapies. Since some outpatient drug benefit is likely to be included in plans for universal coverage, now is a particularly inappropriate time to introduce price regulation.

References

Andersson, Fredrik, and Peter McMenamin. "International Price Comparisons of Pharmaceuticals: A Review of Methodological Issues." Battelle Medical Technology and Policy Research Centre paper prepared for the U.S. Pharmaceutical Manufacturers' Association, March 3, 1992.

Danzon, Patricia, and Jeong D. Kim. "International Price Comparisons for Pharmaceuticals." Working paper. Philadelphia: Health Care Department, The Wharton School, University of Pennsylvania, 1993.

---

13. "Appropriate" insurance means some copayment to deter unnecessary use, with a stop-loss on out-of-pocket costs for necessary drugs. This could be provided as a managed drug benefit, but with the option for the beneficiary to pay more (without additional public subsidy) if he desired greater choice. Similarly, Medicare beneficiaries could be given incentives to enroll in a managed drug program.

Diewert, W. E. "The Economic Theory of Index Numbers: A Survey." In *Essays in the Theory and Measurement of Consumer Behaviour in Honour of Sir Richard Stone*, edited by Angus Deaton. London: Cambridge University Press, 1981, pp. 163–208.

———. "Microeconomic Approaches to the Theory of International Comparisons." Technical working paper no. 53. Cambridge: National Bureau of Economic Research, 1986.

———. "The Theory of the Cost-of-Living Index and the Measurement of Welfare Change." In *Price Level Measurement*, edited by W. E. Diewert and C. Montmarquette. Ottawa: Statistics Canada, 1983, pp. 163–233.

DiMasi, Joseph A., Ronald W. Hansen, Henry G. Grabowski, and Louis Lasagna. "The Cost of Innovation in the Pharmaceutical Industry." *Journal of Health Economics* 10 (1991): 107–42.

General Accounting Office. "Prescription Drugs: Companies Typically Charge More in the United States than in Canada." Washington, D.C.: Government Printing Office, 1992.

———. "Prescription Drugs: Companies Typically Charge More in the United States than in Great Britain." Washington, D.C.: Government Printing Office, 1994.

Pollak, R. A. "The Social Cost of Living Index." *Journal of Public Economics* 15 (1981): 311–36.

———. "Subindexes of the Cost of Living." *International Economic Review* 16 (1975): 135–50.

Thomas, Lacy Glenn, III. "Implicit Industrial Policy: The Triumph of Britain and the Failure of France in Global Pharmaceuticals." Unpublished manuscript, School of Business, Emory University, 1993.

6
Industrial Policy and International Competitiveness in the Pharmaceutical Industry

Lacy Glenn Thomas III

This chapter examines government industrial policy and international competitiveness in the pharmaceutical industry. That industry is of particular interest as it is one in which the United States maintained competitive preeminence in the 1980s, while Japan suffered clear competitive inferiority. The world market share of U.S. ethical drug firms is roughly 40 percent, more than double that of the second strongest nation. The U.S. export share is roughly 20 percent, slightly ahead of Germany and far ahead of other nations. Indeed, the U.S. competitive position arguably improved over the past decade, in terms of world sales shares, export shares, and shares of significant innovations. At the opposite extreme, Japan spent the 1980s as a laggard in the industry, with minimal exports, a negative trade balance, and virtually no direct sales presence in either North America or Europe. Thus, pharmaceuticals represent a distinctive and powerful competitive triumph for the United States.

With the adoption of proposed health care reforms of the Clinton administration, U.S. industrial policy toward the pharmaceutical industry would change, perhaps drastically. Amid the debate over those proposed reforms, it is useful to review the outcomes and underpinnings of U.S. competitive performance in pharmaceuticals, and the industrial policy lessons that experience holds.

The following section examines the nature and sources of competitive success in the global pharmaceutical industry and documents the preeminence of the United States and the corresponding failure of Japan. Next we consider the underlying theoretical foundation for industrial policy. The analysis of those two sections is adapted from Thomas (1994). Then we turn to three key aspects of industrial policy for pharmaceuticals that lay behind the divergent performances of those two nations: regulation of product safety, setting of prices for new drugs, and government investment in basic research. The fourth section examines the effects of U.S. pharmaceutical industrial policy in more detail by contrasting the U.S. and Japanese pharmaceutical industries. The analysis of that section is adapted from Thomas (1990). In the fifth section we speculate on the potential impact of proposed health care reforms in the United States.

Competitive Performance in Global Pharmaceuticals

Table 6–1 reports various measures of competitive performance for the nine major competitor nations in the global pharmaceutical industry. Those nations are the source of virtually all new drugs launched anywhere in the world during the years 1965 to 1985. For the data reported in table 6–1, ownership defines nationality. For example, the sales of drugs by Pfizer in the United Kingdom, Merck & Co. in Japan, or Eli Lilly in France are American because those three firms are based in the United States. Likewise, the sales or products of Wellcome in the United States or Glaxo in Germany are British, because those two firms are based in the United Kingdom. The leftmost column of table 6–1 reports the world share of sales achieved by firms based in the nine competitor nations. U.S. firms are clearly the leader with a 43 percent market share of the global pharmaceutical industry, and Japanese firms are second with a 20 percent share of world sales. This column initially suggests that Japan is a strong performer in pharmaceuticals. Actually, world sales by Japanese firms are almost entirely located in a large home market that is protected by extensive nontariff trade barriers. The market share of 20 percent thus represents Japanese protectionism far more than it does the superior competitive performance of Japanese pharmaceutical firms.

To avoid bias from protectionist measures in measuring competitiveness, we instead use the column of table 6–1 that reports the external market shares of firms in 1985. External share represents the sales that firms of a given nation achieved outside that nation's borders as a share of pharmaceutical sales in all external markets. Thus, on average, U.S. firms achieved 19 percent of sales in such foreign markets as Britain, Germany, Italy, and Japan. Using that external market share measure, we find that the nine nations clearly segregate themselves into two tiers. The first tier of *strong competitive performers* includes the United States, Switzerland, Britain, and Germany, with the United States in almost a class by itself as an exceptionally strong competitor. In the second tier of *weak competitive performers* we have France, Italy,

TABLE 6-1
COMPETITIVE PERFORMANCE, MARKET STRUCTURE, AND INNOVATION TYPE FOR NINE MAJOR COMPETITOR NATIONS

Nation	World Market Share 1985	External Share 1985	Number of Firms That Innovate	Number of Firms That Innovate per R&D	Percentage Discovery, Global	Percentage Discovery, Local
United States	43.3	19.1	20.1	3.6	44	28
Switzerland	8.0	7.4	3.1	2.2	38	41
United Kingdom	7.4	5.8	5.8	4.8	51	25
Germany	10.2	6.2	13.2	5.9	18	49
France	4.1	1.0	15.6	13.0	13	60
Italy	2.5	.5	20.1	26.8	10	75
Japan	20.2	.1	27.5	12.2	9	77
Sweden	1.0	.7	2.9	9.7	38	32
Netherlands	.6	.4	3.1	10.3	33	35

SOURCE: Thomas (1992).

Japan, Sweden, and the Netherlands, with Japan in almost a class by itself as an exceptionally weak performer.[1]

In table 6–1 we can additionally examine the diverse strategies of various national pharmaceutical firms that lead to either strong or weak performance. The middle column gives the number of firms that on average per year discovered new pharmaceutical products from 1965 through 1985. That measure in and of itself demonstrates a clear scale effect, reflecting the difference in sheer size of operations among nations, for example, between the United States and Sweden. To better compare competitive strategies across nations, we divide the data of this middle column reporting the number of firms by billions of dollars of domestic pharmaceutical research and development for each of the nine nations. The resulting normalized numbers are reported in the column immediately to the right. Provocatively, we again find a stark two-tiered structure. For the strong competitive performers, the United States, Switzerland, Britain, and Germany, innovative effort is concentrated in a handful of firms, with the Swiss firms being the most concentrated of all. Conversely, in the five other nations, innovative effort is fragmented into many more firms. At the extreme, in Italy each billion dollars of pharmaceutical R&D expense is fragmented into as many as twenty-seven different firms. On average, the strong competitive performers have only one-third as many firms per dollar of research expense as the weak competitive performers.

A second attribute of the strategies pursued by strong competitive performers is the type of innovations discovered. The two rightmost columns of table 6–1 give the percentage of drugs discovered by each nation from 1965 through 1985 that are either *global products* or *local products*. We define global products as new drugs that diffuse to at least six nations, out of a maximum possible twelve nations measured for this study. Those products are sometimes called "consensus drugs." Global products represent relatively significant innovations that can be effectively marketed in diverse medical environments. In contrast, local products are minor innovations that diffuse to only one or two nations out of the maximum possible twelve. Local products are either directly imitative of existing products, are ineffective or unsafe products that can not clear regulatory hurdles in many nations, or are products that fill minor local niches.

In table 6–1 we find that strong competitive performers tend to innovate predominantly global products. Roughly 40 percent of the innovations discovered by strong performers are global products,

---

1. For a more extensive review of competitive performance, see Burstall (1985) and Thomas (1992).

FIGURE 6–1

PRODUCTION POSSIBILITY FRONTIER FOR PHARMACEUTICAL INNOVATION

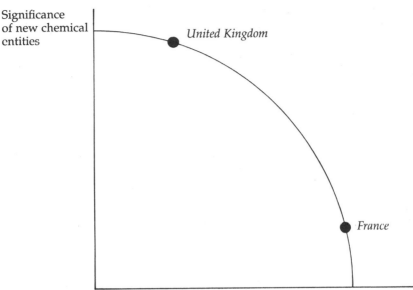

Significance of new chemical entities

United Kingdom

France

Number of new chemical entities

while only 30 percent are the less significant local products. In contrast, France, Italy, and Japan fragment their innovative effort so that as many as 70 percent of their discoveries are minor local products, while only roughly 10 percent of their innovations are global products.

We may highlight those difference between the two strategies based on innovation type by specifically comparing the United Kingdom and France. Figure 6–1 summarizes the different strategies pursued by British and French pharmaceutical firms during this time period. The production possibility frontier traced in figure 6–1 notionally gives the different ways of spending a comparable amount of pharmaceutical research expenditures. On the one hand, a nation can discover a great many minor derivative new chemical entities. On the other hand, the nation could take the same dollar volume of pharmaceutical research expenditure and discover only a small handful of very significant products. The production possibility frontier traces the full range of innovative options for a given level of pharmaceutical R&D expense. For a lower level of expense the frontier would lie entirely inside the one shown in figure 6–1, and for a higher level of expense it would lie entirely beyond that of figure 6–1.

It is straightforward to apply figure 6–1 to British and French firms because in recent decades, British and French firms have collectively expended roughly the same amount on pharmaceutical innovation each year, although this common amount has increased over time. From 1965 to 1985, French firms discovered 204 new chemical entities or roughly ten new drugs a year. In contrast, British firms discovered in total only eighty-one new chemical entities or roughly four a year. As a price for their numerous discoveries, however, French firms innovated only 13 percent global products and 60 percent local products. In contrast, 51 percent of the British discoveries were global products and only 25 percent local products.

It is this key strategic difference that accounts for the divergent performances of various national industries. Concentration of innovative effort into a handful of products discovered by a handful of firms in strong competitors, like the United States and Britain, leads to significant global success. Conversely, the fragmentation of innovative effort into large numbers of minor derivative products discovered by many weak firms leads to competitive failure in nations like Japan and France.

Why have U.S. and British firms adopted this successful strategy? Why have Japanese and French firms adopted a strategy that leads to failure? To understand the reasons for the differences in the strategies pursued by firms based in those nations, we now turn to the underlying theoretical foundation for industrial policy and then to the actual industrial policies practiced by various nations toward pharmaceuticals.

Industrial Policy and the Theory of the Firm

Industrial policy is a controversial concept, at the heart of an extensive debate over the proper interface between government and industry. On the one hand, opponents of industrial policy like the Reagan and Bush administrations in the United States argued that government has no role to play in direction of industry activity and ought to be "neutral" in its economic impact.[2] By "neutrality," opponents believe that government should not favor one firm over another firm, one industry over another industry, or one technology over another, all relative to some (quite conceptual) market in the absence of government. At best, such a view represents a principled opposition to socialism, or government ownership of corporations. Yet the last decade has brought a collapse of intellectual support for socialism throughout much of the

---

2. For discussions of this view, see Council of Economic Advisers (1984, 87–111), Lawrence (1984), Quick (1984), Schultze (1983), and Weidenbaum (1988).

world, including Western Europe, Eastern Europe, Latin America, and East Asia. Virtually no U.S. advocate of industrial policy seeks government ownership, and this debate is now muffled, however important it was historically.

Advocates of industrial policy reject this false dichotomy of capitalism or socialism. They counter that government neutrality is simply impossible (Johnson, Tyson, and Zysman 1989; Kuttner 1983; Reich 1983, 1985; and Zysman and Tyson 1983). There are innumerable ways for government to organize and administer taxation, government procurement, labor markets, capital markets, technology development, international trade, antimonopoly restrictions, and corporate governance. In the very act of defining national institutions that constitute the market, government inescapably favors certain firms, industries, and technologies, and that favoritism is large and durable. Put bluntly, there are many forms of capitalism, and the very act of choosing a particular form creates predictable favoritism. Industrial policy does not imply government ownership (or micromanagement) of industry but rather the government definition of the network of relations surrounding firms. Thus, the only real choice for government is not yes or no as to pursuit of industrial policy, but rather either to recognize and optimize government impact on industry explicitly or to ignore government impact blindly so that it occurs in a fragmented and conflicting manner. In other words, the only choice for government is explicit versus implicit industrial policy.

At the heart of the debate over industrial policy is a more fundamental debate over the theory of the firm. At one extreme, underlying the traditional Reagan-Bush views of industrial policy, is the neoclassical economics theory of the firm. The neoclassical model is precisely the firm as a black box, or as a production function relating inputs to outputs and stripped of any institutional detail. That exogenously given production function is essentially the same for all firms in the industry, and for potential entrants. Nothing impedes movement along that production function, and there is thus no role for the competitive environment or industrial policy. In contrast, a new set of views is coalescing around an organizational economics model of the firm, depicted in figure 6–2. From this new perspective, the firm is regarded as a collection of resources and skills embedded in a network of relations with other agents. The resources and skills of the firm are accumulated in the process of interactions with agents in the network, and that network of relations is precisely the domestic competitive environment.[3] As long as the firm has a certain specific form of relationship

---

3. For studies that view the firm as a collection of resources and skills, see

FIGURE 6–2
VIEW OF THE FIRM WITH SKILLS IN NETWORK

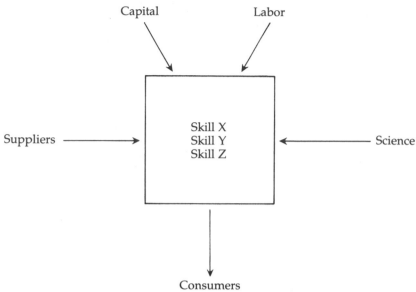

with capital providers, with labor, with science, with consumers, and with suppliers, the firm will perform in a particular way. It is not free to alter itself in isolation, and, indeed, the firm is its relationships with those local transactors.

This organizational economics theory of the firm has several important implications. First, firms have distinct national identities, based on the very different institutions that constitute the firm in various nations, and thus the different skills accumulated in each nation. Second, firms have durable competitive advantages. Highly skilled firms will outperform others, and those skills may be quite difficult for less skilled firms to imitate. Third, firm strategies and skills are dependent on the environment. The activities of transactors in the local network generate large externalities, and individual firms are heavily influenced by them. Fourth, competition among firms is dynamic, concerned with the accumulation and application of skills needed for superior performance. From those four points on firm constitution and conduct, the role of industrial policy follows directly. Appropriate in-

Barney (1991), Rumelt (1984), Wernerfelt (1984), and Teece, Rumelt, Dosi, et al. Winter (1992). For studies that present the firm as a network of relations with other local transactors, see Chandler (1990), Freeman (1987), Nelson (1993), and Porter (1990).

dustrial policy structures the national network to encourage rapid accumulation of appropriate corporate skills. Government plays a pervasive and inescapable role in *constructing* national competitive advantage.

The neoclassical perspective on the firm is quite different. Firms have no national identity, no sustained competitive advantage, no environmental dependence, and no dynamic competition. Critics of the neoclassical perspective would point out that those features are absent from neoclassical analysis because they are baldfacedly assumed away, and with those features goes any semblance of the modern firm and realistic corporate strategy. As a consequence, there is little room for any industrial policy in the neoclassical model other than correction of expectedly rare and isolated market failures.

In the end, the debate over industrial policy and the theory of the firm will be resolved on an empirical basis. Systematic studies of individual industries will indicate which theories best predict the strategies and performances of individual firms and the patterns of national success and failure across industries. As we return to the pharmaceutical industry in the next section, we shall find a tight fit between the industrial policies of various nations and the competitive strategies and skills followed by firms operating under those industrial policies.

Pharmaceutical Industrial Policy

Numerous government actions determine the character of the domestic competitive environment. Below we outline the major policies that shape the domestic competitive environments of pharmaceuticals.

Safety Regulation. There is considerable variation in the nature of safety regulations across most nations. In the United States and the United Kingdom, new drugs receive access to the market only after well-controlled (double-blind) clinical trials establish both safety and efficacy of the product. Such stringent requirements for premarket testing directly screen out many products that cannot demonstrate safety and efficacy. Additionally, the large cost and lengthy testing period indirectly screen out many products with moderate earnings insufficient to cover the testing and time costs. Finally, safety regulations in the United States and United Kingdom screen out entire firms that lack a strong scientific base and thus are unable to scale the rigorous testing hurdles (Thomas 1990). Thus, the tightening of safety regulations in the United States in 1962 and in the United Kingdom in 1964 led to shakeouts of smaller, less innovative firms and a concentration of innovative effort in larger firms.

115

In contrast, in Japan and France the stringency of access regulations has been drastically lower, with the difference being more pronounced for efficacy than for safety. Access to the French market required only that a recognized "expert" pronounce the drug safe and effective. Those expert judgments were often not reached after well-controlled tests, but only after some form of observation of patient usage by the expert—hence the derisive term "French Impressionist School" of safety regulation. More lenient regulation makes the launch of ineffective new products possible and also sharply reduces the costs of imitation of successful effective products. Such a regulatory environment has preserved numerous, small French firms that lack a strong scientific base for participating in the global industry but can successfully compete in the local market. In Japan safety is stringently regulated, but efficacy almost not at all. Further, clinical safety trials must be completely replicated in Japan on Japanese citizens, a nontariff barrier to trade that artificially shelters domestic Japanese firms. Again, domestic firms with a weak scientific base have been able to succeed locally without developing skills to penetrate the global marketplace.

The effects of those regulations on introduction and consumption give rise to widely varying patterns of new-drug availability, as listed in the middle of table 6–2. On one hand, some nations such as France and Italy are quite open to entry of new drugs, with very high access rates for drugs of all types. Other nations, including Sweden, the United States, and Japan, are drastically less open to new drugs, and post sharply lower access rates. Thus, there are variations in pure restrictiveness across nations. A second look at table 6–2, however, exposes an additional dimension of access. If we contrast in each nation the access rate for local products with that of global products, we also find significant variations across nations. In France, Italy, and now also Japan, the ratio of local to global access rates is 1 to 3. In contrast, in the United Kingdom it is 1 to 10, and in Sweden and the Netherlands it is 1 to 20. We may label this second dimension of access quality restrictiveness. Note that a nation may be purely restrictive without restricting quality (Japan), may be quality restrictive without being purely restrictive (the United Kingdom, where the global access rate is extremely high), or may be restrictive in both dimensions (Sweden and the Netherlands).

Comparisons between tables 6–1 and 6–2 indicate a very strong link between access rates and mix of innovations discovered by each competitor nation. Those nations that are quality restrictive, such as the United Kingdom, Sweden, and the Netherlands, have domestic markets dominated by global products, with few local products. The reverse relations hold for France, Italy, and Japan.

TABLE 6–2
COMPETITIVE PERFORMANCE AND INDUSTRIAL POLICY FOR NINE MAJOR COMPETITOR NATIONS

Nation	External Share, 1985	Access, All Drugs	Access, Global	Access, Local	Share of Public R&D, 1980	Price Level, 1980
United States	19.1	33.8	72.7	16.9	55.4	.98
Switzerland	7.4	38.2	78.4	13.1	1.1	1.62
United Kingdom	5.8	39.2	90.3	9.6	3.7	.97
Germany	6.2	59.4	96.3	26.5	15.3	1.19
France	1.0	54.3	86.5	32.3	6.2	.62
Italy	.5	54.9	86.2	33.5	2.6	.74
Japan	.1	39.3	65.0	22.1	11.6	2.35
Sweden	.7	19.1	59.6	2.9	2.4	.70
Netherlands	.4	25.1	61.0	3.9	2.6	1.24

SOURCE: Thomas (1992).

117

Government Funding of R&D. In the United States, the National Institutes of Health receives multibillion dollar annual funding that provides a significant competitive advantage for American firms. In part, the benefits of public R&D improve the productivity of domestic commercial innovation through spillovers. But also in part, public R&D in health care significantly alters consumption patterns by making medical personnel more sophisticated and "scientific" in deciding among alternate therapies. That consumption effect actually is arguably more important than the more expected productivity effect in determining the performance of national pharmaceutical industries.

Price Levels. If we contrast the levels of average prices across various nations, we find an important correlation between local price levels and the strategies and skills pharmaceutical firms follow—hence their global competitiveness. Nations with strong competitive performance (the United States, the United Kingdom, Switzerland, and Germany) have prices above the international median. Nations with weak competitive environments (France and Italy) tend to have prices below the median. This pricing-performance correlation is not perfect, however. For example, Japan has high prices with a weak competitive performance. Further, the extremely high prices of Switzerland did not buy Swiss firms an especially improved performance. Clearly, other government policies (principally access regulations) affect competitive performance. Nonetheless, it is clear that nations with low domestic prices do not sustain a globally competitive industry. In Thomas (1992), a study that excludes most nations with noncompetitive environments—Canada alone is included—national price levels explain roughly 10 percent of the variation in domestic competitive environments and global success. If we were to include more of the low-price nations, such as Australia, Austria, or Spain, the impact of pricing policies would presumably be significantly larger.

U.S. Pharmaceutical Industrial Policy since 1962

At the core of the findings above on industrial policies in nine nations is the imperative of stringent access regulation. In the United States, those regulations arose from the 1962 Amendments to the Food, Drug, and Cosmetic Act. Put bluntly, if greater government regulation (for safety and efficacy) in 1962 not only did not harm the U.S. drug industry but actually laid a foundation for its international success, might not new government regulation (for cost control) have comparable positive results? The answer to this question will be possibly yes, but probably no. To provide that answer, it is useful to examine in more detail the industrial policy the United States followed toward pharmaceuticals.

Since adoption by Congress of the 1938 Food, Drug, and Cosmetic Act, new ethical drugs are sold in the United States only after premarket safety tests, reviewed and approved by the FDA. The nature and magnitude of the required premarket testing changed drastically after adoption in 1962 of the Kefauver amendments to the 1938 act. Those amendments included the following key features:

• *Proof of Effectiveness:* New drugs had to demonstrate substantial evidence of effectiveness for indicated uses; only safety had to be demonstrated before 1962.

• *Clinical Testing:* FDA authority was extended to cover premarket testing in humans; no such guidelines existed before 1962.

• *Good Manufacturing Practice:* The FDA was authorized to set and enforce minimum standards for the operation of pharmaceutical research and manufacturing facilities in the United States; no such standards existed before 1962.

• *"Me-Too" Drugs:* Premarket testing for both safety and efficacy was required of all new drugs; before 1962, identical (generic) and similar (me-too) drugs could avoid premarket testing through certification by the FDA that the new product was in effect an "old drug."

How would the uniform FDA enforcement of this greater premarket testing alter the U.S. competitive environment and promote concentration of the market into large, highly innovative firms? The effects of the 1962 amendments on imitative firms producing only generic and me-too products were immediate and severe. Before 1962, those firms performed only perfunctory premarket testing and received from the FDA certification that their product was effectively identical to an established, successful drug. After 1962, those firms had to generate all their own premarket testing for both safety and efficacy and had to market their drugs on the strength of those tests alone. Unsurprisingly, the vast majority of firms on the imitative fringe of the industry completely ceased innovation after 1962, with a resulting sharp drop in total number of drugs approved after 1962.

For those firms that continued to develop new drugs after 1962, the amendments required a large and increasing interaction with physicians and pharmacologists on the staffs of medical research hospitals. It is those "superexperts" who would conduct the clinical trials for safety and efficacy necessary for regulatory approval. Those tests, and the reputations of the superexperts conducting them, would also, however, be the basis for the ultimate marketing of new drugs to U.S. physicians. Yet the accessibility of this class of superexperts varied

119

enormously among drug firms, despite the importance of this access. For the large firms with extensive R&D facilities and the best industrial research scientists searching for significant new therapies, the tasks of attracting the attention of and communicating with the necessary superexperts were relatively easy. For smaller firms with less extensive R&D efforts aiming for more imitative products, those interactive tasks were much harder. This formal integration of academic medicine and pharmaceutical marketing created a severe deterioration in competitive advantage for imitative drug firms in the U.S. market.

To illustrate how severely FDA regulations restricted smaller, imitative firms in the United States, it is useful to contrast the U.S. market with the vastly less stringently regulated Japanese market. For that contrast, we shall consider a single example, that of beta-blockers, a category of cardiovascular products that revolutionized care after their introduction. Let us compare the aggregate market shares of the first four successful products in the United States and Japan. In the United States, powerful first-mover advantages sustain the market shares of the earliest entrants, even in the face of generic competition. As a consequence, in the early 1990s, over fifteen years after the introduction of major beta-blockers, the first four products to reach the market retained an aggregate U.S. share of over 80 percent. In contrast, in Japan the market shares of the first four successful entrants fell quite rapidly, reaching 10 percent by the early 1990s. Easy entry because of lenient access (safety and efficacy) regulations and minimal physician brand loyalty enabled subsequent entrants to gain significant market presence. Even the second four successful entrants into the Japanese beta-blocker market suffered rapid erosion of market share.

Consider the incentives to U.S. firms for cardiovascular innovation. Clearly, there are only minimal incentives to expend research effort on imitative products, such as yet more beta-blockers. Instead, there are powerful incentives to be early in launching entirely new categories of cardiovascular products, such as calcium channel blockers or ace inhibitors, where U.S. firms are important innovators. As a consequence, even counting generics, only eleven beta-blockers were successfully launched in the United States by 1992, and all but two of those remain as successes over time. Facing such incentives in their home market, it is not surprising that U.S. firms have concentrated their R&D on significant innovations with global marketing potential. Conversely, in Japan there are great possibilities for imitative entry, and as a consequence the beta-blocker market in Japan is a whirl of entry and exit. By 1992, over thirty different beta-blocker products, most of them distinct molecules, had successfully entered the Japanese market, although over half of those once successful entrants had ceased to be successful by that year. Over 130 products, both successes and failures, had entered this cardiovascular segment in Japan. Facing such incentives, it is not surprising that Japanese firms have shied away from significant innovation and have instead fragmented their R&D efforts into a multiplicity of imitative products that are of little value outside their home market.

In short, U.S. industrial policy toward pharmaceuticals after 1962 generated two key mechanisms:

• *Marketing Technology #1:* Physician choice among competing drugs in the United States was brand loyal, price insensitive, and technology driven. Brand loyalty generated strong first-mover advantages that gave large market shares to early entrants and punished late, imitative entry with low market shares. Price insensitivity rewarded early entrants with high prices that would cover the discovery and marketing costs of innovative new products. And the strong scientific training of U.S. physicians made clinical trials generated by FDA requirements a key marketing tool for new pharmaceutical products.

• *Regime of Appropriation:* An innovator is competitively successful in the long run when it can appropriate a significant share of the benefits from its innovation. Absent such appropriation, the innovator cannot recoup the upfront costs of research and is unable to continue innovation. A regime of appropriation is a mechanism that accomplishes this appropriation (Teece 1986). Common regimes of appropriation are producer experience effects, consumer switching costs or brand loyalty, first-mover advantages, and patents and copyrights (Levin, Klevorick, Nelson, and Winter 1987). While patents are clearly important in pharmaceuticals, first-mover advantages and FDA barriers to imitation have been powerful supplements since 1962.

What we find then is that industrial policy is a complex whole. Yes, the 1962 amendments created a demanding competitive environment for U.S. firms by drastically raising safety and efficacy standards. But the FDA also simultaneously drove from the market dozens of imitative or generic firms, created strong economies of scale in innovation, and inadvertently transformed the marketing of new drugs in the United States by providing a concrete mechanism (clinical trial results) for doctors to scientifically choose among products. Equally important, FDA regulations were supplemented by powerful first-mover advantages in marketing and by price flexibility in demand that enabled higher prices to cover mounting research costs. To pick out an isolated component of this industrial policy is to risk misrepresenting its individual impact. U.S. drug firms were simultaneously challenged and

121

nurtured by their home market, targeted toward a winning strategy of concentrated innovative effort.

U.S. Pharmaceutical Industrial Policy after 1993

Explicitly intended or not, the large-scale intervention by the U.S. government into the pharmaceutical industry in 1962 was a great competitive success. Those regulations directly and indirectly demanded new skills from U.S. firms, and by closing the market to less skilled firms made the desired skill accumulation a profitable enterprise. What are the prospects for the impact on this industry of health care reform? Might new reforms have a comparable positive effect by demanding new skills at cost control?

For two reasons, there is merit to this question. First, the technology of pharmaceutical innovation has enabled the discovery of unusually expensive products. One of those products, Centoxin, developed by the biotechnology firm Centocor, illustrates the issues involved.[4] Centoxin was designed to treat septic shock—usually an infection acquired in a hospital—that strikes 400,000 Americans and kills 100,000 of them every year. The cost is extravagant: $4,000 per treatment, for a total potential cost of $1.6 billion per year. And for two-thirds of the patients treated (one-third of those who die), Centoxin provides no benefit, as their septic infection is not caused by the bacterium targeted and killed by Centoxin. For patients affected by this bacterium, Centoxin provides a quick recovery that is almost miraculous. Tests for the presence of the relevant bacterium take two to three days at the moment, and thus the decision to deploy the drug must be made blindly. Further, almost 80 percent of those patients whose lives were saved by Centoxin die within the year after treatment, as they were extremely sick to begin with, which is why they were in the hospital where they contacted septic infection.

An expenditure of $1.6 billion to save 70,000 lives is actually well within standard U.S. expenditures for life-saving activities (Viscusi 1993). Yet several issues immediately are raised. First, Centoxin is a new product that provides an expansion of care at an increase in costs, and therefore increases the share of GDP that flows to health care ex-

---

4. Centoxin has been subsequently removed from the market to assess potentially severe side effects. Rather than be drawn into the debate over existing products, this chapter considers Centoxin as a hypothetical example of the medical, economic, and ethical issues that will be confronted in cost control. Several other products currently on the market pose similar conundrums, and more such products will be introduced over time.

penditures. A proliferation of such products would mean a significant increase in health care expenditures, and a concomitant marketing-political problem of justifying to whoever is going to pay the bill that this increase is appropriate. Additionally, while Centoxin may well have marginal benefits to society that exceed marginal costs, it is straightforward to imagine permutations of aspects of this drug that will not pass such a test. The traditional U.S. health care system encourages consumption of any health care product or service with positive marginal benefit, regardless of cost, and thus would provide a welcome market for new products that are not cost-effective. Finally, cost-benefit decisions of the type that surround Centoxin are highly complex and center on such unpleasantries as comparing the values of life for a severely ill eighty-year-old adult and a healthy eight-year-old child.

A second reason that sensible reform of the U.S. health care system would benefit the U.S. competitive advantage in pharmaceuticals arises from health care reforms abroad. The last several years have seen widespread efforts at cost control in Europe including reference pricing, fixed prescription budgets, indicative prescribing, and direct price controls. Those approaches have proliferated across countries and have sharply increased in intensity during the past five years. A near crisis mentality has set in as health care expenditures in general, and pharmaceuticals in particular, have risen faster than general inflation or GDP growth for Europe at a time of significant macroeconomic recession and government budgetary shortfalls. As in the United States, rising expenditures are not unique to the pharmaceutical sector of health care, and pharmaceuticals represent only a small fraction of overall health care expenditures. Thus, the current European government focus on pharmaceuticals may well be driven more by political expediency and administrative convenience than by any real solution to fundamental problems.

An example of the extreme tactics used in Europe can be seen in Germany, where until recently pharmaceutical prices were unregulated. Beginning in 1993, the German government abruptly adopted a variety of extremist tactics to hold down pharmaceutical expenditure. Those included an outright though supposedly temporary price freeze for all products. Additionally, Germany set a national medicines budget for drug expense; physicians themselves would directly pay for any expenditures in excess of that fixed budgetary cap through fines levied on doctors who "excessively" prescribed. Finally, doctors who "excessively" prescribe pharmaceuticals will be individually audited by the state to suggest corrections for their inappropriate behavior. As a consequence of those tactics, the monetary value of German pharmaceutical consumption fell by almost 20 percent from 1992 to 1993, although that may well be a short-term response to the initial scare tactics used to present the new cost-control regime to doctors.

The contrast of cost-control hysteria in Europe with the biotechnology explosion in the United States is quite profound. Were the United States to ignore all issues of cost control, it would risk decoupling its domestic market from the rest of the world. The proliferation of cost-is-no-object niche markets filled with products not saleable in the rest of the world would provide a lucrative but ultimately uncompetitive set of incentives for U.S. product strategy, especially for entrepreneurial biotechnology firms. And a U.S. home market oblivious to drug costs would encourage U.S. firms to remain mired in a marketing strategy that paid no attention to costs and was increasingly out of touch with foreign markets. The current U.S. marketing strategy relies on skills of selling specific pharmaceutical products in isolation based solely on safety and efficacy concerns of individual physicians.

With current and proposed changes in health care in the United States, individual physician choice among competing drugs in the United States will be supplemented and in many ways replaced by choice of large vertically integrated providers. From an optimistic perspective, the old marketing technology in the United States will be changed as follows:

• *Marketing Technology #2.* Choice among competing drugs by new health care providers will become price conscious, analytically responsive, and technology driven. Providers will choose among products based on demonstrations of safety, efficacy, and cost effectiveness from excellent and widely respected studies. Drug companies without the capacity to convincingly provide this complex set of information in their marketing efforts will be slowly excluded from the nongeneric market. The bias in favor of all new technology will be replaced with a bias in favor of all cost-effective new technology.

Such a new marketing technology will have a variety of implications. On the one hand, the pronounced first-mover advantages that encourage early innovation in the United States and discourage imitation will be essentially eliminated. Successful late entry will now be vastly more feasible, as will price competition as a means of stealing market share from established early innovators. The number of entrants will arguably increase, although not to the degree seen in the Japanese domestic market, and the profitability for all entrants will decrease. Because much of the organizational superstructure of U.S. pharmaceutical firms exists to obtain early launch advantages, significant cutbacks in corporate overheads in both research and marketing

124

will occur. On the other hand, the new environment will require a transformation of U.S. firms' marketing skills: new staff, new systems, and new networks of academics producing cost-effectiveness studies. Drug firms marketing products like Centoxin will need to produce studies showing which patients should receive the drug under which circumstances and to convince MBA-trained administrators in large, vertically integrated providers that the product is appropriate. Those complex marketing skills will be difficult for smaller, less sophisticated firms in a manner very similar to the challenges posed for smaller firms by the 1962 amendments.

Thus, one critical regime of appropriation will disappear in the United States, while another of highly uncertain value will arise. The net effect of the change on the overall volume of innovative investment by the U.S. pharmaceutical industry and on the distribution of this investment along the innovation possibility frontier given in figure 6–1 is unclear. The central variable in determining the outcome will be the medical conduct of the large, vertically integrated providers. If those providers legitimately promote high-quality care and aggressively seek technological advances in health care, then the outcome will be arguably positive. Under those optimistic circumstances, the imprimatur "sold in America" will have powerful worldwide impact; it will signal that new drugs have passed a brutal but fair test of cost-effectiveness in the U.S. market and that they are thus worthy of consumption abroad.

Yet there are many aspects of the Clinton plan that would threaten significant deterioration of the U.S. environment for pharmaceuticals and, thus, the long-term global competitiveness of U.S. ethical drug firms. Again, the most important issue is the conduct of the vertically integrated providers. The very reason we regulate the safety of pharmaceuticals (and automobiles and airplanes) is that in markets where consumers have difficulty judging the quality or safety of products, there is a marked incentive by producers to underprovide quality or safety. However complex individual products may be, a health care provider that marshals innumerable products and services under a variety of highly uncertain contingencies is arguably by several orders of magnitude the most complex purchasing decision an individual can make. The legal framework created by health care reform will be vital in determining how well consumer choice among those new health care providers will function. Numerous details of the Clinton proposal are quite troubling in this regard, for example, the budget caps (after 1996) that set maximum prices for average health plans, the prohibition on providers' charging more than 20 percent of this average plan, the ban on individuals' buying their own health care, and the practice guidelines set by a national regulatory board that create medical rationing. All of those details would worsen, not reduce the innate tendency of a market for complex products to underprovide quality, mostly by price controls and rationing. As troubling as those details is the general philosophy of the Clinton plan that seeks to limit overall medical spending to a fixed share of GDP. Both the details for health care providers and the general philosophy are inherently anti-innovative in nature and represent a confusion of "cost suppression" with "cost effectiveness." Whatever the short-term need to wring minor excesses out of the U.S. health care system, in the long term the real issue will be a regulatory framework to address the potentially chronic underprovision of quality care. The provider organizations that will emerge under whatever reforms the United States adopts will create cultures, staffing, reputations, and internal routines that will be quite durable. Should those organizations somehow be established with anti-innovative biases, the long-term effects on U.S. drug firms would be quite negative and severe.

A second cluster of administration proposals would create formal price controls specifically for pharmaceuticals. An Orwellianly named Breakthrough Drug Committee would encourage "reasonable" drug prices by "jawboning" drug firms and vertically integrated health care providers into setting lower prices. That committee would presumably target for implicit regulation precisely the products that are the current basis of U.S. global competitive success—blockbuster products. Further, the "reasonableness" of prices would be determined by considering only the discovery costs of each drug in isolation and ignoring the multiplicity of dead ends inescapably reached in the process of discovering any one particular drug. Additionally, the secretary of the Health and Human Services Department would be empowered to bargain directly with drug firms in setting prices for products purchased by Medicare and to refuse to buy those products if not given the requested price. Of course, some level of negotiation and price setting is expected should the U.S. government extend Medicare coverage to prescription drugs. Yet the anti-innovation and cost-suppressive aspects of the Clinton plan suggest that those negotiations would be executed in a highly destructive manner.

The perversity of the Clinton approach as industrial policy, if followed completely, would create a completely new competitive environment in the United States.

• *Marketing Technology #3:* Choice among competing drugs by new health care providers will become price conscious, analytically indifferent, and technology repressive. Providers will choose among established products primarily on the basis of cost. Price wars will predominate in most drug categories, and drug innovation will focus on imitation of existing products. New drug products that do not directly and clearly reduce costs, regardless of benefit, will face slow and grudging adoption.

The consequences of that marketing technology would be severe. The demanding and sophisticated competitive environment of the United States that so effectively elicits breakthrough drugs from U.S. firms would now discourage such behavior and instead reward a very different pattern of competitive performance. In this new competitive environment, existing U.S. firms, with their fixations on science, their ponderous development schedules, and their armies of sophisticated marketing staff, would be at a distinct competitive disadvantage. Instead, competitive advantage would shift to those firms with extensive experience with cost-suppression, such as the Japanese, French, and Italian firms that have been so disadvantaged in a proinnovation environment yet have thrived at home in their own low-price, unsophisticated domestic markets.

Conclusions

Neoclassical economics lulls us into regarding markets as the inescapable equilibration of given preferences and technologies. Yet the environments in which modern firms compete are significantly constructed by myriad public policies, so that economic activity is organized, not simply aggregated from given supply and demand. Some aspects of this competitive environment, such as FDA regulation for safety and the historical price-indifference of U.S. doctors, are explicit and well known. Other aspects of the competitive environment are implicit and much less well known. For example, few Americans seem to grasp that FDA regulation of efficacy has a far larger economic impact than safety regulation, or that first-mover advantages for new drugs are historically as important as patents in securing returns for pharmaceutical innovators in the United States, or that FDA regulation has created enormous economies of scale that have secured the global competitive position of larger U.S. firms only by driving smaller firms from the U.S. market.

As the contrasting experiences of the United States and Japan well illustrate in pharmaceuticals, there is really very little that is inevitable about the trajectory over time of technology in an industry or the corresponding global success of firms from a given nation. In pharmaceuticals the domestic U.S. competitive environment, as formed by both explicit and implicit industrial policies, created and sustained the observed superior global performance of U.S. ethical drug firms. Proposed reforms of U.S. health care offer significant changes in the competitive environment for pharmaceuticals ranging from modest improvements that encourage cost-effectiveness to severe degradations that could end the historically superior innovative performance of U.S. firms and drastically reduce their international competitive advantage.

Perhaps the most important historical lesson the United States should keep in mind as it reforms its health care sector is that "producer protection" is disastrous industrial policy. Appropriate industrial policy encourages firms to adopt strategies that create value for consumers in the long run and punishes firms that offer inferior or uninnovative products. The 1962 amendments succeeded as industrial policy in the United States precisely because they forced firms operating in the U.S. pharmaceutical market to focus their efforts on significant, safe, and effective products that would enjoy worldwide demand. To the extent that U.S. health care reform attains its important mandate of promoting true cost-effectiveness in demand for medical products and services, U.S. industrial policy may not only sustain but may strengthen the global competitiveness of U.S. pharmaceutical firms. If, however, U.S. health care reform falters and seeks cost suppression regardless of the merit of new technologies, then not only will the value and quality of health care service deteriorate in the United States, but the competitive position of U.S. ethical drug firms will slowly but surely follow.

References

Barney, J. B. "Firm Resources and Sustained Competitive Advantage." *Journal of Management* (1991): 99–120.

Burstall, Michael L. *The Community's Pharmaceutical Industry*. Luxembourg: Office for Official Publications of the European Communities, 1985.

Council of Economic Advisers. *Economic Report of the President, 1984*. Washington, D.C.: Government Printing Office, 1984.

Chandler, Alfred. *Scale and Scope: The Dynamics of Industrial Capitalism*. Cambridge: Harvard University Press, 1990.

Freeman, C. *Technology, Policy, and Economic Performance*. London: Francis Pinter, 1987.

Johnson, Chalmers, Laura D'A. Tyson, and John Zysman, eds. *Politics and Productivity: How Japan's Development Strategy Works*. New York: Harper Collins, 1989.

Kuttner, Robert. *The Economic Illusion*. Boston: Houghton Mifflin, 1984.

Lawrence, Robert Z. *Can America Compete?* Washington, D.C.: Brookings Institution, 1984.

Levin, Richard C., Alvin K. Klevorick, Richard R. Nelson, and Sidney G. Winter. "Appropriating the Returns from Industrial Research and Development." *Brookings Papers on Economic Actitity, Microeonomics* (1987): 783–832.

Nelson, Richard R. *National Innovation Systems: A Comparative Analysis*. Oxford: Oxford University Press, 1993.

Porter, Michael E. *The Competitive Advantage of Nations*. New York: Free Press, 1990.

Quick, Perry D. "Business: Reagan's Industrial Policy." In *The Reagan Record: An Assessment of America's Changing Domestic Priorities*, edited by John L. Palmer and Isabel V. Sawhill. Cambridge, Mass.: Ballinger, 1984.

Reich, Robert B. *The Next American Frontier*. New York: Penguin Books, 1983.

————. "Bailout." *Yale Journal on Regulation* 2 (1985): 163–224.

Rumelt, Richard P. "Towards a Strategic Theory of the Firm." In *Competitive Strategic Management*, edited by David J. Teece. Englewood Cliffs, N.J.: Prentice-Hall, 1984.

Schultze, Charles L. "Industrial Policy: A Dissent." *Brookings Review* (Fall 1983): 3–12.

Teece, David J. "Profiting from Technological Innovation: Implications for Integration, Collaboration, Licensing, and Public Policy." *Research Policy* 15 (December 1986): 285–305.

Teece, David J., Richard P. Rumelt, G. Dosi, and Sidney G. Winter. "Understanding Corporate Coherence: Theory and Evidence." Working paper, 1992.

Thomas, Lacy Glenn III. "Implicit Industrial Policy: The Triumph of Britain and the Failure of France in Global Pharmaceuticals." *Industrial and Corporate Change* 3 (1994).

————. "Regulation and Firm Size: FDA Impacts on Innovation." *Rand Journal of Economics* 21 (1990): 497–517.

————. "Spare the Rod and Spoil the Industry: Vigorous Regulation and Vigorous Competition Promote Global Competitive Advantage." Working paper, Emory University, 1992.

Weidenbaum, Murray. *Rendezvous with Reality: The American Economy after Reagan*. New York: Basic Books, 1988.

Wernerfelt, Berger. "A Resource-Based View of the Firm." *Strategic Management Journal* (April–June 1984): 171–80.

Zysman, John, and Laura D'A. Tyson, eds. *American Industry in International Competition: Government Policies and Corporate Strategies*. Ithaca: Cornell University Press, 1983.

7
R&D Productivity and Global Market Share in the Pharmaceutical Industry

Donald L. Alexander

Over the past several decades, the ethical pharmaceutical industry has been an important source of new products as firms compete to develop and market drugs that are consumed for a wide range of medical reasons.[1] At the same time, the rising cost of new drug development and the adverse effect of Food and Drug Administration regulations on pharmaceutical R&D expenditures have forced firms to improve R&D productivity so as to remain competitive in the global marketplace.[2] The empirical evidence reported in the economics literature, however, suggests that firms are able to realize small gains in R&D productivity by getting larger, but only up to a certain size. Comanor (1965), for example, finds no evidence that marginal productivity diminishes as firm size increases when the scale of the R&D operation is held constant, but finds that R&D productivity falls as the scale of the R&D operation increases when firm size is held constant. By contrast, Vernon and Gusen (1974) find that increasing firm size increases the mar-

This chapter is drawn from a paper that I have written with Joseph Flynn and Linda Linkins of the U.S. International Trade Commission. Many thanks to Robert Rogowsky, John Ratner, and Brian Healy for their comments and suggestions on an earlier draft of that paper. I assume all responsibility for any errors contained herein.

1. Cocks (1975) describes the dynamic elements of product innovation and competition in the pharmaceutical industry.

2. DiMasi et al. (1991) find that it costs approximately $231 million to develop a new drug that may never sell in the marketplace. Wiggins (1981, 1983) reports that FDA regulations have had an adverse impact on R&D spending and, consequently, on the flow of new product innovation. Wiggins (1984), however, acknowledges that other factors have contributed to the decline in new drug innovation.

ginal productivity of the staff when the size of the R&D staff is fixed, but that increasing the size of the R&D staff within a given firm size eventually gives rise to diminishing returns. Addressing certain econometric problems in those previous studies, Jensen (1987) reports that firm size has no discernable effect on the marginal productivity of R&D expenditures when the level of R&D spending is constant and that increasing R&D expenditures within a given firm size has no effect on productivity.[3] At best, the empirical evidence regarding the relationship between firm size and R&D productivity in the pharmaceutical industry is inconclusive.

The primary objective of this chapter is to reexamine the relationship between firm size and R&D productivity empirically by using a representative sample of twenty-six international pharmaceutical firms. In addition to using more recent data, this research differs from the aforementioned studies in two important respects. First, I use a new measure of R&D output in the empirical analysis that reflects the number of compounds that a firm has in its R&D pipeline in a given year to avoid the problem that there may be a zero value when using new chemical entities as the R&D-output measure. This new measure, however, has several limitations as well that are discussed in the empirical section below. Second, I use total employment per firm instead of a sales measure to proxy firm size, because the relationship between firm size and R&D productivity involves real rather than nominal factors. Moreover, the use of sales data to proxy firm size may be problematic because of fluctuations in the demand for a firm's product(s) in a given year or because differences in demand conditions faced by firms in different markets would affect sales even though the physical size of the firm did not change.[4] Total employment, in contrast, is closely related to the physical size of the firm and thus provides a real measure of firm size. Furthermore, total employment and diversification are likely to be correlated for firms in the pharmaceutical industry, since those firms often diversify into other chemically related activities that are likely to have spillover effects on R&D conducted in the pharmaceutical area. Larger firm size may also allow those firms to diversify their R&D across several therapeutic classes, which may increase productivity as well. To the extent that firm size and diversification are

---

3. These studies use the number of new chemical entities per firm as the R&D output measure. In any given year, however, a firm may not develop a successful new chemical entity, which means that the dependent variable equals zero and that classical least squares estimation is inappropriate.

4. See Alexander, Flynn, and Linkins (1994) for a discussion of demand variations across seven countries.

related, the employment measure should pick up those additional effects.[5]

The second objective of this chapter is to examine empirically the determinants of global market share, since market share is an important performance indicator in a competitive marketplace. I estimate an empirical model that captures the relationship between firm size, R&D productivity, and global market share in a straightforward and theoretically consistent manner.

This chapter is organized in the following manner. The second section presents the empirical model and a discussion of the regression results. The third section presents the empirical model that is used to estimate the determinants of global market share and a discussion of the empirical results. The final section summarizes the major findings and discusses some policy implications that may be drawn from this research.

An Empirical Analysis of the Relationship between Firm Size and R&D Productivity

The regression analysis in this section examines the relationship between firm size and R&D productivity by using a pooled, cross-section sample of firm-specific data for twenty-six international pharmaceutical firms that sell ethical and over-the-counter (OTC) drugs.[6] Those firms accounted for approximately 50 percent of the global ethical pharmaceutical sales in 1989, with global market shares ranging from .43 to 4.41 percent. Pooling those data over the period 1987 to 1989 increases the number of observations (seventy-eight) used in the estimation procedure.

A Description of the Empirical Model. Fisher and Temin (1973) describe the basic theoretical model idea underlying the construction of the empirical model in this analysis. In simple terms R&D productivity is a function of a vector of firm-specific characteristics related to the R&D process that are likely to affect a particular firm's productivity. Since pharmaceutical firms are located in different countries that have specific industrial policies that are likely to affect their firms' competi-

---

5. I included a measure of the size of a firm's R&D operations (discussed below) to control for the fact that diversification across therapeutic classes may be more closely correlated with the size of the R&D operation than with the total size of the firm.

6. Ten of these firms have headquarters in the United States, seven have headquarters in Western Europe, and nine have headquarters in Japan. I describe all data and their respective sources in the data appendix.

tive performance in the global marketplace, I have attempted to account for the effect of those external (to the firm) policies in the empirical model by including a dummy variable distinguishing firms headquartered in the United States from firms headquartered elsewhere.[7] I did not include a specific variable for each policy either because the policy is too difficult to quantify or because the policy is roughly the same across several countries, which then makes it difficult to capture any variation that is necessary in the regression analysis. Thus, the general specification of the empirical model is shown as

R&D productivity =
f(firm-related R&D factors, firm size, U.S. dummy variable).

In the regression model I used two different measures of R&D productivity. The first is the ratio of a firm's R&D compounds to the firm's R&D employees (*OUTPUTEMP*), in which case the numerator represents the total number of compounds patented but not yet approved for marketing that are in a firm's R&D pipeline in a given year,[8] and the denominator (*RDEMP*) represents the total number of employees involved in the R&D process—scientists, technicians, and managers. Since it is likely that no single group is entirely responsible for the discovery and development of any compound, *RDEMP* is a reasonable measure to use in the empirical analysis. *OUTPUTEMP* is also a reasonable measure to use because it is consistent with the traditional productivity measures used in economic theory.

The second measure that I use is the number of R&D compounds per firm (*OUTPUT*). The rationale is that variations in *OUTPUTEMP* may reflect only variations in the denominator or numerator, and I avoid this potential problem by using the *OUTPUT* measure just described. Since I did not normalize the number of compounds by the

---

7. Thomas (1995) provides an excellent discussion of the various ways in which a country's industrial policies affect the firms in its domestic pharmaceutical industry.

8. These data exclude any R&D compounds that have been licensed from other firms. This measure, however, has several limitations. First, the compounds in the pipeline differ in terms of quality. This is an important factor that I am unable to control for in the regression analysis, since, ideally, one should weight each compound in terms of whether the compound is a pure innovation or simply an imitation of an existing compound. Second, a compound's ultimate success as a new drug is frequently the result of serendipity, which may vary widely across firms. Unfortunately, I am unable to identify and then select the successful compounds from this sample. Nevertheless, it is a reasonable measure to use because it reflects the output of R&D employees for a given pharmaceutical firm.

number of employees (*RDEMP*), I included *RDEMP* as an explanatory variable in the empirical model.

In the first regression model using *OUTPUTEMP* as the dependent variable, I included the following independent variables to control for firm-specific differences that are likely to affect R&D productivity. The first is the level of R&D expenditures, in which case I used the ratio of real R&D expenditures to R&D employees per firm (*RDEXPEMP*). Firms that invest in higher levels of R&D per employee should be more productive although not necessarily more successful, if all other things are equal. I also included $RDEXPEMP^2$ in the model, because firms that spend large amounts for R&D will eventually experience diminishing returns from additional real R&D spending per employee. Thus, those two measures should capture the overall resources that R&D personnel use to develop new compounds.[9]

To control for differences in overall firm size, I included the total employees per firm as an explanatory variable (*TOTALEMP*). It is expected that larger firms are likely to be more diversified in the R&D process and, therefore, are likely to gain from the specialization of R&D personnel in several different therapeutic classes. Furthermore, it is expected that R&D staffs in larger firms are likely to achieve higher levels of productivity because they are likely to have access to more resources. To test this second hypothesis, I interacted *RDEXPEMP* with *TOTALEMP* to determine whether real R&D spending per R&D employee has a differential effect on productivity in larger as compared with smaller firms.

The fourth explanatory variable that I included is a measure of past R&D expenditures to capture the dynamic effects of previous spending on current output (*PASTRDEMP*). This variable is likely to have a positive effect on current output because firms that have spent more per employee in the past are likely to produce more R&D compounds in the current period because of lags in the discovery process.

Finally, I included a dummy variable (*FOREIGN*) to control for differences in government regulations that may affect R&D productivity across firms. This variable has a value equal to one if the firm's headquarters are located outside the United States and zero otherwise. I do not expect that variable to capture the precise difference in regulations between the United States and the rest of the world because of its crude construction. Nevertheless, despite this limitation, it does reflect to some extent the broad policy differences between the United States and other major countries. Thomas (1995), for example, finds that strin-

---

9. This assumes that R&D expenditures and capital equipment used in the R&D process are positively correlated.

gent FDA safety and efficacy regulations, higher than average market prices in the United States, important first-mover advantages because of patent laws and FDA policy limiting imitative drugs, and R&D spillovers because of generous subsidies channeled through the National Institutes of Health have all combined to make U.S.-based firms more competitive in the global marketplace as compared with firms headquartered in other countries. Of course, this crude measure may simply reflect differences across countries that are completely unrelated to any regulatory differences. If, for example, U.S.-based firms have easier access to a larger pool of R&D scientists because of the high-quality university system in the United States, that access may provide U.S. firms with more productive employees and, hence, a competitive advantage. I do not wish to overstate that point because many foreign firms have R&D facilities located in the United States. Therefore, the expected sign for this measure is uncertain.

In the regression model with *OUTPUT* as the dependent variable, I included a similar set of explanatory variables. The first two variables are the number of R&D employees (*RDEMP*) and a squared term (*RDEMP*^{2}) to capture any diminishing returns in the relationship between R&D employees and R&D output. Second, I included a measure of real R&D expenditures to control for spending differences across firms (*RDEXP*). That measure includes expenditures on new capital equipment that are likely to have some impact on a firm's R&D output. Third, I included a measure of total employment (*TOTALEMP*) to control for differences in firm size and an interaction term between *TOTALEMP* and *RDEMP* to test whether firm size has a differential effect on R&D productivity. Finally, I used a measure of past R&D to capture the dynamic effects of past R&D spending on current output.[10] The next section presents the empirical results for the two econometric models.

Empirical Results for the Firm Size and R&D Productivity Regression Models. Table 7–1 presents the summary statistics for the variables used in the regression analysis. I estimated each model using a fixed-effects approach (time-specific effects) and ordinary least squares. After correction for heteroskedasticity, however, the F-tests revealed that the time-specific effects did not add any additional ex-

---

10. I did not normalize the *PASTRD* measure by R&D employees as I did in the first regression model since *RDEMP* is included as a separate independent variable.

TABLE 7–1
SUMMARY STATISTICS FOR THE REGRESSION ANALYSIS

Variable	Mean	Standard Deviation	Coefficient of Variation
MKTSHARE	1.50	.89	.59
OUTPUTEMP	.03	.01	.33
OUTPUT	43.74	20.66	.47
RDEXP	235.63	124.87	.53
RDEXPEMP	143.50	91.86	.64
RDEMP	2.25	1.45	.64
SALESEMP	3.36	2.05	.61
TOTALEMP	37.77	43.15	1.14
LICDRUG	15.80	7.09	.45
PASTRD	809.70	490.95	.61
PASTRDEMP	439.63	223.24	.51

NOTE: These data and their respective sources are described in the text. MKTSHARE is expressed in percent; OUTPUTEMP is expressed as the number of R&D compounds per R&D employee; OUTPUT is expressed as the number of R&D compounds; RDEXP is expressed in millions of 1982–1984 dollars; RDEXPEMP is measured in thousands of 1982–1984 dollars per R&D employee; RDEMP is measured in thousands of R&D employees; SALESEMP is measured in thousands of sales employees; TOTALEMP is measured in thousands of total employees; PASTRD is measured in millions of 1982–1984 dollars; and PASTRDEMP is measured in thousands of 1982–1984 dollars per R&D employee.

planatory power to the model.[11] I then reestimated the models by using a modified version of Kmenta's (1986) estimation procedure for pooled data that corrects for cross-sectional heteroskedasticity. The parameter estimates appear in table 7–2.

Column (1) of table 7–2 shows the estimates for the log-log specification; column (2) displays the results for the linear specification. In either specification the model performs well as it explains at least 50 percent of the variation in the dependent variable. Moreover, the explanatory variables all have the expected signs, and many are significant at conventional levels. The positive and negative parameter estimates shown respectively for RDEXPEMP and $RDEXPEMP^2$ in col-

---

11. I tested for autocorrelation by using the Durbin-Watson test statistic and found that either I was unable to reject the hypothesis of no positive autocorrelation or the test statistic fell in the inconclusive range. I also tested for heteroskedasticity by using the Breusch-Pagan-Godfrey test statistic and found that I was able to reject the hypothesis of homoskedasticity, which I corrected for by using the HETCOV procedure in SHAZAM.

umn (1) indicate the presence of diminishing returns from additional R&D expenditures per R&D employee. By differentiating the regression equation shown in column (1) with respect to changes in *RDEXPEMP*, we find that diminishing returns set in at approximately $118,449 of R&D spending per R&D employee (evaluated at the mean values for *OUTPUTEMP* and *RDEXPEMP*).[12]

$$\frac{\partial OUTPUTEMP}{\partial RDEXPEMP} = (4.547 - .674 \ \ln RDEXPEMP \tag{1}$$

$$- .366 \ \ln TOTALEMP) \ \frac{OUTPUTEMP}{RDEXPEMP}.$$

The average pharmaceutical firm in this sample spends only $143,500, which suggests that the average firm may be operating in the range where changes in average productivity from additional R&D spending per employee are negative. The second partial derivative, however, is negative for all values of *RDEXPEMP*, which is consistent with the fact that profit-maximizing firms operate in the range where diminishing returns have occurred.

The results also reveal that the impact of additional R&D spending per employee on R&D productivity varies according to firm size. By differentiating equation (1) above, we find that increases in firm size (*TOTALEMP*) have a negative effect on changes in the average productivity of R&D employees (evaluated at the mean values for *OUTPUTEMP*, *RDEXPEMP*, and *TOTALEMP*), which suggests that larger firms obtain less output for an additional dollar spent per R&D employee than smaller firms for the same additional dollar spent per R&D employee. One plausible explanation may be that the additional dollar spent per R&D employee is partially offset by bureaucratic inefficiencies that often arise in larger, more diversified firms.

In addition, by differentiating the regression equation in column (1) with respect to changes in *TOTALEMP*, we find that increases in firm size have a positive effect on the average productivity of an R&D employee (evaluated at the mean values for *TOTALEMP* and *OUTPUTEMP*).[13]

$$\frac{\partial OUTPUTEMP}{\partial TOTALEMP} = (1.584 - .366 \ \ln RDEXPEMP) \ \frac{OUTPUTEMP}{TOTALEMP}.$$

$$\tag{2}$$

---

12. It is important to recognize that the interaction term includes *RDEXP-EMP*, which requires that we differentiate it also with respect to changes in *RDEXPEMP*.

13. The effect is positive as long as *RDEXPEMP* is less than $75,783.

TABLE 7-2

REGRESSION ESTIMATES FOR THE DETERMINANTS OF R&D PRODUCTIVITY FROM A POOLED, CROSS-SECTIONAL TIME-SERIES ANALYSIS BY FIRM, 1987–1989

	(1) log(OUTPUTEMP)	(2) OUTPUTEMP	(3) log(OUTPUT)	(4) OUTPUT
Constant	−18.936 (−5.89)	−.003 (−.87)	2.412 (5.19)	18.203 (4.00)
RDEXPEMP	4.547 (4.08)	.0003 (6.55)		
RDEXPEMP^2	−.337 (−3.74)	−.0000003 (−3.74)		
RDEMP			.380 (5.81)	15.344 (4.29)
RDEMP^2			−.098 (−2.37)	−2.667 (−3.54)
RDEXP			.169 (2.09)	.030 (1.72)

	(1)	(2)	(3)	(4)
TOTALEMP	1.584	.0001	−.240	−.308
	(4.06)	(3.46)	(−4.59)	(−2.78)
RDEXPEMP*TOTALEMP	−.366	−.000001		
	(−4.69)	(−4.97)		
RDEMP*TOTALEMP			.005	.100
			(4.63)	(2.91)
PASTRDEMP	.294	.00001		
	(4.07)	(1.21)		
PASTRD			.156	.011
			(2.26)	(2.28)
FOREIGN	−.290	−.001	−.346	−9.340
	(−4.54)	(−.92)	(−6.10)	(−3.20)
Buse R^2	.65	.50	.64	.39
SSE	1.03	1.02	1.02	1.04

NOTE: t-statistics are in parentheses and SEE is the standard error of estimate. 2.33 = 1 percent significance level (one tailed). 1.67 = 5 percent significance level (one tailed). 2.66 = 1 percent significance level (two tailed). 2.00 = 5 percent significance level (two tailed).

139

The interpretation of this result is that, given the same dollar spent per R&D employee, larger firms produce more R&D compounds per R&D employee than smaller firms, which may simply reflect the fact that as firms get larger, their growth is associated with resource expenditures that improve the productivity of the firm's R&D employees.[14] The main difference between that result and the previous result is that the former describes the effect of firm size on changes in the average productivity of an R&D employee, given an additional dollar spent for R&D, while the latter describes the effect of firm size on the average productivity of an R&D employee when R&D expenditures are held constant.

The positive and statistically significant parameter estimate for *PASTRDEMP* supports the view that current output is a function of past resource commitments made in the R&D process, which is not surprising, since it takes pharmaceutical firms an average of twelve years to develop a new drug to sell in the marketplace.[15] The negative and statistically significant coefficient for *FOREIGN* indicates that firms not headquartered in the United States are on average less productive than U.S.-based firms. That finding is consistent with Thomas's analysis (1995), in which he shows that U.S.-based firms accounted for 44 percent of the global products (new drugs that are diffused in at least six of the twelve countries in his study) discovered over the period 1965 to 1985. Alternatively, those results may reflect firm-specific or country-specific differences for which the empirical model does not explicitly control.

The parameter estimates I report for the linear specification of the model in column (2) are qualitatively similar to the results shown for the log-log specification in column (1) with two exceptions that are worth mentioning. First, by differentiating the regression equation shown in column (2) with respect to changes in *RDEXPEMP*, we find that increases in R&D expenditures per R&D employee have a positive effect on changes in average productivity for all values of *RDEXPEMP* less than $260,000 (evaluated at the mean value for *TOTALEMP*).

$$\frac{\partial OUTPUTEMP}{\partial RDEXPEMP} =$$

$$.0003 - .000001\ RDEXPEMP - .000001\ TOTALEMP. \quad (3)$$

Since the mean for *RDEXPEMP* is only $143,500, that result suggests that firms in the sample could spend additional funds on R&D before

---

14. This result is consistent with the findings in earlier research. See, for example, Comanor (1965) and Vernon and Gusen (1974). Jensen (1987), however, finds no evidence that firm size matters.

15. See Office of Technology Assessment (1993) for more details.

the effect on average productivity becomes negative. In comparison with the log-log specification in column (1), this result spans a wider range of values for *RDEXPEMP* in which changes in R&D expenditures have a positive effect on average productivity.[16]

The second difference is that *PASTRDEMP* and *FOREIGN* are both insignificant in the linear specification of the model. Apparently, the significance of those two variables is sensitive to the specification of the regression model that is used. The results shown in columns (3) and (4) of table 7–2, however, indicate that past R&D expenditures do matter and that there is a difference between U.S.-based and non-U.S.-based firms in terms of R&D productivity.

I report the parameter estimates for the regression model with *OUTPUT* as the dependent variable in columns (3) and (4) of table 7–2. Column (3) shows the parameter estimates for the log-log specification; column (4) displays the results for the linear specification. At least with respect to the log-log specification, the model performs well: it explains 64 percent of the variation in the dependent variable. Moreover, the parameter estimates all have the expected signs and are statistically significant at conventional levels. The positive and negative signs for *RDEMP* and *RDEMP²* indicate the presence of diminishing returns in the R&D process. By differentiating the regression equation shown in column (3) with respect to changes in *RDEMP*, we find that the marginal productivity of an additional R&D employee is positive as long as *RDEMP* is less than 7,619 (evaluated at the mean value for *TOTALEMP*).[17]

$$\frac{\partial OUTPUT}{\partial RDEMP} = (.380 - .196 \ln RDEMP$$

$$+ .005 \ln TOTALEMP) \frac{OUTPUT}{RDEMP}. \quad (4)$$

Because the average number of R&D employees is 2,246, this result suggests that firms in this sample have opportunity for expansion before diminishing productivity occurs.[18] Moreover, by differentiating equation (4) with respect to changes in *TOTALEMP*, we find that increases in firm size have a negative effect on marginal productivity of

---

16. The second partial derivative is also negative for all values of *RDEXP-EMP*, which is consistent with profit-maximizing behavior.

17. It is important to recognize that the interaction term includes *RDEMP*, which requires that we differentiate it also with respect to changes in *RDEMP*.

18. The second partial derivative for equation (4) is negative, which is consistent with profit-maximizing firms operating in the range of diminishing returns.

R&D employees, which again may reflect the fact that, as firms get larger, the effect of an additional dollar spent per R&D employee is partially offset by bureaucratic inefficiencies that often arise in larger, more diversified firms.[19]

Differentiating the regression equation shown in column (3) with respect to changes in TOTALEMP reveals that increases in firm size have a negative effect on the total number of R&D compounds in the firm's pipeline for a wide range of plausible values for the number of R&D employees.[20]

$$\frac{\partial OUTPUT}{\partial TOTALEMP} = (.005 \ln RDEMP - .240) \frac{OUTPUT}{TOTALEMP}. \tag{5}$$

That result is puzzling to the extent that we would expect a positive effect for firms with smaller R&D staffs and a negative effect for firms with larger R&D staffs. Nevertheless, for a firm with a small R&D staff, increasing the total firm size may involve adding more non-R&D employees, which would reduce the effectiveness of the research staff. For a firm with a large R&D staff, however, increasing the total firm size may involve increasing the physical capacity of the R&D operation and hiring new non-R&D employees. Thus, changes in firm size for firms with small R&D staffs may not involve additions to capacity, whereas changes in firm size for firms with larger R&D staffs may involve some expansion of physical capacity to accommodate the increase in employees. Unfortunately, the requisite data to test this explanation are not available.

The results also reveal that real R&D spending (RDEXP) has a positive and statistically significant effect on the number of compounds in the firm's pipeline in the log-log specification (column (3)), although it is insignificant at conventional levels in the linear specification (column (4)). This variable may be picking up the effects of expenditures on R&D resources other than R&D personnel.[21]

The effect of PASTRD on R&D compounds is positive and significant at conventional levels, which again supports the hypothesis that past spending has some effect on current R&D output. Similarly, the negative and statistically significant coefficient for the FOREIGN dummy variable further confirms the argument that U.S.-based firms are more productive relative to the Western European and Japanese

---

19. Comanor (1965) finds that marginal productivity is inversely related to firm size.

20. The effect is positive for all values of RDEMP that exceed 1.44×10^{24}, which is unlikely.

21. The correlation coefficient between RDEXP and RDEMP is only 0.78.

firms included in the sample. Whether we can attribute that finding completely to the regulatory differences across those countries is a question that requires further investigation.

The pattern of parameter estimates for the linear regression model shown in column (4) is qualitatively similar to that reported in column (3). The findings show that: increases in *RDEMP* have a positive effect on R&D output as long as R&D staff size is less than 3,585; firms are operating in the range where diminishing marginal productivity has set in; changes in firm size (*TOTALEMP*) have a positive effect on marginal productivity; and increases in firm size lead to increases in the number of R&D compounds in the firm's pipeline, provided the R&D staff size exceeds 3,080 employees. All in all, the results presented in table 7–2 indicate that firm-specific factors explain part of the variation in R&D productivity and that differences between U.S.-based firms and other firms not explicitly controlled for in the model contribute to explaining part of the variation in R&D productivity as well.

An Empirical Analysis of the Relationship between R&D Productivity and Global Market Share

This section examines the determinants of global market share by using a regression model that includes the explanatory variables for the R&D productivity models (*OUTPUTEMP* and *OUTPUT*) that are discussed above. Such an approach seems reasonable to the extent that productivity is likely to be an important factor explaining competitiveness as measured by global market share and to the extent that the firm-specific factors (discussed above) are likely to affect market share indirectly through the productivity relationship. I also included several additional explanatory variables that are likely to affect market share directly and shall discuss them below. Thus, the regression model that I used in this section captures, to a certain degree, the relationship among firm-specific characteristics, R&D productivity, and global market share.

A Description of the Empirical Model. The dependent variable is a firm's market share of the worldwide total of ethical pharmaceutical sales in each year from 1987 to 1989 (*MKTSHARE*). In addition to the determinants of R&D productivity discussed above, several other firm-specific factors are likely to have an influence on a firm's global market share. The first factor is the number of marketing personnel that a firm employs when selling new drugs in the marketplace. To control for differences in sales staffs, I included the number of sales personnel for each firm as an explanatory variable (*SALESEMP*). Firms that employ

143

more salespersons are likely to have a larger market share, when all other things are equal. Moreover, it is plausible that sales employees in larger firms may be more effective to the extent that larger firms offer a wider range of complementary products and, perhaps, provide greater support services for their employees. To test for this potential effect arising from firm size, I interacted *SALESEMP* with firm size (*TOTALEMP*) and included it in the regression model. For larger firms the interaction term may also pick up any economies in the distribution of drugs that increase the effectiveness of the representative salesperson and that are not likely to be realized in smaller firms.[22]

The second factor is the number of compounds that a firm has licensed from other firms (*LICDRUG*). The rationale is that a firm's own drugs are likely to have a positive and larger effect on market share as compared with a drug licensed from another firm because the licensing firm is likely to keep only those compounds that it expects to be successful. A firm may, however, have a compound in its pipeline that has potential for success but may not have the requisite expertise or resources to develop the drug for sale in the marketplace. Consequently, the firm may be inclined to license the compound to some other firm. Those explanations suggest that the expected sign for *LICDRUG* is uncertain.

The third factor is a dummy variable (*FOREIGN*), which equals one if the firm is headquartered outside the United States and zero otherwise. That measure is intended to control for any country-specific differences that may directly affect a firm's market share. The countries represented by the firms in this sample are similar in terms of their economic development, but, as Thomas (1995) shows, the countries differ markedly with regard to the various industrial policies affecting the pharmaceutical industry; for example, the United States and West Germany permitted unrestricted pricing for most ethical pharmaceutical products from 1987 to 1989. Because those firms compete in a global marketplace and because industrial policies vary widely across those countries, it is not clear how such a distinction will affect global market shares. Therefore, the sign for *FOREIGN* is uncertain.

A firm's relative performance in the R&D process is a major determinant of the firm's success in global competition. Performance is difficult to model in one respect because it involves a combination of luck,

---

22. It is possible that global market share determines the number of salespersons that a firm is willing to hire, which suggests that *SALESEMP* is endogenous. Given the limited firm-level data that are available for the pharmaceutical industry, however, I am unable to construct an appropriate instrumental variable to account for this potential problem.

foresight, resource commitment, and having a productive R&D staff. Having a productive R&D staff, however, is not sufficient to increase a firm's market share, because the firm may be efficient at producing low-quality, imitative drugs that diffuse in few markets. Nonetheless, although I am unable to determine the quality of the compounds that are in a firm's R&D pipeline, a firm's productivity in producing those compounds remains as one of several likely determinants of its global market share. Thus, I only include the determinants of productivity (*OUTPUTEMP* or *OUTPUT*) and other firm-specific factors like the number of sales personnel and the number of drugs that a firm licenses from other firms in the global market share regression model presented in this section.

Empirical Results for the R&D Productivity and Global Market Share Regression Model. In table 7–1 I present the summary statistics for the variables used in the regression analysis. I estimated each model by using a fixed-effects approach (time-specific effects) and ordinary least squares. After correction for heteroskedasticity, however, the *F*-tests revealed that the time-specific effects did not add any additional explanatory power to the model.[23] I then reestimated the models by using a modified version of Kmenta's (1986) estimation procedure for pooled data, which corrects for cross-sectional heteroskedasticity. The parameter estimates appear in table 7–3.

Columns (1) and (2) present the results for the global market-share equation that used the determinants for *OUTPUTEMP* (see table 7–2) as explanatory variables. The first column shows the parameter estimates for the log-log specification, whereas the second column presents the parameter estimates for the linear specification of the model. In either case the model performs well as it explains 43 percent of the variation in *MKTSHARE* in column (2) and 72 percent of the variation in *MKTSHARE* in column (1). Nevertheless, only a few of the explanatory variables have the expected sign and are significant at conventional levels. The results in column (1), for instance, show that increases in a firm's sales employees will increase global market share provided the total size of the firm is less than approximately 221,000 employees.[24] Since the mean value for *TOTALEMP* is 37,772 employees,

---

23. I tested for autocorrelation by using the Durbin-Watson test statistic and found that either I was unable to reject the hypothesis of no positive autocorrelation or the test statistic fell in the inconclusive range. I also tested for heteroskedasticity by using the Breusch-Pagan-Godfrey test statistic and found that I was able to reject the hypothesis of homoskedasticity, which I corrected for by using the HETCOV procedure in *SHAZAM*.

24. A similar result holds for the regression equation shown in column (2).

TABLE 7–3
REGRESSION ESTIMATES FOR THE DETERMINANTS OF GLOBAL MARKET SHARE FROM A POOLED, CROSS-SECTIONAL TIME-SERIES ANALYSIS BY FIRM, 1987–1989

	(1) log(MKTSHARE)	(2) MKTSHARE	(3) log(MKTSHARE)	(4) MKTSHARE
Constant	1.310 (.31)	−.536 (−1.59)	−1.019 (−2.40)	.580 (4.00)
SALESEMP	1.245 (5.80)	.471 (8.35)	−.420 (−1.55)	−.081 (−1.24)
SALESEMP* TOTALEMP	−.059 (−.80)	−.0002 (−.09)	.262 (3.34)	.007 (4.20)
LICDRUG	.025 (.50)	−.004 (−.86)	−.040 (−1.27)	−.004 (−.77)
RDEXPEMP	−.106 (−.07)	.005 (2.47)		
RDEXPEMP^2	.002 (.02)	−.00001 (−3.31)		
RDEMP			.542 (7.46)	.040 (.34)

	(1)	(2)	(3)	(4)
RDEMP²			−.081 (−2.47)	.063 (3.17)
RDEXP			.654 (8.39)	.004 (8.49)
TOTALEMP	−1.052 (−2.04)	−.012 (−1.56)	−.635 (−10.09)	−.018 (−3.72)
RDEXPEMP* TOTALEMP	.164 (1.65)	.0001 (3.12)		
RDEMP* TOTALEMP			−.0004 (−.25)	−.005 (−3.93)
PASTRDEMP	−.170 (−2.41)	−.0002 (−0.67)		
PASTRD			−.138 (−2.05)	−.0002 (−1.00)
FOREIGN	.374 (4.20)	.640 (4.53)	−.113 (−1.33)	−.038 (−.41)
Buse R²	.72	.43	.80	.83
SSE	1.00	1.00	1.04	1.02

NOTE: t-statistics are in parentheses and SSE is the standard error of estimate. 2.33 = 1 percent significance level (one tailed). 1.67 = 5 percent significance level (one tailed). 2.66 = 1 percent significance level (two tailed). 2.00 = 5 percent significance level (two tailed).

147

the effect will likely be positive for most firms in the pharmaceutical industry, although the magnitude of the effect will likely be very small. By contrast, the results indicate that increasing *TOTALEMP* reduces the impact of an additional sales employee on *MKTSHARE*, which suggests that the inefficiencies of working in larger firms may offset, to some extent, the effectiveness of hiring an additional sales employee.

In column (2) *RDEXPEMP* and *RDEXPEMP*^{2} have the expected signs and are statistically significant. Those results suggest that additional R&D expenditures, which were found to increase R&D productivity, have a positive but diminishing effect on global market share. Since the interaction term (*RDEXPEMP*TOTALEMP*) includes firm size (*TOTALEMP*), the effect increases with increases in firm size, which simply means that an additional dollar spent on R&D per employee has a much greater impact on global market share in larger firms—firms with a large number of total employees—as compared with smaller firms. One reasonable explanation may be that larger firms are spending their R&D funds on resources other than hiring additional employees, which improves the productivity of their R&D staffs and consequently increases their market share.

The number of drugs that a firm licenses in is insignificant at conventional levels in both models and suggests that those drugs do not affect a firm's global market share. The estimates for *PASTRDEMP* indicate that past R&D has a negative effect on market share (column (1)) or, at the very least, no effect at all (column (2)). Finally, the *FOREIGN* dummy variable indicates that the mean market share for non-U.S.-based firms is larger than for U.S.-based firms in both columns (1) and (2). That result is puzzling to the extent that I found that the same dummy variable had a negative effect in three of the four productivity equations in table 7–2. One might expect that if firms not headquartered in the United States are on average less productive than U.S.-based firms, then the former are likely to have on average smaller market shares than the latter. Such a finding, however, may simply reflect the composition of the sample of firms used in this analysis. The sample includes: ten firms headquartered in the United States that have an average market share equal to 2.11 percent; seven firms headquartered in Western Europe that have an average market share equal to 2.49 percent; and nine firms headquartered in Japan that have an average market share of 1.05 percent. The weighted-average market share of the non-U.S.-based firms is greater than that for the U.S.-based firms, which is consistent with the finding in Thomas (1995) that firms based in the United Kingdom, Switzerland, and Sweden are competitive in the global marketplace. In any event, that result does not support the hypothesis that country-specific differences not explicitly controlled for in the model (perhaps, for example, industrial policies) disadvantage foreign firms.

Columns (3) and (4) present the results for the global market share equation that used the *OUTPUT* determinants (see table 7–2) as explanatory variables. The first column shows the parameter estimates for the log-log specification, whereas the second column presents the parameter estimates for the linear specification of the model. Again, each model performs well as it explains at least 80 percent of the variation in *MKTSHARE*. Interestingly, the pattern of results shown in columns (3) and (4) is somewhat similar when compared with the pattern shown in columns (1) and (2). In columns (3) and (4), for example, the *SALESEMP* variable is insignificant, but the interaction term (*SALESEMP*TOTALEMP*) has a positive sign and is statistically significant. With respect to the equation shown in column (3), as long as firm size is greater than 5,000 employees, adding an additional sales person will have a positive, but relatively small, effect on global market share. The evidence also indicates that productivity differences matter in determining global market share. The parameter estimates reported in column (3) for *RDEMP* and *RDEMP²* reveal that increasing the number of R&D employees will increase a firm's market share, but the effect is diminishing. Those results are consistent with the explanation that hiring additional R&D employees increases a firm's R&D output, although at a decreasing rate. Finally, the results in columns (3) and (4) show that increasing R&D expenditures (*RDEXP*) will also increase a firm's market share. In fact, the elasticity for *RDEXP* in column (3) is approximately 13.86, which is relatively large. In summary, the results presented in table 7–3 support the hypothesis that productivity matters in the determination of global market share, but that other factors like the number of sales employees are also important.

Table 7–4 presents the parameter estimates for the global market-share regression models using only the firm-specific variables such as *SALESEMP* and a productivity measure (*OUTPUTEMP* or *OUTPUT*) as explanatory variables. This simpler version of the previous model may provide additional insight concerning the relationship between R&D productivity and market share. Three patterns emerge from the results presented in table 7–4. First, the number of sales employees matters and additional sales employees have a greater impact in smaller than in larger firms. Second, the number of drugs that a firm licenses in may improve market share, but the effect is relatively small. Third, productivity differences, as measured by the number of R&D compounds per R&D employee, explain variations in a firm's market share. Firms that have higher levels of productivity are likely to have larger market shares, all things considered.

TABLE 7-4

REGRESSION ESTIMATES FOR THE DETERMINANTS OF GLOBAL MARKET SHARE FROM A POOLED, CROSS-SECTIONAL TIME-SERIES ANALYSIS BY FIRM, 1987–1989

	(1) log(MKTSHARE)	(2) MKTSHARE	(3) log(MKTSHARE)	(4) MKTSHARE
Constant	-.630	-.054	-1.246	-.073
	(-2.13)	(-.22)	(-5.23)	(-.45)
SALESEMP	1.464	.459	1.221	.399
	(7.40)	(8.49)	(8.45)	(8.67)
SALESEMP* TOTALEMP	-.279	-.002	-.254	-.003
	(-6.82)	(-5.89)	(-6.98)	(-6.22)
LICDRUG	.170	.007	.099	-.001
	(3.14)	(1.28)	(2.00)	(-.19)
OUTPUTEMP	.018	-.756		
	(.19)	(-.29)		
OUTPUT			.246	.008
			(3.19)	(4.14)
FOREIGN	.178	.459	.131	.390
	(1.64)	(3.29)	(1.66)	(3.00)
Buse R^2	.52	.38	.57	.42
SSE	.99	.95	.98	.97

NOTE: t-statistics are in parentheses and SSE is the standard error of estimate. 2.33 = 1 percent significance level (one tailed). 1.67 = 5 percent significance level (one tailed). 2.66 = 1 percent significance level (two tailed). 2.00 = 5 percent significance level (two tailed).

Summary and Conclusions

This study uses a recent sample of international pharmaceutical firms and a new measure of research productivity to reexamine the relationship between firm size and R&D productivity in the pharmaceutical industry. Three major conclusions emerge from the empirical analysis. First, the evidence reveals that firm size is an important determinant of R&D productivity in the pharmaceutical industry. For plausible R&D staff sizes, increases in firm size have a positive effect on average R&D productivity but a negative effect on marginal R&D productivity. Moreover, the marginal effect of an additional dollar spent on R&D becomes smaller as firm size increases, perhaps owing to the bureaucratic inefficiencies associated with larger firms. Second, the evidence indicates that R&D productivity does have an impact on a firm's global market share, but that other factors, such as the location of the firm's headquarters, matter also. Third, the evidence shows that the number of sales employees a firm commits to marketing its products has a positive impact on a firm's global market share, but the effect varies according to the size of the firm. Again, the marginal effect gets smaller as firm size increases.

The empirical results may interest public policy makers for several reasons. First, the evidence reported in the economics literature suggests that FDA regulations have reduced the R&D productivity of U.S.-based firms, and, in addition, that the effect has been to disadvantage smaller firms relative to larger firms.[25] Although this analysis does not test for the effects of FDA regulation on firm productivity, the results provide an interesting contrast to that conclusion because I find that firm size affects R&D productivity only up to a certain size. Second, to the extent that policy makers are seriously debating implementing price controls, they should consider the likely effects of those controls on firm size, R&D productivity, and global market share. Clearly, this is an issue that warrants additional research to guide public policy.

Appendix 7–A

Data.

OUTPUT: the number of R&D compounds that have been patented, but not yet approved for marketing. Those data are found in the *Scrip Yearbook*, various years.

---

25. Grabowski, Vernon, and Thomas (1978), for example, find that FDA regulation has reduced the R&D productivity of U.S. pharmaceutical firms. Moreover, Thomas (1990) finds that FDA regulation has shifted sales toward larger firms and away from smaller firms.

RDEMP: the number of R&D employees. The 1989 data are reported in *Shearson Lehman's Pharma Profiles* (1990). Since 1988 and 1987 data are not available for all firms in the sample, I used the ratio of R&D employees to total employees (*TOTALEMP*) in 1989 and then multiplied that ratio by *TOTALEMP* in 1988 and 1987 to estimate *RDEMP* in 1988 and 1987, respectively.

RDEXP: nominal, firm-level pharmaceutical R&D expenditures. The 1989 data are found in *Shearson Lehman's Pharma Profiles* (1990); the 1987 and 1988 data are found in the 1990 and 1989 *Japan Data Book*, respectively. The 1987 and 1988 data include all R&D expenditures. Therefore, I estimated pharmaceutical R&D expenditures by multiplying those data by the ratio of pharmaceutical sales to total sales (which are also reported in the *Japan Data Book*). I then deflated those data to constant 1982–1984 dollars and normalized by the R&D employee data described above.

TOTALEMP: the total number of firm employees. The 1987 and 1988 data are reported in the *Japan Data Book* (various years). I constructed the 1989 data by applying the growth rate for 1987–1988 to the 1988 figures.

PASTRD: cumulative R&D expenditures over the previous six years (including 1989). These data are found in *Shearson Lehman's Pharma Profiles* (1990). To construct *PASTRDEMP* for 1989, I deflated the aforementioned data to constant 1982–1984 dollars, and then subtracted 1989 *RDEXP* from that value to obtain cumulative expenditures for the previous five years. Then I normalized those data by *RDEMP* to yield *PASTRDEMP*. I repeated that procedure for the 1987 and 1988 data.

MKTSHARE: the 1989 sales data are taken from *Shearson Lehman's Pharma Profiles* (1990), and represent ethical sales only. I computed the ratio of ethical to over-the-counter (OTC) sales for 1989 and applied that ratio to the 1987 and 1988 ethical and OTC sales data to estimate ethical sales for those years. The 1987 and 1988 sales data (ethical and OTC) are found in the 1990 *Japan Data Book*. I divided the sales data for each firm in a given year by the global ethical sales in that year to estimate the firm's respective market shares. The global sales data are found in Glaxo's *Annual Report*, various years.

SALESEMP: the total number of sales employees. The 1989 data are reported in *Shearson Lehman's Pharma Profiles* (1990). Those data are not available for 1987 and 1988, however. To estimate the data for those years, I computed the ratio of *SALESEMP* and *TOTALEMP* for 1989 and then applied that ratio to *TOTALEMP* in 1988 and 1987.

LICDRUG: the number of compounds that are patented, but not yet approved for consumption, that have been licensed in from other firms. Those data are found in the *Scrip Yearbook*, various years.

References

Alexander, Donald L., Joseph E. Flynn, and Linda A. Linkins. "Estimates of the Demand for Ethical Pharmaceutical Drugs Across Countries and Time." *Applied Economics* 26 (1994): 821–26.

Cocks, Douglas. "Product Innovation and the Dynamic Elements of Competition in the Ethical Pharmaceutical Industry." In *Drug Development and Marketing*, edited by Robert B. Helms. Washington, D.C.: AEI Press, 1975.

Comanor, William S. "Research and Technical Change in the Pharmaceutical Industry." *Review of Economics and Statistics* 47 (1965): 182–90.

DiMasi, Joseph, Ronald Hansen, Henry Grabowski, and Louis Lasagna. "The Cost of Innovation in the Pharmaceutical Industry." *Journal of Health Economics* 10 (1991): 107–42.

Fisher, Franklin M., and Peter Temin. "Returns to Scale in Research and Development: What Does the Schumpeterian Hypothesis Imply?" *Journal of Political Economy* 81 (1973): 56–70.

Glaxo's Annual Report, various years.

Grabowski, Henry, John Vernon, and Lacy Glenn Thomas III. "Estimating the Effects of Regulation on Innovation: An International Comparative Analysis of the Pharmaceutical Industry." *Journal of Law and Economics* 21 (1978): 133–63.

Japan Data Book, various years.

Jensen, Elizabeth J. "Research Expenditures and the Discovery of New Drugs." *Journal of Industrial Economics* 36 (1987): 83–95.

Kmenta, Jan. *Elements of Econometrics*, 2nd ed. New York: Macmillan, 1986.

Scrip Yearbook, various years.

Shearson Lehman's Pharma Profiles, 1990.

Thomas, Lacy Glenn III. "Industrial Policy and International Competitiveness in the Pharmaceutical Industry." In *Competitive Strategies in the Pharmaceutical Industry*, edited by Robert B. Helms. Washington, D.C.: AEI Press, 1995.

———. "Regulation and Firm Size: FDA Impacts on Innovation." *RAND Journal of Economics* 21 (1990): 497–517.

Vernon, John M., and Peter Gusen. "Technical Change and Firm Size: The Pharmaceutical Industry." *Review of Economics and Statistics* 56 (1974): 294–302.

Wiggins, Steven. "The Effect of U.S. Pharmaceutical Regulation on New Introductions." In *Pharmaceutical Economics*, edited by Bjorn Lindgren. Stockholm, Sweden: Swedish Institute for Health Economics, 1984.

———. "The Impact of Regulation on Pharmaceutical Research Expenditures: A Dynamic Approach." *Economic Inquiry* 21 (1983): 115–28.

———. "Product Quality Regulation and New Drug Introductions: Some Evidence from the 1970s." *Review of Economics and Statistics* 63 (1981): 615–19.

U.S. Congress, Office of Technology Assessment. *Pharmaceutical R&D: Costs, Risks and Rewards.* Washington, D.C.: Government Printing Office, February 1993.

Commentary on Part Two

Robert Rogowsky

Don Alexander's study provided a thorough analysis of the factors affecting competition in the pharmaceutical industry. His results are not extremely surprising. He finds that firm size is important, which is not surprising for an industry that needs to come up with more than $260 million (some estimates exceed $300 million) to produce a marketable drug that will take eight to twelve years to produce. He finds that productivity increases with size up to a point and then bureaucratic inefficiency starts to be a factor. That is useful for us to know because it has implications for policy and should be of interest to senior managers in the industry. Alexander also gives us some sense of the magnitudes of the economies of scale in the industry.

It is unfortunate that Alexander's data stop at 1989 because changes in the industry warrant the effort to get more recent numbers, particularly with respect to the differences between pharmaceutical firms headquartered in the United States and those headquartered elsewhere.

The Senate Finance Committee directed the International Trade Commission to conduct a series of studies on the international competitiveness of U.S. high-technology industries. One of the first industries we studied was the pharmaceutical industry, in part because we wanted to look at an industry that was doing very well in the United States and in the global marketplace.

One illuminating thing about studying pharmaceuticals was that in many ways the same things that affect the pharmaceuticals and explain its successes are the flip side of what explains the lack of success in other industries and even in some pharmaceutical companies. It is not always the government policies that firms face that matter, but how businesspeople perform as entrepreneurs in the marketplace.

This finding does not suggest that regulatory behavior, cost-

---

My views are not necessarily those of the U.S. International Trade Commission or of any individual commissioner.

155

containment measures, health care practices, and drug approval mechanisms are not important, because they are very important in the pharmaceutical industry. But at the same time, much of the industry's success depends on the effectiveness of its scientists in the laboratory and on the innovativeness of its business and marketing managers.

The pharmaceutical industry is one of the perfect examples of Robert Reich's question, Who is us? The industry is global, and all firms face much of the same kinds of market pressures and regulatory constraints internationally. The questions then become: How well do you produce in your labs? How do you keep inventiveness and inspiration at a high level in a bureaucracy? How do you stay entrepreneurial when your organization becomes very large?

The International Trade Commission study of the pharmaceutical industry required that we spend quite a good deal of time visiting the companies, talking to the scientists, and learning the creative and productive processes. I left that study impressed by the evidence of the tremendous uncertainty involved in creating successful market outcomes. Starting a search for drugs with literally 10,000 possible chemical permutations, the research team tries to put on the market one effective, profitable drug. I was impressed by the reliance the pharmaceutical manufacturer has, and indeed a healthy society has, on the ability of the R&D staff to develop the curative compounds that the firm produces. The R&D staff's success really drives the company. Because only a small portion of the drugs that finally reach the market are actually profitable, the economic reality is that occasionally one must be very profitable—a blockbuster.

Nor can one not be impressed by both the incredible investment in technology and the importance of serendipity. A firm has to have good sales people and outstanding scientists. The firm must still hope that those scientists find the effective, marketable drug. There certainly have been firms with very good scientists that invested heavily in R&D but saw no return for a long time. The pipeline was just dry.

We presented the consequence of this business phenomenon in what came to be called the "fabulous spaghetti graph," which simply shows the market share of the top ten pharmaceutical firms in three distinct periods approximately ten years apart. The graph reveals the remarkable rising and falling of the market shares, and hence fortunes, of the firms over the two-decade period. Thus, the graph takes on a decidedly untidy look, much like a plate of spaghetti. Firms are at the bottom one time, at the top the next, and then in the middle. Some simply drop off the chart as time passes; others enter. The chart shows that pharmaceuticals are a tough business. Success is by no means certain. Policy makers cannot always understand the difficulty of operating under that uncertainty. Nor are they always able to understand how to measure accurately the economic return in the face of such great uncertainty.

I do not want to minimize the importance of government policy, particularly the difference in the economic environment pharmaceutical manufacturers face in different countries due to disparate government policy. It becomes clear very quickly that the kinds of health care systems and the kinds of cost-containment measures in foreign countries matter. Given the necessary reliance on blockbusters to finance research for new breakthrough drugs, the success of cost-containment measures in major markets targeted to pharmaceuticals that will tend to level those profits must affect the ability of firms to produce new drugs.

The United States becomes a very important market, not simply for its size but for its unconstrained markets. It is very valuable to have the kind of research that Alexander is conducting.

Patricia Danzon carefully studies some of the problems of comparing drug prices across nations. The International Trade Commission has experienced difficulty comparing not only pricing data but any data across countries. First of all, getting data sets that cross national borders is no easy task. Getting ones that actually reflect reality borders on heroic. Nevertheless, in our numerous studies at the International Trade Commission, we have found that global competition stimulates high productivity and that protectionism causes industries to stagnate.

Jonathan Ratner

My responses to the studies of Donald Alexander, Patricia Danzon, and Lacy Glenn Thomas divide into two groups. First, some thoughts on objectives and methodology in international price comparisons, such as the one conducted by Professor Danzon and the studies I directed at the U.S. General Accounting Office. Second, my observations—triggered by all three studies—on pharmaceutical pricing, research, and policy.

Insight and Controversy in International Price Comparisons

International price comparisons have been in the spotlight of public debate over the U.S. pharmaceutical marketplace. While advocates of

---

My views are not necessarily those of the General Accounting Office.

regulating U.S. drug prices have, in making their case, appealed to international price comparisons, opponents of such intervention have disputed the policy relevance of those comparisons and have criticized their methodology. Despite often spirited disagreement over methodological points—for example, which package size to compare—international comparisons of prescription drugs generally conclude that U.S. prices typically exceed prices charged for the same drug product in other countries. For example, Professor Danzon's table 5–2 implies that U.S. prices of all drugs (brand-name and generic) are 47.5 percent higher than U.K. prices (Laspeyres index, price per kilogram, MOL/ACT). The GAO found that U.S. prices for its narrower sample of brand-name drugs were on average 60 percent above U.K. prices. The GAO's sensitivity analysis (1994a, 26) found that the overall price differential was 50 percent, when the availability of generic equivalents in its sample was accounted for.

Differences of this magnitude between the GAO and the Danzon studies suggest that the cash value of methodological differences is less than might be supposed.[1] Nonetheless, methodological squabbling can shed light on more basic issues, particularly the purpose of international price comparisons. Several issues that wear the tag methodological (such as whether to include generic drugs in the sample) really rest on one's purpose in conducting the comparison. For example, studies such as the GAO's that examine prices a given manufacturer charges should exclude any generic drug that has different manufacturers in the two countries studied. Research exploring the cost of drug therapy, such as Professor Danzon's, should include generics. An unconditional claim that a price comparison should never—or always—include generics is valid if the claimant's preferred objective for international comparisons is the only sensible one. I find such a monist view unconvincing.[2]

In any case, the researcher's purpose in conducting a price comparison may not correspond to the reader's. For example, some readers of the GAO's 1992 U.S.-Canadian price comparison wanted answers to different research questions from those the GAO studied. To help such readers, the GAO's second study—the U.S.-U.K. comparison—(GAO

---

1. Professor Danzon's wide-ranging research suggests that U.S. prices of brand-name drugs, and probably of all drugs including generics, tend to exceed prices of comparable drugs in many industrialized countries. She finds that U.S. prices per gram of active ingredient exceed the comparable prices in six of eight foreign countries (Laspeyres index, MOL/ACT).

2. To some analysts and observers, a researcher's "purpose" implies (or is the same as) his "policy agenda." This notion is ubiquitous but misguided.

1994a, 24–26) provides supplementary analyses. For example, the study recalculates the overall differential based on substituting generic prices for the prices of multisource, brand-name drugs in its sample. The study also estimates differentials based on U.S. prices including discounts.[3]

Another methodological disagreement that focuses on purpose concerns Professor Danzon's contention that the GAO's aim of illuminating the "pricing practices of manufacturers" is illogical because, when prices are controlled, pricing behavior is involuntary. That argument is overdrawn for two reasons. First, assume that in country A a manufacturer treats its controlled price as a parameter, but that in country B it can select its price at will. Then, the price differential $(P_A/P_B - 1)$ reflects at the very least the manufacturer's "voluntary" pricing practices in the free-market country, A. Second, even in countries that regulate drug prices, manufacturers and the authorities often engage in a bargaining game over the product price.[4]

Observations on Pharmaceutical Economics and Policy

According to conventional wisdom, a finding of large international price differentials provides aid and comfort to advocates of U.S. drug

---

3. Two narrowly technical criticisms remain to be examined: the weighting of prices and the pack size. With respect to the weighting of prices, Professor Danzon notes that the first GAO study employs an unweighted price index. She neglects to mention, however, that the GAO states that constructing the conventional, weighted index was impossible because data on sales volume were not publicly available. Furthermore, in this case, evidence suggests that the GAO's use of an unavoidably imperfect index did not cause a substantial error. An ordinal proxy for sales volume is each drug's ranking by sales volume. If the price (per prescription) of each drug is weighted by the inverse of its sales ranking, the total U.S.-Canadian differential falls from an unweighted 32 percent to 29 percent.

With respect to the pack size, Professor Danzon points to problems with "nonrepresentative packs," a vexing issue but one whose quantitative importance is unclear. The GAO's two studies acknowledge in different ways the relationship of unit price to pack size. For example, the earlier study reports that the median price differential fell from 43 percent to 35 percent when the U.S. unit price was recalculated by using the largest U.S. pack size. Although 35 percent represents the lower bound of the estimates, 43 percent is not the upper bound. In the second study, the GAO accounts for package size with a method that generally uses larger package sizes in the United States than in the United Kingdom. See General Accounting Office (1994a, 45–48).

4. In addition, lack of discretion in pricing does not imply that it is purely involuntary. Whenever a firm treats price as a parameter—whether the price

price regulation. Nonetheless, whatever the public reaction to such a finding, large differentials are as logically consistent with defense of the status quo as with advocacy of price regulation. Determining appropriate policy calls for information beyond price disparities. For example, researchers should examine whether the current U.S.-foreign price differentials are desirable. On the one hand, as Professor Danzon argues, some degree of international price discrimination seems desirable. She makes a persuasive case that poor countries benefit from a wider array of drug products when manufacturers are able to finance innovation by charging affluent countries higher prices. On the other hand, whether current differentials are better than ones 20 percent smaller, or larger, is unknown. In particular, are the price gaps between the United States and other relatively wealthy, industrialized countries desirable? An answer requires examining both the merits of the international cross-subsidies involved and the optimality of the current level of research and development.

Conflicting theoretical arguments exist about whether the current level of pharmaceutical R&D is optimal, inadequate, or excessive.[5] No empirical model exists that could help resolve the theoretical dispute. In particular, the arguments for pharmaceutical R&D's being too little or too much have missing empirical links: the strength of the relationship between past R&D and the flow of new drugs, and the extent to which a decline in R&D would reduce future breakthrough drugs versus "me-too" products. Professor Thomas's insightful study takes a step toward analyzing the second issue. He explores the determinants of the quality of new drugs developed by the industry in any given country and identifies as factors not only drug prices but the goals of the drug approval process (safety versus efficacy). The difficult next step—an econometric analysis of the R&D–drug quality linkage—must build on Professor Thomas's work.

Notwithstanding the unresolved state of the analysis of the optimality of R&D, many believe that, as a practical matter, the current high levels of world and U.S. pharmaceutical R&D are desirable. Moreover, they believe that relatively high U.S. drug prices are themselves desirable, indeed critical, in sustaining high levels of world pharmaceutical R&D. This belief raises the empirical question of how responsive pharmaceutical R&D is to the price of drugs. Unfortunately, the extent to which R&D varies with the average world price of brand-

---

is regulated or emerges from a competitive market—the firm retains the option to withhold supply.

5. See Office of Technology Assessment (1993, 32), for a discussion of the implications of "first-to-the-finish-line" R&D and R&D as a collective good.

name drug products has not been researched. A recent econometric study by the GAO (1994b, 37–44, 78–99) examines a related issue—the link between firms' R&D spending in a given country and the average drug price in that country.[6] Professor Thomas's study explores that relationship qualitatively.

Whatever policy makers decide about the appropriate level of drug prices, the public debate over drug price policy should distinguish targets from instruments. That rarely occurs. For example, advocates of price regulation implicitly assume the desirability of both a target (lower U.S. drug prices) and an instrument for attaining that target (price regulation). Likewise, others criticize the reliance on that regulatory instrument in part because it would depress U.S. drug prices below the critics' preferred target level. A different instrument—a shift toward a more competitive pharmaceutical marketplace—might well cause a similar drop in U.S. drug prices, however. Is the debate over targets, instruments, or both? Greater clarity would help.

In sum, vis-à-vis pharmaceutical policy, decisions must be made despite gaping holes in information. In this area the level of research is never enough.

References

General Accounting Office. *Prescription Drugs: Companies Typically Charge More in the United States than in Canada.* GAO/HRD-92-110, September 1992.
———. *Prescription Drugs: Companies Typically Charge More in the United States than in the United Kingdom.* GAO/HEHS-94-29, January 1994a.
———. *Prescription Drugs: Spending Controls in Four European Countries.* GAO/HEHS-94-30, May 1994b.
U.S. Congress, Office of Technology Assessment. *Pharmaceutical R&D: Costs, Risks, and Rewards.* Washington, D.C.: Government Printing Office, 1993.

W. Brian Healy

When I joined the international division of Merck & Co., Inc., in 1976, all the industrialized nations except the United States practiced socialized medicine. In Europe, Japan, Canada, and our other foreign mar-

---

6. The GAO's point estimates of the domestic price elasticity of R&D are in the neighborhood of .5, but the estimates and their confidence intervals are consistent with priors that are both substantially smaller and larger than .5.

kets, governments were offering the "free" medicine that is now so attractive to the Clinton administration.

Clearly, many aspects of the economic side of state-provided health care were highly distorted. The history of medical care in Europe over the past ten to fifteen years should serve to inform national policy in the United States, and act as a cautionary tale. For a long time Europe provided free medical care and social services. Now, however, Europe faces the same cost-containment pressure as the U.S. health care sector and is moving away from free physician visits and prescriptions toward a medical care regime with copayments.

I was in charge of international pricing at Merck headquarters for seven or eight years. Subsequently, some seven years ago, I transferred to Brussels, where I set up our European Community offices. At that time, our concern was solely new and existing product pricing. We focused on pharmaceutical budgets and on whether Merck could gain a competitive edge in the various countries in which we operated. I realized, however, that those concerns were only part of the current debate on the need to reform the health care system.

I am very happy to see that the pharmaceutical industry is now broadening the scope of its debate on health care reform. The industry no longer focuses narrowly on negotiating with governments about the proportion of pharmaceutical budgets allocated to innovative medicines. We now consider such macro issues as the total reform of health care systems. That broader view is important, because if policy makers consider drugs in isolation, the industry may ultimately bear the financial brunt of health care cost containment.

Many of the discussions I had with European governments focused on international price comparisons, as might be expected when dealing with a monopsonistic buyer. Such a buyer, whether a nation's government or sick fund association, was in an especially powerful position and would often cite prices from other countries. Unfortunately, that would be done in a way that lacked the scientific rigor of Patricia Danzon's study. One of our products, or a comparable item in another country, would be selected, with the inevitable query, Why can't you match that price? We experienced numerous negotiations of that kind, few of which were done in a transparent manner.

About three years ago, however, the European Commission passed a directive—European law—mandating transparency in pharmaceutical price regulation. That directive is very important for us because we, as a foreign multinational operating in those countries, do not know the criteria those governments or sick funds use to establish our prices. Without such transparency, we have been unable to argue our case and have been placed at a particular disadvantage vis-à-vis domestic companies. Since enactment of the directive, however, we have had the ability to complain either to national courts or the European Commission about unfair treatment, which is often related to international price comparisons.

Although Danzon's methodology is extremely useful to us in such discussions, they often become, in effect, political debates. Thus, we need to consider industrial policy, the topic of Lacy Glenn Thomas's study. When negotiations turn political, the government, or the group of sick funds that represent the monopoly purchaser in the particular country, acts as though it were in the public procurement business. Because it is spending public funds or national tax revenues, it feels political pressure to buy domestically. Therefore, we are selling in a market that is hardly competitive; the government wants to ensure that the products it purchases are manufactured in its country, even though in many cases that practice goes against the basic rationale of the single European Common Market. The government also wants to ensure that any price controls imposed not only keep prices down, especially for imported products, but also support local industry. So the practice of price control in a number of countries has an industrial policy dimension that creates prices that are by no means pure market prices.

I had the opportunity to represent American pharmaceutical companies on a task force on industrial policy that included the European pharmaceutical industry, other industries, and the European Commission. Experts on industrial policy for all the key European industries see the pharmaceutical industry as one whose competitiveness must be preserved. They view it as one of the few in which Europe has a competitive advantage vis-à-vis the United States and Japan. To maintain that edge, Europeans know that they must balance cost-containment pressures, which experts believe are becoming excessive, with the need to ensure the flow of truly competitive products.

Don Alexander's study considers precisely that—the productivity of research and development. Research in France, Italy, Spain, and now Germany is becoming too risky for many firms and weakens the prospects for the development of blockbuster drugs. Firms in those countries know that local pricing systems will limit the price they can charge for their new product at the time of introduction and that they will consequently not earn the appropriate return on a very risky investment. It is now much easier to develop a different molecular version of a new product, and hope to gain, via therapeutic substitution or a manufacturer's status as a domestic company, an advantage in the local pricing system. The result is not only a diminution in the number of new chemical entities originating in Europe, especially continental Europe, but a diminution in the number of original blockbuster prod-

163

ucts on a global basis. Instead, noninnovative domestic products, meant only to circumvent the local pricing system, take their place.

That trend forced the European Commission to acknowledge that European cost containment is not equivalent to cost efficiency. Such cost containment is simply government intervention in the form of direct price controls. Those price controls have upset the nature of pharmaceutical research and development, the productivity of European research, and European competitiveness.

The studies of Danzon, Thomas, and Alexander are thus very much interrelated. The pharmaceutical industry uses international price comparisons to negotiate with individual countries about the price of new product offerings. Industrial policy permeates the way we do business, especially in the countries of southern Europe. The productivity of research and development flourishes only under a system in which a firm can expect to get a fair price for a new product. A fair price, in turn, is one that will continue to provide incentives to seek cures for difficult diseases, such as Alzheimer's and AIDS.

As both sides of the Atlantic tend to converge in their approach to the economic regulation of the pharmaceutical industry, both the industry and policy makers can benefit from additional research along the lines of the stimulating studies by Danzon, Thomas, and Alexander.

PART THREE

The Risks of and Returns to Pharmaceutical Investment in Research

8
The Determinants of Research Productivity in Ethical Drug Discovery

Rebecca Henderson and Iain M. Cockburn

In 1971 the members of the Pharmaceutical Manufacturers Association spent about $360 million dollars on research and development.[1] In 1991 they spent $8.9 *billion*, an increase of over 2300 percent. While industry sales have grown in line with research expenditures, however, there has been no significant increase in the number of new drugs introduced. Why have costs increased so dramatically? Breakthroughs in pharmaceutical research can lay the groundwork for qualitative improvements in the quality of life and for significant reductions in the cost of health care, but escalating health care costs have focused attention on every aspect of health care expenditure and have led several observers to question the apparent decline in the productivity of pharmaceutical research. This chapter hopes to contribute to the debate by exploring the issue in the context of a broader study of the determinants of research productivity in the discovery of ethical drugs.

We draw upon a detailed data set compiled from the internal records of ten major pharmaceutical firms. The data set allows us to distinguish between research (or discovery) and development expenditures at a highly disaggregated level. For example, within the general class of cardiovascular therapies we can observe the distinc-

This research was funded by four pharmaceutical companies and by the Sloan Foundation. We gratefully acknowledge their support. We would also like to express our appreciation to all of those firms that contributed data to the study and to Allan Afuah for his outstanding work as our research assistant. The conclusions and opinions expressed in this chapter are our own, and any errors or omissions remain entirely our responsibility.

1. Here and throughout the chapter, all amounts are denominated in deflated 1991 dollars.

tions among fields such as hypertension, cardiotonics, and blood-related conditions.

This chapter first presents some descriptive statistics from the sample. Our sample firms display the long-term decline in productivity that is characteristic of the industry as a whole. Both research and development expenditures have increased dramatically in real terms, while the output of important patents has fallen,[2] and the number of drugs discovered has remained approximately constant.

We then explore the degree to which the escalation in real research costs may reflect a change in the mix of research projects that firms are pursuing. Real research costs may have increased, for example, if resources have shifted away from "easy" fields toward "more difficult" fields such as oncology and gerontology. The disaggregate data suggest, however, that such an effect is probably not very important as a driver of falling productivity. While on average there has been a shift of resources across fields, there is no evidence that this shift has been to fields in which it has been on average more difficult to obtain results.

Next we explore the degree to which rising real research costs reflect increased competition in the industry. Some economic theory suggests, for example, that an increase in the expected returns to an industry will encourage firms to increase their investment in research in the hope of capturing those returns from their rivals. In the extreme, such theories suggest that private returns in the industry will be driven to zero as competing firms dissipate all the available returns by over-investing in research.

That is an important issue for public policy because it highlights the dangers of relying on the research cost per drug as a useful measure of research costs. On the one hand, if there is significant overinvestment in research, so that competing firms are racing each other to market by investing in substantially identical research, average research costs per drug per firm substantially *overstate* the actual expenditure required to discover a new drug. On the other hand, if there are significant spillovers among firms and among research projects within the same firm, and if firms do not immediately dissipate anticipated returns through excess investment, then mean research costs substantially *understate* the resources required to discover a new drug.

Unfortunately, it is difficult to test those ideas systematically because the theoretical models very quickly become fundamentally indeterminate. As a first step toward a richer understanding of the issue, we focus on exploring the assumptions on which the theoretical litera-

---

2. We define important patents as those granted in two of the three major world markets: the United States, Japan, and the European Community.

ture rests. The rather extreme conclusion that free entry unambiguously leads to overinvestment in research is crucially dependent on at least five key assumptions: that entry will occur until marginal private returns have been driven to zero, that there is no spillover of knowledge among firms, that there is total appropriability of consumer surplus, that competing projects are perfect substitutes for each other, and that there are no efficiency gains to multifirm competition.

Testing the validity of the last three assumptions is beyond the scope of this chapter, but we do explore the first by examining the dynamics of investment behavior. Following methodology pioneered by Scherer (1992) and Meron and Caves (1991), we distinguish among a leader, core followers, and fringe firms. We find some weak evidence that core followers invest in response to investment by the leading firm, while fringe firms reduce the investments in research as follower firms increase their research expenditures. Those effects are only marginally significant, however, and of very small magnitude. Our results suggest that by far the most important determinant of one year's research spending is the previous year's spending: a finding consistent with a world in which investment decisions are driven much more by heterogeneous firm capabilities, adjustment costs, and scientific opportunity than by strategic interactions. We interpret our finding as suggesting that while firms may respond strategically to each other, such reactions are probably not sufficiently important to drive marginal private returns to zero.

We then investigate the nature of spillovers in the industry by studying the determinants of the output of important patents. Our results are consistent with the presence of substantial spillovers, both within and across firms, and thus suggest that the entry of additional firms into the R&D race does not unequivocally destroy welfare.

The final section of this chapter presents our conclusions and explores their implication for formulating public policy. Our results suggest that the apparent decline in the pharmaceutical industry's long-term productivity is probably a function of the escalating real costs of research. There is no evidence of a shift from easier to more difficult classes, or of an increase in racing behavior across firms. Our research does, however, highlight the complexity of pharmaceutical research. In the absence of good measures of the returns to innovation in the industry, we cannot know whether firms, on average, make excessive expenditures on R&D. Our results do, however, suggest that while the pharmaceutical industry is sometimes held up as a textbook example of dissipative racing behavior in R&D competition, the reality is probably considerably more complex. In some cases we find evidence consistent with the kinds of correlated patterns of investment at the research

FIGURE 8–1
MEAN R&D SPENDING PER FIRM

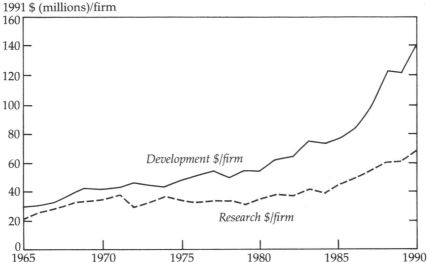

program level that we would expect to see if R&D spending decisions were dominated by strategic interaction of the kind captured by game-theoretic models. But we also find evidence consistent with significant R&D project complementarities and other spillover benefits across firms, which suggests that correlated investment strategies may create significant externalities. While our results must be interpreted with care, they suggest that the simple characterization of the costs of R&D by an average dollars per drug figure is almost certainly incorrect.

Long-Term Trends in Industry Productivity

Figure 8–1 plots average spending on R&D by the firms in our sample from 1965 to 1990.[3] While research spending has increased in real terms, the lion's share of the increase in pharmaceutical research costs is a function of the accelerating cost of clinical development. Figure 8–2 plots R&D spending as a share of sales: while research expenditures are increasing roughly in line with sales, development expenditures have far outstripped them.

Figure 8–3 plots average outputs per dollar from 1965 to 1990. The number of important patents granted to the mean firm in our sample has fallen dramatically. This mirrors trends observed for the economy as a whole, but while the number of patents the Patent and Trademark

---

3. Appendix 8–A describes the construction of the data set in detail.

FIGURE 8–2

R&D AS SHARE OF SALES AND SAMPLE AVERAGE SALES

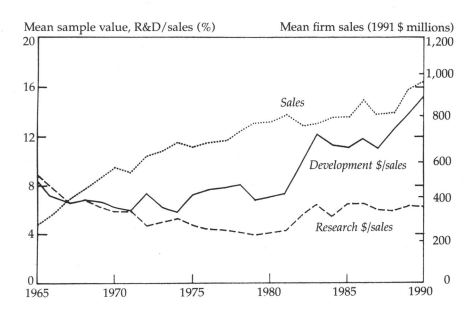

FIGURE 8–3

PATENTS, INVESTIGATIONAL NEW DRUG APPLICATIONS, AND
NEW DRUG APPLICATIONS PER R&D DOLLAR

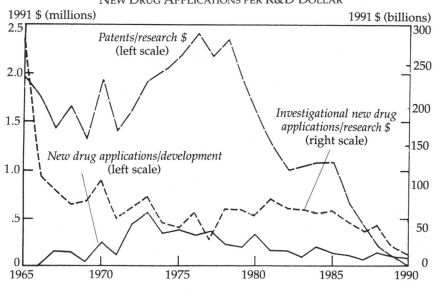

Office granted to U.S. firms fell in every industry in the 1970s, a number of the firms in our sample are European, and the decline in patenting rates by our sample firms is significantly greater than this more general trend (Griliches 1990).[4]

On average, the number of investigational new drug applications and new drug applications obtained for each dollar invested in R&D by the firms in our sample has steadily declined.[5] We must interpret that trend with caution because firms can take more than ten years to file a new drug application after the Food and Drug Administration has granted an investigational new drug application. Thus, it is possible that the acceleration in development spending that we observe in the late 1980s will be followed by an outpouring of new drug applications over the next decade. In general, however, our data are in line with the aggregate statistics in suggesting that increases in spending on R&D have not been accompanied by a proportionate increase in the easily tracked measures of output: patents, investigational new drug applications, and new drug applications.

Heterogeneity across Therapeutic Classes

Wiggins (1979) first demonstrated the importance of distinguishing among therapeutic classes in modeling the determinants of productivity in the pharmaceutical industry. In table 8–1 we begin the process of disaggregating the data to reveal the heterogeneity of pharmaceutical research. We show the ratio of cumulative outputs to cumulative inputs by therapeutic class for the years 1975 through 1990. We must approach those numbers with caution, because they are subject to both left and right censoring. In the early years, for example, the outputs from each class are partially the result of spending before 1975, and many of the inputs to the process in the second half of the period will not yield results until after 1990. The numbers do, however, illustrate

---

4. The very low patenting rates from 1988 through 1990 may reflect two complicating factors. On average, patents are granted two years after firms apply for them. We graph the number of patents granted by year of application, so there may well be patent applications still outstanding for those years. Derwent Publications Inc., the firm that provided the data, must classify each patent once the Patent and Trademark Office grants the patent. Because this process is not instantaneous, the number of patents reported for recent years may be further undercounted.

5. To test a drug on humans in the United States, firms must file an investigational new drug application. If the firm successfully completes clinical trials, it then files a new drug application. We count only investigational new drug applications for original indications.

TABLE 8–1

CUMULATIVE OUTPUTS OVER CUMULATIVE INPUTS BY CLASS, 1975–1990

Class	Patents/ Research ($ million)	Investigative New Drugs/Research ($ billion)	New Drug Applications/R&D ($ billion)
Alimentary	1.7	34	13
Blood	.8	32	8
Cardiovascular	1.0	41	11
Dermatology	2.6	81	34
Anti-infective	.2	25	13
Hormones	1.9	96	16
Cytostatics	.6	61	25
Musculoskeletal	1.1	36	6
Central nervous system	1.6	49	14
Respiratory	1.7	43	9
Sensory organs	1.1	38	32

the variation that is hidden by aggregating the data. The number of important patents obtained per million dollars invested in research, for example, varies from a high of 2.6 in dermatological drugs to a low of .2 in anti-infective drugs. Similarly, the ratio of investigational new drug applications obtained per billion dollars varies from twenty-five for anti-infective drugs to eighty-one for dermatological drugs, and the ratio of new drug applications to cumulative R&D spending varies from a low of six per billion in musculoskeletal research to a high of thirty-four per billion in dermatology.

Those variations translate into significant differences in the average "cost per drug" in each class. If we assume, for example, that investment in each program is constant across the sixteen-year period and that the time value of money is 9 percent, they translate into an approximate cost per new drug application of over $370 million for a musculoskeletal drug, $200 million for a cardiovascular drug, and $66 million for a dermatological drug.[6]

Thus, differences in costs across therapeutic classes are one possible explanation for the apparent decline in the productivity of research

---

6. These numbers are reassuringly in line with those calculated by Di Masi et al. (1991). Note, however, that they are *very* approximate and indicate no more than an order of magnitude. The Di Masi et al. study uses a much more sophisticated methodology and more detailed project data to calculate the cost per drug.

FIGURE 8–4
Share of the Discovery Portfolio by Therapeutic Class

Mean share of discovery portfolio

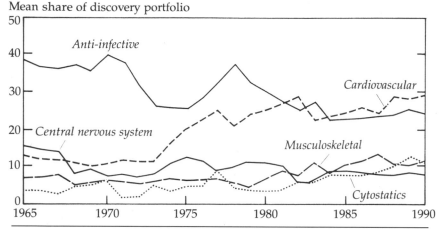

FIGURE 8–5
Mean Share of Development Portfolio by Therapeutic Class

(%)

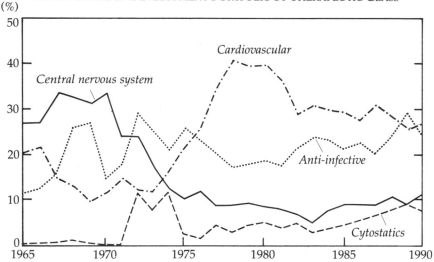

in the pharmaceutical industry. If firms have shifted resources away from "easy" fields such as dermatology toward "hard" fields such as anti-infective research, then research costs would rise and output would fall solely as a result of a change in portfolio composition. Figures 8–4 and 8–5 explore that issue. Figure 8–4 graphs the mean share of the research portfolio by therapeutic class over time, while figure 8–5 plots the mean share of the development portfolio. Both figures suggest that it is very unlikely that shifts in portfolio composition drive the increases in research costs. In general, firms have shifted investment in research from anti-infective drugs to cardiovascular drugs. The results reported in table 8–1 suggest that this shift should have *increased* research productivity, when all other things are equal. In development the firms in our sample have been shifting from central nervous system drugs to cardiovascular drugs, while the share of resources devoted to anti-infective drugs has remained more or less constant. Again, the summary statistics of table 8–1 suggest that this shift should have left research productivity approximately unchanged, all other things equal.

Thus, although research productivity differs systematically across therapeutic classes, there is little evidence to suggest that shifts among classes is at the root of the long-term "decline" in the productivity of pharmaceutical R&D. To gain insight into changes in industry productivity, we next explore the dynamics of investment behavior and of differences in firm productivity.

The Dynamics of Investment Behavior

Escalating real costs of research in the pharmaceutical industry may reflect increasing competition and "overinvestment" in research. The theoretical literature exploring the relationship between competitive dynamics and investment strategy is both voluminous and inconclusive, but many of the models raise the concern that free entry into R&D competition will result in overinvestment relative to both the privately and the socially optimal investment levels. Intuitively, those results are driven by the assumption that in deciding to invest in research, firms consider only their own marginal returns and do not take into account the externality that they impose on other firms in reducing their chances of success. In the extreme, those models suggest that entry will occur until all expected profits are dissipated (Dasgupta and Stiglitz 1980; Loury 1979; Reinganum 1982, 1989).

Unfortunately, it is difficult to test those ideas. Models that attempt to incorporate all the relevant variables quickly become dauntingly complex, and we have, as yet, no general results about the relationship among market structure, scientific or technological regime, and the realized and optimal levels of research investment (Harris and Vickers 1987; Reinganum 1989).

The literature does, however, highlight several factors that determine whether the entry of an additional firm into the research race will raise or lower social welfare. For example, one can show that in markets characterized by perfectly competitive behavior, complete appropriability, and research projects that are perfect substitutes for each

175

other, there will be considerable overinvestment in research (Dasgupta and Stiglitz 1980). Conversely, in industries characterized by weak appropriability, where investment in research is more cooperative than competitive and in which research projects are largely complements, there is likely to be underinvestment relative to the social optimum (Dasgupta and Maskin 1987; D'Aspremont and Jacquemin 1988, 1990; Fraja 1993; Suzumura 1992).

Because theoretical models that attempt to capture simultaneously the interaction among all of those factors quickly become intractable, we instead explore the validity of two of the core assumptions on which the models of rent dissipation rely: first, that under free entry firms will respond strategically to each other and will invest in research until marginal returns fall to zero, and second, that there are no spillovers of knowledge either across projects within the firm or among firms. A more complete discussion of the theoretical issues involved and of the relationship between our research and the existing literature is given in our study "Racing to Invest?: The Dynamics of Competition in Ethical Drug Discovery" (Cockburn and Henderson 1995).

In general, the literature suggests that two plausible types of investment behavior are consistent with dissipating behavior. On the one hand, Reinganum (1982) presents a model in which symmetric oliogopolistic firms race for a well-defined prize. Under those conditions, firms' reaction functions slope upward, and one firm's marginal increases in spending are met by increases in its rivals' spending. On the other hand, Harris and Vickers (1987) develop a model of rivalry among asymmetric firms in which increased spending by the leader evokes a submissive response by the followers.

The distinction between the two behaviors builds on earlier work by Scherer (1967) and is confirmed by previous empirical work. Grabowski and Baxter (1973), for example, found that in the chemical industry, the two largest firms responded quickly to changes in each other's R&D policies, while rivalry among the smaller firms was less clear-cut. Meron and Caves (1991) found that in a sample of twenty-eight U.S. manufacturing industries, leaders and followers reacted positively to each other's increases in R&D expenditures, while fringe firms' investment decreased with their larger rivals' investment. Scherer (1992) found that firms with greater domestic sales in more concentrated U.S. markets were likely to react much more aggressively to increasing import competition than smaller firms or firms in less concentrated markets.

In tables 8–2, 8–3, and 8–4 we present our analysis of the investment dynamics that characterize our sample. Table 8–2 contains results

TABLE 8–2
DETERMINANTS OF INVESTMENT IN RESEARCH AT THE PROGRAM LEVEL

	(1)	(2)	(3)
Dependent variable	$Research_t$	Δ $Research_t$	"News" in $research_t$
Intercept	.174[a]	.197[a]	.174[a]
	(.072)	(.075)	(.072)
$Research_{(t-1)}$	.984[a]		
	(.034)		
$\Delta Research_{(t-1)}$		.008	
		(.049)	
"News" in $research_{(t-1)}$			.824[a]
			(.034)
Research $stock_{(t-1)}$	.000	−.004	.005
	(.012)	(.006)	(.006)
"News" in $patents_{(t-1)}$	.013[b]	.013[b]	.013[b]
	(.008)	(.008)	(.008)
"News" in key $papers_{(t-1)}$	.003	.004	.003
	(.007)	(.007)	(.007)
Class dummies	Sig.	Sig.	Sig.
Firm dummies	Partial	Partial	Partial
	sig.	sig.	sig.
Time	−.020[a]	−.021[a]	−.020[a]
	(.007)	(.007)	(.006)
Time * time	.001[a]	.001[a]	.001[a]
	(.000)	(.000)	(.000)
Adjusted R-squared	.879	.007	.648

NOTE: O.L.S. regression. Dependent variable = investment in discovery. 4597 observations. Heteroskedastic-consistent standard errors in parentheses.
a. Significant at the 1 percent level.
b. Significant at the 5 percent level.

from regressing investment onto control variables suggested by the qualitative analysis. They include: the stock of research, which is intended to capture, among other things, unobserved differences in the quality of the program; firm and therapeutic class dummies; a time trend; and variables intended to capture shocks to scientific opportunity—"news" in own patents and in important papers. We define *news* as the excess of the current year's flow over the amount necessary to maintain the stock, given a depreciation rate δ:

$$News_t = Flow_t - \delta\, Stock_t.$$

177

This formulation is intended to capture activity in excess of normal levels.[7] Of all the control variables, only news in patents is significant.

We use three specifications for the dependent variable. In model (1) the dependent variable is just the level of research spending, and the explanatory variables include lagged research to capture the adjustment costs. This variable dominates the regression, and its coefficient is indistinguishable from one. In model (2) we constrain it to be one by using the first difference of R as the dependent variable. We include a lagged difference of R in this specification, but it is insignificant. Model (3) uses a news version of R and lagged news on the right-hand side. Lagged news is strongly significant, which suggests that changes in research strategy are correlated from year to year.

In table 8–3 we introduce competitors' expenditures into the regression to test for the presence of strategic interactions.[8] We reproduce model (3) from table 8–2 for purposes of comparison. Model (4) tests the hypothesis that every firm responds to every other firm by including news in competitors' research as an independent variable. It is insignificant. Model (5) tests the hypotheses that the leading firm responds only to core followers, while core followers respond both to each other and to the leading firm, and fringe firms respond both to the leader and to the core followers.[9] All the coefficients except that of the leader's response to the core followers have the expected sign, but only one is significant: fringe firms appear to react submissively to investment by core followers. Moreover, the standard test for the significance of additional variables cannot reject the hypothesis that competitive spending adds no additional explanatory power to either model (4) or model (5). While we must temper our interpretation of this result because our firms together comprise only about 28 percent of the industry, the result provides only very limited support for the presence of strategic interactions among firms.

In table 8–4 we test for the idea that racing behavior may have increased over time, even if it is not significantly present in the sample

---

7. Experimentation with various combinations of lags, depreciation rates, and other factors added little to our analysis.

8. Obviously, there is potential simultaneity among competitors' and own research investments. Plausible instruments are hard to find, however. Rather than use weak instruments, we simply present the ordinary least squares results here. We are actively pursuing this issue in our research.

9. One firm in our sample consistently spent more on discovery research than all the others. Following Caves and Meron (1991), we defined this firm as the leader. We defined firms that consistently invested more than 30 percent of the leader's investment as core followers and firms that spent less as fringe firms. There are three fringe firms and six core followers in the data set.

TABLE 8–3
DETERMINANTS OF INVESTMENT IN RESEARCH AT THE PROGRAM LEVEL

	(3)	(4)	(5)
N	4597	4597	4115
Intercept	.174[a]	.148[b]	.145[b]
	(.072)	(.072)	(.084)
"News" in research$_{(t-1)}$	.824[a]	.825[a]	.825[a]
	(.034)	(.034)	(.036)
"News" in competitors' research$_{(t-1)}$		.006 (.006)	
Leader* News in core followers' research$_{(t-1)}$			−.007 (.016)
Follower* News in core leaders' research$_{(t\ 1)}$			.026 (.019)
Follower* News in core followers' research$_{(t-1)}$			.004 (.009)
Fringe firm* News in core leaders' research$_{(t-1)}$			−.003 (.017)
Fringe firm* News in core followers' research$_{(t-1)}$			−.010[b] (.006)
Research stock$_{(t-1)}$	.005	.004	.005
	(.006)	(.007)	(.007)
"News" in patents$_{(t-1)}$	.013[b]	.012	.012
	(.008)	(.007)	(.008)
"News" in key papers$_{(t-1)}$	.003	.004	−.006
	(.007)	(.007)	(.011)
Class dummies	Sig.	Sig.	Sig.
Firm dummies	Partial sig.	Partial sig.	Partial sig.
Time	−.020[a]	−.019[a]	−.018[a]
	(.006)	(.007)	(.008)
Time * time	.001[a]	.001[a]	.001[a]
	(.000)	(.000)	(.000)
Adjusted R-squared	.648	.649	.645
Sum of squared residuals	3029.1	3026.8	2868.7

NOTE: O.L.S. regression. Dependent variable = "news" in research. Heteroskedastic-consistent standard errors in parentheses.
a. Significant at the 1 percent level.
b. Significant at the 5 percent level.

TABLE 8–4
DETERMINANTS OF INVESTMENT IN RESEARCH AT THE PROGRAM LEVEL

	(6)	(7)	(8)
Sample	1961–1988	1961–1974	1975–1988
N	4170	1360	2810
Intercept	.131[a]	.091	−.220
	(.071)	(.086)	(.622)
"News" in research$_{(t-1)}$	.825[b]	.744[a]	.827[b]
	(.036)	(.056)	(.039)
Leader*	−.005	.010	−.012
News in core followers' research$_{(t-1)}$	(.016)	(.035)	(.017)
Follower*	.028	.056	.029
News in core leaders' research$_{(t-1)}$	(.019)	(.040)	(.021)
Follower*	.006	−.016	.007
News in core followers' research$_{(t-1)}$	(.016)	(.022)	(.010)
Research stock$_{(t-1)}$	.005	.029[b]	.003
	(.007)	(.013)	(.008)
"News" in patents$_{(t-1)}$	.012	.018[a]	.007
	(.008)	(.011)	(.010)
Class dummies	Sig.	Sig.	Sig.
Firm dummies	Partial sig.	Insig.	Partial sig.
Time	−.017[a]	−.010	.011
	(.008)	(.019)	(.060)
Time * time	.001[b]	.001	.000
	(.000)	(.001)	(.001)
Adjusted R-squared	.646	.701	.639
Sum of squared residuals	2874.6	296.3	2554.1

NOTE: Compares competitive dynamics before and after 1975. O.L.S. regression. Dependent variable = "news" in research. Heteroskedastic-consistent standard errors in parentheses.
a. Significant at the 5 percent level.
b. Significant at the 1 percent level.

as a whole. Model (7) is run using the data from 1961 to 1974, while model (8) tests for the significance of competitive investment from 1975 to 1988.[10] Competitive investment is insignificant in both specifications, and a Chow test cannot reject the hypothesis that there is no difference in the dynamics of the two periods.

---

10. The results in table 8–4 rely on a more limited set of explanatory vari-

Thus, we find only very limited evidence of strategic interaction in investment behavior. Moreover, the magnitude of those reactions is very small: together, in the most successful specification, they add only .1 percent to the explanatory power of the regression, and our results suggest that the overwhelmingly most important determinant of a period's investment is the preceding period's investment.

Those results are consistent with our qualitative findings. Highly trained personnel are expensive to hire and to let go, and dramatic increases in the size of a program are unlikely to lead to equally dramatic increases in its productivity.[11] Discovery research is a highly uncertain process, and our quantitative finding that investments are highly serially correlated is consistent with a world in which investment decisions are driven by heterogeneous firm capabilities, by adjustment costs, and by the evolution of scientific opportunity.

Spillovers and Research Productivity

In an industry characterized by straightforward duplicative racing behavior, one firm's success is another's loss since each firm invests in identical research programs and there are no spillovers of knowledge across firms. If there are, however, significant spillovers of knowledge across firms, research productivity may be correlated with competitive investment, and additional entry into the R&D race may enhance welfare.

We test for the presence of spillovers in our data by regressing important patents onto a variety of control variables and a set of measures designed to capture competitive activity in the field. We can usefully think of those equations as a production function for important patents in which competitors' research successes enter as inputs to each other's R&D.

Table 8–5 sets out our results. Models (9) and (10) use our full sample. Model (9) suggests that own output and the success of rival firms' efforts are positively and strongly significantly correlated. Using competitors' discovery spending in place of their patents gives very similar results: competitors' investment has a positive and significant impact on own research productivity.[12] The model fails, however, to control for changes in scientific opportunity and thus raises the possibility that the observed correlations across firms merely reflect exoge-

---

ables than those in table 8–3 because we do not have data for key articles before 1975, and the fringe firms in our data set appear relatively late.

11. There is no evidence of increasing returns to scale in our data.

12. We do not report those results here.

TABLE 8–5
DETERMINANTS OF PATENT OUTPUT AT THE RESEARCH PROGRAM LEVEL

	Full Sample (9)	Full Sample (10)	C.V. Only (11)	C.V. Only (12)
N	4879	4879	491	491
Intercept	−2.807[a]	−3.114[a]	−1.651[a]	−1.359[a]
	(.149)	(.158)	(.269)	(.344)
ln (discovery)	.030[a]	.026[a]	−.026	−.009
	(.010)	(.010)	(.023)	(.030)
ln (stock of discovery)	.035[a]	.040[a]	.121[a]	.068
	(.009)	(.009)	(.029)	(.035)
SCOPE: number classes firm is active	.105[a]	.123[a]	.107[a]	.112[a]
	(.016)	(.016)	(.038)	(.040)
SCOPE * SCOPE	−.006[a]	−.007[a]	−.006[a]	−.005[a]
	(.001)	(.001)	(.001)	(.002)
ln (SIZE): Total disc. spending by firm	.244[a]	.283[a]	.223[b]	.229[b]
	(.042)	(.043)	(.093)	(.104)
Stock own patents in this class	.032[a]	.031[a]	.038[a]	.037[a]
	(.001)	(.001)	(.002)	(.002)
News in patents in related classes	.033[a]	.032[a]	.053[a]	.061[a]
	(.003)	(.003)	(.007)	(.007)
News in competitors' patents in this class	.007[a]	.006[a]	.018[a]	.010[a]
	(.001)	(.001)	(.001)	(.002)
News in competitors' patents in related classes	.002[a]	.002[a]	−.003[a]	.002
	(.000)	(.001)	(.001)	(.001)
Key papers$_t$		−.002		
		(.005)		
Key papers$_{t-1}$		.011		
		(.001)		
Key papers$_{t-2}$		−.003		
		(.005)		
Key public sector C.V papers$_t$				−.055
				(.164)
Key public sector C.V. papers$_{t-1}$				.006
				(.161)
Key public sector C.V. papers$_{t-2}$				−.145
				(.136)
Key private C.V. papers$_t$				.286[a]
				(.105)
Key private C.V. papers$_{t-1}$				.074
				(.098)

(Table continues)

TABLE 8–5 (continued)

	Full Sample (9)	Full Sample (10)	C.V. Only (11)	C.V. Only (12)
Key private C.V. papers$_{t-2}$				.135 (.097)
Firm dummies	Sig.	Sig.		Sig.
Class dummies	Sig.	Sig.		Omit.
Time	.069[a]	.078[a]		−.017
	(.010)	(.009)		(.025)
Time * time	−.003[a]	−.003[a]		−.001
	(.001)	(.000)		(.001)
Log-likelihood	−8026.9	−7595.4	−1347	−977.1

NOTES: Poisson regression. Dependent variable = PATENTS. Standard errors in parentheses. The ln (variable) is set = 0 when variable = 0, and an appropriately coded dummy variable is included in the regression. The omitted therapeutic class dummy is class 60, systemic anti-infectives.
a. Significant at the 1 percent level.
b. Significant at the 5 percent level.

nous shifts in opportunity that make it easier to obtain patents in any given class. Model (10) includes key papers as a measure of scientific opportunity. There is no significant correlation between those measures and own output, and important competitive patents remain a significant predictor of own patents.[13] Models (11) and (12) repeat those analyses using cardiovascular data alone; model (12) uses the more detailed measures of scientific opportunity.[14] Patent output is not significantly correlated with key papers in the public sector, which suggests that major shifts in the stock of public knowledge are not immediately translated into patents. Patent output is, however, significantly correlated with the flow of key papers published by researchers in the private sector. Nonetheless, controlling for that effect *strengthens* the correlation between own research productivity and competitors' output.

13. An alternative measure of opportunity, citations of key articles, performed very similarly.

14. We used secondary sources and consultation with industry experts to identify those papers that had a seminal influence on the field and that represented an order of magnitude change in scientific opportunity. We divided those papers into two classes: those for which a majority of the authors were employed in the public sector—key public papers—and those for which a majority of the authors were employed in the private sector—key private papers.

Thus, our results are consistent with the idea that there are significant spillovers of knowledge across firms. Important patents per discovery dollar are likely to be significantly higher if competitors have recently obtained a number of important patents in the area, and far from leading to a "mining out" of opportunities, competitors' research appears to be a complementary activity to own R&D. Thus, the entry of additional firms into a therapeutic area may enhance welfare.

We must qualify that result by observing that not all patents are equally important. If, for example, a major discovery in an area makes it easier to obtain patents in the area, and if our measures of scientific opportunity do not capture that effect, then correlation in output across firms may reflect no more than the generation of "me-too" patents for "me-too" drugs. Two factors moderate this problem. The first is that so-called me-too drugs may offer important additional therapeutic benefits such as reductions in side effects or improved efficacy with different segments of the population. The second is our finding that output is positively associated with competitive *investment* as well as with competitive *output*, which suggests that we are capturing the effect of genuine spillovers of knowledge.

Conclusions

Over the past twenty years, the pharmaceutical industry appears to have suffered a dramatic decline in productivity. We have used disaggregated data at the research program level to explore that decline in the context of the drivers of productivity in drug discovery. Our results suggest that the decline is probably not a function either of a shift to research in more difficult areas or of an increase in racing behavior in the industry. Rather, our results are consistent with the hypothesis that rising real costs of research in the industry reflect decreasing returns. The switch to more science-intensive methods of drug research appears to be a major contributor to increasing costs, but the most important driver of cost escalation appears to be the rocketing costs of developing clinical drugs. We speculate that this probably reflects both a shift to the treatment of conditions that require more complex clinical trials and increasing regulatory stringency, but we have no data about those issues.[15]

In general, our results must be interpreted with caution. Our anal-

---

15. The decline in measured productivity may also reflect inadequate measures of output. The move to more rational drug design, for example, may have resulted in the introduction of drugs that were more expensive to discover but that have more valuable therapeutic effects.

ysis of investment behavior and spillover effects applies only to competition in research or drug discovery: we plan to explore the determinants of productivity in development in later work. Moreover, the validity of our spillover analysis is crucially dependent on our use of important patents as a measure of output. We plan to extend our analysis by using alternative measures of output. We also hope to enrich our understanding of the ways in which the dynamics of the industry have evolved over time.

Those results have potentially important implications for public policy. Most important, they suggest that the presence of several competitors in any given area may increase social welfare. While it may be tempting to think that one could rationalize the amount of R&D conducted by the industry or set prices on the basis of the research expenditures of a single firm, our analysis suggests that it may be dangerous to think of research costs in terms of some measure of "dollars per drug" deduced from the spending of any single firm. A reduction in the number of firms conducting research in any given area may have significant negative externalities, if R&D spending complements rather than substitutes for rivals' investment. Intuitively, the true cost of a drug may include the costs of those programs in rival firms that apparently failed but that contributed to the industry's common pool of knowledge by spilling information across the boundaries of the firm.

Appendix 8–A

Sources and Construction of Quantitative Data. This research relies on a data set obtained as part of a larger study of research productivity in the pharmaceutical industry. It draws on data about spending and output at the research program level that we obtained from the internal records of ten pharmaceutical firms. We were able to obtain data about every program in which those firms invested for a period of up to thirty years—a total of more than 180 programs. Although for reasons of confidentiality we cannot describe specifics of the total size or nature of the firms, we can say that they cover the range of major pharmaceutical manufacturers that perform R&D and that they include both American and European manufacturers. In aggregate, the firms in our sample account for approximately 28 percent of U.S. R&D and sales, and we believe that they are not markedly unrepresentative of the industry in terms of size or of either technical or commercial performance.

Inputs. Our data on inputs to the drug discovery process come from the internal records of participating companies and consist primarily of annual expenditures on exploratory research and discovery by research program. Several issues arise in dealing with those data.

Discovery versus development. The distinction between discovery and development is important. We define resources devoted to discovery as all preclinical expenditures within a therapeutic class and development as all expenses incurred after a compound has been identified as a development candidate. Where exploratory research was attributable to a particular research program, we include it in the discovery category. We include nonprogram exploratory research in the overhead allocation for each research program. We include clinical grants in the figures for development and grants to external researchers for exploratory research in the total for discovery.

In some cases the companies supplied us with data already broken down by discovery versus development by research program. In others, we had to classify budget line items for projects and programs into the appropriate category. We did this on the basis of how the original sources described each item and where the items were located within the structure of the company's reporting procedure.

Overhead. To maintain as much consistency in the data collection process as possible, we tried to ensure that these figures include appropriate overhead charges directly related to discovery activities, such as computing, R&D administration, and finance, but exclude charges relating to the allocation of central office overhead. The overhead also includes some expenditures on discipline-based exploratory research such as molecular biology, which appeared not to be oriented toward specific therapies. We allocated overhead across therapeutic classes according to their fraction of total spending.

Licensing. We treat upfront, lump-sum payments for the licensing of compounds and participation in joint programs with other pharmaceutical companies, universities, or research institutes as expenditures on discovery. We exclude royalty fees and contingent payments.

Outputs. We focus on patent grants as our measure of research output. We count patents by year of application. Our interest here is on determinants of technical success, defined in terms of producing new, potentially important compounds, rather than on the ultimate commercial success or failure of new drugs. Since patent examiners award grants based on slowly changing objective criteria of novelty, nonobviousness, and potential industrial application, we believe that patent grants are an appropriate basis for measuring research output in the pharmaceutical industry. Pharmaceutical companies patent prolifically, and patents are, of course, a rather noisy measure of research success, in part because the significance of individual patents varies widely. We partially control for this by counting only important patents, where we define importance by the fact that the patent was granted in two of the three major markets: the United States, Japan, and the European Community.

We obtained those data from Derwent Publications Inc. We asked that firm to use its proprietary classification and search software to produce counts of important patents broken down by therapeutic class for twenty-nine U.S., European, and Japanese pharmaceutical manufacturers for the twenty-six years preceding 1990. Those firms include the ten firms that provided us data and nineteen other firms that we selected on the basis of their absolute R&D expenditures, R&D intensity, and national home base to develop a representative, rather than an exhaustive, assessment of worldwide patenting activity. Those nineteen firms have been consistently in the top thirty worldwide pharmaceutical firms in terms of R&D dollars and sales.

Note that many of those patents will be defensive patents in that firms may patent compounds they do not intend to develop in the short term but that may have competitive value in the longer term. Alternative measures of importance include citation weighting and more detailed international filing data, since very important patents are usually filed in nearly every major potential market. We hope to explore those alternative measures in later work.

Classification. Classification of inputs and outputs by therapeutic class is important because this drives our measure of spillovers. There are essentially two choices: to define programs by physiological mechanisms, for example, prostaglandin metabolism, or by indications or disease states, for example, arthritis. We have chosen to classify on the basis of indication, largely because that corresponds well to the internal divisions used by the companies in our sample (which is conceptually correct) and because classification by mechanism is much more difficult. In further work we intend to repeat the analysis using the classification by mechanism. We classified both inputs and outputs according to a scheme that closely follows the worldwide classes used by the market research firm IMS. This scheme contains two tiers of aggregation: a detailed research program or research area level, and a more aggregated level that groups related programs into therapeutic classes. For example, the therapeutic class cardiovascular includes the research programs antihypertensives, cardiotonics, antithrombolytics, and diuretics.

There are some problems with that procedure. First, some projects

187

and compounds are simply very difficult to classify. A particular drug may be indicated for several quite distinct therapies: consider serotonin, which has quite different physiological actions on either side of the blood-brain barrier. As a neurotransmitter, it is believed to play important roles in mediating motor functions. As a systemic hormone, it has a variety of effects on smooth muscle; for example, it functions as a vasoconstrictor. Some companies report expenditures in areas that are very difficult to assign to particular therapeutic classes. For example, a company doing research using recombinant DNA technology might charge the expenditure to an accounting category listed as gene therapy/molecular biology, which is actually specific research performed on cystic fibrosis, but we have no idea about which diseases the research is directed toward treating and are forced to include those expenditures in overhead. Second, our two-tier classification scheme may not catch all important relationships between different therapeutic areas. We believe that we are undercounting, rather than overcounting in this respect, so that the importance of spillovers will be underestimated rather than overestimated. Third, where firms supplied us with data that they had already classified, they may have used substantively different conventions in classifying projects. One firm may subsume antiviral research under a wider class of anti-infectives, while another may report antivirals separately. Indeed, there are major changes within companies in internal divisional structures, reporting formats, and so forth that may also introduce classification errors. After working very carefully with those data, we recognize the potential for serious misassignment of outputs to inputs, but we believe that such errors that remain are not serious. The use of patents as the output measure should reduce vulnerability to that problem, because we observe relatively large numbers, and a few misclassifications are unlikely to affect our results seriously. When we move to investigational new drug applications and new drug applications as our output measures, the much more sparsely distributed data are likely increase our vulnerability.

Matching. We matched the data series on inputs and outputs for each firm at the research program level. Such a procedure appears to match outputs and inputs unambiguously for the great majority of programs. In a very few cases, however, we ended up with research programs in which patents, investigational new drug applications, or new drug applications were filed, but where there were no recorded expenditures. Of those, the majority were obviously coding errors or reflected dilemmas previously encountered in the classification process, and we made the appropriate corrections. In other cases, it was clear that those reflected spillovers—research done ostensibly in, for example, hypertension, may generate knowledge about the autonomic nervous system that prompts patenting of compounds that may be useful in treating secretory disorders such as ulcers. In such cases we set own inputs for the program equal to zero and included those observations in the data base.

Deflation. Since our data sources span many years, it is important to base the analysis on constant dollar expenditures. We used the R&D price deflator constructed by Edwin Mansfield (1987) for his oil and chemicals industry grouping. That index is based on wage rates for R&D employees and a price index for equipment and instrumentation purchases, and though its movement is quite different from the CPI or the GNP deflator, it varies much less across industries, which leads us to believe that it may be a reasonable approximation to the correct index for pharmaceuticals. Mansfield's index exists only for the period 1969 through 1983. We extended it back to 1966 and forward to 1990 by using movement in the CPI. The periods from 1966 through 1969 and from 1983 through 1990 saw relatively little price inflation, so our approximation is unlikely to be a serious problem. In future research we intend to exploit the information that some companies were able to give us on R&D inputs in units of labor hours to construct an index specifically for research costs in the pharmaceutical industry.

Demand. We attempt to measure cross-sectional and time series variation in the state of demand for drug treatments for the different therapeutic classes by using a variety of publicly available data. First, we compiled statistics on disease incidence and mortality in the U.S. population from a variety of sources, including the information provided by bodies such as the National Institutes of Health and the National Cancer Institute. Unfortunately, those data are not entirely comprehensive and consistent. Some diseases or conditions are underreported because they are not sufficiently serious or because there is a social stigma attached to them, as in depression. In many cases data appear to have been gathered only at five-year or longer intervals, and in others there were serious inconsistencies in series over time that presumably reflect differences in reporting requirements. There are also problems in comparing, for example, diseases that have low incidence but high mortality rates with those with high incidence and low mortality rates (for example, thyroid cancer and the common cold), or indeed in comparing diseases that are merely uncomfortable with those that are life-threatening, or chronic conditions with acute conditions.

Second, we compiled data on the number of doctors in the United

189

States who specialize in particular areas of medicine. Those data are at best available only at a rather high level of aggregation (cardiology versus neurology), and their usefulness is also limited by the classification of many doctors into specialties such as internal medicine or pediatrics, which have no information about therapeutic classes.

Those data are far from satisfactory measures of demand: they are not so detailed as we would like, nor do they show much variation over time (trend is driven by demographics), nor are they necessarily directly comparable in the cross section, nor do they capture the potential market size for alternative treatments such as drug therapy or surgery. Our hope is that they pick up gross variation in levels of demand, or shocks to demand such as the appearance of AIDS.

An alternative measure of demand is actual dollar sales of pharmaceuticals in the class. We compiled those data from the reports of the market research firm IMS America for each of the therapeutic classes in our data.

A final, and perhaps more fundamental, problem with those demand measures is that their usefulness as measures of incentives to do R&D may be rather limited. Ideally, we would like some measure of the total consumer surplus available to be captured, based on market characteristics such as the price elasticity of demand, potential for drug therapies to enhance patients' quality of life or extend their life expectancy, and the efficacy of currently available therapies. Our measures fall far short of that ideal, but they may be the best that we can do with limited time and resources.

Scientific Opportunity. We use two sources of data to measure discrete shocks to scientific opportunity: bibliometric data based on the citation databases of the Institute for Scientific Information and the identification of key events in the evolution of the science base for particular therapeutic classes. The ISI publishes an annual list of the most significant articles published in the life sciences. For each year and each therapeutic class we noted the number of articles in that area that made the top 100 list and also the frequency with which those articles were subsequently cited in the next two years. Problems with such measures of shocks to opportunity include matching articles to therapeutic classes, which is often difficult if the article refers to generic aspects of molecular biology or physiology rather than to specific diseases or organ systems. In addition, the scientific community often fails to identify key advances until much time has passed, and advances may be of great importance to researchers in a narrowly defined field but lack sufficient general interest to attract enough citations to make the top 100 list. Nevertheless, those measures have the advantage of being con-

TABLE 8A–1
DEFINITION OF VARIABLES USED IN THE REGRESSION ANALYSIS

Measures of Scientific Opportunity

Articles	Total articles in the class listed in the ISI list of "top 100 papers" in the biological sciences.
Key private articles (cardiovascular only)	Number of papers signaling major breakthroughs in the field published by authors employed by private firms.
Key public articles (cardiovascular only)	Number of papers signaling major breakthroughs in the field published by authors employed by the public sector.

Measures of Demand

Cases	Reported U.S. incidence of the disease.
Deaths	Reported U.S. mortality.
Doctors	Number of doctors identifying themselves as specialists in the area.
U.S. sales in class	Wholesale U.S. sales of drugs in the class.

Measures of Competitive Activity

Competitors' patents in this class	Important patents applied for by twenty-eight major (worldwide) competitors.
Competitors' patents in related classes	Important patents applied for by twenty-eight major (worldwide) competitors in related classes.

Firm-Specific Variables

Competitors' investment in this class	Investment in discovery research by the other nine firms in the core database.

Firm-Specific Variables

Investment	Expenditures by this firm in this research area, relating primarily to production of new compounds, by year, in millions of constant 1986 dollars.
Patents in this class	Important patents granted to this firm in this research area, by year, from the Derwent database. Note that throughout the analysis we count patents by year of application.

(Table continues)

191

TABLE 8A–1 (continued)

Patents in related classes	Important patents granted to this firm in the related therapeutic class, net of the patents granted in this research area.
Firm sales in class	Total U.S. sales in the class.
Scope	The number of research areas in which this firm has spent at least $.5 million dollars on discovery this year.
Total investment (size)	Total research expenditure by this firm in this year across all therapeutic classes.

NOTE: Observations are identified by (encoded) *FIRM, CLASS,* and *YEAR.*

sistent and comparable over time, and they are reasonably well matched to specific therapeutic classes.

For cardiovascular therapies, we attempted to identify key events. Although that process is more subjective than citation analysis, it is more comprehensive. We examined standard texts on pharmacology such as Gilman et al. (1990) and texts on cardiovascular therapies, including Bristol (1986) and Kostis and De Felice (1984) and attempted to identify significant advances in scientific understanding, such as the discovery of entire classes of compounds showing desirable activity in vitro or in animal models, or the identification of important enzyme pathways. We then cross-checked our results with experts in the field.

In table 8A–1 we define the variables used in the regression analysis.

References

Bristol, James A., ed. *Cardiovascular Drugs.* New York: John Wiley and Sons, 1986.

Cockburn, Iain, and Rebecca Henderson. "Racing to Invest? The Dynamics of Competition in Ethical Drug Discovery." *Journal of Economics and Management Strategy* 3 (1995): 481–519.

Dasgupta, P., and Eric Maskin. "The Simple Economics of Research Portfolios." *Economic Journal* 97 (1987): 581–95.

Dasgupta, P., and Joseph E. Stiglitz. "Uncertainty, Industrial Structure, and the Speed of R&D." *Bell Journal of Economics* 11 (1980): 1–28.

D'Aspremont, Claude, and Alexis Jacquemin. "Cooperative and Noncooperative R&D in Duopoly with Spillovers." *American Economic Review* 78 (1988): 1133–37.

———. "Cooperative and Noncooperative R&D in Duopoly with Spillovers: Erratum." *American Economic Review* 80: 641–42.

DiMasi, Joseph A., Ronald W. Hansen, Henry G. Grabowski, and Louis Lasagna. "The Cost of Innovation in the Pharmaceutical Industry." *Journal of Health Economics* 10 (1991): 107–42.

Fraja, Giovanni. "Strategic Spillovers in Patent Races." *International Journal of Industrial Organization* 11 (1993): 139–46.

Gilman, Alfred G., Louis S. Goodman, Theodore W. Rall, and Ferid Murad, eds. *The Pharmacological Basis of Therapeutics.* New York: Macmillan, 1985.

Gilman, Alfred G., Theodore W. Rall, A.S. Nies, and Taylor Palmer. *The Pharmacological Basis for Therapeutics.* New York: Macmillan, 1990.

Grabowski, Henry, and Nevine Baxter. "Rivalry in Industrial Research and Development." *Journal of Industrial Economics* 21 (1973): 209–35.

Griliches, Zvi. "Patent Statistics as Economic Indicators: A Survey." *Journal of Economic Literature* 28 (1990): 1661–1707.

Harris, C., and J. Vickers. "Racing with Uncertainty." *Review of Economic Studies* 54 (1987): 1–22.

Henderson, Rebecca, and Iain Cockburn. "Scale, Scope, and Spillovers: The Determinants of Research Productivity in Ethical Drug Discovery." NBER Working Paper #4466, revised September 1994.

Kostis, John B., and Eugene A. De Felice, eds. *Beta Blockers in the Treatment of Cardiovascular Disease.* New York: Raven Press, 1984.

Loury, Glenn. "Market Structure and Innovation." *Quarterly Journal of Economics* 93 (1979): 395–410.

Mansfield, Edwin. "Price Indices for R&D Inputs, 1969–1983." *Management Science* 33 (1987): 124–29.

Meron, Amos, and Richard Caves. "Rivalry among Firms in Research and Development Outlays." Unpublished manuscript, Harvard University, 1991.

Reinganum, J.F. "A Dynamic Game of R and D: Patent Protection and Competitive Behavior." *Econometrica* 50 (1982): 671–88.

———. "The Timing of Innovation: Research, Development, and Diffusion." In *Handbook of Industrial Organization,* vol. 1, edited by R. Schmalensee and R. Willig. Amsterdam: North Holland, 1989.

Scherer, Frederic M. *International High-Technology Competition.* Cambridge: Harvard University Press, 1992.

———. "Research and Development Resource Allocation under Rivalry." *Quarterly Journal of Economics* 81 (1967): 359–94.

Suzumura, K. "Cooperative and Noncooperative R&D in an Oligopoly with Spillovers." *American Economic Review* 82 (1992): 1307–20.

Wiggins, Steven. "Regulation and Innovation in the Pharmaceutical Industry." Ph.D. dissertation, Massachusetts Institute of Technology, 1979.

9
Prospects for Returns to Pharmaceutical R&D under Health Care Reform

Henry G. Grabowski and John M. Vernon

Pharmaceuticals are currently the focus of vigorous cost containment in almost all countries. Those efforts tend to be driven by short-term budgetary considerations. In particular, price regulators try to obtain big-selling new drugs at break-even prices while letting other countries bear the high fixed costs of research and development. The proposed provisions for the pricing of breakthrough new drugs under the Clinton administration's health reform plan are a prime example of that type of behavior. In the Clinton plan the secretary of the Department of Health and Human Services would create an advisory council on breakthrough drugs that would have the authority to solicit information from firms about the factors underlying pharmaceutical prices so that the council could issue reports about the "reasonableness" of those prices. The plan would also give the secretary of HHS the authority to negotiate a special rebate to the Medicare program for any new drug that the secretary determines is excessively or inappropriately priced. If a manufacturer is unable to negotiate a price that the secretary determines to be reasonable, the particular drug may be excluded from coverage under Medicare. This negotiated price is likely to become the model for other health care providers.[1]

The introduction of those proposed control measures in the Clin-

---

1. Beyond these specific measures focused on new drug launch prices, there are several other general cost-containment measures in the Clinton plan that can be expected to significantly influence the usage of new drugs. The most prominent of these are the constraints on the annual growth in premiums for the basic benefit package. Premium increases are limited to the rate of inflation after a phase-in period. This can retard the adoption of pharmaceuticals which are cost increasing to the health care system, but which provide long-term net benefits to patients and society. For further analysis, see Grabowski (1994).

ton plan follows an intense public policy debate on drug profits and pricing. President Clinton and several congressmen have contended that the pharmaceutical industry's high return on shareholder equity is evidence of its excessive prices. In addition, a highly publicized report by the Office of Technology Assessment (1993) fueled the perception of high industry profits when one of its congressional sponsors, Representative Henry Waxman, incorrectly concluded from the study's results that pharmaceutical firms earn "more than two billion dollars a year in excess profits."

This chapter briefly summarizes our findings (Grabowski and Vernon 1994) on the returns to pharmaceutical R&D for a cohort of new drugs introduced in the period 1980 through 1984 and then uses the model from that study to perform several simulations of what might result from Clinton's proposed health care reform—what we might term "extreme case" scenarios. The main finding of our 1994 study is that the mean internal rate of return for that cohort is within one percentage point of the industry's cost of capital. Therefore, according to our results, large excess returns do not exist for the 1980 to 1984 cohort. The distribution of returns is highly skewed, however. The top decile of new chemical entities—the Food and Drug Administration's designation for chemically distinct new drugs approved for marketing— earns very high returns. When we use our 1980 to 1984 data and returns model as the base case in our simulations, we consider the effect on returns if there should be a government policy that results in constraining the top decile of drugs to "break even." We also examine a scenario in which generic competition after patent expiration leads to unusually severe losses of sales by the brand-name firms.

Returns on R&D for U.S. Introductions of New Chemical Entities

We have been engaged in a continuing study of the returns on R&D for chemically distinct new drugs approved for marketing that have been introduced in the United States since 1970. A key issue that we address in this chapter is whether the average new drug earns a return on R&D investment that is commensurate with the pharmaceutical industry's cost of capital. We also examine the distribution of returns. We base our analysis on a comprehensive sample of U.S. new drug introductions and make our computations on a real after-tax basis.

In our initial study (Grabowski and Vernon 1990) we analyzed the returns on R&D for new drugs introduced during the 1970s. We found that the average new chemical entity earned returns roughly equal to the industry's cost of capital. The distribution of returns was highly skewed, however. In particular, only the new drugs from the top three deciles had present values on postlaunch cash flows that exceeded the estimated R&D costs for a new chemical entity.

Using a comparable methodology, we studied the returns on R&D investment for new drugs introduced from 1980 through 1984. This section summarizes the nature of our analysis and our major findings.

Modeling R&D Returns. The R&D investment costs for the representative new drugs introduced from 1980 through 1984 in our sample are based on a recent study by DiMasi et al. (1991). That study used cost data for a random sample of drugs undergoing testing and found that the average successful new chemical entity introduced during the 1980s incurred $73 million of preclinical testing expenditures and $53 million during clinical testing. We should note that those are the uncapitalized out-of-pocket costs but do include the cost of failures. Indeed, only 23 percent of drugs tested in man become successful new chemical entities. Those costs are spread over an R&D investment period of approximately twelve years.

The first step in analyzing the returns to R&D investment is to construct life-cycle sales revenue profiles for each new drug introduction in the sample. We obtained U.S. sales data over the product lifetime to date from audit sources. We used information on each new chemical entity's patent expiration and related economic data to estimate sales over future years of the product life cycle. We projected sales to worldwide levels by using an international sales multiplier.

Figure 9–1 shows the sales profiles for the median, mean, and top few deciles. These curves exhibit a life-cycle pattern frequently observed in pharmaceuticals. In particular, there is rapid growth in the early years of market life, a sales peak in the tenth or eleventh year, and then continual decline over the mature phase of the life cycle. Most of the drugs in the sample have effective patent lifetimes of nine to thirteen years. This accounts for the peak in sales revenues in the range of ten to eleven years. Sales erosion rates in the postpatent period are based on our study (Grabowski and Vernon 1992) of generic competition for leading new chemical entities.

Figure 9–1 also illustrates the highly skewed nature of the sales distribution for new drugs introduced in the 1980s. The sales profile of the top decile drug is several times higher than that of the second decile. Furthermore, the mean sales curve is much higher than the median one. We observed the same pattern of skewness for new drugs introduced in the 1970s.

We derived cash flows after product launch from sales values by applying a drug industry profit margin on sales. During the late 1980s,

FIGURE 9–1
U.S. SALES PROFILES OF 1980–1984 NEW CHEMICAL ENTITIES

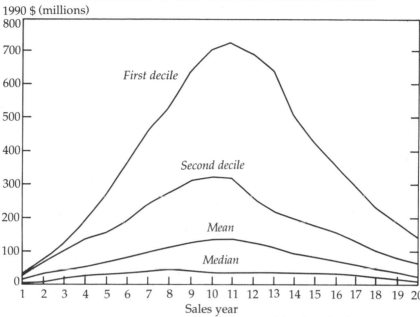

we estimated those margins to be in the neighborhood of 40 percent. Our model also includes capital expenditures in fixed plant and equipment as well as above-average promotional expenditures in the early years after the market launch. We transformed the stream of R&D expenditures and net cash outflows to after-tax values by using an average tax rate of 33 percent.

On the basis of the above assumptions and data inputs that we discuss in more detail in Grabowski and Vernon (1994), the representative new chemical entity introduced in the 1980 to 1984 period has the pattern of cash flows presented in figure 9–2. Cash flows are negative over the preclinical and clinical R&D period and become increasingly so in the years before marketing because firms have large launch and capital investment outlays. By the third year after the launch, cash flows become positive. They then escalate rapidly and reach a peak in the eleventh year. Subsequent generic competition and product obsolescence cause cash flows to decline in value until the final year of market life—the twentieth year.

The baseline values shown in figure 9–2 provide the basis for computing the internal rate of return and net present value for the mean new chemical entity introduced during the 1980 to 1984 period. To do this we use a 10.5 percent real cost of capital for pharmaceutical firms,

FIGURE 9–2

TOTAL CASH FLOWS FOR MEAN 1980–1984 NEW CHEMICAL ENTITY

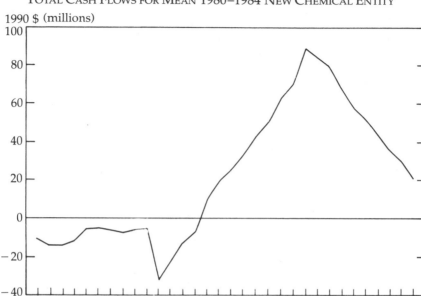

a figure Myers and Shyam-Sunder derived in a study they performed for the OTA that they report in chapter 10. Specifically, they found that the real cost of capital on total investments of the pharmaceutical industry varied between 10 percent and 11 percent during the 1980s.

Findings for the 1980 to 1984 New Drug Cohort. The results for the base case appear in the first row of table 9–1. In particular, the capitalized value of R&D investment costs is $201.9 million (in 1990 dollars). The discounted value of net cash returns resulting from that R&D investment is $224.1 million. Hence, the net present value for the mean new drug in that cohort is $22.2 million.[2] The internal rate of return for the mean new drug is 11.1 percent—only slightly above the 10.5 percent cost of capital.

Of course, there is uncertainty about some parameters. In table 9–1 we demonstrate the effect of changes in important parameters on the net present value and the internal rate of return. For example, re-

2. Our findings indicate a lower net present value than the $36 million reported in the 1993 OTA study, which uses a shorter interval for its sample period (1981 through 1983) and also makes some different assumptions. We provide a detailed comparison of the two studies in Grabowski and Vernon (1994).

TABLE 9–1
RETURNS TO 1980–1984 NEW CHEMICAL ENTITIES

Case	Present Value Cash Flows (after tax)	Present Value R&D Costs (after tax)	Net Present Value	Internal Rate of Return
Baseline	224.1	201.9	22.2	11.1
At 35% margin	187.6	201.9	(14.3)	10.1
At 45% margin	260.6	201.9	58.8	11.9
At 1.8 international multiplier	201.7	201.9	(0.2)	10.5
At 2.2 international multiplier	246.5	201.9	44.6	11.6
At .25 tax rate	257.1	226.0	31.2	11.2
At .40 tax rate	195.2	180.8	14.4	10.9

NOTE: Baseline case assumes 10.5 percent cost of capital, international multiplier of 2.0, tax rate of .33, and margin of .40.

ducing the contribution margin from the baseline case of 40 percent to 35 percent reduces the internal rate of return from 11.1 percent to 10.1 percent. Raising the margin from the baseline case to 45 percent raises the internal rate of return to 11.9 percent. We vary two other important parameters—the international multiplier and the tax rate. Varying the international multiplier from 1.8 to 2.2 causes the internal rate of return to vary from 10.5 percent to 11.6 percent. The tax rate has a much smaller effect. A 25 percent rate yields an internal rate of return of 11.2 percent, and a 40 percent rate yields a 10.9 percent internal rate of return.

To conclude this section, we present figure 9–3, which shows the distribution of present values of net cash returns by decile. The dashed line represents the average R&D cost per new drug. It is clear that this distribution is highly skewed. The top decile has an estimated present value of $1 billion, or more than five times the capitalized value of average R&D costs. We also see that only the top three deciles have present values that exceed average R&D costs. Such extreme skewness of returns has an important implication for the simulation experiments that we consider in the next section. If, as proposed, a type of price regulation develops under the new health care plan that focuses on the "big winners"—the top few deciles—then the returns to new drugs will be reduced significantly.

Sales Trends on New Drugs Introduced from 1985 through 1989. Before turning to those simulations, we report briefly on the sales trends

FIGURE 9–3
PRESENT VALUES BY DECILE FOR 1980–1984 NEW CHEMICAL ENTITIES

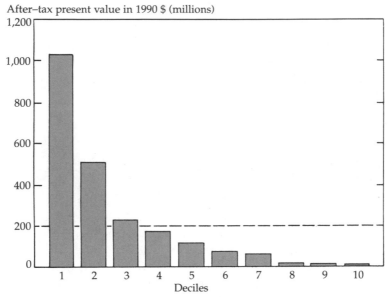

After–tax present value in 1990 $ (millions)

of more recent new drug introductions. To evaluate current policy issues, we prefer using information from the most recent cohort of new chemical entities. Using a more recent cohort limits the extensiveness of the data, however. Therefore, it is still too early to do a comprehensive rate of return analysis for the 1985 through 1989 cohort of new drugs. Nevertheless, we can compare the performance of those new drugs with that of the 1980 through 1984 cohort at similar points in their initial market life.

Our first preliminary finding is that the distribution of sales for the 1985 through 1989 new drugs is as highly skewed as distributions were for earlier cohorts: the top decile accounts for over half of that group's total fourth-year sales. Second, the "big winner" drugs among those introduced from 1985 through 1989 have higher average sales in the first few years of market life than the drugs introduced from 1980 through 1984, but their growth in sales declines much earlier in the market life cycle than was the case for the preceding cohort. Thus, we can expect sales for the 1985 through 1989 cohort to peak sooner and at lower levels than the eleventh-year maximum sales point exhibited in figure 9–1 for the drugs introduced from 1980 through 1984.[3]

---

3. In this regard, it is useful to note that although the level of sales per new drug for the three most recent years—1987, 1988, and 1989—are significantly

Therefore, evidence suggests that even without enactment of Clinton's health care proposal, market pressures are depressing the sales of new drugs. While more recent new drug introductions are experiencing increasing cost-containment pressures, they are also characterized by the same basic skewed distribution of outcomes. Hence, there is no real loss of generality in using our 1980 through 1984 analysis as the base case for our simulation experiments in the next section.

Simulation Experiments of Health Care Reform

We shall now analyze some scenarios that we can view as long-term implications of President Clinton's proposed health care reform. That plan appears to establish a regulatory framework for drug price controls and, in particular, one that focuses on commercially important new drugs. The plan's other measures to contain drug costs include having accountable health plans and government agencies encourage formularies so as to promote price discounts in pharmaceuticals. The plan also strongly encourages the use of generic drug products.[4]

First, we consider the effect on returns on R&D for new drug introductions if there should be a government policy that results in constraining the top decile of new drugs to "break even." Second, we examine some scenarios in which the erosion of sales from generic competition becomes unusually great—in particular, sales fall by 70 percent to 90 percent in the year after the patent expires.

Top Decile of New Drugs Constrained to Break Even. The simplest way to describe this simulation is to refer to figure 9–3, which shows the present values by decile for the sixty-seven new drugs in our 1980 through 1984 sample. We assume that the government focuses its attention on the top decile of new drugs. As a result of constraining the top decile's prices, government policy actions eliminate the present

---

higher in the early years than the 1980 through 1984 average, they all tend to show declining rates of sales increase by the sixth year of market life. This is in contrast to the 1980 through 1984 cohort, which shows no such tendency until the tenth year of market life. (See figure 9–1.) Clearly, to project a complete product life cycle for the 1985 through 1989 cohort would be extremely speculative. Nevertheless, it seems to be fairly obvious that the market environment in pharmaceuticals is changing, and product life cycles for more recent new drug introductions are shortening as a consequence.

4. For example, Medicare coverage for multisource drugs would reimburse at generic price levels unless the physician specifically indicates that a brand-name medication is required. Even when the physician indicates this, the secretary of HHS may require physicians to obtain prior approval before prescribing brand-name products when a generic substitute is available.

TABLE 9–2
IMPLICATIONS OF PRICE CONSTRAINTS ON TOP DECILE DRUGS FOR
MEAN NEW CHEMICAL ENTITY'S INTRODUCTION
(1990 $ millions)

Case	Present Value Cash Flow	R&D Costs	Net Present Value	Δ Net Present Value
Baseline	224.1	201.9	22.2	—
Top decile constrained to break even	141.7	201.9	−60.2	−82.4
Top two deciles constrained to break even	110.8	201.9	−91.0	−113.2
Top three deciles constained to break even	107.8	201.9	−94.0	−116.2

value of cash flows of the top decile above the average R&D cost. In particular, under the first scenario analyzed, the top decile of drugs has present values reduced from $1,026 million to $201.9 million. That is, government policy has constrained the present value of cash flows to equal average R&D costs. This also means that the internal rate of return for the top decile of drugs is exactly equal to the cost of capital in our model, 10.5 percent. We assume that all other deciles are unaffected.

In table 9–2 we show the implication of government price constraints for the mean new drug introduction. Our main result is that the net present value falls from the base case value of $22.2 million to −$60.2 million.[5] In other words, constraining the internal rate of return for the top decile of drugs to the cost of capital causes the mean new drug to lose more than one-third of its total present value ($82.4 million/$224.1 million), and the net present value goes from a moderately

5. It is relevant to ask what type of revenue reductions would cause the top decile to just cover average R&D costs. This would depend on a number of factors including the price elasticity of demand for these drugs, induced shifts in marketing and administrative costs, as well as other parameters. Under a set of polar assumptions in which output and costs are assumed to remain constant as prices decline, we computed that a 23 percent reduction in total revenues in each year would cause the top decile to just cover R&D costs. For comparative purposes under these same assumptions, revenue reductions of 17 percent and 3.8 percent would reduce the second and third deciles' net present value to zero.

positive value to a highly negative one. With such large losses for the representative or mean new drug introduction, firms would be expected to respond by curtailing expenditures on future R&D projects until expected returns again become positive.

In addition, in table 9–2 we show the effect of broader restraints that eliminate the excess returns to the second and third deciles, respectively. The net present value falls from − $60.2 million, when only the top decile is restrained, to − $91 million and − $94 million, when the restraint extends to the next two deciles. Hence, there would be further losses as additional drugs are constrained to break-even status, but at a sharply diminishing rate. This latter result reflects the extreme skewness in the returns distribution shown in figure 9–3.

Going beyond the effects on mean returns reported in table 9–2, we would expect important shifts in R&D investment allocations for new pharmaceuticals. If we regard R&D investment as somewhat like a lottery—with low probabilities of achieving huge returns—top-decile regulation clearly changes the attractiveness of the "R&D lottery." Winning the lottery now provides only a break-even return. As a consequence, firms would be expected to devote more of their R&D and marketing activities to certain incremental or "niche" advances that entail fewer technological and regulatory risks. To the extent that prospective social gains are positively correlated with risk bearing in pharmaceutical R&D, these are precisely the wrong signals to create in the U.S. market.

Severe Generic Competition upon Patent Expiration. An alternative cost-containment approach would be for the government to encourage the use of lower-priced generics when they become available after patent expiration. Some components of the Clinton administration's health care plan use such a strategy, and for many reasons it is preferable to the price regulation of important drugs. First, the market is likely to evolve strongly in this direction in any case, and the government would be reinforcing rather than retarding market forces.[6] Second, a large number of the current top-selling drugs will experience patent expiration over the next several years and thus provide opportunities

---

6. Pharmacy benefit management plans and managed care organizations are growing rapidly, and this will contribute to a more rapid diffusion of generic price levels after patent expiration in future years (Morrison 1993). In terms of overseas markets, generic reimbursement limits for multiple-source drugs are also being implemented in many European countries (Mattison 1993).

for large cost savings.[7] Finally, and most relevant to the current analysis, we expect that encouraging the use of generic drugs will less adversely affect incentives to innovate than will price regulation.

To illustrate the last point, we examine the effects of two scenarios in which name-brand drug manufacturers face keen competition by manufacturers of generic drugs. In our base case we assumed that the average percentage declines in sales in the first four years following patent expiration were 30 percent, 21 percent, 12 percent, and 12 percent. We derived those numbers from the sales losses major products experienced in the period immediately after Congress passed the Drug Price Competition and Patent Term Restoration Act of 1984. We now assume that firms expect that far more severe government and market pressures will develop to force the use of lower-priced generics by the time patents expire on new drug candidates currently in R&D, whose patents will not expire for a least a decade.

In the first scenario we assume that firms expect sales to fall 70 percent in the year after patent expiration and remain at that level for four years. Thereafter, sales follow a 10 percent decline for the remainder of market life.[8] In the second we assume that sales are expected to fall 90 percent in the first year after patent expiration and 10 percent thereafter.

Figure 9–4 presents the sales profile for our base case compared with the case of the most severe generic competition. As we show in table 9–3, in the 70 percent case the net present value for the mean new drug falls to $8.8 million from the base-case value of $22.2 million, and the internal rate of return falls from 11.1 percent to 10.7 percent. In the 90 percent sales loss scenario, the net present value for the mean drug falls to −$7.4 million and the internal rate of return to 10.3 percent.[9]

The observed change in net present value for the mean new drug under the most severe generic erosion scenario (−$29.9 million) is, therefore, significantly less than the change when only the top decile drugs are constrained to a zero net present value (−$82.4 million).

---

7. According to a 1993 survey in *Medical Advertising News*, 54 of the top-selling 100 drugs will go off patent by the year 2000.

8. We assume that severe generic erosion applies to all new chemical entities for which we applied patent erosion in the text (the top thirty new chemical entities); however, the price cuts are restricted to the top decile only.

9. In a world dominated by managed care institutions and drug formularies, the first patent expiration for a class of therapeutically similar drugs is likely to trigger severe sales erosion, not only for the brand going off patent but also for all the other new chemical entities in that class. This is an interesting issue to consider in future research assessments of the growth of managed care organizations and health care reform scenarios.

FIGURE 9–4
BASE-CASE MEAN SALES VERSUS SEVERE EROSION

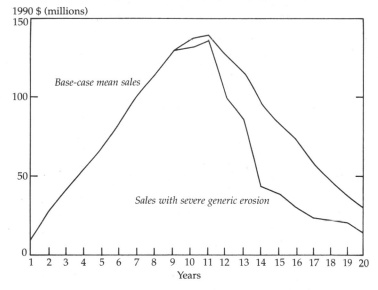

1990 $ (millions)

Base-case mean sales

Sales with severe generic erosion

Years

TABLE 9–3
IMPLICATIONS OF ALTERNATIVE SCENARIOS ON GENERIC PRICE EROSION FOR MEAN NEW CHEMICAL ENTITY'S INTRODUCTION

Case	Mean Net Present Value (1990 $ millions)	Δ Net Present Value (1990 $ millions)	Mean Internal Rate of Return (%)	Cost of Capital (%)
Baseline	22.2	—	11.1	10.5
Severe erosion after patent expiration				
70 percent case	8.8	− 13.4	10.7	10.5
90 percent case	− 7.4	− 29.9	10.3	10.5

That reflects the fact that the severe erosion cases take effect only after a patent life of approximately ten to twelve years, and sales losses that occur later in the product life cycle are heavily discounted in a net present value analysis.

More generally, the scenarios in table 9–3 are consistent with the primary public policy strategy for encouraging technological advances in this country—an unregulated period in which there is patent exclusivity followed by a period of vigorous competition after the patent expires. By contrast, over the past two decades, policy makers have generally moved away from the economic regulatory approaches of the sort reported in table 9–2. One reason is to prevent the adverse consequences for industrial innovation that are inherent in such regulation.

Concluding Remarks

If enacted, the Clinton administration's health care reform proposal can be expected to lead to many fundamental changes for the pharmaceutical industry. The objective of our simulation analysis was not to model those changes in a comprehensive fashion. Rather we have selected a few policy directions presented in the plan and have attempted to highlight their potential consequences by analyzing some extreme value scenarios. Of particular interest is the specter of the incipient price controls, oriented toward the most commercially successful new drugs.

As our experiments have shown, limiting the net present value of top decile drugs to average R&D cost, so that those drugs just earn the industry cost of capital, implies that the net present value of the average new drugs introduced from 1980 through 1984 will drop dramatically (− $82.4 million). Of course, this is before any compensatory adjustments in other costs. Our findings do, however, illustrate the disproportionate effect on R&D returns of the top decile of new drugs and the highly skewed distribution that characterizes new drug returns. By contrast, an alternative extreme case scenario, involving almost total use of generic drugs after the patents expire, leads to a much smaller negative effect (− $29.9 million) on expected returns to the mean new drug. The impact of different cost-containment approaches on the incentives for innovation remains an important topic for further research and policy analysis.

References

DiMasi, Joseph A., Ronald W. Hansen, Henry G. Grabowski, and Louis Lasagna. "The Cost of Innovation in the Pharmaceutical Industry." *Journal of Health Economics* 10 (1991): 107–42.

Grabowski, Henry G. *Health Reform and Pharmaceutical Innovation.* Washington, D.C.: AEI Press, 1994.

Grabowski, Henry G., and John M. Vernon. "Brand Loyalty, Entry and Price Competition in Pharmaceuticals after the 1984 Act." *Journal of Law and Economics* 35 (1992): 331–50.

————. "A New Look at the Returns and Risks to Pharmaceutical R&D." *Management Science* 36 (1990): 804–21.

————. "Returns to R&D on New Drug Introductions in the 1980s." *Journal of Health Economics* 13 (1994): 383–406.

Mattison, Nancy. "Health Care Systems and Methods for Controlling Pharmaceutical Expenditures in Eight OECD Countries." Basel, Switzerland: F. Hoffman-La Roche Ltd., March 1993.

Morrison, Sylvia. "Prescription Drug Prices: The Effect of Generics, Formularies and Other Market Changes." Washington, D.C.: Congressional Research Service, August 17, 1993.

Myers, Stewart C., and Lakshmi Shyam-Sunder. "Cost of Capital Estimates for Investment in Pharmaceutical Research and Development." Washington, D.C.: Office of Technology Assessment, 1990.

"100 Powerhouse Drugs." *Medical Advertising News* (May 1993).

10
Measuring Pharmaceutical Industry Risk and the Cost of Capital

Stewart C. Myers and Lakshmi Shyam-Sunder

This chapter summarizes what modern finance can say, using publicly available data, about the cost of capital for investment in pharmaceutical R&D. We provide benchmark estimates for 1980, 1985, and 1990, and discuss how the estimates could change under different assumptions about financing and risk. We also discuss some of the practical difficulties encountered in evaluating commitments to R&D programs. The chapter is an overview of standard theory and good current practice on these topics.

We first briefly review the standard theory and then provide preliminary estimates of the overall cost of capital for major U.S. pharmaceutical companies. Current practice would use those estimates as benchmarks and would adjust them up or down to set the cost of capital and discount rate or "hurdle rate" for particular classes of capital investments. After commenting on cost of capital estimates used in past studies of costs and returns in pharmaceutical R&D, we discuss the special risks that could justify a cost of capital for pharmaceutical R&D higher than the benchmark total cost of capital for major pharmaceutical companies. We note some of the practical problems encountered in evaluating investments in pharmaceutical R&D. For example, the skewed payoff distributions encountered in R&D investments often make application or interpretation of standard discounted cash flow analysis exceptionally difficult.

Theory

The two key concepts in describing the theory and practice of asset valuation with specific emphasis on the methods for estimating the

We wish to thank Dr. Judith L. Wagner of the Office of Technology Assessment for helpful comments.

cost of capital used for discounting forecasted cash returns to investment are the capital asset pricing model (CAPM) and the weighted average cost of capital. These are not necessarily the "best" or most advanced developments in finance theory, but they are consistent with the theory and represent current practice in financially sophisticated companies.

Net Present Value and the Cost of Capital. The relevant corporate financial objective is to find and invest in assets, projects, or programs that have positive net present value (NPV):

$$NPV = \text{asset value} - \text{required investment.}$$

Positive NPV means simply that the asset is worth more than it costs.

Financial analysis of capital investment decisions thus rests on a theory of valuation. We shall not develop that theory but instead state three results as axioms. First, value ultimately depends on incremental, after-tax cash flows. Second, a dollar today is worth more than a dollar tomorrow. Third, a safe dollar is worth more than a risky dollar. These axioms lead naturally to the discounted cash flow (DCF) method, in which forecasted project cash flows (axiom 1) are discounted for the time value of money (axiom 2) and for risk (axiom 3). Discounting converts risky future cash flows into present value.

DCF analysis does not require that the proposed investment be in tangible assets or be recorded on the company's books. It looks only to cash flows, not to accounting earnings or balance-sheet entries. It applies equally to investments in R&D and in blast furnaces.

The appropriate discount rate is investors' opportunity cost of capital, defined as the expected rate of return offered by other investments subject to the same degree of risk as the project under consideration. Other investments include *all* the economy's real and financial assets, including shares of other companies. Financial managers generally look to expected returns on traded financial assets to set discount rates for the real investment opportunities open to their firms.

Figure 10–1 plots expected returns against risk. At the extreme left, risk virtually disappears and gives an intercept equal to the Treasury bill rate. From that point, risk and return go up together. We indicate three risk levels on the horizontal axis: market risk (the average risk of all stocks), the average risk of the assets and operations of a particular firm, and the risk of a hypothetical project open to that firm, which in this example happens to have the highest risk of all. There are three corresponding levels of expected return on the vertical axis: the market return, the expected rate of return that would be demanded by investors in the company as a whole, and the expected rate of return

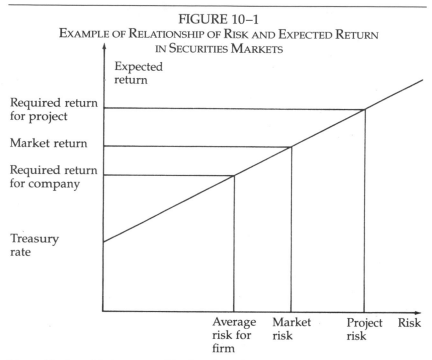

FIGURE 10–1
EXAMPLE OF RELATIONSHIP OF RISK AND EXPECTED RETURN
IN SECURITIES MARKETS

NOTE: Project risk is assumed higher than the risk of the total market and also higher than the average risk of the firm's assets.

they would demand in the specific project. This last return is the opportunity cost of capital and the correct discount rate for the project's forecasted cash flows. If the project's expected return embodied in those forecasted flows falls short of the discount rate, the project should be rejected: there are other assets "out there" in the stock market that *do* offer the opportunity cost of capital. The opportunity cost of capital is *defined* as the expected rate of return investors demand at a given level of risk. They will demand at least as high an expected return from the project as they could obtain from investment in equivalent risk common shares. Thus, the appropriate discount rate depends on project risk and does not generally equal the average cost of capital of the company undertaking the project.

Since the correct project discount rate is based on returns offered by alternative investments, it does not depend on financing. In principle, it does not matter whether project funding is borrowed, raised by issuing new shares, or drawn from internally generated funds.[1]

---

1. Once money is in hand, there is no justification for investing inside the

Questions and Answers about Measurement. Now we come to problems of measurement and the practical compromises taken to address them. We shall address the problems in a series of questions and answers.

Q: How are project risk and project discount rates estimated?

A: They usually are *not* explicitly estimated project by project. A company cost of capital is estimated and used as a benchmark. Since many projects are viewed as average risk, the company cost of capital is often the appropriate discount rate. Judgmental adjustments are made for projects that are materially higher or lower than average risk. Sometimes the adjustment is in the discount rate. Sometimes the discount rate is held constant, and the degree of conservatism applied to the cash flow forecasts is varied. Thus, projected cash flows for an especially risky project may be given an especially severe haircut by decisionmakers; this is crudely equivalent to setting a higher discount rate.[2]

Companies operating in two or more distinct industries often set divisional costs of capital based on analysis of risks and returns of stocks of "pure play" companies in the respective industries. The divisional rates then serve as benchmarks for specific projects within each division.

Q: How is the company cost of capital estimated? The company's assets are not usually traded securities.

A: One looks at a portfolio of securities with the same risk as the assets. Think of a simplified market value balance sheet:

Net working capital	Long-term debt	(D)
Present value of assets, operations, and future opportunities	Market value of shares	(E)
Market value of firm	Market value of firm	(V)

firm in projects offering returns inferior to those the firm or its shareholders would expect outside the firm from equivalent-risk shares or other assets. Thus, the opportunity cost of capital depends on the proposed use, not the source, of funds.

This statement ignores the tax advantages of debt financing, which we discuss later.

2. Adjusting cash flows downward to reflect risk is not the best practical solution. It is better to generate an unbiased forecast of expected cash flows and to discount these by an expected rate of return that reflects the risk of the cash flows.

211

This balance sheet has no necessary connection with the firm's books. It is just a way of showing that the value of all the firm's assets—including the value of intangibles and opportunities for profitable growth—must equal the market value of all the securities issued against those assets. If one buys up all the debt and all the shares, he owns all the assets.

Thus, the rate of return (r) on a portfolio of all the company's debt and equity securities equals the rate of return demanded by investors in the firm's assets:

$$r = r_D D/V + r_E E/V,$$

where r_D and r_E are expected rates of return offered by the firm's debt and equity securities. Note that the weights D/V and E/V are based on *market* values, not on the company's historical cost balance sheet.

Q: Is this the company cost of capital?

A: Not quite. The tax-deductibility of corporate interest payments is usually recognized in the discount rate. Let T_c be the marginal corporate tax rate. The weighted average company cost of capital is

$$r^* = r_D (1 - T_c) D/V + r_E E/V.$$

For most public companies, all the inputs to r^* except r_E can be estimated with reasonable confidence. But r_E is defined as an expectation, usually long-term, of dividends and capital gains on common shares. The stock market is so volatile, and uncertainty about future cash flows so massive, that few investors could express their subjective beliefs numerically. Even if they did, we still would not understand how to combine them into an unbiased market consensus.

Q: How can r_E be estimated?

A: By starting with a model relating risk and return and extrapolating from historical evidence.[3] We shall use the capital asset pricing model. The CAPM states that the expected return on an asset is equal to the

---

3. An alternative discounted cash flow approach is often used for mature, high-payout firms, for example, electric utilities. If expected future growth (g) in dividends is assumed constant, then the expected rate of return to stockholders is

$$r_E = (DIV_1/P_0) + g,$$

where DIV_1 is next year's cash dividends and P_0 is current stock price. There are variants of this formula and several approaches to estimating g.

We have not tried the DCF approach to pharmaceutical companies. We doubt the industry is mature enough for the approach to be reliable.

risk-free rate plus a risk premium that is positively related to the risk (beta) of the asset being valued:

$$r_E = r_f + \beta_E \, (r_m - r_f),$$

where r_f is the risk-free (Treasury) rate, β_E measures risk, and $(r_m - r_f)$ is the expected return premium offered by the market portfolio of all stocks. The CAPM puts β on the horizontal axis of figure 1 and draws a straight line between the Treasury bill rate r_f and the market return r_m. Given β_E, r_E can be read from the vertical axis.

The CAPM states that investors will (or can easily) hold well-diversified portfolios. As a result, they demand a risk premium based not on the total risk or variance of an asset but only on that asset's contribution to the variance of the return on a well-diversified portfolio. The statistical measure of this contribution is the covariance of the stock's return with the portfolio's, standardized by the variance of the market return. This measure is *beta*. The beta of the market portfolio itself is one. An asset that has average risk has a beta of one.

Q: What kinds of risks does beta measure?

A: Beta is a summary statistic for the macro risks affecting a company or project, including uncertainty about aggregate industrial production, international competitiveness, inflation, energy costs, interest rates, and foreign exchange rates. Micro risks peculiar to a company and project are not included in beta because they wash out in diversified portfolios.

Managers worry about both micro and macro risks, but only the latter affect the cost of capital.

Many projects that appear to be extremely risky do not have an unusually high opportunity cost of capital. For example, a wildcat oil well is naturally regarded as riskier than a development well. The wildcat's geological and technical uncertainties fade away, however, when that one venture is held in a diversified portfolio with hundreds or thousands of other assets.

The wildcat well also faces macro risks, for example, uncertainty about future oil prices. Changes in oil prices affect the entire economy. Even diversified investors cannot escape. Of course, this risk affects development wells, too.

Q: Suppose wildcats end up with the same cost of capital as development wells. Will they also have the same discounted present value?

A: No, because forecasted cash flows will differ. If successes in the wildcat and development ventures generate the same revenues, then

213

the *expected* cash flows to the wildcat are lower because the probability of actually finding oil is less.

To repeat, managers and investors must recognize both macro and micro risks in forecasting future cash ventures. But only the macro risks affect the discount rate.

Take one further example. Pharmaceutical R&D is generally regarded as extremely risky because of the technical, clinical, and regulatory hurdles facing any new drug. Thousands of compounds may have to be investigated to obtain one successful drug. The most obvious risks facing pharmaceutical R&D are "micro," however. They must be recognized in cash flow forecasts but do not require a higher cost of capital. We shall discuss in a subsequent section the real reasons why pharmaceutical R&D faces a higher-than-average cost of capital.

Q: Do we identify the relevant macro risks and work out each one's impact on the cost of capital?

A: That is rarely practical. Instead, we appeal to the CAPM, which takes fluctuations in the market portfolio as a proxy for all the macro risks relevant to investors. Beta gives the contribution of an asset or security to the risks of the market portfolio.

Q: How is the CAPM applied?

A: Suppose that the market portfolio has an expected rate of return that is 8 percent greater than the risk-free rate and that a stock has a beta of 1.5. The risk premium to be added to the risk-free rate would be 1.5 times 8, or 12 percent. If the Treasury rate is 9 percent,

$$r_E = 9 + 1.5 \, (8) = 21\%.$$

Betas are typically estimated by regressing excess rates of return for individual stocks on excess returns for the overall market. Excess returns are the differences between experienced returns (including capital gains and losses as well as dividends) and the return on Treasury bills. Five years of monthly rates of return are generally used.[4] The market is defined by a broadly based index. A number of organizations produce beta estimates. Merrill Lynch's *Security Risk Evaluation,* for example, has published betas monthly since the early 1970s. Our betas are based on ordinary least squares regressions of firms' monthly excess returns against excess returns on the S&P 500 Composite Index.

We use the CAPM in the empirical section of our study not be-

---

4. Daily or weekly rates of return are also used, particularly when year-to-year changes in beta are expected. In this exercise betas seem to be reasonably stable.

cause it is truth—it has both theoretical and empirical weaknesses—but because it reflects the main ideas of modern valuation theory, it is widely used, it seems to generate sensible discount rates, and other models are extremely difficult to implement in practice.[5] The following CAPM-based empirical analysis expresses good current practice, and we believe that it generates cost-of-capital estimates in the same ballpark as those corporate financial managers actually use.

Costs of Capital for Major Pharmaceutical Companies

We now present estimates of company costs of capital for major U.S. pharmaceutical companies. We give estimates for the beginning of 1980, 1985, and 1990.

Before discussing bottom-line estimates, we present a step-by-step summary of sample selection and measurement assumptions and procedures.

Step-by-Step Summary of Sample Selection and Measurement Procedures.

Sample selection. We obtained a list of firms in the pharmaceutical industry from Value Line for the start of years 1980, 1985, and 1990. We screened each list for data availability for five prior years from Compustat and the Center for Research in Security Prices (CRSP). Those screens yielded a sample consisting largely of major pharmaceutical firms. A few newer and smaller firms were present, particularly in 1989. A $250 million lower limit on the market value of equity produced a set of firms that, with a few exceptions, were available for all three periods. We base our analysis on that set of firms.[6]

Betas. We estimated equity betas by regressing excess returns against excess returns on Standard and Poor's 500 Composite Index for sixty months ending in December 1979, December 1984, and December 1989, respectively. We report the estimates for the period ending December 1989 in table 10–1. The second column of that table gives the standard error of the beta estimates.

---

5. The arbitrage pricing model (APT) is often cited as a competitor. However, reliable estimates of the factors and factor-risk premiums required to implement the APT are not publicly available.

6. Although data for A. H. Robins were available from 1984 through 1988, we excluded that firm because it filed for Chapter 11 bankruptcy in 1985. After bankruptcy, debt takes on the properties of equity, and common shares no longer measure the value of the company as a going concern. The company had an extremely large off-balance-sheet liability as defendant in the Dalkon Shield litigation.

TABLE 10–1
ESTIMATES OF COMMON STOCK BETAS AND NOMINAL EXPECTED RETURNS ON
EQUITY FOR MAJOR PHARMACEUTICAL COMPANIES, JANUARY 1990

Firm	β_E	Standard Error	r_E
Abbott Laboratories	1.01	.13	15.6
American Home Products	.89	.11	14.6
Bristol-Myers[a]	.81	.10	13.9
Johnson & Johnson	.93	.11	14.9
Eli Lilly and Co.	1.24	.12	17.6
Merck & Co., Inc.	.85	.12	14.2
Pfizer Inc.	1.02	.14	15.7
Rorer Group	1.18	.23	17.1
Schering-Plough	.84	.11	14.1
SmithKline Beecham	.93	.16	14.9
Squibb[a]	1.18	.20	17.1
Syntex Corp.	1.41	.15	19.1
Upjohn Company	1.19	.18	17.2
Warner-Lambert	1.05	.13	16.0
Equally weighted average	1.04		15.9
Market-value-weighted industry portfolio	0.98		15.4

NOTE: β_E is obtained by regressing the excess returns on each stock against excess returns on the S&P 500 market index over sixty months ending December 1989. The expected return on equity, r_E, is $r_E = r_f + \beta(r_m - r_f) = 8.02 - 1.21 + \beta_E (8.73)$. The risk-free rate is estimated by subtracting a historical term premium from the twenty-year Treasury bond yield.
a. Bristol-Myers and Squibb merged on October 4, 1989. They are treated here as separate companies until that date.
SOURCE: Figures for the Treasury bond yield are from Moody's *Government and Public Finance Manual* and figures for the term and risk premiums are from Ibbotson Associates, *Stocks, Bonds, Bills and Inflation: 1990 Yearbook*, exhibit 22.

Cost of equity capital. We use those betas to estimate the cost of capital using the CAPM equation,

$$r_E = r_f + \beta(r_m - r_f).$$

The CAPM is a one-period model, so r_f should be interpreted as a short-term Treasury bill rate. We want a discount rate for R&D investments that may span more than a decade, however. We should use a forecast of Treasury bill rates over the relevant period. We based this forecast on the average yield on twenty-year Treasury bond rates quoted for December 1989 in Moody's *Government and Public Finance*

Manual. Since long-term governments have on average yielded 1.2 percent per year more than Treasury bills, we subtracted this term premium from the twenty-year rate.

The risk premium, $r_m - r_f$, is a historical average of the excess of the market return over the Treasury bill rate. The arithmetic mean was 8.7 percent over the period 1926 to 1989.[7]

For example, the cost of equity capital for Abbott Laboratories was:

$$r_E = (8.0 - 1.2) + 1.01(8.7)$$
$$= 15.6 \text{ percent.}$$

The cost-of-equity-capital estimates appear in column (3) of table 10–1.

The weighted average cost of capital. The weighted average cost of capital requires market-value debt ratios and costs of debt capital. We defined the debt ratio as the ratio of long-term debt, capitalized leases, and preferred stock to the value of the firm. We defined the value of the firm as the book value of those liabilities plus the market value of equity. We obtained all figures from the Compustat tapes as averages over the period December 1985 to December 1989. We report the debt ratios in column (3) of table 10–2.

Most companies in our sample are consistently profitable. We assumed that they will pay taxes at the full marginal rate. At the start of 1990, this was $T_c = .34$.[8]

We based costs of debt capital on bond ratings for each of the firms collected from Moody's *Industrial Manuals.* We also collected average yields to maturity in December for each rating from Moody's. If a rating was not available, we assigned a AAA rating if the firm was large and had a low debt ratio. Otherwise, we assigned a AA rating. We assumed that preferred stock and leases have the same costs as debt capital. We report the cost of debt, r_D, in column (1) of table 10–2.

---

7. The term premium (the excess of long-term Treasury rates over short-term rates) and risk premium are given in *Stocks, Bonds, Bills and Inflation, 1990 Yearbook,* exhibit 22. The extreme volatility of the stock and bond markets makes long measurement periods essential. Estimates based on postwar data would also be acceptable, however. Risk and term premiums for 1947 through 1988 are 8.3 percent and −.15 percent, respectively. We believe that the latter figure is unreasonable and have used the longer-term average here.

Average real returns implied by those risk premiums match up fairly well with long-run average rates of return from the National Income and Product Accounts for the nonfinancial corporate sector. See Holland and Myers (1984).

8. Some companies adjust T_c by, say, two percentage points to account for state income taxes. We did not have sufficient information for this refinement.

TABLE 10–2

ESTIMATES OF RATES OF RETURN ON EQUITY, DEBT, AND WEIGHTED AVERAGE
COST OF CAPITAL FOR MAJOR PHARMACEUTICAL COMPANIES, JANUARY 1990

Firm	r_D	r_E	D/V	r^*
Abbott Laboratories	9.1	15.6	.03	15.3
American Home Products	9.1	14.6	.05	14.2
Bristol-Myers	8.9	13.9	.01	13.8
Johnson & Johnson	8.9	14.9	.05	14.5
Eli Lilly and Co.	8.9	17.6	.03	17.3
Merck & Co., Inc.	8.9	14.2	.01	14.2
Pfizer Inc.	9.1	15.7	.03	15.4
Rorer Group	9.9	17.1	.31	13.8
Schering-Plough	9.1	14.1	.04	13.8
SmithKline Beecham	9.4	14.9	.06	14.4
Squibb	9.1	17.1	.03	16.8
Syntex Corp.	9.1	19.1	.04	18.6
Upjohn Company	9.1	17.2	.07	16.5
Warner-Lambert	9.1	16.0	.07	15.3
Averages (nominal)				
Equally weighted	9.1	15.9	.06	15.3
Market-value-weighted				
industry portfolio	9.1	15.4	.04	15.1
Averages (real)				
Equally weighted	4.1	10.9	.06	10.3
Market-value weighted				
industry portfolio	4.1	10.4	.04	10.2

NOTE: r_D is the average nominal yield quoted in Moody's *Industrial Manuals* for corporate bonds of the appropriate rating class. If a bond rating is not available, then a rating of AAA has been assigned for large firms with low debt ratios; otherwise a rating of AA has been assigned. r_E is the nominal expected rate of return on equity (from table 10–1). D/V is the debt ratio defined as long-term debt, preferred stock, and capitalized leases, divided by the value of the firm. Firm value equals the market value of the firm's equity plus the book value of other liabilities. r^* is the weighted average cost of capital given by $r_E = r_D(1 - T_c)D/V + r_E(1 - D/V)$, where T_c, the marginal corporate tax rate, is .34. An expected rate of inflation of 5 percent has been assumed.

For example, the weighted average cost of capital for Abbott Laboratories was:

$$r^* = r_D(1 - T_c)D/V + r_E(1 - D/V)$$
$$= 9.11(1 - .34).03 + 15.63(1 - .03)$$
$$= 15.3\%.$$

We show the weighted average costs of capital for each of the firms in the 1985 through 1989 sample in column (4) of table 10–2.

These figures are point estimates of the discount rates for investments that those companies would see as average risk. The estimates are largely based on historical data, but they are not retrospective. We used historical evidence to infer investors' expectations at the start of 1990.

Real rates of return. The estimates discussed above are nominal. We obtained a real or inflation-adjusted rate of return by subtracting a contemporary expected rate of inflation. We assumed a figure of 5 percent for 1990. For 1985 and 1980, survey data on expected rates of inflation for ten-year horizons were available.[9] The forecast we used for January 1980 was an average of 6.75 percent (as of June 1979) and 8.61 percent (as of July 1980). This produces an estimate of 7.71 percent for the start of 1980. We used an average of 5.61 percent (December 1984) and 5.23 percent (January 1985) for 1985, which gives us an estimate of 5.4 percent.

We show real weighted average costs of capital in tables 10–2 and 10–3. The average weighted average cost of capital is 15 percent in nominal terms and about 10 percent in real terms at the start of 1990.

Discussion. Table 10–1 shows that the mean equity beta for the period 1984 to 1989 is 1. A beta of one means average risk.[10] A firm's equity beta reflects both business and financial risk, however. As shown in table 10–2, debt ratios for the firms in our sample are extraordinarily low (.06 on average), much lower than for manufacturing firms generally. The financial risk of those firms' equity is therefore significantly *lower* than average. Since the equity betas are average, the pure *business risk* for those pharmaceutical firms is *higher* than average.

The equity betas are well behaved. There are no unusual differences over time or within the samples. The cross-sectional variation in the sample is not large, and there is no significant relationship of estimated betas with firm size. As we show in table 10–3, value-weighted estimates of the equity beta are not appreciably different from equally weighted averages in any of the three periods. Average equity betas during the period 1980 to 1984 appear to be lower than those for the other two periods, however.

---

9. The source for these rates of expected inflation is Hory and Hotchkiss (1985).

10. Financial risk is the extra risk imposed on shareholders by debt financing. Since debt is a senior claim, the risk of the residual claim, equity, increases with the debt-to-equity ratio.

TABLE 10–3
ESTIMATES OF COSTS OF CAPITAL FOR START-OF-YEAR 1980, 1985, AND 1990 FOR MAJOR PHARMACEUTICAL COMPANIES

Firm	1980			1985			1990		
	β_E	r_E	r^*	β_E	r_E	r^*	β_E	r_E	r^*
Abbott Laboratories	.98	17.9	16.6	.81	17.7	17.0	1.01	15.6	15.3
American Home Prod.	.89	17.1	17.2	.44	14.6	14.6	.89	14.6	14.2
Bristol-Myers	1.27	20.5	19.8	.71	16.9	16.6	.81	13.9	13.8
Johnson & Johnson	.97	17.9	17.7	.71	16.9	16.7	.93	14.9	14.5
Eli Lilly and Co.	.96	17.8	17.8	.62	16.1	16.0	1.24	17.9	17.3
Merck & Co., Inc.	1.02	18.3	17.9	.47	14.9	14.6	.85	14.2	14.2
Pfizer Inc.	.90	17.3	15.4	.71	16.9	15.9	1.02	15.7	15.4
Rorer Group	.90	17.3	17.2	.56	15.6	15.2	1.18	17.1	13.8
Schering-Plough	1.11	19.1	19.0	.51	15.2	14.5	.84	14.1	13.8
SmithKline Beecham	.71	15.6	15.1	.56	15.6	15.4	.93	14.9	14.4
Squibb	1.23	20.1	17.5	.65	16.4	15.1	1.18	17.1	16.8
Syntex Corp.	1.22	20.0	19.1	1.06	19.8	18.8	1.41	19.1	18.6

Upjohn Company	.72	15.7	14.5	1.00	19.3	16.9	1.19	17.2	16.5
Warner-Lambert	1.15	19.4	17.7	.89	18.4	15.8	1.05	16.0	15.3
Sterling Drug	.76	16.1	15.6	.43	14.5	14.2	—	—	—
A. H. Robins	.87	17.0	16.4	.85	18.0	17.2	—	—	—
Searle	—	—	—	.87	18.2	17.3	—	—	—
Averages (Nominal)									
Equally weighted	.98	17.9	17.2	.70	16.7	16.1	1.04	15.9	15.3
Value weighted	.97	18.0	17.2	.66	16.4	16.1	.98	15.4	15.1
Industry portfolios									
Standard error	(.14)			(.09)			(.07)		
Averages (Real)									
Equally weighted	.98	10.3	9.7	.70	11.3	10.8	1.04	10.9	10.3
Value weighted	.97	10.3	9.9	.66	10.9	10.7	.98	10.4	10.2

NOTE: β_E, r_E, and r^* are derived as described in tables 10–1 and 10–2. The marginal corporate tax rate for 1980 and 1984 is $T_c = .46$. Expected rates of inflation are 7.7 percent for 1979 and 5.4 percent for 1984. These are obtained from Hory and Hotchkiss (1985). Figures for 1989 are from table 10–2.

Average ratios of long-term debt to capital are about the same in the three periods we examined. The ratio of R&D to sales is higher in the last period. We do not report those statistics firm-by-firm in table 10–3, but we give averages.

	1975–1979	1980–1984	1985–1989
Simple averages			
debt to value	.06	.07	.06
R&D to sales	.05	.07	.11
Value-weighted averages[11]			
debt to value	.04	.04	.04
R&D to sales	.06	.07	.12

The total estimate of the real weighted average cost of capital is 9.9 percent in January 1980, 10.7 percent in January 1985, and 10 percent in January 1990. Those are market-value-weighted averages across the sample. In table 10–3 we show that equally weighted averages are almost identical.

Gross and Net Debt Ratios. Many pharmaceutical companies have large sums invested in marketable securities. Some are net lenders rather than net borrowers.

We have defined the debt ratio as the ratio of *long-term* debt to the total market value of debt and equity. The implied market-value balance sheet is

Net working capital	Long-term debt
Assets	Equity
Firm value	Firm value

Net working capital normally includes some cash and marketable securities. Cash is needed to support operations, and most companies find it prudent to hold marketable securities in anticipation of future outlays, or as a reserve to affect the ups and downs of their business. But when marketable securities persistently exceed those requirements, the firm ends up partly in the business of lending money.

Thus, a company with the following balance sheet really has *negative* net debt of $10 - 15 = -5$. In other words, it is a net lender.

---

11. Debt ratios were weighted by total market value of debt and equity. R&D to sales rates were weighted by sales.

Net working capital:			
"Excess" marketable securities	15	Long-term debt	10
Other	10		
Assets	75	Equity	90
Market value of firm	100	Market value of firm	100

In this situation calculating r^*, the weighted average cost of capital, at a debt ratio of $D/V = 10/100$ would *understate* the proper hurdle rate for investments in the company's regular business. The resulting r^* would be correct for investment in a *blend* of the (relatively safe) marketable securities and (risky) business. Investment in the business alone, rather than in the blend, would face higher risk and require a higher discount rate.

As table 10–4 shows, many pharmaceutical companies do have

TABLE 10–4

ESTIMATES OF COST OF CAPITAL FOR MAJOR PHARMACEUTICAL COMPANIES USING NET DEBT MEASURES, JANUARY 1990

Firm	r_D	r_E	Long-Term Debt Ratio	Cash and Marketable Securities Ratio	Net Debt Ratio	r^*
Abbott Laboratories	9.1	15.6	.03	.04	−.01	15.8
American Home Products	9.1	14.6	.05	.09	−.04	15.1
Bristol-Myers	8.9	13.9	.01	.15	−.14	15.1
Johnson & Johnson	8.9	14.9	.05	.06	−.01	15.0
Eli Lilly and Co.	8.9	17.6	.03	.06	−.03	18.1
Merck & Co., Inc.	8.9	14.2	.01	.06	−.05	14.7
Pfizer Inc.	9.1	15.7	.03	.09	−.06	16.4
Rorer Group	9.9	17.1	.31	.06	.27	14.4
Schering-Plough	9.1	14.1	.04	.16	−.12	15.2
SmithKline Beecham	9.4	14.9	.06	.10	−.04	15.3
Squibb	9.1	17.1	.03	.12	−.09	18.3
Syntex Corp.	9.1	19.1	.04	.11	−.07	20.1
Upjohn Company	9.1	17.2	.07	.04	.03	16.9
Warner-Lambert	9.1	16.0	.07	.06	.02	15.9
Averages (nominal)						
Equally weighted	9.1	15.9	.06	.09	−.02	16.1
Market-value-weighted	9.1	15.4	.04	.08	−.04	15.9

negative net debt ratios. Therefore, the r^*s shown in figure 10–2 understate the appropriate hurdle rates for their regular businesses.

We can calculate the approximate magnitude of the understatement by recalculating weighted average costs of capital at a *net* debt ratio.[12] (In the numerical example, the debt and equity ratios would be $D/V = -5/85 = -.059$ and $E/V = 90/85 = 1.059$.) This increases some individual companies' costs of capital by as much as 1 percent. The market-value-weighted r^* increases from 15.1 percent to 15.9 percent in nominal terms.

Financing and the Weighted Average Cost of Capital. The debt ratios of most of our sample companies are usually low. This is true even if they are measured in gross, not net, terms. Therefore we pause to ask whether they might enjoy lower weighted average costs of capital if they moved to less conservative capital structures.

Figure 10–2 summarizes the standard view of optimal capital structure, the "static trade-off" theory. The horizontal baseline expresses Modigliani and Miller's idea that V, the market value of the firm—the aggregate market value of all its outstanding securities—should not depend on leverage when assets, earnings, and future investment opportunities are held constant. But the tax-deductibility of interest payments induces the firm to borrow to the margin where the present value of interest tax shields is just offset by the value loss due to agency costs of debt and the possibility of financial distress.

Costs of financial distress should be most serious for firms with valuable intangible assets and growth opportunities. We should observe that *mature* firms holding *tangible* assets should borrow more, other things constant, than growth firms or firms that depend heavily on R&D, advertising, or other intangible assets.[13] Thus, we would expect a pharmaceutical company to borrow less than a chemical manu-

---

12. This procedure may exaggerate the extent of understatement because it implicitly assigns a substantial tax disadvantage of lending to the project. We argue below that the tax advantages of borrowing are less than they seem. The corresponding tax disadvantages of lending are also less.

13. This predicted inverse relationship between (proxies for) intangible assets and financial leverage has been confirmed empirically by Long and Malitz (1985). Titman and Wessels (1988) find that debt ratios are negatively related to marketing and selling expenses and R&D expenses. Those expenses are obvious proxies for intangible assets, although Titman and Wessels interpret them as proxies for "uniqueness," following Titman (1984). Myers (1990) provides a survey and interpretation of the evidence on alternative theories of optimal capital structure.

FIGURE 10–2
STATIC TRADE-OFF THEORY OF OPTIMAL CAPITAL STRUCTURE

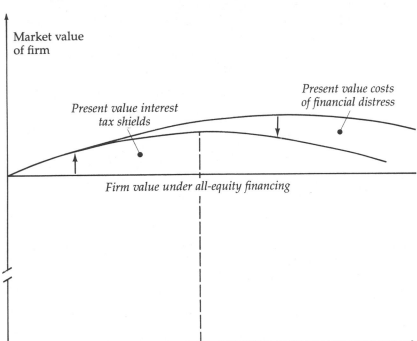

facturer, even if the two firms' business risks (measured by asset beta, for example) are the same.

Thus, the character of their assets, as well as their relatively high business risk, tends to explain the low debt ratios observed in the pharmaceutical industry. Yet, it is difficult to believe that those firms are at optimal positions in the trade-off shown in figure 10–2—most of them are so conservatively financed that the odds of a threat of financial distress seem remote.[14]

This leaves us with two possible explanations. One is that major pharmaceutical companies could increase value, and lower their company costs of capital, by taking on more debt and retiring equity. The other is that the standard static trade-off theory is a poor guide to ac-

---

14. A. H. Robins was forced into bankruptcy by product liability claims, so the risk of financial distress cannot be completely dismissed. The surviving firms' exceptionally low debt ratios and good debt ratings suggest, however, that they are still conservatively financed.

tual corporate behavior; better theories would reveal the companies' low debt ratios to be reasonable and efficient.

Suppose the first explanation is correct. How much could the cost of capital be reduced by moving from a 4 percent debt ratio (the average shown in table 10–2) to, say, 25 percent?

The following formula due to Miles and Ezell (1980) connects the company cost of capital to leverage:[15]

$$r^* = r - r_D T_C [(1+r)/(1+r_D)] \, D/V,$$

where r is the company cost of capital for an all-equity financed firm. Using value-weighted nominal numbers from table 10–2, we get

$$.151 = r - .091(.34)[(1+r)/(1.091)](.04),$$

which implies that $r = .152$ or 15.2 percent. At $D/V = .25$,

$$r^* = .152 - .091(.34)(1.152/1.091).25$$
$$= .144 \text{ or } 14.4\%,$$

.7 percent less than the comparable figure in table 10–2. This illustrates the static trade-off theory's implication that major pharmaceutical companies could reduce their general costs of capital by more aggressive borrowing. The reduction reflects the tax advantage of corporate borrowing.

Is a reduction of .7 percent economically significant? Probably not. In our experience, subtracting 1 percent, say, from the discount rate has little impact on project rankings or values. Moreover, the range of possible measurement error in our—or any—estimate of the cost of capital is more than plus or minus 1 percent.

Moreover, we question the empirical relevance of the static trade-off theory. It is not clear that taxes are a first-order determinant of optimal capital structure.

The difficulties with the theory are illustrated by the following evidence. *Within an industry,* the most profitable firms borrow less, and the least profitable borrow more. Kester (1986), in an extensive study of debt policy in U.S. and Japanese manufacturing corporations, finds that return on assets is the most significant explanatory variable for

---

15. This and other formulas are reviewed in Brealey and Myers (1988, chap. 19). All of the formulas incorporate strong simplifying assumptions. For example, the Miles-Ezell formula used here considers only corporate taxes, in particular the value of interest tax shields, and ignores the tax advantages to equity investors, that is, the privilege of deferring payment of capital gains taxes until shares are sold.

actual debt ratios. Baskin (1989) and Titman and Wessels (1988) report similar results. Baskin cites about a dozen other corroborating studies.

Thus, high profits mean low debt. Yet, the static trade-off theory would predict just the opposite relationship. Higher profits mean more dollars for debt service and more taxable income to shield. They should mean *higher* target debt ratios.

We cite this evidence not to dismiss the static trade-off theory or the tax advantages of borrowing, but to suggest caution before concluding that pharmaceutical firms are inefficiently financed. We do not view the tax-driven ratio trade-off theory as a reliable guide to corporate behavior.[16]

"Small"-Firm Sample for 1988. We also constructed a sample of smaller pharmaceutical firms for the period ending December 1988. Table 10–5 summarizes the betas and costs of capital for these firms. The equity betas are higher for this group, averaging 1.54 compared with 1.0 for the sample of major firms. The standard error of the beta estimates is also higher. A few firms' higher equity betas reflect high debt ratios and substantially greater financial risk, for example, ICN Pharmaceuticals. The debt ratios for most of the other firms, however, are comparable to the major firms' ratios. This suggests that the pure business risk of these firms is higher.

The weighted average cost of capital for the equally weighted portfolio is 19.1 percent in nominal terms compared with 16.0 percent for the major firms. The market-value weighted averages are 17.9 percent versus 15.9 percent.

The higher company costs of capital for those "small" firms may be due to differences in asset composition (for example, less cash and marketable securities), their investment portfolios (more "biotech"), and higher R&D intensity. While the ratio of R&D to sales has risen appreciably for the larger firms, to levels of 17 percent for Upjohn and 14 percent for Merck in 1988, this ratio is much higher for some of the firms in the "small" sample. For example, for Biogen the ratio is 346 percent. It is 26 percent for Cetus and 40 percent for Genentech.

There appear to be important differences in the characteristics of smaller, start-up or biotechnology firms compared with the larger, well-established pharmaceutical firms that lead to significantly higher company costs of capital for the smaller firms.

Summary of Company Cost of Capital Estimates. To sum up, our estimate of the weighted average cost of capital for major pharmaceutical

---

16. This is perhaps a minority position.

TABLE 10–5
ESTIMATES OF COST OF CAPITAL FOR "SMALL" PHARMACEUTICAL FIRMS,
JANUARY 1989

Firm	β_E	Standard Error	r_E	r_D	D/V	r^*
Scherer	1.08	.26	17.2	10.1	.35	13.7
Biogen	2.02	.36	25.2	10.7	.03	24.7
Cetus Corporation	1.70	.28	22.5	10.7	.11	20.7
Forest Laboratories	1.51	.28	20.9	10.7	.01	20.7
Genentech	1.51	.38	20.9	10.7	.04	20.3
ICN Pharmaceuticals	1.53	.33	21.0	11.0	.55	13.4
Mylan Laboratories	1.41	.29	20.0	10.7	.01	19.9
Portfolio returns (Nominal)						
Equally weighted	1.54		21.1	10.7	.16	19.1
Value weighted	1.54		21.1			17.9
Portfolio returns (Real)						
Equally weighted	1.54		16.1	5.7	.16	14.1
Value weighted	1.54		16.1			12.9

NOTE: Betas for Biogen and Mylan Laboratories are from *Security Risk Evaluation* (New York: Merrill Lynch, January 1989). All other figures were obtained as described in the notes to tables 10–1, 10–2, and 10–3. We assumed that Biogen, Cetus, Forest Laboratories, and Mylan Laboratories have the same cost of debt (r_D) as Genentech.

firms in January 1990 is 15.1 percent in nominal terms and 10.1 percent in real terms. The corresponding estimates for January 1980 and January 1985 are 17.2 percent and 9.9 percent and 16.1 percent and 10.7 percent, respectively. The changes over time reflect primarily variation in the risk-free rate of interest and expectations of inflation.

Cost of Capital Estimates in Prior Studies. Most prior studies of pharmaceutical R&D devote more space and analytical effort to measuring profitability than to estimating the cost of capital. For example, Clarkson (1979) estimates a real, after-tax opportunity cost of capital of 10 percent on the grounds that "this is the prescribed rate for U.S. government investment decisions on deferred cost and benefits." The derivation of that rate and its relevance to private investment decisions are unclear.

Baily (1972) compares internal rates of return of 35 percent in the 1950s and 25 percent in 1961 to an 18 percent–20 percent pretax required return for capital goods investment. Schwartzman (1975) employs a real after-tax rate of 10 percent, which he reports is a decision criterion other industries often use. Grabowski and Vernon (1982) *assume* alternative costs of capital ranging from 5 percent to 15 percent, with most of their discussion centered around 10 percent and 8 percent. In their study of the impact of the 1984 Drug Act (1986), they employ a discount rate of 10 percent. Virts and Weston (1980) use a discount rate of 8 percent, which they state is a reasonable estimate of the true value of money for the period 1963 to 1976.

The main difficulty with those studies' estimates of the cost of capital is not that they are numerically inappropriate, but that the numbers have either been arbitrarily assumed or employed without adequate justification. Although many of those authors recognize the positive relationship between risk and return, they do not attempt to determine a discount rate that quantifies this relationship.

Some other studies do, however, justify the numerical values employed. Brief comments on their methods follow.

Joglekar and Paterson (1986) take the opportunity cost of capital to be the yield on long-term corporate bonds, which they estimate as a nominal, pretax rate of 13 percent. With an assumed inflation rate of 6 percent and a tax rate of 34 percent, this is equivalent to a real after-tax rate of 2.3 percent. That figure clearly does not incorporate a risk premium appropriate for the pharmaceutical business. Corporate bonds are relatively safe investments whose yields do not fully reflect business risks. Overall weighted average costs of capital for the pharmaceutical industry are significantly higher than bond yields. From table 10–2, for example, the pretax bond return in January 1989 was 9.8 percent, corresponding to an after-tax real return of 3.2 percent at a 5 percent inflation and 34 percent tax rate. The real after-tax weighted average opportunity cost of capital was, by comparison, 11 percent.

Grabowski and Vernon (1989) base their estimate of the cost of capital on the CAPM, although they do not provide detailed information on their sample of firms or on how they estimated equity betas. The authors recognize that the measured equity betas reflect financial as well as business risk, but point out that since pharmaceuticals are overwhelmingly equity-financed (over 90 percent), the equity cost of capital is a good approximation to the weighted average cost of capital. There is similar lack of detail concerning procedures for estimating real risk-free interest rates.

Statman (1983) estimates a market-value-weighted average cost of capital based on the CAPM for a sample of twelve pharmaceutical firms for the years 1951 through 1977. His methods are essentially similar to ours and also to common practice. His estimate of the nominal weighted average cost of capital for 1977 is 14 percent. This compares with our 1980 figure of 17.2 percent. (Both figures incorporate the contemporary tax rate of 48 percent.)

Project versus Company Costs of Capital

As we stressed above, the opportunity cost of capital depends on the risk of the project under consideration, not on the risks of the firm's other assets or on the source of financing. There is no reason, in principle, why the company's average cost of capital should be used to discount any particular project's cash flows.

In practice, project-specific discount rates are rare. Sometimes different rates are set for classes of investment, for example, a lower rate for new cost-reducing equipment than for launching new projects. Sometimes the company takes the path of least resistance and writes its average cost of capital into its capital budgeting manual for all projects.

This does not mean that managers ignore differences in project risks. Higher returns are demanded of riskier projects, but the adjustments are judgmental and implicit. For example, managers may discount at the company cost of capital for an especially risky project, yet penalize the project for its risk by working with especially conservative cash flow forecasts.

None of that excuses us from considering the discount rates that should in principle apply to investment in pharmaceutical R&D. Those rates may be implicit in practice and not quantified here, but they are clearly higher than the benchmark rates given above.

Relative Risk of Pharmaceutical R&D. R&D is generally regarded as riskier than production and sale of existing products, especially so in pharmaceuticals where the incubation period is especially long and perhaps one in 10,000 compounds tried is an eventual commercial success. The variance of possible payoffs to any particular research project is extremely high.

High variance does not necessarily imply that *beta* is high, however. In fact, many of the uncertainties that drive intuition to regard R&D as especially risky do not contribute to beta. There *are* reasons to expect high betas for R&D, but they are *not* what intuition first suggests.

Macro and micro risks. Most of the risks that trouble a pharmaceutical manager or scientist are technical or regulatory and have nothing to do with the macroeconomic risks that move the stock market and therefore concern diversified investors. The micro or diversifiable risks—for example, the chance that a new drug will work without unacceptable side effects—should be recognized in cash flow forecasts but not the discount rate.

Technical risks tend to wash out across R&D projects. For example, the uncertainty of returns from an R&D *program*—a portfolio of projects—is less than the uncertainty surrounding individual R&D projects. Of course, the annual output of commercially successful drugs from any one company's program is still hard to predict. Almost all the remaining technical and firm-specific risks are washed out in *investors'* portfolios, however. An investor holding dozens or hundreds of securities, perhaps through a mutual fund or pension plan, does not demand a high expected rate of return because a particular drug may or may not work.

The implication at the project level is that investment in a drug with a one-in-ten chance of working is no less risky to investors than another facing odds of one in one hundred. Of course, the long-shot drug is worth only one tenth of the other, assuming the payoff to success is the same, because the payoff is multiplied by the probability of success in each case. But so long as the difference in the risk of failure depends only on technology and biology, the discount rate is exactly the same.

Amplification of risk in sequential investment. The real reason why R&D projects tend to be high-risk assets is quite different. It follows from the *sequential* nature of R&D. Every R&D program, even if it is sure to succeed, carries a future liability. The fruits of R&D do not come free and clear; additional funds are required for production capacity, start-up costs, inventories, and marketing. Those future outlays create a kind of leverage that increases the risk of—and the appropriate discount rate for—the net final value from a successful R&D program.

We can best introduce the argument with a simple example. Assume the payoff to a successful research project is an asset worth $PV = \$100$ million, representing the present value of future cash flows generated by an effective and approved drug. The drug is just beginning its commercial life cycle. The firm has just spent $40 million on required production capacity. At that point, the $40 million is a sunk cost. Just before that point the drug's NPV was $100 million − $40 million = $60 million. That was the payoff to the R&D program.

We suppose that production and sale of the drug have a beta of .75, reflecting less than average exposure to market and macroeconomic risks. A company formed to produce and sell the drug, with no further R&D, would have a common stock beta of .75. If the risk-free rate is 8 percent and the market risk premium also 8 percent, the opportunity cost of capital of such a company will be:

$$r = r_f + \beta(r_m - r_f) = 8 + .75(8) = 14\%.$$

Now back up one year (to year 0) and assume for the moment that the drug is sure to work and be introduced. The prospect is:

Year 0   Year 1

$\llcorner$—R&D Program——$\llcorner$——Commercial Production———$\longrightarrow$

Invest 40

PV = 100

NPV = +60

At year 0, the value of the drug when it is finally introduced is only a forecast. Its present value is found by discounting at one year at 14 percent.

$$PV = 100/1.14 = \$87.7 \text{ million.}$$

Suppose the $40 million investment is known ahead of time. We treat it as a fixed liability and discount at the 8 percent risk-free rate:

$$PV_{investment} = 40/1.08 = \$37 \text{ million.}$$

Thus, the net present value of the drug one year before commercialization is $87.7 million − $37 million = $50.7 million.

Notice that we have implicitly discounted the $60 million forecasted future NPV at about 18.4 percent:

$$50.7 = 60/1.184.$$

Betas before and after commercial production. The *net* payoff to R&D—viewed one year before commercialization—is a riskier asset than the ultimate value of the drug. In fact, the beta of the R&D project at time minus one is not .75 but about 1.3. The R&D project does hold a promised future asset with $\beta = .75$, but this asset is offset by a fixed liability—the $40 million required investment—with $\beta = 0$ and present value of $37 million.

The betas of the fixed liability and the net position must "add up":

$$\beta_{asset} \times PV_{asset} = \beta_{investment} \times PV_{investment} + \beta_{net} PV_{net}$$
$$.75 \times 87.7 = 0 \times 37 + \beta_{net} 50.7$$
$$\beta_{net} = 1.3$$

This explains the discount rate:

$$r = r_f + \beta_{net} (r_m - r_f)$$
$$= 8 + 1.3(8) = 18.4\%.$$

Thus, the R&D project is risky *not* because of worries about effectiveness or regulatory approval—the example treats commercialization as a sure thing—but because the R&D project faces a future liability, the additional investment required before the drug is produced and marketable.

The required investment acts as a debt claim. The "balance sheet" for the R&D project at year 0 is:

PV of cash flows from future commercial production	87.7	*PV* required for future investment	37
		NV	50.7
	87.7		87.7

The risk of the net value is higher than the risk of the underlying asset, the present value of cash flows from future commercial introduction. The discount rate for the residual *net* payoff to R&D is higher than the rate appropriate for the underlying asset, for the same reason that equity investors demand higher returns from leveraged firms, even when the risk of the firms' assets is held constant.

Technical and regulatory uncertainty. Of course, uncertainty about whether the drug will "make it" would reduce the present value of the R&D project. Suppose that there is only a one-in-ten chance that the drug will work and receive FDA approval:

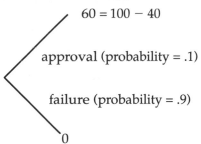

$$60 = 100 - 40$$

approval (probability = .1)

failure (probability = .9)

0

In this case, the project's net present value would fall to $5.1 million:

$$NPV = (.1 \times 60)/1.184 = \$5.1 \text{ million.}$$

The discount rate does not change, because the risk of failure is diversifiable.

R&D as a Call Option. We can easily formalize the simple example. Investing in pharmaceutical R&D is equivalent to purchasing a ticket

233

in a lottery on a call option. The ticket wins if the drug works and is approved. In that case the company decides whether to invest to produce. Thus, the payoff to winning the lottery is a call option, giving the firm the opportunity, but not obligation, to invest in production, marketing, and other costs necessary for commercial production.

In the numerical example, the call was so far in the money that exercise was taken as certain. If it is uncertain, the example's main point still holds: just as the beta of a call option always exceeds the beta of the security it is written on, the beta of an R&D program is greater than the risk of the assets the program is aiming to produce. The only critical (and generally reasonable) assumption is that the beta of the future investments necessary to produce those assets be less than the beta of the asset itself.

The analysis can be extended to R&D projects that, if successful, proceed through two or more stages, with investment at each stage. The analogy here is to compound lotteries and compound options. In general, as we back up from the time that a successful R&D project goes commercial, beta and the opportunity cost of capital increase. This is the sense in which sequential investment amplifies risk.

Other things equal, beta should be higher in the early research stages than in later development stages. Thus, it is no surprise to find high betas for "small" pharmaceutical companies, many of which have made massive investments in R&D but have few established products.

The betas we estimate for major pharmaceutical companies are weighted averages of their R&D betas and the betas of their established products. We cannot observe their R&D betas separately, but they are surely higher than the estimates presented in tables 10–1 and 10–3. Therefore, we must take the company costs of capital given at the bottom of table 10–3 as lower-bound estimates of the cost of capital for pharmaceutical R&D.

Estimates of the "true" cost of capital for pharmaceutical R&D would be helpful in calibrating the profitability of R&D programs. But such estimates would require a way to split pharmaceutical companies' market value between their R&D in process and their commercial products. There is no easy or accurate way to do this, and the effort is in any case beyond the scope of this study. Moreover, the usefulness of such estimates for decisions about R&D investment would be limited, for reasons we now explain.

Problems with DCF Analysis of R&D Projects. Discounted cash flow analysis is now standard practice for most capital investment decisions, yet it is rarely applied to investments in R&D. Managers are often heard to say that most R&D investments could not make the cut if forced to compete on DCF criteria in the usual capital budgeting process.

Discounted cash flow analysis does not work for R&D investments because they are (lotteries on) complex options. Discounted cash flow analysis was designed for assets that generate well-defined streams of symmetrically distributed cash flows. The usual (implicit) assumption of DCF is that detrended cash flows follow a geometric walk with constant drift and variance rate. The probability distribution of future cash flows is supposed to be lognormal.

The payoff distribution to an option is truncated and therefore not symmetrical. A call, for example, pays off only if the value of its underlying asset exceeds its exercise price; otherwise, the call is worth nothing. The call is a bet on the "upside" of the underlying asset's distribution; the "downside" below the exercise price is irrelevant. Thus, the call's payoff distribution is strongly skewed right.[17] The option pricing formulas necessary to value such distributions look nothing like standard DCF.

Option pricing methods could in principle value R&D investments properly, but we know of no serious applications. The options in R&D are extremely complex. They are also "fuzzy" and therefore difficult to describe with the definiteness required by the formulas.

Conclusion

In table 10–3 we show estimates of company costs of capital for major U.S. pharmaceutical companies at the start of 1980, 1985, and 1990. The estimates for 1990 are about 15 percent nominal and 10 percent real. We must take those figures as lower-bound estimates of the cost of capital for pharmaceutical R&D. The sequential investments required for R&D amplify its risk compared with the risk of producing and selling established drugs. The cost of capital for R&D is correspondingly higher.

Small pharmaceutical companies tend to be evaluated to a greater extent on the promise of their R&D than on the profitability of their established products. Thus, their betas and company costs of capital are higher than for our sample of major companies. The equally weighted average company cost of capital for the small firm sample at the start of 1989 is about 19 percent nominal and 14 percent real.

The risk and cost of capital of any particular R&D project will

---

17. The value of the call before exercise can still follow a random walk, but its mean and variance must change continuously as the value of the underlying asset changes.

depend on the stage of the project—how close it is to a commercial product—and on the amount, timing, and other characteristics of the investments required to achieve success. The scientific risks faced in a pharmaceutical R&D project reduce the odds of success—and therefore reduce the value of the project—but they do not directly contribute to its cost of capital.

R&D projects are extremely difficult to evaluate by discounted cash flow. R&D is best viewed as a series of scientific lotteries and commercial options, not as an asset generating a well-behaved stream of uncertain cash flows. Option valuation methods may in due course be used to evaluate R&D investments.

References

Baily, Martin N. "Research and Development Costs and Returns: The U.S. Pharmaceutical Industry." *Journal of Political Economy* 80 (1972): 70–85.

Baskin, Jonathan. "An Empirical Investigation of the Pecking Order Hypothesis." *Financial Management* 18 (1989): 26–35.

Brealey, R. A., and Stewart C. Myers. *Principles of Corporate Finance.* New York: McGraw-Hill, 1988.

Clarkson, Kenneth W. "The Use of Pharmaceutical Profitability Measures for Public Policy Actions." In *Issues in Pharmaceutical Economics,* edited by R. I. Chien. Lexington, Mass.: Lexington Books, 1979.

Grabowski, Henry G., and John M. Vernon. "Longer Patents for Lower Imitation Barriers: The 1984 Drug Act." *American Economic Review* 76 (1986): 195–98.

———. "A New Look at the Returns and Risks to Pharmaceutical R&D." Working paper, Duke University, 1989.

———. "A Sensitivity Analysis of Expected Profitability of Pharmaceutical Research and Development." *Managerial and Decision Economics* 3 (1982): 36–40.

Holland, Daniel M., and Stewart C. Myers. "Trends in Corporate Profitability and Capital Costs in the United States." In *Measuring Profitability and Capital Costs,* edited by D. M. Holland. Lexington, Mass.: Lexington Books, 1984.

Hory, R. B., and H. Hotchkiss. "Decision-Makers' Real Yield: A Key Decision Variable." Drexel Burnham Lambert, March 13, 1985.

Joglekar, P., and M. L. Paterson. "A Closer Look at the Returns and Risks of Pharmaceutical R&D." *Journal of Health Economics* (1986): 153–77.

Kester, W. Carl. "Capital and Ownership Structure: A Comparison of United States and Japanese Manufacturing Corporations." *Financial Management* 15 (1986): 5–16.

Long, Michael, and I. Malitz. "Investment Patterns and Financial Leverage." In *Corporate Capital Structure in the United States*, edited by B. Friedman. Chicago: University of Chicago Press, 1985.

Miles, James, and John Ezell. "The Weighted Average Cost of Capital, Perfect Capital Markets, and Project Life: A Clarification." *Journal of Financial and Quantitative Analysis* 15 (1980): 719–30.

Myers, Stewart C. "Still Searching for Optimal Capital Structure." In *Are the Distinctions between Debt and Equity Disappearing?* edited by R. W. Kopke and E. S. Rosengren. Boston: Federal Reserve Bank of Boston, 1990.

Schwartzman, David. "Pharmaceutical R&D Expenditures and Rates of Return." In *Drug Development and Marketing*, edited by Robert B. Helms. Washington, D.C.: AEI Press, 1975.

Statman, M. *Competition in the Pharmaceutical Industry*. Washington, D.C.: AEI Press, 1983.

Titman, S. "The Effect of Capital Structure on a Firm's Liquidation Decision." *Journal of Financial Economics* 13 (1984): 137–51.

———, and R. Wessels. "The Determinants of Capital Structure Choice." *Journal of Finance* 43 (1988): 1–19.

Virts, John R. and J. Frederick Weston. "Returns to Research and Development in the U.S. Pharmaceutical Industry." *Managerial and Decision Economics* 1 (1980): 103–11.

11

The Effects of Research and Promotion on Rates of Return

Kenneth W. Clarkson

For several decades rapidly rising prices have prompted increasingly careful inquiry into the relationships between prices and profits (U.S. Congress 1963, 3). The recent extensive investigation of the pharmaceutical industry by the Office of Technology Assessment, for example, illustrates the continuing concern about the effects of rising prices and profitability on invested capital (Office of Technology Assessment 1993). Because such investigations have occasionally prompted administrative or judicial action, or the passage of legislation altering the rules regulating economic activity in industries with high reported rates of return, it is important to understand the interrelations among investment in research and development, prices, and profitability.[1]

This study updates our knowledge of the relationships among intangible capital, rates of return, and investment.[2] In determining those relationships, we give special attention to the nature of the industry, especially the nature of the pharmaceutical industry (Office of Technol-

---

1. Some of the provisions of the Kefauver-Harris drug amendments of 1962 (Public Law 87–78), for example, resulted from the Senate's investigations of administered prices during the late 1950s and early 1960s. More recent examples include investigations of the oil and natural gas industry and the legislation empowering the Federal Energy Agency to regulate prices of petroleum products and crude oil. Activities by administrative agencies, based on views of the relationship between prices and profits and the meaning of various levels of profit, can be seen in the inquiries and associated decisions by U.S. antitrust agencies and the President's Council on Wage and Price Stability in the 1970s and by Great Britain's National Board for Prices and Incomes and its Monopolies Commission. There is, of course, significant variation in the rate of return among industries and over time when viewing traditional measures.

2. The results in this chapter update an earlier study (Clarkson 1977) that measured the relationship of profitability to invested capital (tangible and intangible) between 1959 and 1973.

ogy Assessment 1993, chap. 4),[3] the decision-making process, and the measurement of economic activities. Researchers have recognized the accounting rate of return in pharmaceutical firms as being abnormally biased, and a number of studies have singled out the industry for special attention (Office of Technology Assessment 1993, table 4.7). We single it out here also with a somewhat wider-than-usual cast of the net to capture the effects of intangible capital. First, we use accounting data from a pharmaceutical firm with intangible capital unrecognized on accounting statements to correct rate-of-return measurements. The analysis incorporates both R&D capital and marketing and promotion capital. Second, we examine the consequences of correcting rate-of-return measurements in other industries as well as in the pharmaceutical industry. Finally, we investigate the consequences of altering the accumulation and depreciation periods on the economic rate of return.

This study sets out to correct accounting rates of return to remove some of the differential effects of unrecorded intangible capital. Since the pharmaceutical industry has had persistently high accounting rates of return, the study examines a pharmaceutical firm, Merck & Company, in detail and removes as much bias from its accounting as possible by taking account of its outlays on R&D and on promotion. Without correcting for that source of bias, the average accounting return on book equity for Merck & Company is 27.5 percent over the 1980 through 1993 period. Correcting accounting income for the expensing of investment outlays and correcting equity for the omission of intangible assets purchased by outlays on research and on promotion result in a return of 14.3 percent on equity, a decrease of 13.2 percentage points. Despite Merck's decline in rate of return when we correct for outlays on intangible capital, it is still possible that the pharmaceutical industry would stay at its high standing among industries ranked by *corrected* rates of return. Firms in other industries might also show a decline in return on equity if their research and promotion outlays were appropriately capitalized and depreciated, and thus would remain in lower ranks. The pharmaceutical industry is our most research-intensive industry, however. One would expect it to show a greater decline in correct rate of return from accounting return than other industries.

This study recomputes return on equity in fourteen industries for which data are available. The average 1980 through 1993 corrected return on equity in pharmaceuticals drops by 9.2 percentage points from

---

3. An earlier review of much of this literature may be found in Comanor (1986).

the accounting return. The high profitability of the pharmaceutical industry turns out to be, in large part, an accounting illusion.

Our findings suggest that existing measures of profitability are significantly and differentially biased. Applying appropriate corrections to conventional accounting rates of return substantially affects the measured rate of return and the relative rates of return among industries. Those findings indicate that even minor adjustments made to eliminate biases resulting from expensing advertising and research expenditures produce marked changes in measured rates of return in some industries.

Since those adjustments are consistent with economic theory and reflect determinants of managerial choices, corrected returns rather than unadjusted accounting returns are appropriate for public inquiries. Furthermore, since applying those corrections decreases major differentials among the returns of firms and industries, it is evident that congressional hearings and the economics literature have overemphasized the monopoly explanation of firm behavior. We should give more attention to obtaining economically sound measurements of profit rates in each firm and industry. At this point—on the basis of the information assembled here—it seems likely that the traditional reasons given for differences in rates of return among industries where prices and entry are not regulated (entry barriers and concentration) do not produce major differentials in rate of return. Observed differences in profitability for the most part seem to be the consequence of systematic (and correctable) measurement errors.

Pharmaceutical Manufacturing

Using the appropriate price level adjustments, capital outlay levels, and capital accumulation and depreciation periods is relatively straightforward once the data are in hand. Unfortunately, except for price-level adjustments, the data are elusive; conventional accounting procedures do not make it possible for us to identify all of the transactions that should be included as capital outlays, nor do they make it possible for us to determine accumulation and depreciation periods.

In the pharmaceutical industry only a fraction of capital outlays incurred for manufacturing plants (and some other capital outlays) is capitalized and depreciated. For some firms, capital invested in manufacturing plants may represent less than 50 percent of the true economic capital of the firm (table 11–1). First, advertising and other promotion activities are chosen partly according to their ability to augment revenues over long periods of time. Various studies indicate that the economic life of advertising capital ranges from less than one year

TABLE 11–1
ANNUAL PHYSICAL AND INTANGIBLE CAPITAL EXPENDITURES IN THE
PHARMACEUTICAL PREPARATIONS INDUSTRY, 1962–1987
($ millions)

Year	New Plant and New Equipment	R&D	Advertising
1962	71.5	259.0	126.9
1967	169.6	461.0	215.1
1972	166.7	726.0	272.0
1977	419.3	1,276.0	714.6
1982	861.2	2,774.0	2,339.5
1987	1,471.1	5,376.0	3,345.4

NOTE: Standard industrial classification (SIC) 2834. Figures include research and development outlays for veterinary pharmaceutical research. Advertising data for 1977 and 1987 are calculated from SIC 28 data.
SOURCE: U.S. Department of Commerce, *Census of Manufactures* (Washington, D.C.: U.S. Government Printing Office, various dates); Pharmaceutical Manufacturers Association, *Annual Survey Reports* (Washington, D.C.: various dates); and Bureau of the Census, *Statistical Abstract of the United States* (Washington, D.C.: U.S. Government Printing Office, various dates).

in one industry to more than ten years in some (Peles 1971; Palda 1965; Telser 1962; Borden 1952, 105, 135, 137, 140; Hollander 1949; Vidale and Wolfe 1957; Tull 1956; Nerlove and Waugh 1961), depending on such factors as the media used, the scope and clarity of the information, the nature of the product, and the life of the product itself.

In the pharmaceutical industry, where new products are patentable and do not become obsolete or reach a commodity status for ten to twenty years, advertising and other promotional activities would be directed toward long-term effects. It is also likely that information received through direct personal interaction has a more durable effect and correspondingly longer economic life than information received through print or broadcast promotion. The pharmaceutical industry channels the majority of its promotion expenditures into direct personal interaction. The lower bound on the economic life of pharmaceutical advertising and promotion activities is, therefore, likely to be at least two to three years. At the same time, the impact of promotion and marketing is likely to be greatest during the first year and to diminish thereafter. The depreciation periods for advertising and promotion expenditures for a typical pharmaceutical manufacturing enterprise will thus be (conservatively) set at 70 percent for the first year, 21 percent (70 percent of the remaining balance of 30) in the second year, and 9 percent in the third year.

241

More important, pharmaceutical enterprises allocate large expenditures for research on and development of new products. Those expenditures produce no revenues for some years. Then, if successful, they provide revenues over the remainder of the product's life cycle. A small amount of each research dollar is allocated for basic research with no immediate commercial application. Most pharmaceutical firms allocate basic research budgets to investigations covering broad therapeutic areas, to the synthesis of naturally occurring pharmacologically active compounds, and to related investigations of compounds. The remainder of the funds allocated to general research activities are more specifically directed to development of products which, it is hoped, will become marketable. The preliminary testing, the evaluation, the additional testing to meet FDA regulations, and other related activities are included in this development stage. Once a compound becomes a commercial product, research activity on that compound does not cease automatically. Additional research activities continue during the remainder of the compound's economic life, including (but not limited to) the introduction of improved manufacturing procedures, new quality control, and the identification of new uses, new dosages, and the effects and interactions with other drugs. Estimates of the average life cycle of a pharmaceutical product, including R&D time, range from twenty to thirty years (Grabowski and Vernon 1995; Clymer 1970). A representative life cycle for research expenditures, displayed in figure 11–1, shows basic research accumulating for ten to twelve years and development for five to seven years before the compound is marketed. Since most compounds can be patented, and the remaining patent life after a compound reaches the market is usually ten to twelve years (Schwartzman 1976, chap. 9),[4] the total life cycle can be approximately twenty to thirty years. In our initial corrections for the pharmaceutical enterprise's research expenditures, we shall choose a minimum twenty-one-year life for basic research and eleven-year economic life for development. We assume that basic research expenditures accumulate for eleven years and that development expenditures accumulate for the last eight of the eleven years before the compound is marketed.[5] When data are not available for basic research, we assume that expenditures for basic research are 9.6 percent of total research expenditures.

Table 11–2 gives the current dollar sales, current operating ex-

---

4. If a product does not become obsolete before its patent expires, it may continue to contribute a modest return to research and development investment.

5. Recent experience with the 1962 drug amendments indicates that the period of accumulation should be longer. See, for example, the summary of DiMasi, Hansen, Grabowski, and Lasagna (1991).

FIGURE 11-1
ECONOMIC LIFE CYCLE FOR RESEARCH AND DEVELOPMENT EXPENDITURES

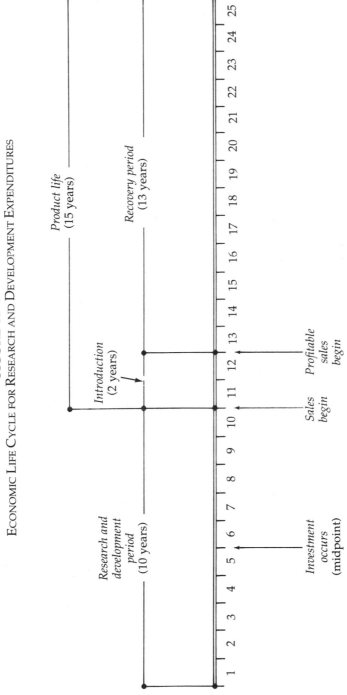

SOURCE: Vernon A. Mund, "The Return on Investment of the Innovative Pharmaceutical Firm." In *The Economics of Drug Innovation*, edited by Joseph Cooper (Washington, D.C.: American University, 1970), p. 131.

TABLE 11–2
Rate-of-Return Accounting Input Data for Merck & Company, Inc.
(current $ millions)

Year	Sales	Cost of Sales	Depreciation	Research Development	Promotion Marketing[a]	Income Tax	Net Income	Total Assets	Equity	ROR on Assets	ROR on Equity
1965	457.35	329.15	16.48	35.77	16.92	57.07	71.13	404.87	297.97	17.57%	23.87%
1966	542.93	381.31	18.37	43.24	20.09	75.11	86.51	440.74	328.50	19.63%	26.34%
1967	590.48	419.60	21.37	49.44	21.85	77.31	93.57	483.66	369.53	19.35%	25.32%
1968	611.22	419.24	23.66	56.35	22.61	94.73	97.24	521.09	402.27	18.66%	24.17%
1969	691.45	475.54	23.97	61.10	25.58	109.27	106.65	601.48	451.03	17.73%	23.64%
1970	761.11	534.40	27.82	69.71	28.16	108.83	117.88	664.29	493.21	17.74%	23.90%
1971	832.42	582.34	31.09	71.62	30.80	118.70	131.38	736.50	542.98	17.84%	24.20%
1972	942.60	670.36	35.20	79.69	34.88	121.04	151.20	834.80	621.79	18.11%	24.32%
1973	1,104.00	787.25	39.50	89.10	40.85	134.05	182.70	988.99	709.61	18.47%	25.75%
1974	1,260.40	900.60	45.10	101.00	46.63	149.30	210.50	1,243.30	822.78	16.93%	25.58%
1975	1,402.00	1,025.50	51.10	121.93	51.87	147.70	228.80	1,539.00	950.00	14.87%	24.08%
1976	1,561.12	1,146.52	57.00	133.83	57.76	159.10	255.50	1,759.40	1,102.20	14.52%	23.18%

244

Year										
1977	1,724.40	1,273.60	65.80	144.30	63.80	173.30	277.50	1,993.40	1,260.20	13.92%	22.02%
1978	1,981.40	1,475.80	74.50	161.40	73.31	198.10	307.50	2,251.40	1,455.10	13.66%	21.13%
1979	2,384.60	1,778.30	80.60	188.10	88.23	224.50	381.80	2,649.10	1,645.00	14.41%	23.21%
1980	2,734.00	2,080.50	91.30	233.30	101.16	238.10	415.40	2,907.70	1,841.00	14.29%	22.56%
1981	2,929.50	2,343.60	105.00	274.20	108.39	187.60	398.30	3,317.20	1,978.20	12.01%	20.13%
1982	3,063.00	2,462.10	121.10	320.20	113.33	185.80	415.10	3,655.40	2,180.20	11.36%	19.04%
1983	3,246.10	2,550.10	135.20	356.00	120.11	245.10	450.90	4,214.70	2,409.90	10.70%	18.71%
1984	3,559.70	2,772.90	151.60	393.10	131.71	293.80	493.00	4,590.60	2,518.60	10.74%	19.57%
1985	3,547.50	2,690.50	163.60	426.30	131.26	317.10	539.90	4,902.20	2,607.70	11.01%	20.70%
1986	4,128.90	3,055.60	167.20	479.80	152.77	397.60	675.70	5,105.20	2,541.20	13.24%	26.59%
1987	5,061.30	3,656.10	188.50	565.70	187.27	498.80	906.40	5,680.00	2,116.70	15.96%	42.82%
1988	5,939.50	4,068.50	189.00	668.80	219.76	664.20	1,206.80	6,127.50	2,855.80	19.69%	42.26%
1989	6,550.50	4,267.50	206.40	750.50	242.37	787.60	1,495.40	6,756.70	3,520.60	22.13%	42.48%
1990	7,671.50	5,211.30	254.00	854.00	283.85	679.00	1,781.20	8,029.80	3,834.40	22.18%	46.45%
1991	8,602.70	5,649.30	263.80	987.80	318.30	831.70	2,121.70	9,498.50	4,919.20	22.34%	43.13%
1992	9,662.50	6,634.50	303.60	1,111.60	357.51	1,043.80	1,984.20	11,086.00	5,002.90	17.90%	39.66%
1993	10,498.20	6,901.60	386.50	1,172.80	388.43	1,430.40	2,166.20	19,927.50	10,021.70	10.87%	21.62%

NOTE: Fiscal year ends December 31.
a. Estimated by using industry averages.

penses (including depreciation on plant and equipment), capital outlays (including promotion, other marketing, and R&D), income taxes, uncorrected profits, equity, and total assets for a pharmaceutical manufacturing enterprise for the years 1965 through 1993.[6] This table also shows the accounting rate of return on total assets and equity. While most comparisons of current expenses with sales or other relationships for each year are valid, inflation will bias interyear comparisons so that they will not reflect the real use and exchange of resources and goods. For example, the uncorrected profit in 1965 was $71,130,000 in 1965 dollars. Before we can usefully compare that amount with the 1993 uncorrected profit—$2,166,200,000 in 1993 dollars—we must adjust those amounts for price-level changes. Using 1993 as the base year for a price index, we adjust the 1965 uncorrected profit for inflation by dividing it by the relative price index (with 1993 = 1) for that year ($71,130,000 divided by .273, calculated from price indexes given in appendix 11–A). The 1965 uncorrected profit becomes $260,560,000 in 1993 dollars. Table 11–3 gives the results of using the price indexes for all values of sales, cost of sales, depreciation, R&D, promotion and marketing, income taxes, net income, total assets, and equity.

Table 11–3 also shows the conventional accounting rate of returns on equity and on assets for each year. They are calculated by dividing the entries in column (7) (net income) by those in column (8) (assets) and column (9) (equity), respectively. The average accounting rate of return from 1965 through 1993 was 16.1 percent (with a standard deviation of 3.6 percent) when based on assets, and 21.1 percent (with a standard deviation of 8.5 percent) when based on equity.

Effects of Capitalization. In table 11–4 we show the effects of capitalizing and depreciating advertising, promotion, and R&D expenditures in the pharmaceutical firm. All amounts are expressed in constant 1990 dollars. The importance of price-level correction becomes apparent when we recognize that some research expenditures may not begin depreciating (that is, may not begin being charged against the revenues they produce) for ten years or more after the outlay occurs, inasmuch as the research is not applied to revenue-producing activity for that length of time.

We may find corrected profits and equity for each period by solving

---

6. We estimate research and development expenditures for 1965 through 1967 by using the industry average (8.2 percent). In addition, we estimate advertising and marketing expenditures by using the industry average (3.7 percent).

$$CP = OP + (AE - DA)(1 - TR)$$
$$+ (RE - DR)(1 - TR) + (AR)(r) \qquad (1)$$

$$CW = OW + BE + BR + AR, \qquad (2)$$

where
CP	=	corrected profits
OP	=	original profits
AE	=	current advertising expenditures
DA	=	depreciation of current and past advertising expenditures
RE	=	current research expenditures
DR	=	depreciation of past research expenditures
AR	=	accumulated research expenditures
TR	=	marginal tax rate
r	=	opportunity cost of capital
CW	=	corrected equity
OW	=	original equity
BE	=	balance of undepreciated advertising expenditures
BR	=	balance of undepreciated research expenditures.

Of course, differences between accounting and economic measurements are a function of several variables—including the amount and growth rate of intangible capital outlays, the lag in and length of the R&D cycle, the opportunity cost of capital, and the economic depreciation of capital expenditures—but the general conclusion holds. Corrected rates of return (and associated variances) will differ from the accounting rates of return. In most cases, accounting rates of return are biased upward when capital activities have been expensed.

We report economic rates of return on assets and equity, corrected for capitalization of intangible assets and expressed in constant 1990 dollars, in the two rightmost columns of table 11–4. We take current sales and accounting expenses (operating costs, depreciation on physical plant and equipment, overhead, advertising, marketing, and research expenditures) from table 11–3. Columns (1), (2), and (3) of table 11–4 show current capital expenditures for research, for development, and for advertising and promotion, respectively. We report the economic depreciation for those activities in columns (4) and (5), where we use declining balance depreciation: a 20 percent rate for basic research, a 30 percent rate for development, and a 70 percent rate for advertising and promotion activities. Column (6) provides the corrected income or profits consisting of original income plus corrections discussed earlier. The current total capital value of assets and equity is given in columns (7) and (8), respectively. These current capital values have added R&D and marketing capital to inflation-adjusted equity and assets of the firm.

247

TABLE 11–3
RATE-OF-RETURN ACCOUNTING INPUT DATA FOR MERCK & COMPANY, INC.
(1993 $ millions)

Year	Sales	Cost of Sales	Depreciation	Research Development	Promotion Marketing	Income Tax	Net Income	Total Assets	Equity	ROR on Assets	ROR on Equity
1965	1,675.29	1,205.67	60.36	131.01	61.99	209.05	260.56	1,483.04	1,091.47	17.57%	23.87%
1966	1,925.28	1,352.15	65.14	153.34	71.24	266.35	306.79	1,562.91	1,164.89	19.63%	26.34%
1967	2,071.86	1,472.28	74.98	173.46	76.66	271.26	328.31	1,697.05	1,296.60	19.35%	25.32%
1968	2,078.96	1,426.00	80.48	191.67	76.92	322.21	330.76	1,772.43	1,368.27	18.66%	24.17%
1969	2,267.05	1,559.13	78.59	200.33	83.88	358.26	349.66	1,972.08	1,478.79	17.73%	23.64%
1970	2,416.22	1,696.51	88.32	221.30	89.40	345.49	374.22	2,108.86	1,565.75	17.74%	23.90%
1971	2,561.28	1,791.80	95.66	220.37	94.77	365.23	404.25	2,266.15	1,670.71	17.84%	24.20%
1972	2,813.73	2,001.08	105.08	237.88	104.11	361.31	451.34	2,491.94	1,856.09	18.11%	24.32%
1973	3,016.39	2,150.96	107.92	243.44	111.61	366.26	499.18	2,702.16	1,938.83	18.47%	25.75%
1974	2,986.73	2,134.12	106.87	239.34	110.51	353.79	498.82	2,946.21	1,949.72	16.93%	25.58%
1975	3,002.14	2,195.93	109.42	261.09	111.08	316.27	489.94	3,295.50	2,034.26	14.87%	24.08%
1976	3,199.02	2,349.43	116.80	274.24	118.36	326.03	523.57	3,605.33	2,258.61	14.52%	23.18%

1977	3,322.54	2,453.95	126.78	279.19	122.93	333.91	534.68	3,840.85	2,428.13	13.92%	22.02%
1978	3,538.21	2,635.36	133.04	288.21	130.91	353.75	549.11	4,020.36	2,598.39	13.66%	21.13%
1979	3,833.76	2,859.00	129.58	302.41	141.85	360.93	613.83	4,259.00	2,644.70	14.41%	23.21%
1980	3,872.52	2,946.88	129.32	331.30	143.28	337.25	588.39	4,118.56	2,607.65	14.29%	22.56%
1981	3,799.61	3,039.69	136.19	355.54	140.59	243.32	516.60	4,302.46	2,565.76	12.01%	20.13%
1982	3,819.20	3,069.95	151.00	399.25	141.31	231.67	517.58	4,557.86	2,718.45	11.36%	19.04%
1983	3,982.95	3,128.96	165.89	436.81	147.37	300.74	553.25	5,171.41	2,956.93	10.70%	18.71%
1984	4,278.49	3,332.81	182.21	472.48	158.30	353.13	592.55	5,517.55	3,027.16	10.74%	19.57%
1985	4,223.21	3,202.98	194.76	507.50	156.26	377.50	642.74	5,835.95	3,104.41	11.01%	20.70%
1986	4,986.59	3,690.34	201.93	579.47	184.50	480.19	810.06	6,165.70	3,069.08	13.24%	26.59%
1987	5,989.70	4,326.75	223.08	669.47	221.62	590.30	1,072.66	6,721.89	2,504.97	15.96%	42.82%
1988	6,858.55	4,698.04	218.25	772.29	253.77	766.98	1,393.53	7,075.64	3,297.69	19.69%	42.26%
1989	7,190.45	4,684.41	226.56	823.82	266.05	864.54	1,641.49	7,416.80	3,864.54	22.13%	42.48%
1990	8,024.58	5,451.15	265.69	893.31	296.91	710.25	1,863.18	8,399.37	4,010.88	22.18%	46.45%
1991	8,814.24	5,788.22	270.29	1,012.09	326.13	852.15	2,173.87	9,732.07	5,040.16	22.34%	43.13%
1992	9,779.86	6,715.08	307.29	1,125.10	361.86	1,056.48	2,008.30	11,220.65	5,063.66	17.90%	39.66%
1993	10,498.20	6,901.60	386.50	1,172.80	388.43	1,430.40	2,166.20	19,927.50	10,021.70	10.87%	21.62%

NOTE: Fiscal year ends December 31.

TABLE 11–4

MERCK'S RATE OF RETURN ON ASSETS AND EQUITY BASED ON CORRECTED CAPITAL

(1993 $ millions)

Year	Research Capital	Development Capital	Promotion Capital	R&D Depreciation	Promotion Depreciation	Corrected Income	Corrected Assets	Corrected Equity	ROR on Assets	ROR on Equity
1965	13.835	130.277	18.596	0.000	43.390	378.390	1,645.748	1,254.173	22.99%	30.17%
1966	31.411	295.783	26.949	0.000	62.882	449.715	1,917.051	1,519.037	23.46%	29.61%
1967	52.869	497.853	29.409	0.000	74.199	501.523	2,277.184	1,876.727	22.02%	26.72%
1968	78.396	738.232	29.976	0.000	76.355	539.558	2,619.033	2,214.869	20.60%	24.36%
1969	107.391	1,011.262	32.087	0.000	81.770	593.060	3,122.819	2,629.527	18.99%	22.55%
1970	141.499	1,332.451	34.369	0.000	87.118	628.946	3,617.176	3,074.065	17.39%	20.46%
1971	178.920	1,684.831	36.476	0.000	92.660	693.818	4,166.381	3,570.935	16.65%	19.43%
1972	221.932	2,089.863	39.761	0.000	100.823	791.736	4,843.496	4,207.646	16.35%	18.82%
1973	269.833	2,439.379	42.852	76.162	108.517	821.316	5,454.222	4,690.889	15.06%	17.51%
1974	322.090	2,731.373	43.197	142.455	110.163	798.689	6,042.869	5,046.376	13.22%	15.83%
1975	381.871	2,996.728	43.270	200.559	111.007	787.266	6,717.372	5,456.130	11.72%	14.43%

1976	438.253	3,233.353	45.506	258.993	116.127	810.765	7,322.440	5,975.719	11.07%	13.57%
1977	490.349	3,444.009	47.533	306.871	120.907	811.261	7,822.739	6,410.022	10.37%	12.66%
1978	538.596	3,628.837	50.338	355.800	128.109	814.786	8,238.128	6,816.164	9.89%	11.95%
1979	583.663	3,803.517	54.337	395.683	137.850	878.638	8,700.520	7,086.212	10.10%	12.40%
1980	627.972	3,976.274	55.751	440.101	141.869	856.262	8,778.552	7,267.646	9.75%	11.78%
1981	670.906	4,162.007	55.071	467.755	141.266	796.474	9,190.448	7,453.743	8.67%	10.69%
1982	716.115	4,393.540	55.046	484.878	141.336	833.697	9,722.556	7,883.155	8.57%	10.58%
1983	763.073	4,658.082	56.929	510.486	145.486	899.660	10,649.495	8,435.017	8.45%	10.67%
1984	812.345	4,955.734	60.754	536.682	154.478	971.073	11,346.381	8,855.996	8.56%	10.97%
1985	865.338	5,293.947	61.125	558.629	155.888	1,057.664	12,056.362	9,324.815	8.77%	11.34%
1986	925.187	5,714.900	69.415	580.183	176.215	1,301.670	12,875.202	9,778.584	10.11%	13.31%
1987	994.275	6,239.879	83.091	605.901	207.942	1,644.874	14,039.138	9,822.215	11.72%	16.75%
1988	1,076.915	6,879.112	96.076	639.345	240.782	2,061.265	15,127.738	11,349.794	13.63%	18.16%
1989	1,169.243	7,586.060	102.653	677.940	259.469	2,377.216	16,274.751	12,722.500	14.61%	18.69%
1990	1,273.878	8,364.353	113.017	732.794	286.546	2,677.870	18,150.620	13,762.127	14.75%	19.46%
1991	1,395.827	9,262.765	124.560	793.877	314.584	3,100.089	20,515.222	15,823.316	15.11%	19.59%
1992	1,535.359	10,283.191	137.908	858.718	348.507	3,052.929	23,177.106	17,020.122	13.17%	17.94%
1993	1,685.238	11,369.198	149.097	927.846	377.244	3,295.449	33,131.033	23,225.233	9.95%	14.19%

The current year's basic research and development (where basic research is stipulated to be 9.6 percent of the research budget) do not yield revenues for the current year. They are, therefore, not depreciated in the current year. On the other hand, those activities do represent an asset—conceivably, information collected could be sold—and are, therefore, added to corrected equity and assets. Moreover, until the asset begins to yield revenues to the firm, research expenditures accumulate in value at the opportunity cost of capital (specified as 10 percent unless otherwise stated). This period of accumulation is eight years for development and eleven years for basic research. When the period of accumulation of research capital is completed, the research capital is transferred to the general research capital account (not shown). Thus, we adjust the original $35.8 million (in 1965 dollars) in R&D to $131.0 million in 1993 dollars and accumulate it for its economic life.[7]

We find the corrected profits for each year by adding the original profits and the difference between current advertising, marketing, direct research, and general research, on the one hand, and the depreciation of those accounts in the current year adjusted for changes in taxes (assumed to be 30 percent for 1965 through 1969 and 46 percent thereafter), plus the implicit unrealized income on capital accumulation, on the other hand (see equation (1)). We report the corrected rates of return on equity and assets in columns (9) and (10), respectively.

Comparisons between the accounting and corrected rates of return show striking differences. For example, the accounting rate of return on equity in constant dollars for 1987 through 1991 exceeds 40 percent (see table 11–3). The economic rate of return for the same years, however, is less than 20 percent (see table 11–4). The average rate of return from 1980 through 1993 shows a similar bias: the average accounting rate of return was 30.4 percent on equity and 15.3 percent on assets (calculated from table 11–3). During the same period the estimated economic rate of return averaged 14.6 percent on equity and 11.1 percent on assets (calculated from table 11–4).

We find some indirect evidence of the validity of capitalizing and depreciating advertising, marketing, and direct research when we examine the variance in the rate of return with and without capital outlay adjustments. When markets are relatively competitive, entry and exit—or expansion and contraction by existing firms—will cause the rate of return to move toward the opportunity cost of capital, adjusted for risk (Telser 1975; Cocks 1975). Risk, information and transaction costs, and disequilibrium forces, however, ensure that some variance

---

7. See appendix 11–A for the wholesale price index.

in rates of return will occur. In addition, if rates of return contain systematic biases for some industries, measured variance will tend to be larger than the variance based on corrected rates of return. Since the corrections given above are designed to match economic costs with returns, we would expect calculated variances to decline after the appropriate corrections have been made. An examination of the variance in estimated rates of return when advertising, marketing, and direct research are capitalized confirms the accuracy of this expectation. The standard deviation on the rate of return on equity from 1980 through 1993 falls from 11.4 percent to 3.7 percent, while the standard deviation on the rate of return on assets falls from 4.7 percent to 2.6 percent.

Rate-of-Return Variations and Policy Decisions

Applying correction techniques to a particular firm or industry is necessary to obtain better measurements of the firm's or industry's real activities. We must apply the same corrections to all industries to make valid interindustry comparisons of rates of return and the relative attractiveness of investment in each industry. Before we apply those corrections, we must identify the expected (or hypothesized) outcomes.

Variations in Manufacturing Rates of Return. Differences among rates of return in various industries are the product of many factors. First, the observed rates at any time are dispersed because industries are rarely in static equilibrium for long periods. Second, there may be differences in the nonmoney characteristics that would cause pecuniary rates to differ under competitive market conditions. Third, there are differences in "riskiness" among different industries, with higher average rates of return required for competitive viability in "riskier" industries. Fourth, differences in the quality of resources may cause variation in observed rates of return if superior resources are distributed unequally and earn unequal rents not completely capitalized on the books of the firms owning and using them. Fifth, entry barriers such as those erected by government regulation could cause observed rates of return in some industries to be higher than in others. Finally, differences in rates of return can exist whenever systematic errors in measurement differentially affect firms in some industries.

Given those factors, it would be highly unlikely that observed rates of return among firms within an industry or for all industries would be equal. If we can eliminate or reduce any one or more of those factors, observed rates of return should tend to move closer together if markets are competitive. This study has concentrated on reducing the biases from current measurement techniques. If those biases have been

TABLE 11–5
ADVERTISING AS A PERCENTAGE OF NET SALES BY INDUSTRY

Industry	Percentage
Entertainment	5.0
Industrial/other chemicals	3.7
Pharmaceuticals	3.7
Food and kindred products	2.3
Electronic machinery	1.6
Rubber products	1.5
Engines	1.0
Office machines and computers	1.0
Software	1.0
Motor vehicles	.8
Paper and allied products	.7
Petroleum	.5
Aerospace	.3
Ferrous metals	.3

SOURCE: U.S. Bureau of the Census, *Statistical Abstract of the United States* (Washington, D.C.: Government Printing Office, various dates) and U.S. Treasury, *Statistics of Income: Corporate Income Tax Returns*, various issues

reduced and markets are competitive, we would expect a narrowing of calculated rates of return.

We selected a sample of ninety-nine firms representing fourteen industries to test this hypothesis. Those firms and industries are shown in appendix 11–B. To incorporate proper economic life cycles and to reduce the problems associated with disequilibrium forces, we collected data for each firm from 1965 through 1993 from annual reports as well as from general sources such as Moody's *Industrial Manual*. We obtained average industry advertising expenditures from the *Statistical Abstract* and U.S. Treasury *Statistics of Income* and got average company R&D expenditures for each from the National Science Foundation. Tables 11–5 and 11–6 give these amounts as a percentage of net sales. Whenever R&D expenditures were not available for a firm, we used the industry average in table 11–7. We used a similar rule for advertising expenditures. To determine the amount of basic R&D, we price adjusted and averaged industry data from NSF surveys for several years. We report the results in table 11–7. We estimated the period of accumulation for basic research and for development expenditures in each industry from several industry sources (see table 11–8) with an additional three years added for basic research expenditures.

TABLE 11–6
RESEARCH AND DEVELOPMENT EXPENDITURES AS A
PERCENTAGE OF SALES BY INDUSTRY

Industry	Percentage
Software	20.0
Office machines and computers	11.7
Pharmaceuticals	8.2
Electronic machinery	5.3
Industrial/other chemicals	4.3
Aerospace	3.8
Motor vehicles	3.2
Rubber products	2.2
Engines	2.1
Petroleum	.9
Paper and allied products	.8
Food and kindred products	.7
Ferrous metals	.7
Entertainment	.1

SOURCE: Calculated from statistics reported in National Science Foundation, *Research and Development in Industry*, various years.

TABLE 11–7
BASIC RESEARCH EXPENDITURES AS A PERCENTAGE OF
TOTAL FUNDS BY INDUSTRY

Industry	Percentage
Software	10.0
Industrial/other chemicals	9.9
Pharmaceuticals	9.6
Petroleum	6.0
Paper and allied products	4.0
Ferrous metals	3.4
Rubber products	3.3
Food and kindred products	3.1
Electronic machinery	3.0
Office machines and computers	1.5
Aerospace	1.1
Entertainment	1.0
Engines	.9
Motor vehicles	.4

SOURCE: Calculated from statistics reported in National Science Foundation, *Research and Development in Industry*, various years.

TABLE 11–8
ACCUMULATION PERIODS FOR BASIC RESEARCH AND FOR
DEVELOPMENT BY INDUSTRY

Industry	Basic Research Accumulation	Development Accumulation
Food and kindred products	6	3
Paper and allied products	7	4
Industrial/other chemicals	7	4
Pharmaceuticals	11	8
Petroleum	8	5
Rubber products	7	4
Ferrous metals	7	4
Engines	6	3
Office machines and computers	6	3
Electronic machinery	6	3
Motor vehicles	6	3
Aerospace	7	4
Computer software	6	3
Entertainment	5	2

SOURCE: Author's estimates based on various sources including David Schwartzman, "Pharmaceutical R&D Expenditures and Rates of Return," in Robert Helms, ed., *Drug Development and Marketing* (Washington, D.C.: American Enterprise Institute, 1975), pp. 63–80. Also, Edwin Mansfield et al., *Research and Innovation in the Modern Corporation* (New York: W. W. Norton and Co., 1971), p. 7.

We computed average accounting rates of return from 1980 through 1993 for each company. We report an industry average for each of fourteen industries in table 11–9.[8] We chose economic lives for basic research, development, and promotion to correct for biases as

8. In 1992 the Financial Accounting Standards Board (FASB) issued rule 106 that required U.S. firms to account for the future estimated cost of retirees' health benefits in their current liabilities and current profit and loss statements. That resulted in a one-time charge for many companies in 1992. General Motors, for example, reported a one-time charge of $20.8 billion, which reduced both profit and equity by that amount. That FASB rule results in a negative one-time accounting rate of return on equity of −336 percent for 1992. That compares with a −9.7 percent return in 1992 without the one-time charge. Because the 1992 charge represents actual expected costs over several years, it has been omitted for six companies (Du Pont, Ford, General Motors, Goodyear, Inland Steel, and Rockwell International), where a significant one-time bias would occur if the special charges were left in net revenue and equity calcula-

TABLE 11–9
AVERAGE ACCOUNTING AND CORRECTED RATES OF RETURN ON ASSETS AND
EQUITY BY INDUSTRY, 1980–1993
(in percentages)

Industry	Accounting Rates of Return		Corrected Rates of Return	
	Assets	Equity	Assets	Equity
Foods	8.17	17.58	7.69	14.95
Paper	4.12	9.20	4.32	8.92
Chemicals	5.52	13.43	4.90	8.46
Pharmaceuticals	12.07	24.37	9.86	13.27
Petroleum	9.00	22.03	8.08	15.81
Rubber products	5.26	12.45	4.24	9.05
Ferrous metals	− .73	− 6.77	− .40	− 2.91
Engines	4.95	9.22	4.85	8.26
Office machines	3.37	3.57	4.99	7.47
Electrical machines	6.36	12.26	6.01	9.93
Motor vehicles	.73	.07	1.45	1.54
Aerospace	4.99	10.65	5.18	9.06
Computer software	12.56	22.05	16.70	22.56
Entertainment	4.14	5.49	4.11	5.66
Average	6.27	12.32	6.30	10.19

NOTE: Calculated using 1993 constant dollars. Accumulation periods for basic research and development are found in table 11–8. Advertising and promotion depreciate at 70 percent, basic research depreciates at 20 percent, and development depreciates at 30 percent each year. In each category the appropriate percentages are applied to previously undepreciated balances.
SOURCE: Calculated from individual firm data. Excludes 1992 FASB 106 health care charges for Du Pont, Ford, General Motors, Goodyear, Inland Steel, and Rockwell International.

given in table 11–8 and previously described.[9] As predicted, the corrected average rate of return significantly changes for those industries that were relatively capital intensive in advertising-promotion and re-search-development expenditures. The pharmaceutical industry, which spends relatively more than most other industries on R&D (see

tions. See Warshawsky (1992) for additional information on this issue and others regarding retiree health benefits.

9. Marketing and promotion are depreciated at 70 percent of current expenses plus 70 percent of previously undepreciated balances.

table 11–6), experiences the largest change in its 1980 through 1993 average rate of return.

When we correct accounting rates of return, the estimated average rate of return on equity from 1980 through 1993 in all industries falls from 12.3 percent to 10.2 percent. More important, the variance, when corrections have been made, falls substantially. Unfortunately, until we obtain better information about the economic life of advertising and the life cycle of research activities, we cannot determine the exact levels in each industry. That approach, however, casts serious doubt on previous studies in which interindustry differentials in rates of return were attributed to risk, entry barriers, concentration, and other related variables. Indeed, the results here suggest that if entry barriers exist, they are not particularly effective and that risk may have been overstated in previous inquiries investigating those variables.[10]

Finally, the methodology used to correct accounting rates of return yields extremely robust results. This is true for variations in assumptions in this study and those assumptions employed by other studies of intangible capital.[11] Those independent studies further confirm the proposition that accounting rates of return are differentially biased.

A Sensitivity Analysis to Modified Assumptions. Our results hold even with modifications of the price level adjustments, economic life cycles for research expenditures, depreciation periods, and the opportunity cost of capital. First, if calculations are based on current dollar amounts rather than on price-level-adjusted amounts, there is little change in the outcome. With identical capitalization and depreciation assumptions, the average economic rate of return on equity using current dollars is 11.2 percent for 1980 through 1993, or 1.0 percentage point higher than the average using price-adjusted data.[12]

Second, the effects from respecifying the opportunity cost of capital are trifling. Changes in the opportunity cost of capital do not have any significant impact on the average economic rates of return. When the opportunity cost of capital is raised from 10 percent to 14 percent,

10. The inclusion of these variables is beyond the scope of this study. For example, testing for the consequences of risk requires inclusion of either all or a significantly large random sample of the firms in the industry. For the pharmaceutical industry this entails knowledge about a large number of firms. Furthermore, data limitations further biased this sample toward the more successful larger firms.

11. See Comanor (1986) for a review of those studies.

12. The 1980 through 1993 average economic rate of return on weighted equity rises .8 percentage point to 11.6 percent.

TABLE 11–10
EFFECTS OF ALTERNATIVE OPPORTUNITY COSTS OF CAPITAL AND PROMOTION/
MARKETING DEPRECIATION ON AVERAGE RATES OF RETURN, 1980–1993
(in percentages)

	Corrected Rate of Return on			
Variation	Unweighted assets	Weighted assets	Unweighted equity	Weighted equity
Opportunity cost of capital (interest rate)				
8	6.20	5.50	10.09	11.45
10	6.30	5.59	10.19	11.50
12	6.41	5.69	10.30	11.55
14	6.52	5.80	10.40	11.61
Promotion/ marketing depreciation options				
50	6.24	5.56	10.00	11.37
60	6.28	5.58	10.12	11.45
70	6.30	5.59	10.19	11.50
80	6.33	5.60	10.28	11.56
90	6.34	5.61	10.33	11.58
100	6.36	5.62	10.38	11.61

NOTE: Calculated using 1993 constant dollars. Accumulation periods for basic research and development are found in table 11–8. Advertising and promotion depreciate at 70 percent, basic research depreciates at 20 percent, and development depreciates at 30 percent annually for changes in the opportunity cost of capital.
SOURCE: Computed from individual firm data. Excludes 1992 FASB 106 health care charges for Du Pont, Ford, General Motors, Goodyear, Inland Steel, and Rockwell International.

the inflation-adjusted ten-year average economic rate of return on equity increases from about 10.2 percent to 10.4 percent, as shown in table 11–10.

Third, table 11–10 also shows the effects of modifying the depreciation period for advertising and promotion. As predicted, longer economic lives are generally accompanied by lower average economic rates of return.[13] When advertising and promotion are depreciated at 100 percent, the 1980 through 1993 average return on equity (with price

---

13. If the growth rate of advertising and promotion is very high, the average rate of return can increase with longer economic lives.

corrections) rises about .2 percentage point to 10.4 percent. Average rates of return on weighted equity also produce a small change. With longer advertising and promotion depreciation periods, such as 50 percent per year, the average rate of return falls .1 percentage point to 10.0 percent over the 1980 through 1993 period.

Fourth, shortening the total economic life cycle by decreasing the period for accumulation and depreciation mildly increases yearly and average economic rates of return from the levels of the accounting rates of return. For example, table 11–11 shows that the 1980 through 1993 average economic rate of return on net worth rises .04 percentage point when two years are taken from both the research and development accumulation periods and both depreciation rates increase by 20 percent. Moreover, table 11–11 shows little variation in the 1980 through 1993 economic rates of return for relatively large changes in the economic life cycle, although all variations yield rates of return below the uncorrected accounting rates of return.

Fifth, as table 11–11 shows, combining capitalization of advertising and promotion with capitalization of basic research and development produces a general lowering of both yearly and average rates of return. For example, increasing the research and development period cycles by two years and reducing depreciation by 10 percent when advertising and promotion are depreciated by 70 percent lower the estimated 1993 average rate of return on equity from 10.2 percent to 9.8 percent.

Finally, other corrections—such as replacing the accounting depreciation schedules with schedules that more closely represent true economic depreciation—might increase accuracy but are unlikely to alter the major general effects described above. We should note that combinations of the changes suggested above are generally additive in that the individual effects maintain their expected directions. Table 11–11 shows, for example, that increasing both the economic life of promotion and the life cycle for research and development usually lowers rates of return more than either single correction.

We should also note that under certain conditions, corrected rates of return will be higher than uncorrected rates. For example, comparisons between corrected and uncorrected rates of return for the years when capitalization begins may not be valid unless there were no prior advertising and promotion or R&D capital expenditures—this because the corrected profits in equation (1) will not include depreciation of previous capital expenditures. In addition, if those capital expenditures are rising rapidly, similar biases may be introduced. If the period under analysis is significantly longer than the economic life cycles, and if the earliest years are omitted from comparisons of corrected and uncorrected rates of return, those biases can be decreased.

Other Factors Causing Differential Returns. Measurement error accounts for a major portion of the distance between the pharmaceutical industry's accounting rate of return on equity and the all-industries' average return. Is the residual large enough to induce concern about possible monopoly power in the industry? In our sample of firms and industries, uncorrected accounting figures show the pharmaceutical industry return to be 12.0 percentage points above the average return earned. After removing the measurement error that results from inappropriate accounting for the two varieties of intangible capital, we reduce the distance to 3.1 percentage points (see table 11–9).

Part of the remaining differential between the pharmaceutical rate of return and the average return of the firms in our sample of industries is the consequence of some remaining measurement error. Other varieties of intangible capital—such as investment in the recruitment, selection, and training of a work force—remain unaccounted for. But that error is probably similar in most industries, although Lester Telser (1972) has demonstrated that concentrated industries invest disproportionately in human capital. But the pharmaceutical industry is not a concentrated industry.

There is a variety of promotional capital that is more heavily used in pharmaceuticals than in almost any other industry, and that may be an important source of relative distortion of accounting rates of return. Pharmaceutical firms spend as much on informing doctors of the results of their research—by means other than advertising—as they spend on research itself. Since data on the nonadvertising promotional outlays of other industries are scanty, it is not possible to determine the differential impact of those expenditures.

A second source of relative bias in pharmaceutical industry figures is the risk factor. If risks are greater in the pharmaceutical arena than in most other industries, successful pharmaceutical firms will have a higher rate of return than successful firms in other industries (Mancke 1974).[14]

There is reason to believe that pharmaceutical firms face even greater risks than those firms that explore for and produce crude oil, uranium, gold, copper, and other elusive minerals. The Pharmaceutical Manufacturers Association (now the Pharmaceutical Research and Manufacturers of America) frequently reported that their members

---

14. Government compilations of industry profit rates use the profits of successful or "leading" firms in an industry.

TABLE 11–11

EFFECTS OF ALTERNATIVE CAPITAL EXPENSE CORRECTIONS ON AVERAGE RATES OF RETURN, 1980–1993
(in percentages)

	Corrected Rate of Return on			
Capital Expense Corrections	Unweighted assets	Weighted equity	Unweighted net worth	Weighted equity
Initial corrections[a]	6.30	5.59	10.19	11.50
Basic research accumulation (−1) Development accumulation (−1) Basic research depreciation [+10] Development depreciation [+10]	6.28	5.61	10.40	12.33
Basic research accumulation (−2) Development accumulation (−2) Basic research depreciation [+20] Development depreciation [+20]	6.23	5.62	10.58	13.18
Basic research accumulation (−3) Development accumulation (0) Basic research depreciation [+10] Development depreciation [0]	6.31	5.59	10.23	11.57

Basic research accumulation (+1) Development accumulation (+1) Basic research depreciation [−10] Development depreciation [−10]	6.28	5.52	9.81	10.54
Basic research accumulation (+2) Development accumulation (+2) Basic research depreciation [−10] Development depreciation [−10]	6.34	5.56	9.18	10.26
Basic research accumulation (+1) Development accumulation (+1) Promotion depreciation [−10] Basic research depreciation [−10] Development depreciation [−10]	6.26	5.51	9.75	10.50
Basic research accumulation (−1) Development accumulation (−1) Promotion depreciation [+10] Basic research depreciation [+10] Development depreciation [+10]	6.31	5.63	10.50	12.40

NOTE: Calculated using 1993 constant dollars. Change in accumulation years in parentheses. Percent depreciation change in brackets. Initial accumulation periods for basic research and development are found in table 11–8. Initial advertising and promotion depreciate at 70 percent, basic research depreciates at 20 percent, and development research depreciates at 30 percent each year. In each category the appropriate percentages are applied to previously undepreciated balances.
a. See table 11–9.
SOURCE: Calculated from individual firm data. Excludes 1992 FASB 106 health care charges for Du Pont, Ford, General Motors, Goodyear, Inland Steel, and Rockwell International.

"obtained, prepared, extracted or isolated" thousands of compounds in 1970 and tested thousands of additional compounds for pharmacological activity. Only a few of those compounds proved promising and safe enough after testing in animals to move into clinical testing (Pharmaceutical Manufacturers Association various years). Since fewer than twenty new compounds reach the market in a typical year,[15] this means that the investment in R&D produces an enormous number of "dry holes"—some of them very expensive—for every successful compound.[16] A firm may test thousands of compounds each year for many years and never hit a winner.[17] Those that do happen to hit a winner will appear to be very profitable, while the industry may be relatively unprofitable. Since it is the firms with winners that survive and since their returns are measured to compute industry profitability, a biased figure is produced.

There are grounds for suspecting that the pharmaceutical industry profit rates reported by the Federal Trade Commission and the Securities and Exchange Commission, using a small number of firms and only the largest firms, overstate the industry's attractiveness. From 1947 to 1967, the number of firms in the pharmaceutical preparations industry (SIC 2834) declined from 1,123 to 791, and further declined to 640 in 1987 (U.S. Department of Commerce 1982, 7–24 and 7–25; 1987, 28C-5). If the industry were actually as profitable as reports from a small number of successful firms make it appear, the firms in the industry would find it attractive to remain and new firms would be attracted to the industry. A declining number of firms is not usually found in an industry with true above-average returns or supracompetitive prices. Also, it is notable that the rate of decline in number of firms accelerated following the passage of the 1963 amendments to the Food, Drug, and Cosmetic Act, which increased the cost and riskiness of research (Grabowski and Vernon 1990; Baily 1972; Peltzman 1974) and contributed to a reduction in the expected rate of return on research from 11.4 percent in 1960 to 3.3 percent in 1973 (Schwartzman 1975, 36, 44).

---

15. The number of new chemical entities marketed was sixteen in 1974 and twelve in 1975. The average annual number was fourteen from 1963 through 1975 (Grabowski 1976, 18, table 1).

16. Merck & Company "recently shelved a new drug for gout on which it had spent close to $20 million" (Robertson 1976, 136).

17. Merck has "in the last ten years, brought out only one commercially important drug in the U.S. market. . . . [D]uring this period the corporation has pumped almost $800 million into research" (Robertson 1976, 134–35). "Since 1948, Merck has spent close to $90 million on antibiotics research without producing a . . . commercially successful product" (Robertson 1976, 168).

TABLE 11A–1
WHOLESALE PRICE INDEX, 1965–1993
(1982 = 100)

Year	Price Index	Year	Price Index
1965	34.1	1980	88.0
1966	35.2	1981	96.1
1967	35.6	1982	100.0
1968	36.6	1983	101.6
1969	38.0	1984	103.7
1970	39.3	1985	104.7
1971	40.5	1986	103.2
1972	41.8	1987	105.4
1973	45.6	1988	108.0
1974	52.6	1989	113.6
1975	58.2	1990	119.2
1976	60.8	1991	121.7
1977	64.7	1992	123.2
1978	69.8	1993	124.7
1979	77.6		

SOURCE: Table B-64, Council of Economic Advisers, *Economic Report of the President*, February 1994.

Appendix 11–A

Table 11A–1 shows the wholesale price index from 1965 through 1993.

Appendix 11–B

Industries and Firms Included in Capital Expenditure Sample.

Food and kindred products. Adolph Coors Co.; Borden Inc.; Campbell Soup Co.; CPC International Inc.; Kraft Inc.; Conagra Inc.; H.J. Heinz Co.; Quaker Oats Co.; Kellogg Co.; Sara Lee Corp.; and General Mills Inc.

Paper and allied products: Georgia-Pacific Corp.; Scott Paper Co.; Weyerhaeuser Co.; Boise Cascade Corp.; International Paper Co.; Champion International Corp.; Mead Corp.; and Kimberly-Clark Corp.

Industrial and other chemicals. Dow Chemical Co.; E.I. duPont de Nemours; Koppers Co., Inc.; Monsanto Co.; and Union Carbide Corp.

Pharmaceuticals and medicines. Abbott Laboratories; Bristol-Myers Squibb Co.; Eli Lilly & Co.; Rorer Group, Inc.; Syntex Corp.; Warner

Lambert Co.; Merck & Company, Inc.; Pfizer Inc.; Schering Plough Corp.; SmithKline Beecham Corp.; and Upjohn Co.

Petroleum. Amoco Corp.; Chevron Corp.; Exxon Corp.; Mobil Corp.; Pennzoil Co.; Phillips Petroleum Co.; Shell Oil Co.; Sun Oil Co.; and Texaco Inc.

Rubber products. B.F. Goodrich Co.; and Goodyear Tire & Rubber.

Ferrous metals. Allegheny Ludlum Corp.; Bethlehem Steel Corp.; Inland Steel Co.; National Steel Corp.; Rio Algom Ltd.; USX Corp.; and Armco Inc.

Office machines and computers. International Business Machines; Unisys Corp.; Control Data Corp.; Digital Equipment; Amdahl Corp.; Data General Corp.; and Hewlett-Packard Co.

Engines: Briggs & Stratton; Cooper Industries Inc.; Emhart Corp.; and Ingersoll-Rand Co.

Electronic machinery. General Electric Co.; Motorola Inc.; Westing-house Credit Corp.; Whirlpool Corp.; Emerson Electric Co.; General Signal Corp.; and Grainger (W.W.) Inc.

Motor vehicles. Chrysler Corp.; Cummins Engine Co., Inc.; Ford Motor Co.; General Motors Corp.; Navistar International; and Paccar Inc.

Aerospace. Boeing Co.; Curtiss-Wright Corp.; Lockheed Corp.; Mc-Donnell Douglas Corp.; Northrop Corp.; Rockwell International; United Technologies Corp.; Grumman Corp.; and Martin Marietta Corp.

Computer software. Ashton Tate Corp.; Computer Associates International; Continuum Co., Inc.; Infodata Systems Inc.; Lotus Development Corp.; Microsoft Corp.; and Oracle Systems Corp.

Entertainment. Walt Disney Co.; Handleman Co.; MCA Inc.; Viacom Inc.; and Warner Communications Inc.

References

Baily, Martin N. "Research and Development Costs and Returns: The U.S. Pharmaceutical Industry." *Journal of Political Economy* 80 (1972): 70–85.

Borden, Neil H. *The Economic Effects of Advertising.* Homewood, Ill.: Richard D. Irwin, 1952.

Clarkson, Kenneth. *Intangible Capital and Rates of Return*. Washington, D.C.: AEI Press, 1977.

Clymer, Harold. "The Changing Costs and Risks of Pharmaceutical Innovation." In *Economics of Drug Innovation*, edited by Joseph Cooper. Washington, D.C.: American University, 1970.

Cocks, Douglas. "Product Innovation and the Dynamic Elements of Competition in the Ethical Pharmaceutical Industry." In *Drug Development and Marketing*, edited by Robert B. Helms. Washington, D.C.: American Enterprise Institute, 1975.

Comanor, William S. "The Political Economy of the Pharmaceutical Industry." *Journal of Economic Literature* 24 (1986): 1178–1217.

DiMasi, Joseph A., Ronald W. Hansen, Henry G. Grabowski, and Louis Lasagna. "The Cost of Innovation in the Pharmaceutical Industry." *Journal of Health Economics* 10 (1991): 107–42.

Grabowski, Henry G. *Drug Regulation and Innovation*. Washington, D.C.: AEI Press, 1976.

————, and John M. Vernon. "A New Look at the Returns and Risks to Pharmaceutical R&D." *Management Science* 36 (1990): 804–21.

————. "Prospects for Returns to Pharmaceutical R&D under Health Care Reform." In *Competitive Strategies in the Pharmaceutical Industry*, edited by Robert B. Helms. Washington, D.C.: AEI Press, 1995.

Hollander, Sidney. "A Rationale for Advertising Expenditures." *Harvard Business Review* 27 (January 1949): 79–87.

Mancke, Richard. "Causes of Interfirm Profitability Differences: A New Interpretation of the Evidence." *Quarterly Journal of Economics* 88 (1974): 188–93.

Nerlove, Marc, and Frederick Waugh. "Advertising without Supply Control: Some Implications of a Study of the Advertising of Oranges." *Journal of Farm Economics* 43 (1961): 813–37.

Office of Technology Assessment. *Pharmaceutical R&D: Costs, Risks and Rewards*. OTA-H-522. Washington, D.C.: Government Printing Office, 1993.

Palda, Kristian. "The Measurement of Cumulative Advertising Effects." *Journal of Business* 38 (1965): 162–79.

Peles, Yoram. "Rates of Amortization of Advertising Expenditures." *Journal of Political Economy* 79 (1971): 1032–58.

Peltzman, Sam. *Regulation of Pharmaceutical Innovation: The 1962 Amendments*. Washington, D.C.: AEI Press, 1974.

Pharmaceutical Manufacturers Association. *Annual Survey Report*. Washington, D.C.: various years.

Robertson, Wyntham. "Merck Strains to Keep the Pots Aboiling." *Fortune* 93 (March 1976): 136.

Schwartzman, D. *The Expected Return on Investment in Pharmaceutical Research*. Washington, D.C.: AEI Press, 1975.

267

————. *Innovation in the Pharmaceutical Industry*. Baltimore: Johns Hopkins Press, 1976.

Telser, Lester. "Advertising and Cigarettes." *Journal of Political Economy* 70 (1962): 471–99.

————. *Competition, Collusion and Game Theory*. Chicago: Aldine-Atherton, 1972.

————. "The Supply Response to Shifting Demand in the Ethical Pharmaceutical Industry." In *Drug Development and Marketing*, edited by Robert B. Helms. Washington, D.C.: AEI Press, 1975.

Tull, D.S. "An Examination of the Hypothesis That Advertising Has a Lagged Effect on Sales." Ph.D. dissertation, University of Chicago, 1956.

U.S. Bureau of the Census. *Concentration Ratios in Manufacturing, 1982*. Washington, D.C.: Government Printing Office, 1986.

————. *Census of Manufactures, 1987*. Washington, D.C.: Government Printing Office, 1991.

U.S. Congress, Senate Committee on the Judiciary, Subcommittee on Antitrust. *Administered Prices: A Compendium on Public Policy*. 88th Cong., 1st sess., 1963.

Vidale, M.L., and H.B. Wolfe. "An Operations Research Study of Sales Response to Advertising." *Operations Research* 5 (1957): 370–81.

Warshawsky, M. J. *The Uncertain Promise of Retiree Health Benefits: An Evaluation of Corporate Obligations*. Washington, D. C.: AEI Press, 1992.

Commentary on Part Three

Frederic M. Scherer

There is a central theme lurking in the studies of Henderson and Cockburn, Grabowski and Vernon, Myers and Shyam-Sunder, and Clarkson. I shall attempt to draw it out. The theme, as I see it, is the question of endogeneity, or, in less fancy language, to what extent there is an invisible hand guiding the R&D activities of drug companies. I shall combine observations from the four studies.

First of all, Myers and Shyam-Sunder show that the cost of capital in the drug industry is roughly 10.5 percent. Grabowski and Vernon suggest that the mean rate of return on R&D by pharmaceutical companies in the early 1980s was approximately 11.1 percent. The difference is .6 percentage point, but as Myers and Shyam-Sunder point out, the range of possible measurement error in estimating the cost of capital exceeds plus or minus 1 percent. Thus, observed average R&D returns and the cost of capital clustered within a normal range of measurement error.

To this finding a few further observations must be added. As the Henderson and Cockburn study shows, there was an explosion of drug research and development spending during the 1980s. By my calculations, the average annual real growth rate was close to 10 percent. At the same time, new technologies of drug discovery appeared. Notably, rational drug design came to the forefront during the 1980s. For that reason, or perhaps also because of expanded insurance coverage of prescription outlays, Grabowski and Vernon show, price-cost margins in pharmaceuticals rose from about 33 percent in the early and mid-1970s to 40 percent in the late 1970s and early 1980s.

The central question is, Was the rapid growth of drug research and development an endogenous response to the *actual* rise in gross profitability, or, alternatively, to an *expected* rise in profitability foreseen as the consequence of richer technological opportunities? Query number two, Did that response, the increase in research and development spending, drive profits back to the more or less normal level, despite increased price-cost margins and increased sales of the big winners? I believe the answer to both questions is yes.

Professor Clarkson insists that monopoly is not an issue in drugs. Surely, he cannot be right if he is denying that drug companies seek and win dominant positions in new therapies. Clearly, they are out to secure monopolies of new therapies that lead to high prices and substantial profits, as Grabowski and Vernon show for their top decile of new chemical entities. What Clarkson must mean is that there is competition in the sense that firms bid for monopoly positions until all the rents are dissipated. One might call that phenomenon "Demsetz competition," following the analysis of Harold Demsetz (1968). In this instance, companies bid for monopoly positions by incurring substantial R&D costs.

Such a view of the world would be sufficient to explain the observed facts but for one remaining awkwardness raised by the very interesting and pioneering Henderson and Cockburn study. They find no evidence of rent-dissipating "racing." How can we reconcile their findings with the other three studies? I agree with much that is in the Henderson and Cockburn study. My objection is simply that their conclusion that there is no rent-dissipating racing does not necessarily follow from their analysis. Rather, as is frequently the case in economics, Henderson and Cockburn appear to be blinded by the theoretical model they have chosen.

I agree with their qualitative conclusion that the racing model, as they have specified it, does not apply. But it is a limited and stylized model of racing that by no means characterizes the entire relevant literature. Drug discovery and development are more like a marathon than a 400-meter dash. In a marathon, the runner mostly has to pace himself, or he will drop from exhaustion. But there may be key stages at which he comes into head-to-head rivalry. Moving from that analogy to a closer approximation, firms in the pharmaceutical industry are racing to horizontally differentiated niches in what economists call product characteristics space. If that is true, and I believe it is, it is not an "either he wins or I win" race. It can be an "everybody wins" race—one, to be sure, in which some win more than others.

This poses measurement problems. Each niche captured by a firm with its new products is likely to be blanketed by a cluster of patents—sometimes many, sometimes few. This must be true, since pharmaceutical companies receive far more patents than new drug approvals. The number of patents covering any single niche has a substantial random component. There is no necessary correlation among different participants' outputs, measured under the Henderson-Cockburn model by the patents the firms receive. Henderson and Cockburn's uncorrelated patents result does not falsify the alternative product differentiation model.

Their analysis also overlooks the role of "submission," a concept pioneered in brilliant research on arms races eight decades ago by Lewis F. Richardson (1960). That is, if a firm falls too far behind, it simply drops out of the race and enters another race. Henderson and Cockburn quote a drug company representative as saying, "There's no future in me-too drugs." I believe that is true. I heard the same refrain from Harold Clymer, R&D vice president for Smith Kline & French, in 1969. If there is no future in me-too drugs, what companies do is to seek an unpopulated niche. Given the long lead times in drug discovery and testing, however, they may inadvertently end up with a me-too drug. But they are not trying consciously to duplicate the output of one or more known racing partners.

None of this means that research and development spending is not endogenous, nor does it imply that rent dissipation cannot occur. Consider figure C3–1, adapted from an article I published in 1966. On the horizontal axis is the depth of the profit (or more accurately, quasi-rent) stream realized annually for up to twenty-five years from offering a successful new product. It is scaled from zero to $30 million per year. I assume a kind of needle-in-the-haystack search, where experiments are conducted, and there is some small probability that any given experiment will lead to a successful new product. Each experiment can have single-shot success probabilities ranging from one in one hundred to one in five. Multiple successes are possible. The profit-maximizing number of experiments per time period for diverse success probabilities and profit-stream depths is given by the graph's four curves. The lowest curve is for a .2 probability of success; the highest for .01. The curves' positive slopes reveal that the profit-maximizing strategy will vary systematically with the lucrativeness of the product market to be tapped. The greater the profit potential, the more parallel experimental approaches a decision maker will elect. For a given probability of success, the more approaches pursued, the more likely it is that multiple successes will emerge.

Such a generalization is true if an omniscient social planner were to choose a monolithic R&D strategy. It is also true when individual firms see a big pot of gold out there. But more than one firm may respond in the same way, especially when there is great uncertainty about who is doing what. Thus, firms will pursue numerous approaches in the big-benefit therapeutic classes. And even though no firm is individually conscious of what the other firms are doing—they are not consciously racing—there can very well be substantial, even total, rent dissipation.

271

FIGURE C3–1
PROFIT-MAXIMIZING NUMBER OF EXPERIMENTS

Optimal number of parallel experiments

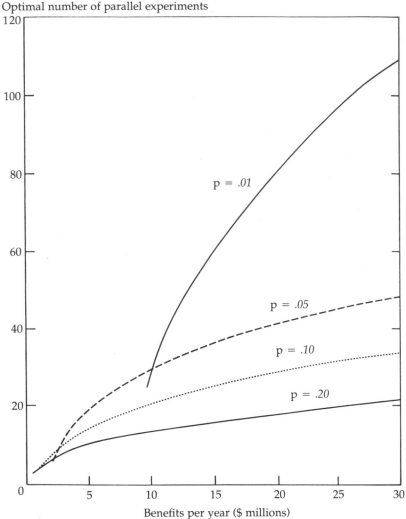

Benefits per year ($ millions)

The only thing that can avoid such dissipation in this differentiated product case with substantial uncertainty is a perfect nominating mechanism—the kind of nominating system about which G. B. Richardson (1960) wrote. Henderson and Cockburn do identify one factor that could serve as such a nominating mechanism. They suggest that individual firms have idiosyncratic capabilities, which might lead each firm to pursue somewhat different leads, perhaps thereby preventing the complete dissipation of rents. How well the nominating mechanism works, and therefore how much rent dissipation is avoided, remains uncertain. That average returns on pharmaceutical R&D come so close to the cost of capital, despite wide-ranging differences in price-cost margins and new product sales trajectories, suggests to me that the invisible hand does lead to rather complete rent dissipation.

To this, one further, very important, normative point must be added. When we move from a homogeneous product model, which is essentially what Henderson and Cockburn assume, to a horizontally differentiated product model, it is not necessarily true that the social returns on investment equal or exceed the private returns on investment. In the differentiated spatial model case, it is likely that some "cannibalization" of other firms' rents will occur (Scherer 1979). In this case it is possible, although not necessary, that private returns could exceed the social returns. If so, rivalry among pharmaceutical companies under conditions of high uncertainty could lead to excessive R&D. I doubt that this happens on average, given the differences among ostensibly similar pharmaceutical entities in therapeutic effects and side effects and the frequently significant consequences of those differences. But it could happen. Determining whether it does happen, and if so, how frequently, is one of the most important unsettled items on the agenda for research on pharmaceutical economics.

References

Demsetz, Harold. "Why Regulate Utilities?" *Journal of Law and Economics* 11 (1968): 55–66.

Richardson, G. B. *Information and Investment*. London: Oxford University Press, 1960.

Richardson, Lewis F. *Arms and Insecurity: A Mathematical Study of the Causes and Origins of War*, edited by Nicholas Rashevsky. Chicago: Quadrangle, 1960.

Scherer, Frederic M. "Time-Cost Trade-offs in Uncertain Empirical Research Projects." *Naval Research Logistics Quarterly* 13 (1966): 71–82.

———. "The Welfare Economics of Product Variety: An Application to the Ready-to-Eat Cereals Industry." *Journal of Industrial Economics* 28 (December 1979): 113–34.

William S. Comanor

Three of the four studies in this part of the volume deal with the long-disputed issue of profitability in the pharmaceutical industry. As most of us know, that issue was raised originally by the Kefauver Committee in hearings held more than thirty years ago. It is still a matter of some concern, for otherwise these studies would not have been undertaken.

The long-standing attention paid to pharmaceutical industry profitability is interesting precisely because there is little doubt about the presence of market power in that industry. Recall that the economic definition of market power turns on the relation of prices to marginal costs, which is why the Lerner index[1] is used to indicate market power. Does anyone doubt that pharmaceutical prices typically exceed marginal costs? I think not. At the same time, would anyone prefer an industry in which prices equaled marginal costs? Again, I think not.

If there is little question regarding market power in the pharmaceutical industry, why should we be concerned about industry profitability? And why do these studies focus on that issue? I think the answer to those questions comes more from the arena of politics than from economics. To many observers there is an issue of legitimacy as to the level of profits earned in any industry. More important than the absolute volume of profits, however, is whether they can be characterized as "legitimate." In the political arena, if not in economics, there is acceptance of the viewpoint that profits earned on certain activities or that promote certain results are legitimate, while monopoly profits are not. In the studies by Henderson and Cockburn, Grabowski and Vernon, Myers and Shyam-Sunder, and Clarkson, and indeed in the entire stream of literature dating back to the Kefauver hearings, the real question is not so much whether substantial profits exist but how they should be characterized. Should they be described in ways that are viewed as politically legitimate or in ways that are considered politically illegitimate?

All four studies seek to answer the political question of whether profits in the pharmaceutical industry are legitimate. That being so, consider how Clarkson, Grabowski and Vernon, and Myers and Shyam-Sunder treat the issue. Clarkson argues that profits in the pharmaceutical industry are legitimate because they are returns to intangible capital. Note that profits which are returns to intangible capital are still profits, but they are now legitimate because they are the expected and "normal" returns on invested capital.

Profits, of course, result from sales on individual products. Therefore, we must aggregate returns on individual products to determine industry profitability. The standard approach is to aggregate returns across all products for the same firm at a single point in time. In this case, the average includes old and new products and patented and

---

1. The Lerner index is defined as $(P - MC)/P$, where P is the price per unit and MC is the marginal cost of producing a unit.

nonpatented products alike. Clarkson adopts that approach. An alternate approach is to consider average profits earned on various products for the same or very similar vintages but across time and across firms. Grabowski and Vernon adopt that approach. It is a different vantage point but essentially looks at the same issue. There is no way of saying that one approach is better than the other. Each has different problems. The two simply represent different ways of looking at average profitability.

Grabowski and Vernon imply that the profitability of new chemical entities should be higher than for other types of products, so that if we do not find high profits for new drugs, we shall not find them anywhere. I agree and therefore find their results of some interest. While they tabulated returns for individual products, their figure on research costs was the average value taken from the well-known study of DiMasi et al. (1991). On this basis, Grabowski and Vernon report a net present value of $22 million per new chemical entity in 1990 dollars.

My only question on their methodology is their applying a factor of 2.0 to indicate the ratio of total world to U.S. sales. I wondered whether this ratio was consistent with aggregate data, so I reviewed statistics from the Organization for Economic Cooperation and Development for the major industrialized countries. That organization provides statistics on total expenditures for pharmaceuticals, limited to ambulatory care, but at purchasing power parity exchange rates rather than at actual exchange rates. As a result, the OECD data are not perfectly compatible with those that Grabowski and Vernon use.

Still, it is interesting to note that the ratio of world sales to U.S. sales, using OECD data, is not 2.0 but rather 2.8. One problem with this estimate, however, is that it includes Japan, and most sales in Japan are not made by U.S. firms, although some are. Even excluding Japan, however, the ratio is 2.3. I am not suggesting that a ratio of 2.3 or even 2.4, if we include some U.S. sales in Japan, is necessarily the right figure. But there is a question of how sensitive the results presented are to that parameter. While Grabowski and Vernon investigate the issue of sensitivity, they only deal with ratios between 1.9 and 2.1. I tried to guess what effect an estimated ratio of 2.3 or 2.4 would have on the average profitability figures. Using their tables, those values might give estimated profit levels of between $55 million and $66 million per product. While those estimates are very rough, they do suggest that Grabowski and Vernon's profit figures may be understated to the extent that they have understated the ratio of foreign to U.S. sales for their sample of products.

Even using a ratio of 2.0, Grabowski and Vernon find a net present value per new product of $22 million, which can be compared with the Office of Technology Assessment figure of $36 million. Given the many assumptions that are needed and the difficulty in making those estimates, the figures are very similar.

To put these values in some perspective, recall another conclusion from the OTA report: resources flowed into pharmaceutical industry research throughout the 1980s at a real rate of increase of approximately 10 percent per year. That is an enormous rate of inflow of resources into any activity. Returning to the political issue with which I started, I do not know how to determine legitimacy, but surely an inducement for such a substantial flow of resources into a very useful activity such as pharmaceutical research is a relevant factor.

With respect to the study by Myers and Shyam-Sunder, I question one assumption that they made. Their analysis used a corporate tax rate of 46 percent in 1980 and 1984 and a 34 percent tax rate in 1990. Again, it is interesting to look at the data. Using Internal Revenue Service data on the pharmaceutical industry, I found that the ratio of income taxes paid in that industry, before credits, divided by net income, is very similar to the values Myers and Shyam-Sunder used. The ratios that I calculated were 34 percent in 1990, 49 percent in 1984, and 46 percent in 1980. The pharmaceutical industry, however, legitimately takes advantage of the possessions tax credit, which has an important effect on the taxes paid. Therefore, if we look at income taxes paid after all credits except the foreign tax credit, which accounts for foreign taxes actually paid, the rates are very different. In 1990 the tax rate is 23 percent; in 1984 it is 30 percent; and in 1980 it is 31 percent. That factor should affect the cost of capital estimates Myers and Shyam-Sunder offer.

With respect to the Henderson and Cockburn study, it is certainly a plausible hypothesis that research and development is carried on in a highly rivalrous context, that firms compete on that basis, and that patent races ensue. Indeed, many economic models rest on that presumption, and this picture has been viewed as the truth. The only difficulty with that hypothesis is that it is wrong—at least in terms of the simplified model that Henderson and Cockburn apply—the Klondike model. Frederic M. Scherer suggests that perhaps they are confronting a straw man, because the right model takes into account more subtleties than they do—for instance, that races take longer periods of time than their study suggests. At the same time, Henderson and Cockburn do point out that the presence of short-run patent races is inconsistent with the data.

Economists tend to emphasize commonalities across firms in an industry, and it is an easy step for us to assume that firms are homogeneous. That assumption facilitates our analysis, but we need to contest and examine it frequently. Unfortunately, we do not do that so often as we should. The basic result of Henderson and Cockburn's study is that firms are intrinsically heterogeneous, particularly in regard to their research and development programs. That is a very important factor which demands more attention as we work on these issues in the future.

Reference

DiMasi, Joseph A., Ronald W. Hansen, Henry G. Grabowski, and Louis Lasagna. "The Cost of Innovation in the Pharmaceutical Industry." *Journal of Health Economics* 10 (1991): 107–42.

PART FOUR

Cost-Effective Information and Promotion

12
New Uses for Old Drugs

J. Howard Beales III

The impact of advertising and other forms of promotion on markets remains a subject of dispute. Some argue that advertising and other producer-provided information facilitate better consumer decisions and enhance market performance. Others, however, doubt the significance of that role of promotional activity. Such skepticism about the social value of marketing efforts underlies many attacks on advertising. This chapter seeks to inform the debate over the significance of seller-provided information by examining a series of markets in which both the information environment and the legal ability of producers to provide information are changing over time.

Since George Stigler's seminal article on the economics of information (1961), a growing body of literature has considered the market effects of seller-provided information. In consumer goods markets, the focus has been on advertising, often the most significant source of seller-provided information. A number of studies have sought to assess the impact of advertising by examining the effects of various regulatory restrictions on advertising.[1] Generally, those studies have considered a particular market before and after restrictions on advertising were removed and have attributed differences in market outcomes to changes in the ability to advertise. Changes in market outcomes have not been linked directly to advertising expenditures.

This research was supported by George Washington University under a contract with Pfizer, Inc. I am grateful to Alison Keith at Pfizer for arranging access to the the necessary data, and to Vincent Ceniccola of IMS America for assistance in developing the nonstandard compilations of the data necessary for this project. I owe a particular debt of gratitude to Caroline Herron for her diligent assistance in compiling the data. Without her help, this project would not have been possible. Responsibility for any errors or omissions is, of course, my own.

1. See, for example, Ippolito and Mathios (1990), Benham (1972), Bond, Kwoka, Phelan, and Whitten (1980). Those and other studies are discussed in Beales and Muris (1993).

Those studies have concluded that advertising restrictions increase prices and that the ability to advertise facilitates product improvements. Nonetheless, doubts remain about the significance or the generality of these effects (Comanor and Wilson 1979).

Outside consumer markets, there is little direct evidence concerning the effects of seller-provided information. In other markets sellers often rely more heavily on channels such as sales representatives to convey information. Moreover, expert buyers may make less use of seller-provided information than consumers and prefer to rely more on neutral third-party information sources. Thus, the significance of restrictions on seller-provided information in such markets remains in doubt.

Pharmaceutical markets provide a valuable set of "natural" experiments on the role of seller-provided information in markets. When the Food and Drug Administration approves the introduction of a new drug, it also approves labeling that identifies the use or uses for which the drug has been found "safe and effective." Because the agency does not regulate physicians' prescribing behavior, however, doctors can prescribe the drug for any condition they deem appropriate. As information emerges about the effectiveness of a drug for other conditions, such off-label uses are likely to increase in significance. Indeed, for some conditions, the drugs of choice are products that have only been formally approved for some other condition.[2]

Although a physician's use of an approved drug is unconstrained, the manufacturer's ability to provide information about appropriate uses is tightly controlled. In particular, manufacturers cannot legally advertise a product for any use that the FDA has not specifically approved in its labeling.[3] Moreover, the FDA has taken an expansive view of what constitutes illegal advertising and promotion, particularly in the past few years.[4]

If a new use of a drug that is already on the market is sufficiently important, and the evidence sufficiently persuasive, a manufacturer can seek the FDA's approval to add that new indication to its product

---

2. In particular, most cancer patients are treated with a course of therapy that includes unapproved drugs (Laetz and Silberman 1991). Overall, an estimated 25 percent of all prescriptions are for unapproved uses ("The FDA's Next Target: Drugs," *Time*, July 15, 1991, p. 56).

3. 21 CFR 202.1(e)(6)(xi) (1991).

4. The FDA's expansive interpretation of its authority and recent activity against such activities as press releases and sponsorship of scientific conferences are discussed in Levine (1993). See Cooper (1992) for an excellent discussion of the limits of the FDA's authority.

labeling. When (and if) the FDA approves the new indication, the manufacturer can then use advertising, detailing, and other forms of promotion to inform physicians of the new use. Changes in the market after promotional activity is permitted provide a natural experiment in the importance of pharmaceutical marketing as a source of information for physicians.

Information Sources Available to Physicians

Given a patient's diagnosis, physicians seek to select the most appropriate therapy. Medically, the most appropriate therapy depends on the balance of the risks and benefits of alternative therapies, both drug and nondrug. Economically, the choice of the optimal therapy requires balancing the net benefits of each therapy against its price.[5] The optimal therapy may well differ from one patient to another because of other conditions, failure to respond to the first-choice therapy, the risks of particular side effects in certain patients, or differences in patient incomes.

Of course, judgments of which therapy is medically most appropriate depend on the state of the scientific evidence, which is changing over time. Equally important, physicians' judgments about the appropriate therapy will depend on the information available to them.

Two primary sources of information are available to physicians: the medical literature and the information manufacturers provide.[6] Information from the medical literature is presumably objective and the peer-review process protects its validity.[7] Using the literature as a source of information, however, is relatively costly. Searching out and reading articles addressing therapies appropriate for a particular patient require substantial amounts of time and effort. Moreover, a single

---

5. This assumes that physicians act as agents to maximize the utility of the patient. It seems unlikely that agency problems would lead physicians to choose medically inferior treatments. Among equivalent products, however, physicians may have incentives to choose more costly drugs that are, because of promotion, easier for them to remember. All of the costs are to the patient, and the physician realizes savings of time and effort. See Leffler (1981).

6. There are, of course, other sources of information available. Physicians discuss treatment options with colleagues and can rely on their own experience with partiular products. These information channels are unlikely to operate any differently before and after approval of a new use.

7. The adequacy of peer review to ensure accuracy is subject to some dispute. Studies that have resubmitted previously approved articles for peer review have found a high incidence of rejections and recommended changes. See, for example, Garfunkel, Ulshen, Hamrick, and Lawson (1990).

article does not necessarily reflect the state of the evidence, and it may be contradicted by other, more reliable studies. Synthesizing various articles to reach conclusions about the relative merits of particular therapies requires additional time and effort. The relatively high cost of using the medical literature should tend to make alternative sources of information attractive to physicians.

The second source of information available to physicians is the drug manufacturer. Although seller-provided information is likely to emphasize the positive aspects of a particular product, it is presented in a form that is designed to be easy to use and remember and offers conclusions based on the literature as a whole. Moreover, the seller's interest in his reputation and concerns about liability, together with regulatory scrutiny of promotional claims, provides some confidence that the information presented is accurate. Thus, seller-provided information can serve as a lower-cost source of information for physicians.

At the very least, seller-provided information can reliably identify drug products that are candidates as the appropriate therapy for an individual patient. The drug's approved labeling, which is readily available in the *Physicians' Desk Reference*, provides a more complete picture of the product's risks and benefits. Similarly, information gleaned from advertising or a sales representative's presentation may increase attention to journal articles discussing similar uses. Thus, seller-provided information may also complement other information sources available to physicians.

Before approval of a particular indication for a drug, the primary source of information available to physicians is the medical literature. After approval of a new use, seller-provided information is likely to become available. The reduced cost of obtaining information should increase the amount of information available in the marketplace.

The enriched information environment after approval has implications for several different market outcomes. First, we would expect to see an increase in the share of patients treated with the newly approved product. Some physicians who become aware of the availability of an alternative therapy are likely to find it the most appropriate therapy for some of their patients.

To some extent, of course, one might expect to see the increased use of a newly approved product simply because the FDA had certified the validity of that use. Such a certification effect should appear as a one-time increase in the use of the product after approval. If increased product use is attributable to the changed information environment, however, it should appear gradually over time and should be related to measures of market information flows.

Second, we should expect to see some increase in the total fraction of patients treated with drug therapy. Such an effect could arise for two reasons. Enhanced information flows would increase the likelihood that a physician who diagnoses the condition is aware of an appropriate therapy. Moreover, the new product may represent the only appropriate drug treatment for some patients. Either effect implies an increase in the fraction of patients treated.

Third, the enhanced information environment should increase competitive pressures on other products used to treat the condition. Although the product is available for use before its approval for the new indication, an effective competitive presence is likely to depend on the ability to inform physicians that the product is safe and effective for the new use. If the availability of an additional treatment option enables better matching of patients to drug treatment therapy, average prices may increase with entry. On the other hand, enhanced competition in the market should reduce the price that consumers pay for drugs used to treat the condition. Thus, with greater promotional expenditures on the new product, we would expect to find average prices lower than they would otherwise have been after a new product is approved.

The Data

The data consist of all drugs that were approved for a second indication between 1984 and 1987 that had previously been on the market for at least four years.[8] For each product, data cover the period from five years before approval of the new indication (or before original approval if the drug had been on the market less than five years) through 1992. The final sample consists of 201 observations on seventeen unique drug and indication combinations.[9] I used multiple regres-

---

8. For 1986 and 1987, the Pink Sheet published a complete list of supplemental approvals of new uses. All products on the list that had been on the market for at least four years were selected. A comprehensive list was not available for 1984 and 1985. Drugs were identified by searching the Pink Sheet for articles about new indications. Thus, the 1984 through 1985 sample may be less comprehensive than the sample for 1986 and 1987 and may be skewed toward new uses that are more commercially significant. With the model reported in table 12–1, however, the data are consistent with the hypothesis that the 1984 through 1985 sample fits the same relationship. Four drugs from the 1986 through 1987 sample were dropped because other necessary data were not available.

9. The sample includes fifteen different indications and sixteen different drugs. Two products, verapamil and captopril, were approved for hypertension within the sample period. Two other products, calcitonin and conjugated

sion analysis to explore the factors determining various outcomes (market share, patient treatment, and average price) across markets.

A new indication might be a distinctly different condition or a distinctly different patient population. Thus, the new indication and the indications for which the drug was originally approved may overlap.[10] In each case, however, the new approval expands the patients for whom the drug is appropriate, given its approved labeling, and should therefore increase its share of the new market.

Because the other data in the analysis are annual observations, I considered a drug to be approved in the first year in which it had been approved for at least six months. The approval dates used in the empirical analysis therefore range from 1985 to 1988. A dummy variable, *APPROVED*, is equal to one in all years in which a product is approved for the indication, and zero otherwise. I define *TREND* as the year minus the year of approval. Thus, *TREND* counts time before and after the year of approval and is zero in the year of approval itself.

The source of data on the use of each drug for the new indication is the National Disease and Therapeutic Index (NDTI), published by IMS America. Using a sample of physicians in office-based practice, NDTI reports all drugs used by patients with a particular diagnosis.[11] I aggregated the different diagnoses for which the drug would be appropriate, given the newly approved indication, to define indication-

---

estrogens, were approved for osteoporosis. One drug, verapamil, was simultaneously approved for treatment of cardiac arrhythmia and hypertension. The other products and markets were acetylcysteine for acetaminophen poisoning, beclomethasone for nasal polyps, bromocriptine for acromegaly, cinoxacin for urinary infections, calcitriol for hypocalcemia and metabolic bone disease in dialysis patients, nystatin for intestinal candida infections, cyclophosphamide for nephrotic syndrome, ketoconazole for recalcitrant dermatophyte infections, naproxen for juvenile arthritis, propranolol for essential tremors, tamoxifen for breast cancer, and daunorubicin for leukemia.

10. The most extreme overlap in the sample involves captopril. Captopril's original approval in 1981 was limited to patients who had not responded to other antihypertensive therapies. Thus, it was a treatment of last resort for hypertension. Revised labeling, approved in 1985, permitted use of captopril as first-line therapy. Although the diagnoses for the original and secondary markets are identical, captopril's potential share of the market was substantially greater after the new indication was approved.

11. The sampling frame for NDTI is patient visits. For each visit, information is collected about the diagnosis and all drugs that the physician has recommended. Prescriptions, however, may have been written on some prior visit.

specific markets for each drug.[12] NDTI provided annual data on the total uses of the drug,[13] uses of each of the top twenty drugs within the market,[14] and the total number of patient visits, divided between visits in which any drug was used and those in which no drug was used.

Using the NDTI data, I defined two outcome measures. *LOVISITS* is the drug's share of all visits with the proper diagnoses. Thus, increases in *LOVISITS* reflect substitution of the drug for other products used for the same diagnosis as well as use of the drug for patients who would not otherwise have been treated. *LOTREAT* measures the share of patients with the relevant diagnoses who are treated with any drug. Thus, it reflects only changes in the incidence of drug therapy, without regard to the products used. Both variables are the logarithm of the odds ratio of the relevant market share.[15]

I measured price as the average price per prescription[16] for the

---

12. Diagnosis codes in the NDTI are based on the World Health Organization's International Classification of Diseases. Data were available for four-digit diagnosis codes. Because the coding scheme was changed in 1986, a handful of diagnostic categories that could not be tracked across the code changes were dropped. I am grateful to Dr. Sal Giorgianni of Pfizer for his assistance in reviewing tentative categorizations of the diagnosis codes and suggesting changes.

13. Uses of all chemically equivalent products, whether identified by brand name or generic name, were included in total sales of the subject drug. Four drugs, with five different newly approved indications, were sold under multiple brand names.

14. NDTI includes, subject to sample size requirements, data on all products used for the diagnosis. As I shall discuss, attention was confined to the top twenty products to make the otherwise overwhelming data collection task manageable.

15. Thus, $LOVISITS = \log (s_{it}/(1 - s_{it}))$, where s_{it} = total uses of the drug for indication i in year t as a fraction of all patient visits with indication i in year t. Nineteen observations were excluded because $s_{it} = 0$. Similarly, $LOTREAT = \log (v_{it}/(1 - v_{it}))$, where v_{it} is patient visits in which any drug is used divided by total patient visits. Logistic regressions were estimated using weighted least squares. In constructing the weights, the actual NDTI sample size for the diagnosis was used.

16. The price per prescription reflects the average prescription filled for all uses of a particular drug, rather than uses for the particular diagnoses that constitute an indication-specific market. The average quantity dispensed for the new indication may differ from the average quantity used for other conditions. The implicit assumption in using average price per prescription is that the relationship between prescription size and diagnosis is the same for the subject drug and competitive products. In any event, there is no apparent reason to expect a change in this relationship before and after approval.

287

newly approved drug relative to the weighted average price of the top twenty drugs in each market.[17] Reflecting the relative price of the subject drug compared with other products in the market, this is the price measure that should influence *LOVISITS*. I obtained the price per prescription from IMS America's National Prescription Audit.[18]

Two other price measures reflect the relative price of drug therapy in a given category. *TOP20PR* is the weighted average price per prescription of the top twenty competitive drugs in the category, deflated by the consumer price index for prescription drugs. *PRICEALL* is the weighted average price per prescription for all products in the market, including both the subject drug and the top twenty competitive products, again deflated by the CPI for prescription drugs. Those price variables should influence changes in *LOTREAT*. I also used them as dependent variables to examine the influence of approval on price.

To determine the number of approved competitors, *NAPPRCOMP*, I counted each of the top twenty drugs that had been approved for the same indication as the subject drug. Just as approval of the subject drug should tend to increase its share of the market, additional approved competitors should tend to reduce its share.[19]

I obtained promotion data for the subject drugs from IMS America's National Journal Audit, which covers advertising in leading medical journals, and its National Detailing Audit, which measures detailing (or sales representative) expenditures. *PROMOTION* is total expenditures on detailing and journal advertising. *JRNLADS* is advertising expenditures in medical journals, and *DETAIL* is total detailing expenditures. In markets where several brands of the newly approved drug were sold, the promotion variables are the total expenditures of

---

17. In markets with generics or multiple brands, the price of the subject drug was calculated as the weighted average of the price of each product, with uses in the market as weights. Uses were also employed as weights in calculating the average price of the top twenty competitive products. For competitive products, however, prices used were the prices for a particular brand, rather than the average price for all brands of a particular molecule.

18. Attention was limited to the top twenty drugs in each market (in each year) to reduce the volume of data needed. Even so, constructing the price of competitive drugs involved collecting data on some 600 products. The top twenty drugs account for an average of 74 percent of all drug uses in the market, but for some observations, they account for as little as 42 percent of all uses in the market.

19. Drugs among the top twenty may well have been approved for other uses that fall within the market. *NAPPRCOMP* counts only those drugs approved for the same indication as the subject drug.

all brands advertised.[20] For all three measures, I deflated expenditures in each year by the implicit price deflator for services to account for changes in the price of promotional activities over time. To provide a measure of scale across markets, I divided real expenditures by the number of patient visits in the market.[21]

Because our interest is in changes in the effects of marketing activities after approval, I used interactions between the marketing variables and approval status to allow for different effects. Those variables are designated with the suffix *AFT*. For example, *PROMOTIONAFT* is equal to *PROMOTION* times *APPROVED*. Thus, before approval, *PROMOTIONAFT* is equal to zero; after approval, it is equal to *PRO-MOTION*. Other *AFT* variables are defined similarly.

The measures of promotional activity are not ideal, primarily because they take no account of the content of the communications involved. In many instances a second indication may be a distinctly smaller market than other uses of the product. Promotional decisions in such instances would presumably be dominated by the needs of the larger market. Even when the second indication is a relatively large fraction of total sales, however, some expenditures presumably promote other uses of the drug. Thus, assigning all promotional expenditures to the new market tends to overstate the manufacturer's expenditures on bringing information about the new use to the attention of physicians.

To explore the influence of information obtained from medical journals, I constructed several measures of the number of English language articles in MEDLINE, a computerized database of the medical literature. The first, *JRNLINDX*, measures the state of scientific knowledge about the new use for the drug over time. For each year in the sample period, I determined the cumulative number of articles discussing therapeutic uses of the drug in connection with the newly ap-

---

20. A series of dummy variables allows the effect of marketing expenditures to differ in these markets. For example, *MULTJRNL* is equal to *JRNLADS* in markets with multiple brands and zero otherwise. Alternative models using the weighted average advertising expenditures of brands in multiple drug markets yielded similar results.

21. Ideally, we would like to measure the average number of messages delivered to an individual physician prescribing in this market. Total expenditures reflect the number of messages, but they also increase with the size of the audience exposed to those messages. Total expenditures per physician would better capture differences across markets in the amount of information conveyed. If patient visits per physician are constant over time and across markets, expenditures per visit would be perfectly correlated with expenditures per physician.

proved indication by a keyword search. I defined *JRNLINDX* as the cumulative number of journal articles in that year, divided by the cumulative number of articles in 1992. Thus, the index of journal articles is always equal to one in 1992.

I developed an additional measure, *PCTTHER*, as a possible measure of the extent to which articles were positive or negative. *PCTTHER* is equal to the percentage of articles mentioning the drug and the indication that also mention therapeutic use. Unlike *JRNLINDX*, *PCTTHER* is based on the flow of journal articles in each year.[22] It was thought that a larger fraction of articles discussing therapeutic uses would reflect more positive results, since reports of adverse reactions or other problems would often not appear under therapeutic uses. In fact, however, as discussed below, the effect of *PCTTHER* is generally negative.

The Results

Marketing and the Drug's Share of Visits. The basic results with the drug's share of visits as the dependent variable appear in table 12–1.[23] Price is negative and significant. Each additional approved competitor reduces share. In five of the seventeen markets, the chemical is sold under multiple brands. Each such brand, measured by *NBRANDS*, significantly increases the chemical's share of the market. *NCATEG* reflects a characteristic of the NDTI data with no obvious economic meaning; it is the number of different diagnostic categories that were combined to build the market data. Share is higher when more categories were combined, which may reflect some double counting of patients with multiple diagnoses.

There is an underlying downward trend in the drug's market share, both before and after approval for the new indication.[24] This trend may reflect the continued introduction of other products that can be used to treat the condition. *JRNLINDX* is positive and highly significant; the time path of use of the product is strongly related to the time pattern of journal articles discussing the use.[25] Thus, despite

22. A similar variable based on the cumulative number of articles was never significant.

23. This model, like all of the other models discussed, included a set of dummy variables that allow the level of market share to differ for each drug and indication combination. These coefficients are not reported.

24. When a separate variable is included to allow trend to differ after approval, it is positive but not significant.

25. Models that allow the effect of *JRNLINDX* to differ after approval indicate that this variable may be slightly less influential after approval, but the effect is not statistically significant.

TABLE 12–1
DETERMINANTS OF THE DRUG'S SHARE OF PATIENT VISITS

Variable	Coefficient (t-statistic)[a]
INTERCEPT	−4.7257 (−8.67)
APPROVED	−.3540 (−2.17)
NAPPRCOMP	−.0622 (−2.00)
TREND	−.1475 (−3.75)
PROMOTION	−.1555 (−3.82)
PROMOTIONAFT	.2440 (6.46)
MULTPROMO	.1592 (2.62)
MULTPROMOAFT	−.2107 (−4.30)
PRICE	−.5349 (−3.64)
JRNLINDX	2.4796 (5.50)
PCTTHER	−.2617 (−1.87)
FLOWAFT	.0150 (6.38)
ADJINTAFT	−.0074 (−2.44)
NBRANDS	.6834 (7.10)
NCATEG	.1314 (3.67)
Adj. R-squared	.8390
F	32.435

NOTE: Dependent variable is log odds share of visits (LOVISITS).
a. All variables significant at .05 or better. Model also included sixteen industry specific dummy variables, not reported. Estimated via weighted least squares.

291

the negative trend coefficient, market share before introduction is essentially flat, with an increasing fraction of journal articles offsetting the negative trend effect. After approval, but not before, the annual flow of journal articles discussing therapeutic use of the drug increases use, as indicated by the coefficient of *FLOWAFT*.[26] In essence, *JRNLINDX* measures the stock of information in medical journals, whereas *FLOWAFT* measures the annual change in the stock after approval. Before approval, only the stock of information matters; after approval, the flow of articles has an additional effect. *PCTTHER* is significant and negative; additional articles about the drug and the indication that do not discuss therapeutic use also tend to increase the drug's share of visits.[27]

The effects of promotional expenditures are complex. Five different variables, each of which is significant, reflect the influence of promotional expenditures.[28] The basic variable, *PROMOTION*, is

---

26. A separate variable measuring the flow of journal articles before approval was not significant.

27. An additional journal article in a given year has effects on prescribing behavior through *JRNLINDX*, *PCTTHER*, and in years after approval, *FLOWAFT*. In any given year,

$$JRNLINDX_t = \frac{\sum_t THERIND_i}{\sum_{92} THERIND_i},$$

$$PCTTHER_t = \frac{THERIND_t}{IND_t},$$

where $THERIND_i$ is the number of journal articles in year i discussing the drug in connection with both the new indication and therapeutic use, and IND_i is the number of articles discussing the drug and the indication. An additional article concerning therapeutic use in year t will increase *LOVISITS* by

$$\beta_j * \frac{\sum_{92} THERIND_i - \sum_t THERIND_i}{(\sum_{92} THERIND_i)^2} + \beta_p * \frac{(IND_t - THERIND_t)}{(IND_t)^2},$$

where β_j = *JRNLINDX* coefficient,
$\quad\quad\beta_p$ = *PCTTHER* coefficient.

Thus, the effect of an additional article through *JRNLINDX* is diminishing over time. Evaluated at the sample means in the year before approval, an additional journal article concerning therapeutic uses increases *LOVISITS* by .002 (t = .95). After approval, there is an additional effect through *FLOWAFT*. The combined effect of one additional article discussing therapeutic use in the year of approval is .016 (t = 4.55).

28. Other models also included the lagged value of postapproval promotion as an independent variable. The lagged value was never significant, however.

TABLE 12–2
EFFECTS OF PROMOTIONAL EXPENDITURES BY TYPE OF MARKET

| | Coefficient (t-statistic) | |
	Before approval	After approval
Single	− .1555[a]	.0085[a]
	(− 3.81)	(2.61)
Multiple	.0037	.0370[a]
	(.08)	(2.18)

NOTE: Calculated from coefficients in table 12–1, neglecting effect of *ADJINTAFT*.
a. Significant at .05.

promotion expenditures per visit and is defined for each observation. The two *MULT* promotion variables allow for different effects of promotion spending in multiple drug markets; the two promotion variables with the *AFT* suffix allow for different effects of promotion spending after approval.[29] To simplify comparisons of the effects of promotion, table 12–2 presents the net effects of promotion spending in each type of market.[30] A fifth variable, *ADJINTAFT*, allows for an interaction between promotional expenditures and the flow of journal articles after approval.[31]

Before approval, the effect of promotional expenditures on the drug's share of patient visits is negative. Because marketing expenditures are limited to approved product uses, higher levels of promotional expenditures, by enhancing physicians' knowledge of approved uses, could tend to reduce unapproved uses of the product.[32] Promotional expenditures before approval of a new indication have significantly greater effects in multiple drug markets, as indicated by the

29. *MULTPROMO* is a slope dummy variable that allows the effect of promotion expenditures to differ in multiple drug markets. It is equal to *PROMOTION* in multiple drug markets and zero in single drug markets. Thus, in multiple drug markets the net effect of promotion expenditures on share before approval is the sum of the *PROMOTION* coefficient and the *MULTPROMO* coefficient.

30. The coefficients are calculated from the data in table 12–1 by adding the coefficients of the relevant variables. Thus, for example, the net effect of promotion spending in single-drug markets after approval is the sum of the *PROMOTION* and the *PROMOTIONAFT* coefficients.

31. Table 12–2 does not reflect this channel of advertising influence.

32. Similar informational spillovers, in which advertising by one producer may actually reduce aggregate demand for the product as a whole, have been documented in a variety of other contexts (Calfee 1993).

coefficient of *MULTPROMO*. Even so, the net effect of promotional expenditures in multiple drug markets is essentially zero, with a combined coefficient of .0037 ($t = .08$).

After the new indication is approved, the influence of promotion expenditures is significantly greater. In both single and multiple drug markets, the total effect of promotional expenditures is to increase the drug's share of the market. The effect is more than twice as great in single drug markets, however.[33]

The reason for the difference between the effects of promotion in single and multiple drug markets is unclear. Before approval, promotion has more influence on sales in the new market when the chemical is sold under several brand names. After approval, however, promotion in such markets is less influential than in markets with only one brand. Reduced influence in multiple drug markets could reflect a measurement problem, since *PROMOTION* measures the total advertising of all competing brands, but even when promotion is measured as the weighted average of brand spending, it is less influential after approval. Alternatively, the information provided in multiple brand markets may tend to focus on the differences between competing products, rather than on the characteristics they share. If so, promotion would convey approved uses less intensively. Before approval, the reduction in demand for unapproved uses would be smaller. After approval, increased use for the new indication would be smaller as well.

The last variable reflecting the influence of promotion is *ADJINT-AFT*, the product of promotional spending per visit and the number of journal articles in each year after approval. Its coefficient is significant and negative, which indicates that additional promotional spending reduces the influence of journal articles and that additional journal articles reduce the influence of promotional spending. Indeed, if more than twelve journal articles appear in a given year (five in multiple drug markets), the calculated influence of advertising after approval is to reduce the drug's share of visits. Intuitively, that result suggests that large flows of information in either channel, whether journal articles or promotional information, tend to reduce the influence of the other channel.

Unlike the other results, however, the estimated effect of ADJINT-AFT is sensitive to a handful of observations. Deleting just six observations with large values of both promotion and journal articles reduces the coefficient to $-.0058$ ($t = -1.03$). Five of those observations are in just one market (bromocriptine for treatment of acromegaly), where

---

33. The coefficient on *MULTPROMOAFT* in table 12–1 indicates that the difference is statistically significant.

TABLE 12–3
EFFECTS OF JOURNAL ADVERTISING VERSUS DETAILING

	Before	After
Single Drug Markets		
Journal advertising	.0977	−.0703
	(.54)	(−.53)
Detailing	−.4527[a]	.1521[a]
	(−2.11)	(2.70)
Multiple Drug Markets		
Journal advertising	−.1417	.0586
	(−.51)	(.50)
Detailing	.0618	.0380[a]
	(.54)	(2.13)

NOTE: Numbers are combinations of coefficients. The t-statistics are in parentheses. Model included same variables as table 12–1. Coefficient combinations neglect effect of *ADJINTAFT.*
a. Significant at .05.

the new indication was approximately 11 percent of total uses of the drug in 1992 and the flow of journal articles was relatively high. Deleting those observations results in virtually no change in other coefficients or their significance. Thus, the apparent interaction appears to be a special feature of a small number of observations.

The results in tables 12–1 and 12–2 combine journal advertising and detailing expenditures in a single promotion measure. Table 12–3 presents the results when we examine those forms of spending separately.[34] It is detailing expenditures that are responsible for the total promotion effects discussed above.[35] Journal advertising, whether in single or multiple drug markets, has no significant influence on share, before or after approval. Detailing expenditures are, on average, substantially larger than journal advertising expenditures ($2.86 versus $.94 per visit). Moreover, detailing expenditures increase in the period after approval ($3.86 after approval versus $1.59 before), while advertising expenditures decline ($.82 versus $1.10).

In short, information provided by the manufacturer after approval for a new indication significantly increases the drug's share of the new

34. Only the coefficients for the promotion variables are presented. Other coefficients change very little.
35. Results are very similar when detailing is measured as detail minutes per visit.

market. Detailing is the more important channel for providing that information. In both single and multiple drug markets, the basic conclusion that manufacturer-provided information significantly increases the drug's share of the market holds.[36]

The results provide little support for the notion that it is approval itself, rather than seller-provided information, that drives the increased use of the product. If diffusion of information about approval through channels other than seller-provided information produced the effects, we would expect to see an upward jump in share upon approval, and the increase in share should depend only on the passage of time rather than on promotional spending. The coefficient of the APPROVED variable, however, is negative.[37] Models allowing for different effects of trend and the stock of articles in medical journals before and after approval (in addition to the effects of promotional spending) found no significant difference in either coefficient. Although the flow of additional articles has a positive and significant effect after approval, physicians learned of the fact of approval from some other source, presumably seller-provided information. Thus, the primary influence of approval on increases in the drug's share of the market is through the ability that approval confers to promote the new use.

Marketing and the Fraction of Patients Treated. A second outcome measure of interest is the effect of approval on the fraction of patients

---

36. It is possible that the results reflect a simultaneity problem to at least some extent, since potential share increases are likely to increase manufacturer's expenditures on promotion. To examine this possibility, I reestimated the model by omitting the promotion variables and allowing trend to differ after approval. If the change in regulatory status is important, trend should be significantly greater after approval than before. In the table 12–1 model, the coefficient of trend after approval is positive and just short of significant at the 10 percent level ($t = 1.63$). The coefficient of APPROVED is positive and insignificant, and NAPPRCOMP is no longer significant. With those two variables omitted, the postapproval trend is significantly greater than the preapproval trend at the 6 percent level ($t = 1.87$). The results are consistent with the conclusion that the ability to promote the use after approval is important.

37. The negative and significant coefficient for APPROVED may be an artifact of the model. The change in the coefficient of promotional spending with approval implies a discrete upward jump in market share coinciding with approval. The negative coefficient of APPROVED may simply mean that the effect is less than the change in the promotion coefficients alone would imply. Consistent with this explanation, if the promotion measures are omitted but trend is allowed to differ after approval, the coefficient of APPROVED is positive but insignificant.

with a relevant diagnosis who receive any drug treatment. Table 12–4 presents the results of this analysis, with various combinations of trend and promotional variables included.[38] Although the differences in fit are slight, the best-fitting model (equation (4.1)) does not include any of the promotional variables.

In most formulations, each approved competitor in the market-place significantly increases the fraction of patients with a diagnosis in the market who are treated with some drug therapy. The price of the top twenty competitive products also influences treatment, with higher prices reducing the fraction of patients treated. The effect, however, is insignificant in most formulations.[39] The time pattern of treatment also reflects the time pattern of journal articles discussing the new product, a relationship that is highly significant. Again, the number of brands in multiple drug markets significantly increases the fraction of patients treated with drugs.

As with the drug's share of visits, there is a significant downward trend in the probability of treatment before approval of the new product. After approval, the trend in the fraction of patients treated is significantly greater than the trend before approval, as indicated by the coefficient on *TRENDAFT*. The postapproval trend is the sum of the *TREND* and *TRENDAFT* coefficients. With the promotion variables excluded, it is only .0090 ($t = .47$). If we omit the preapproval trend, however, *TRENDAFT* is positive and significant (equation (4.4)).[40]

Unlike the drug's share of patients treated, the results do not clearly tie the increase in the fraction of patients treated to the new entrant's promotional expenditures. The promotion variables are uniformly weak.[41] Moreover, journal advertising after approval seems to reduce the fraction of patients treated, an effect that is significant when either trend variable is omitted.

Part of the reason for the weaker promotion results may be the

---

38. The estimates are logistic estimates obtained via weighted least squares. Because patients were treated in every market, the analysis is based on all 201 observations.

39. In other analyses the price of the newly approved drug was also included. Its coefficient was generally positive, but did not exceed its standard error. Results using *PRICEALL* as the price measure are virtually identical to those reported.

40. The *APPROVED* dummy variable, allowing for a one-time increase in treatment upon approval, did not exceed its standard error.

41. None of the variables capturing the effects of promotion before approval ever exceeded their standard errors. They were therefore dropped from the analysis. The same was true of *MULTJRNLAFT*.

TABLE 12–4
DETERMINANTS OF THE FRACTION OF PATIENTS TREATED WITH ANY DRUG

	Coefficients (t-statistics)			
Variable	(4.1)	(4.2)	(4.3)	(4.4)
INTERCEPT	.1718	.2071	.4409	.7996[a]
	(.72)	(.81)	(1.66)	(3.89)
NAPPRCOMP	.0436[a]	.0413[a]	.0279	.0368[a]
	(2.60)	(2.43)	(1.58)	(2.09)
TREND	−.0734[a]	−.0723[a]	−.0282	
	(−4.04)	(−3.64)	(−1.55)	
TRENDAFT	.0850[a]	.0813[a]		.0494[a]
	(4.84)	(4.54)		(3.06)
JRNLADSAFT		−.0557	−.0938[b]	−.1064[a]
		(−1.12)	(−1.81)	(−2.15)
DETAILAFT		.0355	.0469[b]	.0410
		(1.36)	(1.71)	(1.52)
MULTDETAILAFT		−.0258	−.0324	−.0347
		(−1.04)	(−1.24)	(−1.36)
TOP20PR	−.0079	−.0081	−.0038	−.0113[a]
	(−1.43)	(−1.45)	(−.65)	(−1.97)
JRNLINDX	.7785[a]	.7821[a]	.7737[a]	.1957[b]
	(4.17)	(3.95)	(3.70)	(1.63)
PCTTHER	−.1067	−.1041	−.0957	−.0247
	(−1.57)	(−1.52)	(−1.32)	(−.37)
NBRANDS	.0702[a]	.0779[a]	.0578	.0782[a]
	(2.08)	(2.27)	(1.61)	(2.20)
NCATEG	.0659[a]	.0696[a]	.0785[a]	.0753[a]
	(3.69)	(3.73)	(4.01)	(3.92)
Adj. R-squared	.9508	.9506	.9450	.9471
F	161.946	143.478	133.162	138.702

NOTE: Dependent variable is log odds share of patients treated with any drug (LOTREAT), estimated via weighted least squares. $N = 201$. Model also includes industry-specific dummy variables.
a. Significant at .05.
b. Significant at .10.

much smaller variability in the fraction of patients treated compared with the drug's share of all treatments. The coefficient of variation for the share of patients treated is .28, compared with 1.14 for the drug's share of visits. Given reduced variability in the data, determining the separate effects of highly correlated variables is difficult. Consistent with that explanation, omitting either trend variable considerably strengthens the promotion coefficients. The effect of journal advertising, however, remains negative and significant.

Clearly, however, in years after approval of a new product in the market, the fraction of patients treated is larger than it would have been otherwise. The previous downward trend is reversed. Moreover, treatment increases as the fraction of journal articles discussing the new use for the product increases. Thus, the increased use of the newly approved drug is not solely the result of shifting among approved products. The increased treatment may be due in part to detailing expenditures, but the link is weak. Seemingly, the public-good aspects of seller-provided information in the markets in this sample are relatively weak.[42]

Marketing and the Price of Prescription Drugs. The third outcome variable of interest is the impact of marketing expenditures on the price of drugs to consumers. The price most relevant to assessing the impact of a manufacturer's promotional expenditures is the average price per prescription of all products in the market (*PRICEALL*), relative to the consumer price index for prescription drugs. If seller-provided information holds down the average price, consumers clearly benefit, even if nothing else in the market changes. Table 12–5 presents the results.

The time pattern of journal articles discussing the new use is a determinant of prices. As the fraction of total journal articles increases, price declines when other factors are held constant. The effect is just short of significant at the 5 percent level ($t = 1.93$, probability $= .056$). After the subject drug is approved, however, the price-reducing effect of additional journal articles is significantly smaller. Although the combined coefficient of *JRNLINDX* after approval is negative, it is not statistically significant (coefficient $= -.44$, $t = -.08$).

Before approval, journal advertising expenditures appear to increase price, but the effect is not statistically significant.[43] After approval for the new indication, however, additional journal advertising expenditures for the new drug significantly reduce the average price in the marketplace.[44] The combined effect is statistically significant,

---

42. This finding is somewhat weaker than Ippolito and Mathios's findings in the market for fiber (1989). They find that cereal advertising of the health benefits of fiber resulted in an increase in consumption of high-fiber bread, but the increase was less than the effect in the cereal market itself.

43. None of the variables for detail expenditures or for multiple drug markets was significant. Therefore, I omit them.

44. Not surprisingly, the primary effect is on the price of competitive products. In separate regressions with the drug's own price as the dependent vari-

TABLE 12–5
DETERMINANTS OF THE AVERAGE PRICE PER PRESCRIPTION

Variable	Coefficient (t-statistic)
INTERCEPT	18.2139[a]
	(2.92)
NAPPRCOMP	.2359
	(.38)
TREND	.5381
	(1.26)
JRNLADS	.6710
	(1.31)
JRNLADSAFT	−1.9919[a]
	(−2.81)
JRNLINDX	−9.3409[b]
	(−1.93)
JRNLINDXAFT	8.9007[a]
	(3.04)
ADJINTAFT	.0323[a]
	(2.21)
NCATEG	−1.3509[a]
	(−2.28)
Adj R-squared	.5495
F	11.164

NOTE: Dependent variable is weighted average price per prescription, all drugs (PRICEALL), estimated via ordinary least squares. Model also includes industry specific dummy variables.
a. Significant at .05.
b. Significant at .10.

with each additional dollar of journal advertising per visit reducing the average price of prescriptions by \$1.32 ($t = -1.98$, significant at .05). At the average value of the other variables, eliminating journal advertising would increase the average price per prescription by \$.61, or 3.7 percent. In the year of approval itself, when average journal ad-

able, the coefficients of both advertising variables were negative but only about half their standard errors. With the price of the top twenty competitive products as the dependent variable, the postapproval advertising coefficient increases in absolute value, and its t statistic improves. Advertising before approval remains insignificant.

vertising expenditures are higher, the price difference attributable to advertising is 11.4 percent.[45]

The competitive price response to information flows is consistent with the notion that the relative importance of seller-provided information increases upon approval. Before approval, the emerging literature indicating that another product is an effective therapy induces a market response that results in a price lower than it otherwise would have been. After approval, however, seller-provided information induces competitive price responses.

Unlike the drug's share of the market, where detailing seemed to be the primary promotional mechanism driving the increase after approval, it is advertising in medical journals that most affects price. The more visible forms of promotion may have a greater effect in prompting a competitive price response. Mirroring the market share results, there is a significant positive interaction between total promotional spending and the number of journal articles in years after approval.

Throughout the sample period, there is a suggestion of an upward trend in prices. The effect, however, is not statistically significant. Additional approved competitors in the market tend to raise the average price, but again the effect is insignificant.

Conclusions and Implications

Approval of already marketed drugs for new indications offers a series of natural experiments in changes in the information environment. As in other industries, the results of those experiments indicate that seller-provided information offers significant benefits for pharmaceutical consumers.

Before approval, the primary available information channel is the medical journals. By law, seller-provided information is not available. The results indicate that physicians do respond to the medical literature. As the stock of articles increases, so does use of the drug for the new indication, with or without FDA approval. That increase is gradual, however, and, given the trend toward lower share that exists in

---

45. Although additional advertising expenditures reduce price, the average price in the market increases upon approval. In the year before approval, *PRICEALL* is $13.61 versus $14.90 in the year of approval and $19.39 in the year after approval. The regression analysis attributes this increase to the changed coefficient of *JRNLINDX*.

those markets,[46] it is sufficient only to keep the drug's share essentially constant. The emerging medical literature also increases the fraction of patients with the indication who are treated and reduces the average price per prescription for all drugs used for the indication, relative to other pharmaceutical products.

After approval, the drug can be promoted legally for the new indication. Seller-provided information becomes an important source of information to assist physician prescribing. The drug's share of patients with the relevant diagnosis increases substantially, an effect that is tied to promotional expenditures in general and to detailing expenditures in particular. In the average market the newly approved drug's share four years after approval is 2.8 times its share in the year it was approved.[47]

Unquestionably, most of this growth is at the expense of other products already in the market. Nonetheless, it seems clear that growth also represents additional patients treated. After approval, a downward trend in the fraction of patients treated is reversed. Moreover, the likelihood of treatment increases with additional articles discussing the new use of the drug in the medical literature. Although changes in the fraction of patients treated with drugs are not closely linked to seller-provided information, it seems clear that some of the drug's share growth is among patients who otherwise would not have been treated with any drug.

Even if all of the increase in a newly approved drug's share were at the expense of competitive products, it is likely to benefit consumers. In the physician's judgment, informed by both the medical literature and seller-provided information, the newly approved drug is the most appropriate therapy for those patients for whom it is prescribed. Moreover, in six of the seventeen markets in this sample, there were no other drugs approved for the same indication at any time during the sample period; in one additional market there was an approved competitor only in the last year of the sample period. In these markets seller-provided information necessarily diverts sales from unapproved to approved products.

Seller-provided information after approval also increases competition in the marketplace. After entry, additional advertising reduces prices of other products in the market relative to other prescription

---

46. As discussed above, markets are defined on the basis of the specific diagnoses that correspond to the newly approved indication for use.

47. In each market I divided the drug's share in each year by its share in the year it was first approved. I then averaged this index of share growth across the seventeen drug and indication combinations in the sample.

drugs. The average price per prescription is lower, the more seller-provided information is available in the marketplace. Moreover, the reduction in the average price of treatment itself increases the likelihood that patients with the condition will receive some drug therapy.

The data provide no evidence that the increased share of a newly approved product or the reduction in the average price per prescription when entry is more heavily advertised is due to the fact of approval itself. In neither case is the average outcome after approval any better when we hold other factors constant. Nor is there a significantly different trend after approval that might suggest an effect of approval per se. Instead, the increase in share and the reduction in price are closely linked to the flow of seller-provided information in the market. Only in the case of the fraction of patients treated with any drug is there some suggestion in the data of a significantly different trend that may be due to approval itself. Even there, however, the change may well be associated with the flow of seller-provided information.

The measures of seller-provided information do not take account of the actual content of the seller's communication. Undoubtedly, the fraction of communication that discusses the new use varies over time and across markets. Such measurement problems would generally bias the results against finding any effect of seller-provided information. Despite this bias, expenditures are significantly associated with improved outcomes.

The facts substantiating the efficacy of the subject drugs for their new uses were, of course, available before approval. Indeed, in the average market, a majority of the journal articles discussing the new use had already appeared two years before approval. At the time of approval itself, two-thirds of the journal articles had already appeared. Moreover, the new uses were recognized in *U.S. Pharmacopeia Drug Information*, an authoritative compendium of prescription drug information, an average of 2.5 years before approval.[48] FDA review of re-

---

48. I examined past editions of the *USPDI* to determine when the drug was first identified for the new use. Because the *USPDI* is only published every two years, this procedure tends to understate the delay between authoritative recognition and approval. Indeed, for four markets, the product was not listed in the *USPDI* until after approval. Excluding those drugs, the average lag from listing to approval by the FDA is 3.75 years, with a minimum lag of 2 years and a maximum lag of 6 years. The *USPDI* is published by authority of the United States Pharmacopeial Convention, Inc. Once a product is listed in the *USPDI* for a particular use, expenditures for treatment with that product are eligible for reimbursement under Medicaid, regardless of whether the FDA approves the use.

quests for supplemental indications takes an average of almost two years (DiMasi, Kaitin, Fernandez-Carol, and Lasagna 1991).

Before FDA approval of a product's new use, manufacturers could not provide the facts concerning the efficacy of the product to prescribing physicians. Had they been able to do so, the substantial growth in use of effective medications would have occurred sooner, with obvious benefits to consumers. Similarly, the influence of seller-provided information in reducing the average cost of drug treatments would also have occurred sooner. The evidence indicates that the FDA's regulatory policy of insisting on prior approval before information is provided to physicians imposes significant costs on consumers. Its current efforts to expand its control to any means of conveying information supported even partially by seller funding is therefore likely to reduce consumer welfare, not enhance it. Particularly if the FDA seeks to continue those policies, the agency should strive to shorten review times for approval of new indications substantially.

References

Beales, J. Howard, and Timothy J. Muris. *State and Federal Regulation of National Advertising*. Washington, D.C.: AEI Press, 1993.

Benham, Lee. "The Effect of Advertising on the Price of Eyeglasses." *Journal of Law and Economics* 15 (1972): 337–52.

Bond, Ronald S., John E. Kwoka, John J. Phelan, and Ira T. Whitten. *Effects of Restrictions on Advertising and Commercial Practice in the Professions: The Case of Optometry*. Federal Trade Commission, Bureau of Economics Staff Report, 1980.

Calfee, John E. "Free Speech, FDA Regulation, and Market Effects on the Pharmaceutical Industry." In *Bad Prescription for the First Amendment: FDA Censorship of Drug Advertising and Promotion*, edited by Richard T. Kaplar. Washington, D.C.: Media Institute, 1993.

Comanor, William S., and Thomas A. Wilson. "The Effect of Advertising on Competition: A Survey." *Journal of Economic Literature* 17 (1979): 453–76.

Cooper, Richard M. "The Food and Drug Administration's Authority to Regulate Miscellaneous Statements by Pharmaceutical Manufacturers." In *Promotion of Pharmaceuticals: Issues, Trends, Options*, edited by Dev S. Pathak, Alan Escovitz, and Suzan Kucukarslan. Binghamton, N.Y.: Haworth Press, 1992.

DiMasi, Joseph A., Kenneth I. Kaitin, Cecilia Fernandez-Carol, and Louis Lasagna. "New Indications for Already-Approved Drugs: An Analysis of Regulatory Review Times." *Journal of Clinical Pharmacology* 31 (1991): 205–15.

"The FDA's Next Target: Drugs." *Time* (July 15, 1991): 56.

Garfunkel, Joseph M., Martin H. Ulshen, Harvey J. Hamrick, and Edward E. Lawson. "Problems Identified by Secondary Review of Manuscripts." *Journal of the American Medical Association* 263 (March 9, 1990): 1369–71.

Ippolito, Pauline M., and Alan D. Mathios. *Health Claims in Advertising and Labeling: A Study of the Cereal Market.* Federal Trade Commission, Bureau of Economics Staff Report, August 1989.

———. "Information, Advertising, and Health Choices: A Study of the Cereal Market." *RAND Journal of Economics* 21 (1990): 459–80.

Laetz, Thomas, and George Silberman. "Reimbursement Policies Constrain the Practice of Oncology." *Journal of the American Medical Association* 266 (December 4, 1991): 2996–99.

Leffler, Keith B. "Persuasion or Information? The Economics of Prescription Drug Advertising." *Journal of Law and Economics* 24 (1981): 45–74.

Levine, Arthur N. "FDA's Expanding Control over Drug Promotion." In *Bad Prescription for the First Amendment: FDA Censorship of Drug Advertising and Promotion,* edited by Richard T. Kaplar. Washington, D.C.: Media Institute, 1993.

Stigler, George. "The Economics of Information." *Journal of Political Economy* 69 (1961): 213–25.

13
The Leverage Principle in the FDA's Regulation of Information

John E. Calfee

"No federal court has yet been put in a position to issue an opinion construing the meaning or application of the provisions of section 502(n) of the Food, Drug, and Cosmetic Act in an advertising case."[1]

From the standpoint of information, the pharmaceutical market is extraordinary in at least three respects. First, and most obvious, is information's overwhelming importance. The only difference between a pill that cures headaches and one that prevents heart attacks is superior information about aspirin, and much the same is true of numerous other medicines and devices. Second, the Food and Drug Administration's control over information is extremely tight. Third, this control over information has been established through highly indirect means. Essentially, the FDA has leveraged explicit, statute-based control over drugs to construct an elaborate regulatory structure for information about drugs. That leveraged apparatus for regulating information has no more than a tenuous relationship to legislation or any other legal foundation.

There is little reason to expect such regulation by fiat to provide sound public policy. Moreover, the peculiar economic properties of information compound the potential harm that is bound to arise from unchecked power. Property rights to information are so weak that businesses may have little incentive to use commercial methods for dispensing controversial scientific information in the face of governmental intransigence. Many ideas that could improve markets and deter harmful regulatory action are therefore unlikely to emerge in the form of commercial speech unless regulators are strictly limited in their power over speech. The free speech clause of the First Amend-

---

1. From Fisherow (1987). Fisherow was a member of the small FDA staff devoted to reviewing and regulating pharmaceutical advertising.

ment can provide that limitation. But here, too, the FDA's leveraged power has prevailed. First Amendment law has thus far been largely irrelevant in the regulation of information about pharmaceuticals.[2]

This chapter explores the sources of the FDA's leveraged regulation of information, including advertising and promotion. I outline the reasons for believing that the pharmaceutical market would work better in the absence of that type of regulation and recommend means to restore a reasonable legal regime in which to regulate pharmaceutical promotion.

Sources of FDA Control over Information

The legal underpinnings of the FDA's regulatory regime for information are relatively straightforward to describe, although they are not widely known beyond the legal community. The FDA's power over pharmaceutical promotion arises from its authority to prevent misleading labels. Since being granted that authority in 1938, the FDA has systematically expanded this vague statutory basis to comprehend such basic matters as the distinction between prescription and over-the-counter drugs and the requirement that all pharmaceutical advertisements, including those on television, contain a lengthy "brief summary" of medical considerations. When it chooses to do so, the FDA prohibits direct-to-consumer ads of prescription drugs, regardless of whether the ads contain the brief summary. The FDA also prohibits the mention of unapproved uses of approved drugs, even when other branches of the government and the FDA staff endorse those uses, and has imposed a near prohibition on industry-sponsored seminars.[3]

The FDA has achieved that expansion in regulatory power primarily by means that lie outside the legal system. Essential regulatory developments have not been established through legislation, nor have they been the result of formal rule making. Most remarkably, those measures have in recent decades met with essentially no legal challenge whatever from the industry itself. FDA actions range from isolated sanctions, such as shutting down entire production lines or seizing supplies, to large policy initiatives, such as placing severe restrictions on industry sponsorship of seminars or newsletters. These have sometimes aroused verbal objections. Almost never, however,

---

2. On a recent First Amendment challenge to FDA policies, however, see the citation below to the Washington Legal Foundation lawsuit.

3. Much of this history is recounted in Temin (1979) and Kessler and Pines (1990).

have respondents taken the FDA to court.[4] The FDA's prohibition on offering journal articles or reference books describing unapproved uses, to take one example, has never been exposed to a First Amendment test in the courtroom.[5] On the whole, the FDA has operated by administrative fiat in its regulation of information.

Why has the pharmaceutical industry been so compliant? One hypothesis is that the industry, having found the FDA's policy toward information to be in its collective interest, has accordingly decided not to oppose the central principles of that regulation. That hypothesis acquires plausibility from the fact that the stringent drug approval process established by the 1962 amendments to the Food and Drug Act has apparently reduced competition in the pharmaceutical market and increased the profits of the larger firms at the expense of smaller ones (Thomas 1990). Advertising restrictions often work the same way. The historical record of the effects of advertising restrictions in other markets is so consistently anticompetitive that the Federal Trade Commission has for nearly twenty years followed a policy of attacking blanket restrictions on advertising.[6] One might therefore suspect that the industry would wish to establish an implicit agreement not to oppose narrowly drawn restrictions on speech.

Nonetheless, the conspiracy theory seems untenable. The well-documented tendency for production cartels to fold under pressure also applies to implicit agreements to control information in advertising. Even in the cigarette market, which is both highly concentrated and acutely sensitive to the political dangers of unbridled competition through advertising, individual sellers have persistently pursued advertising campaigns that are calculated to help the seller while threatening the collective interests of the industry.[7] That and similar events

---

4. See Fisherow (1987), who discusses in detail the remarkable fact identified at the beginning of this chapter. Fisherow's table on page 231 shows that of several thousand advertising enforcement letters sent out from 1971 through 1983, only seventeen rose to the level of "regulatory letters," the strongest warnings sent by the staff to firms. In each instance litigation was unnecessary to achieve compliance. Another member of the same part of the FDA staff, writing at the same time, counted only four regulatory letters during the previous six years (Yellin 1987).

5. Such a challenge is now underway, however. The Washington Legal Foundation lawsuit is described below in the Conclusions and Recommendations section.

6. See the FTC's 1984 Policy Statement on Advertising Substantiation, printed in *Antitrust and Trade Regulation Report* 47 (August 2, 1984): 234–235, and appended to *FTC v. Thompson Medical Company*, 104 FTC 648, 839 (1984).

7. The tendency for cigarette sellers to pursue self-interest in advertising at

in many other markets—an example being the persistence of discount price advertising during the years in which the FTC frowned on such advertising—reflect the nature of competition through advertising content.[8] Although advertising claims are public, whereas "cheating" on production limits or negotiated prices is hidden, advertising content is sufficiently malleable and open to interpretation that the temptation for firms to push beyond agreed-upon limits is irresistible. History provides little if any support for the view that sellers can maintain an implicit agreement to adhere to strict and ever-changing guidelines on commercial speech, even when the guidelines are suggested by regulatory agencies.

A far more plausible explanation for the FDA's success in regulating information is that pharmaceutical firms are unwilling to challenge the FDA on matters pertaining to speech, because the FDA wields highly discretionary power over the introduction and manufacture of drugs and devices. Anyone who has spent time with attorneys representing pharmaceutical firms is aware of both the extraordinary deference with which the FDA's personnel are treated and the frequently expressed, off-the-record opinion that no pharmaceutical firm is willing to risk offending FDA staff by vigorously opposing FDA regulation of information. In fact, litigation on those matters has been essentially absent during recent decades. Although regulatory staff members are not the most reliable expositors of the motivations of industry, it is worth noting that FDA staffers responsible for regulating pharmaceutical advertising have themselves remarked on the rational reluctance of firms subject to their jurisdiction to resort to legal means for resisting FDA actions. One staff member, after noting that the FDA had seldom been forced to issue its strongest form of written notification to recalcitrant firms and that the agency had *never* been challenged in court on those matters, considered the reasons for the FDA's remarkable success, especially in contrast with the much-challenged FTC. Fisherow (1987, 231) noted that, unlike the FTC,

> the FDA licenses the prescription drug products subject to its regulation and approves labeling which effectively sets the

---

the expense of the industry goes back to the earliest days of that market. See Hanley (1927), Calfee (1985, 1986), and Ringold and Calfee (1989). Examples of this tendency in cigarette advertising continue to emerge: see *Wall Street Journal*, August 25, 1993, on price advertising for Marlboro brand, and *Wall Street Journal*, January 13, 1993, on the controversy over advertising that mentions the ingredients of cigarettes.

8. On the FTC's ill-fated attempt to restrict discount price advertising, and its eventual conclusion that its policy was actually discouraging beneficial competition, see Harkrader (1962) and Pitofsky (1977).

limits on what may be communicated about product performance. This pervasive involvement in the industry's current and
future business means that a corporate decisionmaker needs
to consider more than just the merits of the company's position in the particular advertising dispute at hand. The executive must also weigh how much disagreement with the FDA
staff in a current matter might affect future treatment. No
such continuing relationship exists between the FTC and any
industry.

It is not surprising, therefore, that current FDA Commissioner David
Kessler and Wayne Pines (1990), surveying the scene shortly before his
appointment, noted, "Companies interested in maintaining positive
relationships with the FDA usually agree to the FDA's remedy [in advertising matters]."[9]

Other facts comport with that view. While explicit challenges to
FDA authority over information have in fact been fairly common
through history, they have emanated almost exclusively from nonphar-
maceutical firms. The food market is the apposite example.[10] In the
1960s and 1970s, food sellers defied the FDA's express prohibition on
mentioning the adverse effects of cholesterol and saturated fat or even
the amount of such ingredients contained in foods. The FDA eventually gave up, drawing a new set of rules that permitted statements
about foods' content but not about disease. It is hard to imagine a similar sequence of events in the pharmaceutical market. In 1984, encouraged by the FTC and the National Cancer Institute, the Kellogg
company mounted a dramatic challenge to the FDA's continued prohibition on describing the evidence linking diet to chronic diseases such
as cancer. Again, the FDA backed down, and again it is highly significant that the challenge came from a firm that had no products awaiting
FDA approval. Until evidence to the contrary emerges, the best working assumption is that it is the FDA's power over drug approval and
manufacture that accounts for its unchallenged power over information.

---

9. Fisherow (1987, 230), after noting that the FDA's advertising policies
have never been tested in court, similarly observes: "This capacity to resolve
difficulties to its satisfaction before they reach the courts has delivered what
FDA wants most, the prompt cessation or transformation of a questioned advertising claim or campaign, with a relatively modest expenditure of resources."

10. This section draws on Hutt (1986) and Calfee and Pappalardo (1989,
1991).

What Would Pharmaceutical Information Be Like under a Different Regulatory Regime?

Because the FDA's regulatory regime for information has been constructed more or less without constraint, there is little reason to think that the result is close to a reasonable balance of costs and benefits. The system almost certainly suppresses far more information than it would if it were subject to the same restraints that apply to regulation of advertising and promotion for other products.

It is therefore appropriate to look beyond the effects of marginal changes in regulation—such as relaxing the restraints on direct-to-consumer advertising of prescription drugs—to ask whether the pharmaceutical market would perform better if current FDA regulation were replaced with a system similar to what has been applied to the promotion of other products. Exploring such a hypothetical question raises many difficulties, but it is arguably the most pertinent approach to constructing proposals to reform the regulation of pharmaceutical promotion.

There are at least three ways to assess how the pharmaceutical market would work under a more liberal informational regime. One approach is general, based on economic reasoning and on relevant experience in diverse markets. A second approach focuses specifically on the kinds of information that the FDA has explicitly suppressed and asks whether the market would have been better off if the FDA had allowed the information to go forward. A third approach, less direct but possibly of the greatest interest, examines those markets in which the FDA shares jurisdiction with the FTC, with particular attention to products that are not subject to the FDA's drug approval jurisdiction. Such markets and products can provide insights into what kind of dynamics can occur when the FDA's leverage tools are not available and regulation therefore operates at a level maintained by the FTC rather than at the FDA's more stringent level.[11]

Theory and History in Diverse Markets. The central assumption underlying FDA policy seems to be that the informational aspects of the pharmaceutical market are so unusual, so dominated by difficult scien-

---

11. The FTC has occasionally imposed stronger requirements than the FDA, an example being *FTC* v. *Thompson Medical Company*, 104 FTC 648, 839 (1984). Such cases are undoubtedly rare. Far more common is the situation that emerged in 1984 when Kellogg began its cancer prevention ads for cereals. The FTC explicitly endorsed the ads, while the FDA staff made it clear that they would have prohibited the ads (Calfee and Pappalardo 1989).

311

tific questions, and so characterized by gross disparities of information between buyer and seller, that no other regulatory arrangement is feasible, or at least, that a more traditional regulatory arrangement would bring severely adverse consequences for the market and for consumer health. It is presumably this view that gives rise to such standards as the often impossible requirement that ads must contain "a balanced account of all clinically relevant information—the risks and benefits— that can affect a physician's prescribing decision" (Kessler and Pines 1990).[12] Commissioner Kessler (1992) has even endorsed the results of a study that assumed that pharmaceutical ads should meet the same standards as refereed medical journals. Of course, free markets would not meet such standards, and that presumably is one of the FDA's justifications for pushing its standards so far beyond what a competitive market would provide.

Neither theory nor history provides reason to think that the pharmaceutical market would work badly if information could be used more freely in advertising and promotion. The problems of information in the markets for, say, automobiles, ski boots, or executive aircraft are probably just as difficult to deal with as the analogous problems of the drug market. What makes those diverse consumer markets work— and little evidence has ever emerged indicating that the informational aspects of most consumer markets do *not* work well—is a combination of third-party informational sources and vigorous competition among product sellers, augmented (perhaps necessarily, perhaps unnecessarily) by an FTC advertising regulation process characterized by an absence of prior restraint and a substantial amount of litigation (all the way to final judgments) on the merits of the advertising and the regulation under review.

The central element in the dynamics of advertising and information is the self-correcting nature of competitive information. Even in markets for risky products, competitive advertising spontaneously devises mechanisms to overcome the most essential informational problems. The central logic is relatively straightforward, although not widely appreciated. Much advertising centers on "less bad" or "less harmful" claims. Examples include reduced fat or cholesterol, less dangerous automobiles, shorter waiting times, and lower prices. Such ads call attention to risks as well as benefits and thus provide an informational balance that would be hard to achieve by other means. Even

---

12. I note in passing that FDA policy routinely *prohibits* ads or labels from containing information about well-established off-label uses, even though that information is part of the "clinically relevant information" that can "affect a physician's prescribing decision."

where claims are positive, surveys have consistently shown that consumers approach ads with skepticism. They tend to believe that ad claims are untrue unless there is specific reason to believe otherwise, and they tend to be suspicious of the motives of advertisers (who are correctly perceived as trying to make a sale rather than provide information).[13] Even after credibility has been achieved, it is easily lost in the face of controverting information, as happened in the "oat bran craze" of the late 1980s.[14]

The effect is that advertising competition, like all competition, works more surely for the benefit of consumers than for the benefit of industry. Rather than an inevitable increase in sales, competitive advertising tends to bring better information and sometimes reduced product consumption.[15]

There are substantial reasons for believing that the same self-correcting processes apply to the pharmaceutical market. The pioneering work of Peltzman (1987) has demonstrated that even in nations where uneducated consumers are free to purchase risky antibiotics and other medicines that in the United States are available only with a prescription, consumers do not in fact incur excess risk. Recent case studies have reinforced his conclusions.[16]

The experience with direct-to-consumer ads for prescription drugs in the United States also reflects a normal, self-correcting market rather than one suffering from intractable problems of information. Research by the FDA staff (Brinberg and Morris 1988) indicates that U.S. consumers (like the non-U.S. consumers in Peltzman's work) are able to appreciate the risks involved in prescription drugs featured in ads. Theoretical reasoning and past experience have found that direct-

---

13. On consumer skepticism through the years, see Calfee and Ringold (1988, 1994). On consumers' tendency to suspect advertisers' motives and to make allowances for improvements in advertising techniques, see Bauer (1958, 1963).

14. See "Oat Bran Popularity Hitting the Skids," *Advertising Age*, May 21, 1990, p. 3.

15. On the phenomenon of "demand reduction" from competitive advertising, see Calfee (1992b). On the effects of advertising on total industry sales in cigarettes and alcohol, the two most studied markets, see Calfee and Scheraga (1994). On the tendency in the newly liberated East German market for alcohol advertising to turn consumers toward drinks with lower and no alcohol content, see Breitenacher (1992).

16. See *CIBA-Geigy Pharmaceuticals (A)*, Harvard Business School case 9–589–108 (1990), and *Nigerian Hoechst Limited* case in Kenneth Bernhardt and Thomas Kinnear, *Cases in Marketing Management*, 4th ed. (Homewood, Ill.: BPI/Irwin, 1988), pp. 396–419.

to-consumer advertising can improve consumer health and reduce consumer risk from drugs. Beyond the obvious effect of more quickly matching consumers with the drugs that can help them, advertising and promotion have brought increased emphasis to smaller dosages and avoidance of side effects. Examples range from nonaspirin analgesics that avoid stomach bleeding to anti-allergy medicines that avoid drowsiness and low-dose aspirin to prevent heart attacks. History has shown that it is when drugs move from prescription to over-the-counter status, and thus allow direct-to-consumer advertising, that such risk information becomes paramount in the minds of consumers (Haley 1984).[17]

There is little reason to believe that physicians, who are the targets of most pharmaceutical promotion, are any more susceptible than ordinary consumers to undue persuasion by marketing or advertising. The chapter by Howard Beales in this volume is the latest research to find that the primary effect of pharmaceutical promotion is to move the market toward more informed choices.[18] Research in other nations has found that physicians, like consumers generally, tend to use drug ads for "search" information such as the availability of a specific drug.[19]

The Value of Information Suppressed by the FDA. Another way to assess the effects of the FDA's unusually stringent regulation of information is to assess directly the value of the information that the FDA has sought to keep from the market. A complete survey of the types of pharmaceutical information the FDA suppressed in recent years is beyond the scope of this chapter. It is clear, however, that at least some

---

17. Haley (1984, 19) notes that it was only after Tylenol entered the market that aspirin sensitivity to the stomach became important in the analgesic market.

18. The much-cited work by Avorn, Chen, and Hartley (1982) finds that prescription drug advertising leads to more prescriptions for advertised brands, even in the absence of stronger science based in published journal articles. This finding is consistent, however, with a standard "signaling" model of advertising and information, in which sellers correctly anticipate which drugs are likely to hold up well under physician scrutiny and allocate their advertising expenses accordingly. On signaling through advertising, see Ippolito (1990).

19. Reekie and Otzbrugger (1984, 26) describe survey results indicating that physicians find pharmaceutical ads most useful for learning of the existence of drugs, rather than for information on efficacy. On the distinction between "search" qualities of products, which buyers can assess before purchase, versus "experience" qualities, which they can assess only after purchase, see Nelson (1970).

of the promotional practices in question were probably beneficial. The documented benefits of direct-to-consumer advertising of prescription drugs indicate that consumers have probably suffered from the FDA's historic reluctance to allow such advertising and from the agency's insistence on burdensome disclosures (Masson and Rubin 1985). A recent example is the fact that advertising for nicotine patches was nearly driven from television by the FDA's insistence on excessive within-ad disclosures, even though it was well recognized within the advertising and tobacco industries that such advertising probably constituted a highly effective set of antismoking ads. Similarly, the reverse side of the documented benefits of health claims for foods (discussed in the next section) is the harm that resulted when such advertising was prohibited.

A topic of even greater importance is information on unapproved ("off-label") uses for FDA-approved drugs and devices. When the FDA approves drugs and devices, it does so for specific applications. Physicians, however, are free to prescribe approved products for other, off-label uses. The quick pace of medical research and the rapid accumulation of practical experience, combined with the high costs of obtaining formal FDA approval, guarantee that unapproved uses will always be important. The economic properties of information reinforce that tendency, because manufacturers of off-patent or easily imitated drugs and devices have little incentive to make the investments necessary to incur the cost of obtaining FDA approval for a well-established medical practice when the benefits of such approval would quickly spread to competing manufacturers. It is hardly surprising, therefore, that an American Medical Association official recently estimated that roughly half of all drugs are prescribed for off-label uses, and that for cancer treatment (especially for children) from 60 percent to 90 percent of all drug regimens consist of unapproved uses of approved drugs (Skolnick 1994).

Despite those circumstances, the FDA has in recent years placed substantial emphasis on halting the promotion of off-label uses, and in so doing it has employed an expansive definition of "promotion" (Calfee 1992a). The practices in question include the sponsorship of continuing education seminars that describe new and unapproved uses of approved drugs, sponsorship of newsletters that include descriptions of studies that document unapproved uses, and distribution of journal articles on new uses.[20] The FDA specifically condemned at-

---

20. A prominent provider of continuing medical education seminars has stated, "If you prevent the discussion of off-label uses of medications, there would be little point in holding CME programs" (Skolnick 1994, 335). The FDA's concern is with the role played by industry in funding and in controlling the content of continuing medical education.

tempts to circulate the teachings of respected third-party sources such as the National Cancer Institute or widely respected medical compendia.

The FDA's campaign to eliminate such sources has generated criticism from medical authorities and even from patient advocacy groups, who have found themselves losing access to treatment.[21] Deserving of greater notice is the expansion of this campaign to include medical devices. Information about hardware surgical pins, to take a simple example, cannot easily be assembled and distributed by third parties because what is often needed are hands-on demonstrations, which are best provided by manufacturers. Even as it explicitly recognizes that unapproved uses of surgical pins is widespread and is regarded by the medical community as essential, the FDA continued to attack the provision by manufacturers of relevant information.[22] In the meantime, Consumers Union recommends that consumers stop relying on the widely distributed *Physicians' Desk Reference*, which cannot mention unapproved uses because its information comes from manufacturers, and use instead the "consumer-oriented" *Complete Drug Reference*, which lists "accepted" off-label uses and is distributed by Consumers Union itself.[23]

Experience in Markets Where FDA Leverage Is Hard to Apply. The food market is unusual in that the FTC regulates advertising even when the ads make claims that involve the FDA. This has permitted a limited "natural experiment" in which FTC and FDA regulatory philosophies can be compared. Because most food products do not require FDA approval, tension has often arisen between the FDA's policies and the informational aspects of food marketing. In the 1960s and 1970s the recommendations of the American Health Association and others for consumers to reduce dietary cholesterol and saturated fat prompted sellers to advertise that advice. The FDA attempted to halt all mention of cholesterol or saturated fat, on the grounds that to discuss those ingredients was to invoke a relationship with heart disease, which in turn caused the food to be "labeled" as a drug, which in turn

---

21. Oncologists, including the director of the National Cancer Institute's Division of Cancer Treatment, have attacked FDA actions that restrict off-label uses (*Time*, July 15, 1991, p. 56; and *F-D-C Reports*, June 17, 1991, p. 10). A leading support group for cancer patients has also spoken out (Rosenthal 1991).

22. See "Screws Not Approved for Back Surgery," *FDA Consumer*, March 1994, pp. 2–3. Also see *Wall Street Journal*, March 30, 1992; *Wall Street Journal*, September 9, 1992; *Science*, November 13, 1992, p. 1075.

23. See *Consumer Reports On Health*, August 1993, p. 90.

brought to bear the same FDA approval process that is required for traditional drugs such as antibiotics.[24] Sellers nonetheless persisted in defying that policy, and eventually the FDA compromised by permitting claims about product content but not about the relationship with disease. This advertising has been credited with helping increase consumer knowledge of the importance of fat and cholesterol (Calfee and Pappalardo 1989).

Much the same happened in the 1980s in the wake of Kellogg's ad campaign for fiber as a means to prevent cancer. The FDA almost certainly would have halted those ads, were it not for the support Kellogg received from both the FTC and the National Cancer Institute (which saw advertising as a means for harnessing market forces to solve an information problem). Research by both the FDA and the FTC staffs found that ads by Kellogg and others substantially increased consumer knowledge of health and nutrition (Levy and Stokes 1987; Ippolito and Mathios 1989). The FDA has now formally adopted the position that food advertising on diet and health can improve the market. Nonetheless, its interpretation of the 1990 law on food labeling has had the effect of strongly discouraging the use of such information, especially in claims for individual brands (Ippolito and Mathios 1993).

The food market has therefore provided an arena in which the FDA has attempted to apply its information regulation principles without being able to use its "leverage" mechanism to force firms to adhere to its policies, regardless of market effects. The result has been a demonstration that the market works better when industry opposition has compelled the FDA to relax its principles.

Conclusions and Recommendations

The FDA consistently misunderstands the workings of competitive markets, especially their informational aspects. This can hardly be a surprise. The FDA has never sought to accumulate expertise in economics (except perhaps in the economics of pharmaceutical research and development). One result has been a persistent tendency to overregulate the use of information in advertising and promotion. That tendency has greater consequences in the pharmaceutical market than it would in nearly any other market. The FDA's overwhelming power over drug approval and manufacture has the effect of removing the usual checks and balances on regulatory power over advertising. The

---

24. On this history and the FDA's ability to transform an advertising claim into a legal finding that a food is a drug (a legal ploy called the "squeeze play"), see Hutt (1986).

FDA's pharmaceutical advertising policies have therefore remained unchallenged in court for decades. Yet where an examination of the effects of that policy is possible—as in the food market, where the FDA lacks the leverage given by power over product introduction, or in situations where information first appears in the pharmaceutical market and then is removed at the FDA's insistence—the evidence is very strong that the FDA suppresses a great deal of useful information. Experience from related markets in this nation and abroad also strongly indicates that informational competition involving drugs and devices is likely to work well, and that the pharmaceutical market does not pose unique problems that make it unsuitable for traditional competitive dynamics.

Tensions in the FDA's regulation of information have intensified in the past two decades. We can expect those tensions to continue to increase. Off-label uses, for example, seem likely to assume yet greater importance as the FDA continues its crackdown on medical devices, which often require personal demonstrations rather than third-party instructions. Moreover, older, off-patent drugs will continue to be an important source of medication.[25] The documented role of food and supplements in health will increase, especially if the significance of discoveries on the role of antioxidants and other micronutrients approaches that associated with the discovery of the role of vitamins in deficiency diseases, such as scurvy and rickets.[26] The FDA's "information lag" will increase rather than decrease. A recent example is the extreme reluctance of the FDA to endorse a health claim for folic acid in preventing birth defects, despite the efforts of other public health authorities. Like the widely noted drug approval lag, the information lag tends to be hidden from view because outside observers cannot easily appreciate what is suppressed from the marketplace. The advent of health claims for foods and controversial issues in off-label uses have at least temporarily brought this problem forward, however.

---

25. For a recent example, see Charles A. Peloquin's letter to the editor, "Shortages of Antimycobacterial Drugs," *New England Journal of Medicine*, March 5, 1992, p. 714.

26. For a striking example in this vein, see Chapuy et al. (1992). More generally, a well-regarded university-based health letter stated that until recently its editorial board had been "reluctant to recommend supplementary vitamins on a broad scale for health people eating healthy diets. But the accumulation of research in recent years has caused us to change our minds at least where four vitamins are concerned. These are the three so-called antioxidant vitamins, plus the B vitamin folacin. The role these substances play in disease prevention is no longer a matter of dispute." *U.C. Berkeley Wellness Letter* 10 (January 1994), p. 1. Of course, dispute will continue, given the difficulty of controlled clinical trials for the prevention of such illnesses as cancer and heart disease.

These problems all arise from the FDA's ability to leverage its power over drugs into unchallenged power over information. One potential solution would be to apply the free speech clause of the First Amendment to the provision of some of the information now suppressed by the FDA. But the same leverage that allows the FDA to proceed without challenges to its interpretation of the law has also enabled it to discourage constitutionally based challenges by pharmaceutical firms. Parties not subject to FDA regulation are less easily inhibited, of course, but they cannot bring to bear so large a financial interest. Nonetheless, in a development of great potential significance, the Washington Legal Foundation, a nonprofit institution that receives little if any funding from pharmaceutical firms, recently filed a First Amendment challenge to the FDA's regulation of pharmaceutical labeling. That lawsuit may help fill the void that results from the unwillingness of firms regulated by the FDA to mount legal challenges to FDA policy (Skolnick 1994). The best solution is to separate authority over drug approval from authority over information. One approach would be to establish a separate regulatory agency in the Department of Health and Human Services that would have power over pharmaceutical information but would not report to the FDA commissioner. If properly established, the new agency would be forced to balance traditional concerns with disciplining pharmaceutical manufacturers against larger concerns about public health, just as in 1984 the National Cancer Institute found itself supporting Kellogg's defiance of FDA policy so as to promote the institute's goal of preventing cancer. An alternative—potentially superior but more difficult politically—would be to lodge information regulation at the FTC. That agency has substantial expertise in the workings of markets, has experience in dealing with medical and scientific topics, and most important, does not possess unseemly power over the pharmaceutical market.

References

Avorn, Jerry, M. Chen, and R. Hartley. "Scientific versus Commercial Sources of Influence on the Prescribing Behavior of Physicians." *American Journal of Medicine* 73 (1982): 4–8.

Bauer, Raymond A. "The Initiative of the Audience." *Journal of Advertising Research* 3 (June 1963): 2–7.

———. "Limits of Persuasion: The Hidden Persuaders Are Made of Straw." *Harvard Business Review* 36 (September 1958).

Beales, J. Howard. "Marketing Information and Pharmaceuticals: New Uses for Old Drugs." In *Competitive Strategies in the Pharmaceutical*

319

Industry, edited by Robert B. Helms. Washington, D.C.: AEI Press, 1995.

Breitenacher, Michael. "Ostdeutsche übernehmen suzehends westliche Trinkgewohnheiten." *IFO-Schnelldienst* 24 (1992): 17–20.

Brinberg, David, and Louis A. Morris. "Advertising Prescription Drugs to Consumers." *Advances in Marketing and Public Policy* 1 (1988): 1–40.

Calfee, John E. "Cigarette Advertising, Health Information and Regulation before 1970." Bureau of Economics, Federal Trade Commission, Working Paper #134, December 1985.

———. "FDA Regulation: Moving toward a Black Market in Information." *American Enterprise* (March–April 1992a): 34–41.

———. "Free Speech, FDA Regulation, and Market Effects on the Pharmaceutical Industry." In *Bad Prescription for the First Amendment: FDA Censorship of Drug Advertising and Promotion*, edited by Richard Kaplar. Washington, D.C.: Media Institute, 1992b: 63–86.

———. "The Ghost of Cigarette Advertising Past." *Regulation*, November–December 1986.

———, and Janis K. Pappalardo. *How Should Health Claims for Foods Be Regulated? An Economic Perspective.* Bureau of Economics, Federal Trade Commission, September 1989.

———. "Public Policy Issues in Health Claims for Foods." *Journal of Public Policy and Marketing* 10 (1991): 33–54.

Calfee, John E., and Debra Ringold. "Consumer Skepticism of Advertising: What Do the Polls Show?" *Advances in Consumer Research* 15 (1988): 244–248.

———. "The Seventy Percent Majority: Enduring Consumer Beliefs about Advertising." *Journal of Public Policy and Marketing* 13 (1994): 228–38.

Calfee, John E., and Carl Scheraga. "The Influence of Advertising on Alcohol Consumption: An Econometric Analysis of Selected European Nations." *International Journal of Advertising* 13 (1994): 287–310.

Chapuy, Marie C., Monique E. Arlot, François Duboeuf, et al. "Vitamin D_3 and Calcium to Prevent Hip Fractures in Elderly Women." *New England Journal of Medicine* 327 (December 3, 1992): 1637–42.

Fisherow, Benjamin. "The Shape of Prescription Drug Advertising: A Survey of Promotional Techniques and Regulatory Trends." *Food Drug Cosmetic Law Journal* 42 (1987): 213, 230.

Hanley, R.T. "An Entire Industry Turns to Negative Advertising: Explaining How the Cigarette Business Developed a Coughing Spell." *Printers Ink* (December 19, 1927): 10.

Harkrader, Carleton A. "Fictitious Pricing and the FTC: A New Look at an Old Dodge." *St. John's Law Review* 37 (1962): 1–28.

Hutt, Peter Barton. "Government Regulation of Health Claims in Food Labeling and Advertising." *Food Drug Cosmetic Law Journal* 41 (1986): 3–75.

Ippolito, Pauline. "Bonding and Non-Bonding Signal of Product Quality." *Journal of Business* 63 (1990): 41–60.

Ippolito, Pauline, and Alan Mathios. *Health Claims in Advertising and Labeling: A Study of the Cereal Market.* Bureau of Economics Staff Report, Federal Trade Commission, August 1989.

———. "New Food Regulations and the Flow of Nutrition Information to Consumers." *Journal of Public Policy and Marketing* 12 (1993): 188–205.

Kessler, David A. "Addressing the Problem of Misleading Advertising." *Annals of Internal Medicine* 116 (June 1, 1992): 950–51.

Kessler, David A., and Wayne L. Pines. "The Federal Regulation of Prescription Drug Advertising and Promotion." *Journal of the American Medical Association* 264 (1990): 2409–15.

Levy, A.S., and Raymond C. Stokes. "Effects of a Health Promotion Advertising Campaign on Sale of Ready-to-Eat Cereals." *Public Health Record* 102 (July–August 1987): 398–403.

Masson, Alison, and Paul Rubin. "Matching Prescription Drugs and Consumers: The Benefits of Direct Advertising." *New England Journal of Medicine* 313 (August 22, 1985): 513–15.

Nelson, Philip. "Information and Consumer Behavior." *Journal of Political Economy* 78 (March/April 1970).

Pitofsky, Robert. "Beyond Nader: Consumer Protection and the Regulation of Advertising." *Harvard Law Review* 90 (1977): 661–701.

Reekie, W. Duncan, and Hans G. Otzbrugger. *Advertising and Prescription Medicines.* London: The Advertising Association, 1984.

Ringold, Debra Jones, and John E. Calfee. "The Informational Content of Cigarette Advertising: 1926–86." *Journal of Public Policy and Marketing* 8 (1989): 1–23.

Rosenthal, Elizabeth. "Rules on Approved Uses of Drugs Could Bar Help for Some Patients." *New York Times* (August 11, 1991), p. 1.

Skolnick, Andrew A. "Pro-Free Enterprise Group Challenges FDA's Authority to Regulate Drug Companies' Speech." *Journal of the American Medical Association* 271 (February 2, 1994): 332–35.

Temin, Peter. "The Origins of Compulsory Drug Prescriptions." *Journal of Law and Economics* 32 (1979): 91–105.

Thomas, Lacy Glenn. "Regulation and Firm Size: FDA Impacts on Innovations." *RAND Journal of Economics* 21 (1990): 497–517.

Yellin, Arthur. "FDA Prescription Drug Enforcement Policies and Techniques." *Food Drug Cosmetic Law Journal* 42 (1987): 552–58.

14

Costs and Benefits of Cost-Benefit Analysis in Pharmaceutical Promotion and Utilization Decisions

Ronald W. Hansen

The term "pharmacoeconomics," referring to the application of cost-benefit or cost-effectiveness analysis to pharmaceutical products, has recently entered the pharmaceutical marketing lexicon. A book, *Principles of Pharmacoeconomics* was published in 1991, and the journal *Pharmacoeconomics* appeared in 1992. The introduction of pharmacoeconomics reflects the growing importance of various forms of outcomes or cost-effectiveness analysis to pharmaceutical marketing and utilization decisions. Several firms are conducting economic studies during the clinical trial stage designed to assist in the eventual marketing and promotion of the pharmaceutical candidate. In addition, many pharmaceutical firms have created new positions in pharmacoeconomics, outcomes analysis, or economic analysis.

The growth in cost-benefit, cost-effectiveness, or outcomes analysis[1] coincides with, and is affected by, several other trends in the pharmaceutical marketplace. One important trend is the increased public focus on the price of pharmaceuticals. The introduction of several path-breaking new products at prices that seemed high by historical standards has drawn considerable attention. In large part due to the public concern over the AIDS crisis, the introduction of AZT by Burroughs Wellcome in 1987 at an initial price that implied an annual cost per patient in the range of $8,000[2] generated a major public debate over

---

1. Except where it is important to make a distinction, I shall use these terms interchangeably.

2. "Profiling the Drugs of 1987," *Medical Advertising News*, February 15, 1988.

pharmaceutical prices and profits. Other new product introductions occurred with prices substantially in excess of the products they replaced, but none had quite the impact of AZT. Although the price of AZT has dropped considerably while other AIDS treatment costs continue to increase, it remains a symbol of an expensive drug in the minds of many individuals.

The 1984 Drug Price Competition and Patent Term Restoration Act made it easier to introduce generic versions of many pharmaceuticals with high sales volumes. Publicity over the difference in price between generic and brand-name pharmaceuticals created the perception that the original product was overpriced. Moreover, in the face of competition from generic companies, several of the name-brand companies raised rather than lowered the prices of their products. That move created concern not only among patients using those products but also among congressional leaders involved in the 1984 patent term extension legislation and the subsequent catastrophic health care bill. This latter legislation introduced an outpatient Medicare pharmaceutical benefit program financed by premiums paid by recipients. That program was repealed before implementation primarily owing to opposition from the elderly over the cost of the program.

On the basis of several price indexes for periods after 1980, pharmaceutical prices appeared to increase much more rapidly than general inflation and more rapidly than overall medical care inflation—a perceived trend that added further concern over pharmaceutical prices. Although those same indexes showed that pharmaceutical prices lagged behind most other prices in the decade before 1980, that did little to lessen the concern over the later price increases. In the academic literature, Griliches and Cockburn (1993) have questioned the methods used in constructing pharmaceutical price indexes. Their updated discussion of this issue appears in chapter 2 of this volume.

Historically, outpatient pharmaceuticals were prescribed by independent physicians and paid for by the individual patient. The physician was viewed as the primary decision maker in the selection of prescription pharmaceuticals. Consistent with the reference to those products as "ethical pharmaceuticals," the promotion efforts by firms were directed at the physicians. The perception, right or wrong, was that physicians were primarily interested in medical effectiveness and had little interest in the relative prices of pharmaceuticals. Thus, the promotion efforts for ethical products was focused almost exclusively on medical effectiveness.

Parallel to the public discussions of pharmaceutical prices was the growth of third-party payment for outpatient pharmaceuticals. Pharmaceutical benefits are part of the various state Medicaid programs.

323

Some states established formularies that usually delayed and sometimes denied coverage for new products. Recently, Congress has mandated rebates for pharmaceuticals sold to Medicaid patients.

Pharmaceutical benefits have expanded in private plans, particularly with the growth of health maintenance organizations and related organizational structures such as preferred provider organizations. Some of the private plans include provisions that encourage generic substitution or mail order dispensing. Particularly for HMOs, formularies may be established that exclude coverage for nonapproved pharmaceuticals. Since many physicians are employees of the HMO or have agreed to certain restrictions to participate in PPOs, formulary restrictions can be very important determinants for pharmaceutical sales.

There has been a change in the importance of various decision makers for pharmaceutical sales. The most obvious is the increased role played by third-party insurers and managed health care administrators. Those individuals see pharmaceuticals as a major expense item and are aware of the prices of alternative products, whether a generic version or a therapeutically similar product.

For consumers with no pharmaceutical benefit plan but with hospital and physician insurance coverage, outpatient pharmaceuticals often represent their largest out-of-pocket expense, even if they comprise only a small part of the total cost of the care they receive.[3] They are frequently very aware of prices for competing drugs and may convey those concerns to their physicians. The recent public focus on pharmaceutical prices has undoubtedly made many physicians more concerned about cost in making their prescription decisions.

In general, price has become a more important part of the outpatient pharmaceutical sales equation. Some HMOs have negotiated a deeply discounted price from pharmaceutical firms as the cost of being added to the approved formulary. Those discounts, which have gone beyond normal volume discounts, have become the subject of a recent lawsuit by a group of pharmacies.

But increased price consciousness does not in itself explain why companies should resort to various forms of cost-benefit analysis. The explanation lies in the nature of the pharmaceutical product. If one were marketing a new brand of soft drink, he would have potential consumers sample the product, perhaps through special promotional efforts. On the basis of that experience and the price for the new beverage, consumers would determine whether to purchase the new brand or a competing product.

---

3. Pharmaceuticals represent approximately 8 percent of total health care costs.

Pharmaceuticals cannot be evaluated by such a relatively inexpensive experience. Due to their nature, a patient cannot learn all the important characteristics of the product simply by experiencing it. Not only is the product potentially dangerous to the individual, but the effects of the product may only be learned through repeated or long-term use. This is, in part, the justification for the existence of extensive premarketing clinical studies to determine the safety and effectiveness of the product. In a corresponding manner, the measurement of the benefits of the product are best learned through the experiences of others. Either cost-benefit or cost-effectiveness analysis is a convenient way of summarizing the economic value of using the product.

Brief History of Cost-Benefit Analysis in Pharmaceuticals

Among the earliest cost-benefit studies of pharmaceuticals or related products were the investigations of treatments for syphilis (Klarman 1965) and the use of polio vaccine (Weisbrod 1971). It is important to note that those studies were retrospective in nature. They measured what had happened rather than project to future policies or events. The studies did not affect medical decision making, but confirmed the wisdom of early decisions or measured the value of the medical advances. Those studies tended to take a communitywide perspective; they focused on all costs and benefits the community received and did not dwell on the distribution of costs or benefits. Moreover, they looked at the programs in their entirety to determine whether they were cost-effective. Rarely was the question asked, Under what circumstances is the program cost-effective and under what conditions is it not cost-effective? The studies were useful in demonstrating the potential impact of advances in pharmaceuticals and vaccines but did not have as their primary focus an attempt to affect the use of those products.

Those early studies demonstrated the difficulty in measuring the benefits of improved health, particularly when attempting to quantify the benefits in dollar terms. Thus began the debate over whether researchers should use a human capital approach or a willingness-to-pay approach. Some critics found it reprehensible that economists should try to value health and lives in dollar terms. This lack of consensus on measuring health benefits drove subsequent research in the direction of cost-effectiveness analysis.

The appeal of cost-effectiveness analysis was the ability to finesse the problem of placing an explicit value on health outcomes. The objective measure became values such as "cases prevented," "reductions in disease incidence," or "cases cured." One sought either the least-cost method to achieve a given target or the value-maximizing approach for a given expenditure.

Cost-effectiveness analysis may find the most efficient program, but it does not address the question of whether that solution resulted in a program in which the outcome justified the expenditure. When the outcome measures differ, cost-effectiveness analysis does not identify which program is superior. For example, is a program that reduces ulcers at a cost of $4,000 per case prevented better or worse than a program that reduces the incidence of measles in adults at the cost of $500 per case prevented?

The limitation of cost-effectiveness analysis becomes serious when one encounters cases in which programs designed to reach a targeted objective, say reducing heart attacks, are accompanied by other medical changes. Consider the situation in which one program also produces nausea in 10 percent of the patients and severe ulcers in 2 percent of the treated population. The alternative program results in a one-in-ten thousand chance of kidney failure. Without a mechanism for determining the relative value of avoiding nausea, ulcers, and kidney failure, one cannot determine the most cost-effective program to reduce heart attacks.

Unfortunately, many programs that we want to analyze do not have one-dimensional medical outcomes. That severely limits the usefulness of cost-effectiveness analysis. Translating multidimensional medical outcomes into a single dimension is the focus of recently developed quality-of-life indexes. Although researchers have developed many different indexes, most attempt to scale states of health along a one-dimensional scale in which perfect health takes on a value of one and death a value of zero. Some indexes allow for negative values—states of health that are worse than death.

One of the uses of the indexes is to allow comparisons of states of health that differ in many dimensions. Most indexes are intended to provide not only ordinal but also cardinal values. The difference between .5 and .6 on the scale has the same value as the difference between .2 and .3. The indexes have been used to construct a measure referred to as quality-adjusted life years (QALYs). A treatment program that extends life by three years, in which the average quality of life is .4, generates an outcome value of 1.2 QALYs. In contrast, an alternative treatment that extends life for only two years, but with a higher quality of life of .8, would produce an outcome value of 1.6 QALYs.

Having thus "solved" the multidimensionality problem, the cost-effectiveness analyst can make comparisons across a wide array of medical programs on the basis of costs per QALY. Unfortunately, life is not so simple. There is no consensus on a single index or even on how one should construct the index. Fundamental questions such as who determines values and how those values are defined remain open. Some individuals object to the inclusion of negative values. Others object to the concept of QALYs that trade off length of life for quality of life. Many of the same objections that are leveled at economists who attempt to place a dollar value on life years and states of health are equally applicable to the quality-of-life indexes. The quality-of-life indexes have gained more respectability in the health professions, however, perhaps because health care researchers rather than economists have made the primary developments. In theory, economists could use the same techniques employed to estimate dollar values of life years to translate QALYs into dollars.

Despite the problems inherent in quality-of-life indexes, they have helped to spark a growth in outcomes analysis. Many clinical researchers have found quality-of-life measures a convenient tool in assessing treatment outcomes. A growing literature uses quality-of-life outcome measures as a standard of comparison among treatments with no reference to a cost-effectiveness analysis. If that literature continues to grow, it will be much easier for the cost-effectiveness analysts to conduct their analyses.

The Use of Cost-Benefit Studies in Pharmaceutical Promotions

The willingness of some clinicians to use quality-of-life measures has been of great benefit to pharmaceutical firms wishing to conduct cost-effectiveness studies during clinical trials. The timing is critical. Having the cost-effectiveness study completed by the time of product launch increases its value as a marketing tool in important segments of the marketplace.

As noted earlier, several of the decision makers involved in the selection and purchase of pharmaceutical products are concerned not only with the medical effectiveness of the products but also with the cost of the drugs. Pharmaceutical firms are increasingly being forced to address the cost issue. In some cases the cost issue is simply one of bargaining on the price of the product. That is particularly true where there is a close therapeutic substitute available.

When the pharmaceutical in question differs from the competing products in an important dimension, however, the decision becomes one not of price alone, but the relative value of the differentiating dimension. At this point cost-benefit or cost-effectiveness analysis comes into play. One may be able to charge a higher price for one's product if he can demonstrate that the added value exceeds the added cost. But that is true of other products. What makes pharmaceuticals different?

First, for most other products the decision maker is also the purchaser and the user of the product. For pharmaceuticals the decisions may involve a prescriber, a patient, and a third-party payer. All may influence the decision, and the firm may have to market to three separate, though related, constituencies. An important consideration is how those constituencies relate to each other.

Let us look at the three actors individually. The physician prescriber focuses on the medical effectiveness. The patient is more interested in his out-of-pocket expenditures and the value of the therapy—including pain and suffering, lost income, and effects on his family. The third-party payer is concerned with the full cost of the pharmaceutical as well as any effects on related treatment costs covered by the insurance plan. Although there are some products that simultaneously satisfy each party's objectives, more often there will be conflicting objectives. Most notable is the introduction of a new product with medical superiority but with a substantially higher price.

With three separate actors, the pharmaceutical firm would market not through traditional cost-benefit analysis but rather by convincing each of the actors separately that the product was in their best interest. Companies would market to physicians on the basis of medical effectiveness and to consumers (where marketing is allowed) on the basis of such considerations as improved therapy or lifestyle. If there are no offsetting reductions in other treatment costs, how would a pharmaceutical manufacturer convince a third-party payer with formulary restrictions to add an expensive new product to the formulary?

The key to marketing to the third-party payer is to link decisions back to the patient. In the case of a public-sector payer, such as Medicaid, there is a general presumption that the agency is interested in the welfare of the patient, possibly including any spillovers to the rest of the community. In the public-sector case, classic cost-benefit analysis is relevant. If one views government as broadly promoting the welfare of the community, then the demonstration that a pharmaceutical provides benefits in excess of cost should provide a presumption in favor of including it in a Medicaid formulary. Needless to say, there are other views of decision making in government agencies that predict behavior governed by factors other than maximizing community welfare.

For private-sector insurers, the linkage between extra cost and benefits is different. For the insurer to be willing to add a new pharmaceutical to its formulary, it must be convinced that any additional costs can be recovered in the form of additional premium income. Thus, if the insurer can be convinced that the value to his constituency (either the insured or his employer in the case of employer-paid medical plans) exceeds the additional cost, then it may be possible to raise premiums by enough to cover the added cost. Again, it is at this point that cost-benefit analysis becomes important.

The type of cost-benefit analysis that is useful for marketing a pharmaceutical may differ from the traditional analysis, however. First, traditional analysis took a global perspective, looking at cost and benefits to a total community. For the purpose of marketing in the private sector, some of those costs or benefits may not be relevant. For example, effects on federal tax collections due to higher insurance premiums or earlier return to work will have a negligible impact on decisions made at the personal or local community level. If there is a high turnover of subscribers in health plans, then effects on treatment costs in future years may be discounted heavily.

The above modifications are simply attempts to tailor the analysis to address only those factors that are of concern to the decision maker. This is similar to doing an analysis at the county level and ignoring effects on the state or national budgets. There is a more subtle problem, however. Not only must the insurer be convinced that the benefits of the new therapy exceed the additional costs, but he must be convinced that the insured believes that the new therapy is worth the additional premium. Viewed differently, is there any mechanism by which the failure to include a product on the formulary will result in sufficient dissatisfaction on the part of the insured to force a positive coverage determination?

If a tree falls in the forest and no one is there, does it make a noise? If a product is excluded from a formulary and no patient knows, does the insurer or managed care administrator bear any costs? It is often argued that the FDA has little incentive to speed drug approvals so long as the public is unaware of what is in the pipeline. As an example of the effects of asymmetric information on the behavior of agencies, note the changes in FDA behavior after AIDS activists publicized the potential benefits of therapies in the pipeline. A similar analysis could be applied to coverage decisions in a managed health care environment.

Coverage decisions for new therapies that are relatively minor improvements over existing therapies are rarely an issue of price. Manufacturers tend to price such products at or below the cost of the existing therapies. If priced accordingly, there is little incentive for the managed health care program to exclude those products on a cost basis. There is also little incentive to single those products out for special attention, except as a mechanism to obtain further price concessions from the manufacturers of the new or existing therapies.

329

For major improvements that are accompanied by a significant increase in cost relative to the therapy they replace, an explicit coverage decision often will be made. If there is little public awareness of the product, then there may be little cost to the insurer or managed care administrator if he postpones including it in the formulary. On the other hand, if it is placed on the formulary and a decision is later made to withdraw it, the interim users of the product will be aware of the exclusion.

The ability to maintain asymmetric information will depend in part on the relationship of the physician to the insurer. If the physician is an employee of a managed health care organization, his prescribing habits can be monitored and to a large extent controlled. An independent physician is less bound by the rules of an insurance company and may prescribe a product that the patient learns later is not reimbursable. Limited formularies are more common in staff HMOs and Medicaid programs, in part because of the greater ease of controlling the physician's prescribing habits. Private stand-alone pharmaceutical benefit plans can implement a formulary provision, but they risk a greater level of client dissatisfaction generated by independent physicians prescribing nonformulary products.

Patient knowledge of drug therapies is also key. While many patients rely on physicians to select the appropriate therapy, many patients become aware of therapies through other sources. Patients with chronic conditions, in particular, will invest in learning about treatments for their illness. This may be by discussions with individuals with similar conditions, by consulting medical publications, or by receiving direct-to-consumer advertising. If individuals are members of HMOs with a formulary excluding a therapy the patients consider beneficial, they may press their physicians for the product. Through this bottom-up process, pressure may be brought to include a therapy on the formulary. Cost-benefit or cost-effectiveness analysis can be an important instrument in that process. The potential role of patient awareness of new pharmaceuticals and their characteristics in affecting prescribing and formulary decisions makes the issue of direct-to-consumer advertising of ethical products more important.

Issues in Developing Cost-Effectiveness Studies

Firms naturally want to use cost-effectiveness studies early in the marketing of a product. That puts a premium on conducting the studies during the clinical trial stage and perhaps on incorporating the study into the clinical trials themselves. A literature on the design of economic studies in clinical trials has developed over the past decade (Spilker 1990).

Some individuals view double-blind clinical trial protocols as the gold standard for analysis. That may be true for establishing the safety and effectiveness of the pharmaceutical product. For cost-benefit studies, however, one is usually more concerned with measuring the effects of the product in general use. For example, patients in a clinical trial are usually closely monitored, and attempts are made to ensure compliance with the protocols. Once the drug is released, patients are monitored less frequently, and some may seriously deviate from the recommended regimens. The data from closely controlled clinical trials may be misleading indicators of the product's effects when in general use, particularly where compliance is a major issue. As Arikian (1992, 96) noted, "The traditional clinical trial is an investigational study, while an economic clinical trial is an observational study."

The use of cost-effectiveness studies to affect future utilization decisions brings forward questions that retrospective studies often ignored. For example, if conditions such as the patient's age, occupation, and other medical conditions affect the cost-effectiveness of alternative treatments, one could identify conditions under which a treatment is cost-effective. This opens Pandora's box.

The variables that may determine whether a drug is cost-effective may be "politically sensitive." For example, some studies use the human capital or willingness-to-pay approach to measure the value of reducing illness or speeding recovery. Should a treatment be viewed as cost-effective for an employed or high-income individual but not for individuals not in the work force or with low incomes? Human capital and willingness-to-pay methodologies could prevent unemployed or low-income individuals from receiving treatment. Concerns with equity or public relations may rule out a separation along income lines, even though it affects the calculated benefits in some analyses.

The age of the patient poses another potential problem. If the therapy prevents death from a particular disease, the expected number of life years added by this intervention will be longer for younger patients than for older patients. One may determine a threshold age above which the medical intervention is not cost-effective. Other information about the health of the particular patient may modify the decision to intervene. There are critics who argue that cost-effectiveness studies are inherently biased against elderly individuals. Others argue that this realistically reflects the change in total life years (or quality-adjusted life years), which naturally differs with the age of the patient.

The determination that a treatment is not cost-effective for patients with specific additional medical problems poses fewer difficulties.

331

That is consistent with the general presumption that therapies of choice may be counterindicated when other conditions are present.

From the standpoint of the firm marketing the product, identifying conditions under which a product is cost-effective poses several problems. First, when the key variable is income, age, or another variable that may have a vocal constituency, the firm may face a public relations problem that could spill over to the sales of other products. Unfortunately, under many cost-effectiveness methodologies, those variables can significantly affect the cost-benefit calculations.

Even when the key variables are not "politically sensitive," identifying the cost-effective conditions runs counter to the standard marketing culture. Fundamentally, it is difficult to admit that one's product may be cost-effective in some circumstances but not in others, although the FDA has approved those latter uses for the drug. Naturally, the firm would like to avoid giving up potential sales. Failure to separate out these uses may, however, result in an unacceptable lowering of the overall cost-effectiveness of the product. How forthright should one be?

Potential Biases in Firm-Sponsored Cost-Effectiveness Analyses

One of the biggest dangers is allowing biases in the calculations to occur. Cost-benefit analysis is an inexact science. One cannot include all the possible effects of utilizing different products. Choices have to be made in determining what effects are important enough to be included and what should be ignored (or perhaps acknowledged but not included). There can be honest disagreements about relative importance, and some factors may be inadvertently overlooked.

Biases can also be introduced by the selection of methods to measure the variables. Again, there is honest disagreement over the use of willingness-to-pay versus some modified form of the human capital approach. As noted earlier, the work on quality of life indexes is relatively recent, and there is no consensus on which index to use. For some analyses those differences in measures may have little impact; in others they may have a major impact on the conclusion.

Differences in approaches and conclusions do not imply biased analysis. Moreover, outright dishonesty may be detected and backfire on both the analyst and the client. Unfortunately, there is a natural tendency—whether subconscious or overt—to try to give the client the answer he wants to hear. A healthy skepticism is in order when reviewing a study, whether one is the recipient or the client.

Arikian (1992, 96) argues that while a manufacturer has an important role in the planning process for a pharmacoeconomic study, particularly in reviewing the protocol from a safety and efficacy standpoint, the manufacturer should have no role in the economic analysis. He suggests a neutral, unbiased group. He notes that standards and criteria for quality pharmacoeconomic research are not well established. He does not offer proposals to ensure that biases not enter the analysis, however.

One solution is to subject economic studies to a peer-review process before they are used for marketing or promotional purposes. That may include submitting the studies for publication in respected academic journals. Unfortunately, most major journals will not find such articles of interest unless they have a novel methodological twist.

An open peer-review process that determines that there are major errors in an economic study can be very risky for a firm. Indeed, the correction of the errors may demonstrate that the cost-effectiveness of a competing product is superior. Depending on how open the process is, it may not be possible for the firm simply to close the book and ignore the corrected results. Failure to submit the study to intense review before using it for promotion could result in an even greater embarrassment later. Firms that charge ahead with cost-effectiveness studies without fully considering those potential outcomes may find themselves in serious trouble. Firms will need to develop the expertise in evaluating economic studies that they currently have in evaluating clinical studies.

Long-Term Implications of Cost-Effectiveness Studies

The increased use of cost-benefit or cost-effectiveness analysis as a marketing instrument may have long-term impacts on the pharmaceutical marketplace. For example, there is the danger that regulatory agencies will require a cost-effectiveness analysis as part of the approval process. Since January 1993, Australia has required pharmaceutical firms to include an economic evaluation in support of applications on their schedule of pharmaceutical benefits.[4] The Australian guidelines establish criteria for the costs and benefits a firm may include (Drummond 1992). In particular, the guidelines explicitly exclude indirect costs, such as lost productivity. Drummond's explanation of that exclusion rests with the notion that the productivity is not lost—another worker will take the place of the ill worker in most instances. His argument that replacement is not complete and that some produc-

---

4. Ontario is considering legislation to require cost-effectiveness analysis (Henry 1992).

tivity loss is appropriate is couched in a manner that embraces a productivity view of measuring the indirect costs of illness.

As noted earlier, other methodologies would view the indirect
costs in terms of willingness-to-pay measures, not productivity. In this
chapter I do not discuss the relative merits of each approach except to
note that each has its own proponents. The more important point is
that the government may specify a particular approach—in this case
the exclusion of certain benefits and costs. The particular exclusion is
biased against most modern pharmaceutical innovations. While some
new drugs also reduce treatment costs, the principal benefit of many
new drugs is that they reduce the indirect costs of treatment. Such
stacking of the deck is consistent with a view that the purpose of the
requirements is primarily addressed at reducing pharmaceutical
prices. Indeed, Bloom (1992) criticizes the legislation for singling out
the pharmaceutical industry, which has produced many very cost-
effective products.

To date, the FDA has expressed the view that its job is to assess
safety and effectiveness, not cost. Nevertheless, the agency has hinted
that perhaps cost should be a criterion. If Congress adopts a national
health care plan that includes outpatient pharmaceutical benefits, requiring cost-effectiveness studies as part of the approval process may
not be far behind. Such a measure may significantly increase the cost of
developing pharmaceutical products, in terms of both time and dollar
outlays.

Analyzing the cost-effectiveness of pharmaceutical products
would, on the surface, appear to be an appropriate response to the
concerns with efficiency in health care. One should ask, however, how
cost-effective the studies of cost-effectiveness are. Other than being
used as a tool to help set the price of the product (part of which is a
question of transfers between manufacturers and payers), the major
source of gain stems from changes in the use of pharmaceuticals. Some
of the potential gains in use are lost if the studies are not careful to
outline the boundaries under which a drug is and is not cost-effective.
Using aggregate studies further blurs the distinction between individual and group decisions. Occasionally, the FDA fails to approve a product that some potential users with full knowledge of potential risks
would find acceptable. Using cost-effectiveness analysis may likewise
eliminate products that are cost-effective to some parts of the population.

Currently, many controversies surround the appropriate methods
of studying cost-effectiveness. We should not consider them a justification for abandoning such studies. Rather, we should use the studies
with care. The marketplace will dictate undertaking such studies on a

wide range of innovative therapies. The marketplace may also be the best judge of the value of the studies. The real danger comes in the areas in which the markets are not allowed to work well. A national health plan is high on my list of potential danger areas. The additional costs and uncertainty that cost-effectiveness requirements would bring to a national marketplace might have a chilling effect on R&D that would eliminate all the potential gains from improved utilization decisions.

Costs and Benefits of Cost-Benefit Analysis

Is cost-benefit analysis cost-effective? In part, the answer depends on one's perspective. In a world in which one must perform a cost-benefit analysis to have a product approved at either the FDA level or an individual level, such an analysis may be cost-effective to the individual firm, even if the analysis produces no net benefit from a global perspective.

The global benefit of a cost-benefit or cost-effectiveness analysis rests with the ability of the analysis to improve the use of medical products. Retrospective analysis or analysis read only by academic economists is likely to have little impact on utilization. On the other hand, analysis generated by pharmaceutical firms as part of their marketing efforts is intended to affect utilization decisions. Several questions remain. How effective are cost-benefit studies in influencing utilization decisions, and are the potential changes an improvement in therapy? Can we value the changes in therapeutic decisions? If so, how does the value of the improved utilization compare with the cost of generating the cost-benefit studies?

As we evaluate the benefits of cost-effectiveness studies, we should note that performing those studies adds another layer of cost to an already expensive development process. Such studies may also add to the uncertainty firms face when engaging in pharmaceutical R&D. We should not lose sight of the potential of those added costs to deter the development of cost-effective new technologies.

Many methodological problems still face individuals conducting cost-benefit studies in health care. An additional issue we must address is how extensive the role of cost-benefit studies should be in the delivery of health care.

References

Arikian, Steven R. "The Nuts and Bolts of Pharmacoeconomic Trials: Part 2." *Medical Marketing and Media* 27 (December 1992): 96.

335

Bloom, Bernard S. "Issues in Mandatory Economic Assessment of Pharmaceuticals." *Health Affairs* 11 (1992): 197–201.

Bootman, J. Lyle, Raymond J. Townsend, and William E. McGhan. *Principles of Pharmacoeconomics*. Cincinnati: Harvey Whitney Books Company, 1991.

Drummond, Michael F. "Basing Prescription Drug Payment on Economic Analysis: The Case of Australia." *Health Affairs* 11 (1992): 191–96.

Griliches, Zvi, and Iain Cockburn. "Generics and New Goods in Pharmaceutical Price Indexes." Working Paper No. 4272, National Bureau of Economic Research, Cambridge, Mass., February 1993.

———. "Generics and the Producer Price Index for Pharmaceuticals." In *Competitive Strategies in the Pharmaceutical Industry*, edited by Robert B. Helms. Washington, D.C.: AEI Press, 1996.

Henry, David. "Economic Analysis as an Aid to Subsidization Decisions." *Pharmacoeconomics* 1 (1992): 54–67.

Klarman, Herbert E. "Syphilis Control Programs." In *Measuring Benefits of Government Investments*, edited by Robert Dorfman. Washington, D.C.: Brookings Institution, 1965.

"Profiling the Drugs of 1987." *Medical Advertising News* (February 15, 1988), p. 6.

Spilker, Bert, ed. *Quality of Life Assessments in Clinical Trials*. New York: Raven Press, 1990.

Weisbrod, B. A. "Costs and Benefits of Medical Research: A Case Study of Poliomyelitis." *Journal of Political Economy* 79 (1971): 527–44. (This study also appears in a collection of Weisbrod's cost-benefit studies, Burton A. Weisbrod, *Economics and Applied Research* (Washington, D.C.: American Enterprise Institute, 1983), pp. 65–84.)

Commentary on Part Four

William C. MacLeod

My history in the field of health care marketing reached a climax in a congressional hearing a few years ago, when the Federal Trade Commission was being hauled up before an oversight committee to explain why the commission allows doctors to advertise, lure patients into their offices, and then kill them or maim them with incompetent treatment. The plan for the hearing was to have a couple of very seriously injured patients testify and then to ask the public official, "How could you let this happen?"

The star witness had a heartbreaking story of badly botched plastic surgery. As she described her pain, the mood in the room grew hostile, not just for the doctor, but for the government that allowed her doctor to advertise. After she testified, she was asked, "How did you find out about this doctor?" Everyone in the room expected her to produce a copy of a sensational advertisement. Instead, she answered, "A friend referred me to him." She had no ad, no deception, and no ammunition to fire at me. With her revelation, the fire left the eyes of the lynch mob, the advertising attack withered away, and I did not have to answer for her pain and suffering.

Instead, I was able to discuss the benefits that advertising brings to patients. My testimony drew upon some basic economic principles: ignorance is expensive, smart buyers save money, and information about products and services is valuable.

In most industries those principles are beyond dispute. What I find most fascinating about health care is that the answers are not nearly so obvious, which makes economic inquiry in the industry much more exciting. As I learned in my congressional hearing, there still remains a very distinct divergence of opinion over the value of such things as advertising and the ability of markets to allocate resources in areas of health care and pharmaceuticals.

That brings me to the studies of Ronald Hansen, John E. Calfee, and J. Howard Beales. Professor Hansen's work reminds me of Milton Friedman's (1966) famous example of the pool table: if you construct the right model, you can calculate the odds that Minnesota Fats will sink a bank shot into the corner pocket, even if you cannot explain precisely how he does it.

Economic modeling goes on all the time in the pharmaceutical industry. It is something that a decision maker in a pharmaceutical company has to do. Each doctor and each patient does it, too. Sometimes people do not realize that they are engaging in economics, but deciding whether to develop, sell, prescribe, or use a drug entails cost-benefit analysis. Professor Hansen's analysis tries to predict how the market will work or should work when those decisions are made.

Of course, the market for health care is not exactly the market for wheat, which is why many question whether the health care market works. Economic analysis is essential in this field if we are to answer the questions. Some will always question whether doctors—despite their education and knowledge—know what they are doing when they prescribe a drug. Some will always assert that patients and doctors together cannot select the preferable drug, even with knowledge of each drug's properties and price.

I contend that markets will work, even when they do not behave exactly as the textbooks describe. It does not take too many decision makers at the margin to push markets into a roughly efficient allocation of resources. The problem is that some people and many policy makers do not believe that story.

So my first, most important commentary on Professor Hansen's analysis is that I agree that those studies should be done, and I like the way he does them. They can explain that the decisions made in the marketplace are consistent with decisions that would be observed in properly functioning markets. They can predict that decision makers rationally would decide to opt for a new therapy. I also agree that using such studies as criteria for approval by regulatory authorities can be dangerous. Of course, regulators should be thinking about costs and benefits. But it is always risky when one party undertakes deciding the costs and benefits that other parties should pay and receive. Regulators are human, and they probably make mistakes. So do we all, but regulators' mistakes become law. The examples we have seen overseas, of flawed analyses depriving doctors and patients of choices, should not be transplanted in the United States. Yes, we should have cost-benefit analysis, but if we ignore some of the most important costs or the most important benefits, then we have made the analysis an obstacle to effective health care.

What the health care industry needs to explain about the benefits of pharmaceuticals is very similar to what the congressional committee tried to do in my regulatory encounter—find a victim and propose a rescue. My hearing failed to find a victim of advertising, so the committee failed to sell its "rescue"—more restrictions against advertising. If the pharmaceutical industry fails to show that new drugs can save lives or reduce suffering in a cost-effective manner, it will fail to sell policy makers, not to mention doctors and patients, on the need for innovative products.

Professor Calfee's analysis looks at what controls information about pharmaceuticals. Because the economics of information is a relatively new subject, we are only recently exploring the areas that Professor Calfee has traversed. His subject is important, and his findings are disturbing. The suppression of information causes ignorance that is potentially harmful to the pharmaceutical markets.

I would like to suggest how Professor Calfee might demonstrate his thesis. He describes a fear that exists among pharmaceutical companies because the FDA's drug appproval process controls their economic future. Does this fear exist and is it justified?

The evidence of fear is certainly plausible, especially when the commissioner of the FDA confirms it. The more debatable proposition is the basis for that fear. I would like to see some empirical tests that would explore the relationship between challenges to the FDA and products in the pipeline for approval. Is there a correlation between challenges to the agencies and the time it takes for drug approvals to emerge? Rather than a cross-agency analysis, I would like to see some cross-drug or cross-company analysis. Can we take some measures of what we would regard as misbehavior—perhaps the number of times citations have been issued—and find any relationship between that misbehavior and the speed of a drug approval process or some other measure of the regulatory reaction of the FDA? If, in fact, we do see some evidence of that effect, then we can say that the fear is justified.

Professor Beales's study is an example of the most exciting and impressive work economists can do. His study provides a foundation for the indisputable support for pharmaceutical advertising. Professor Beales has found what appears to be statistically significant evidence that advertising lowers prices of drugs.

The study has a couple of puzzles, but I do not find them disturbing. First of all, Professor Beales finds that the public good element in pharmaceutical advertising was not so pronounced as that found by Pauline M. Ippolito and Alan D. Mathios (1989) in their pathbreaking study of fiber advertising. He did not see such a dramatic growth in the pharmaceutical markets in which the promotions occurred. That does not surprise me. I would not expect to see a growth of prescriptions nearly to the extent I would expect to see a growth in cereal sales. Even before approval of a new drug, we can probably anticipate that

339

most patients being treated by physicians are probably taking a similar drug. Whether they have a prescription painkiller or an antibiotic, patients suffering from a treatable condition are probably receiving some kind of treatment, so I would not expect to see a great deal of growth in the number of prescriptions. By contrast, many people eat breakfast without eating cereal, so there is ample room for those sales to grow.

I would expect to see growth if pharmaceutical manufacturers had access to a promotional method that is available in almost every other market—the ability to inform consumers effectively that a new therapy is available. Advertising to consumers could, indeed, bring people in and expand the markets for the categories of drugs. Because, under the current system, advertising is effectively limited to an audience of doctors, it is likely to improve their selection of drugs, but it will not increase aggregate demand.

The increase in market share of a drug that is advertised is also an incredibly important finding—one that needs to be constantly emphasized to those who will not appreciate the econometric implications. The model says something very important about how the market works: people who had been receiving inferior treatments are finally getting treatments that improve the quality of life.

In short, Professor Beales demonstrates that advertising provides information that results in new prescriptions, Professor Hansen shows how economic analysis can be used to demonstrate the value of the new prescriptions, and Professor Calfee provides disturbing evidence that information that results in new prescriptions may be suppressed, with the result that the prescriptions are never written. What I would like to hear are some real-life stories that make up the numbers Professor Beales measured and that show the benefits that Professor Hansen described. I would like to meet some of the people who benefited from the information that was not successfully suppressed. Those who will not understand the economics will understand a few rescued victims— someone still alive today who would have been dead but for a drug, or someone whose life has been improved immeasurably, thanks to a drug. Those people should be ready when Congress holds the next hearing. Then, perhaps, we shall not have to worry quite so much about the chilling fear that Professor Calfee describes.

References

Friedman, Milton. "The Methodology of Positive Economics." *Essays in Positive Economics*. Chicago: University of Chicago Press, 1966.

Ippolito, Pauline M., and Alan D. Mathios. *Health Claims in Advertising and Labeling*. Washington, D.C.: Federal Trade Commission, 1989.

Pauline M. Ippolito

At the Federal Trade Commission, I have been working on food advertising issues, specifically on the question of what rules should govern nutrition and diet-disease claims for food products (Ippolito and Mathios 1990, 1993). One of the most startling things I have learned in this work is that I can find almost no one in the public health community who has *any* confidence that markets might serve consumers' interests. For instance, few in the public health community seem to think that allowing food producers to make truthful claims in advertising and labeling about the diet-disease advantages of their products would be good policy, with positive effects on product development and consumer purchases. And a surprising number appear to question whether providing anything but the most basic diet-disease information to consumers is prudent, whatever its source.

In such an environment it is important to recognize that the things an economist would take for granted ought not to be taken for granted—such as the idea that a ban on a class of producers' claims will reduce the incentives to develop related products and will reduce the flow of information to the market. When faced with real skepticism, we go to the literature and ask, "What kind of empirical evidence do we have to support these propositions that we all believe to be basically true?"

When the topic is advertising, the answer is often not very much. There are certain ideas that everyone believes to be true, so that no one thinks they are worth proving. Therefore, little evidence exists to establish directly that they are true; consequently, we in the policy setting arena find ourselves in a difficult situation.[1]

Beales's study is one of the very few studies trying to look at the difficult issue of testing whether the introduction of advertising into a market adds information to the market and how big the effect might be. For those of us trying to understand how information spreads in markets and how it affects producer incentives, that is an important area for empirical work.

I would like, however, to raise a few issues in assessing Beales's study. In attempting to test the advertising-information hypothesis, ideally we would like an experiment that would allow us to say with

---

The views in this commentary are my own and do not reflect the views of the Federal Trade Commission.

1. I should hasten to add that evidence shows that advertising has beneficial effects on the market, as typified by the studies of Benham and Benham (1975), Bond et al. (1980), Marvel (1976), and Ippolito and Mathios (1990).

some confidence that a barrier to informational advertising existed and that the barrier was lifted and nothing else has changed, so we can measure the effect of the advertising.

My primary question with Beales's study relates to the purity of his experiment and the way any impurity affects the results. What Beales has is really a joint event: an approved drug has a secondary use for which it does not have FDA approval. As a result, under FDA rules the firm cannot spread information about the drug's other use. Some firms choose to bear the cost of asking the FDA to approve the new use. If the FDA certifies that the drug is effective in the second use, physicians presumably have a greater assurance of the drug's usefulness for that purpose. Thus, we have a joint event: certification that the drug meets the FDA's effectiveness standard for the secondary use, and at the same time, the removal of the ban on producer-provided information about the secondary use.

It is important to address this issue very directly. Beales tries to address it by modeling the quality certification as a discrete event and the removal of the information ban as allowing a continuing flow of information, and he may be right. On the other hand, it is not implausible that it might take time for doctors to find out that the FDA has, indeed, certified the drug as effective for a second use, in which case the way Beales attempts to separate the two events is not completely appropriate.

I would have felt more confident of his specification if other forms of drug certification showed a relatively discrete effect. There might be more we could do to test his specification. For example, the U.S. Pharmacopeia essentially certifies drugs for new uses. When that certification occurs, do we see a relatively quick adjustment or is the reaction to the new listed use a gradual one? Such a test would be an exogenous check on whether the specification is appropriate. Alternatively, I would have liked to see some information on whether FDA certification for a second use is important in and of itself, for liability purposes, for example. If other evidence indicates that FDA certification itself is not very important, the confounding issue is a minor one. If FDA certification is important to a drug's sales, on the other hand, then the confounding issue has the potential to color the advertising results more seriously.

A second issue is the selection process that determines which drugs are in Beales's sample. He did not make clear which drugs are submitted to the FDA for certification for a second use. Presumably, those are drugs that the producer thinks are worth the cost of seeking approval for a second use, because it wishes to spread information to the market or because FDA certification is important for some other reason. So the sample of drugs appears to be a selected sample, and conclusions have to be made carefully.

In addition, there is the obvious cost of dealing with the FDA or any regulatory agency. It would be nice if we had some sense of what that cost is for second-use approval. Obviously, if it is very costly, most firms are not going to seek such approval, and the sample of drugs in Beales's study is going to be quite different from the universe of drugs.

In designing regulations governing producers' claims, the focus is often almost exclusively on preventing potentially deceptive claims, with surprisingly little thought given to the rules' effects on producers' incentives to make truthful claims. This focus may be appropriate, if producers' claims provide little information to consumers and have little effect on the ease of entry by better products, with consequent effects on innovation. But if, as many of us are coming to believe, producers' claims are an important information source and an important spur to innovation in consumer goods markets, a better balance is warranted between the twin goals of stopping deception and facilitating truthful producers' claims.

For this reason, every serious effort to get evidence on how information spreads in markets is of interest to those of us who deal with information issues regularly. And the drug regulations create a unique opportunity to address the issue in a health care setting, where skepticism that producer claims and market forces can play a positive role is especially high.

The Calfee study argues that the range of regulatory powers given to the Food and Drug Administration essentially guarantees that producers' claims for drugs will be regulated inefficiently, because the agency, through its drug approval process, can punish any firm that challenges its information rulings and thus eliminates firms' incentives to challenge the agency. Calfee contends that the information portion of the FDA's duties should be broken off and placed elsewhere—within the Department of Health and Human Services or outside it—to improve the industry's ability to provide an effective check in the regulatory system.

The issue Calfee raises is how an agency's design affects its performance. If we create a government agency to handle a problem that markets do not handle well, how should we structure that agency to best deliver the desired outcome? Calfee focuses on how the range of regulatory authority in a government agency influences performance in particular areas. He considers the interplay between an agency's authority to control some important aspect of a firm's profitability, where considerable discretion is given to the agency—the power to approve a firm's products for market—and the agency's authority to regulate another aspect of the firm's actions under tighter statutory guide-lines—the claims a firm can make for its products, regulated under a deception standard. Calfee's thesis is that the considerable discretion given to the agency in the first area essentially negates any control built into the other portion of the agency's statute. That is an interesting hypothesis that is intuitively plausible. It would be interesting to explore other regulatory agencies with multiple authorities over firms to test whether the pattern predicted by his hypothesis is found.

But I am not so sanguine as Calfee that simply splitting the two functions will produce much benefit. I would expect a few more challenges to agency decisions, but we should remember that information is largely a public good. There are short-term gains to individual firms from being able to make claims, and that is what pushes the industry. But in the end, if all cereal producers, for example, cannot talk about the importance of the fiber in their products, there is little incentive for any individual firm to bear any substantial cost to challenge the rules, since a rule change would allow *all* firms to produce higher fiber cereals and thus earn a competitive return. Consumers are the primary losers of an inappropriate policy, not firms. So I expect that we might need more to discipline the process, such as a positive burden on the agencies to really justify their actions before proceeding.

Moreover, I think there may be special issues raised when a public health organization is placed in charge of markets. In the debate over food claims, the only agencies in the public health community that were willing to think about the market's potential to play a positive role in spreading diet-disease information were the functional agencies, typified by the National Cancer Institute. Their mandates were to bring down rates of particular diseases. Those agencies were essentially given a performance standard. If cancer rates are the focus and the agency is going to be judged accordingly, it has to figure out some way to affect those rates—through treatment or prevention. Possibly, that pressure helps agencies to think more seriously about consumer behavior and how markets really function. That raises the question of whether there is any way to marry the performance standard idea to the mandate to control deception that would achieve a better outcome.

The Hansen study points to a variety of indicators suggesting that cost pressure may be increasing in the pharmaceutical industry. Hansen notes that measuring the cost-effectiveness of drug products is a growth industry, and he reviews the problems in attempting to conduct and interpret such studies.

At the end of his study, Hansen mentions that some researchers have suggested that cost-effectiveness studies should become part of the drug approval process. I am quite dubious of any proposals along that line. There is a wealth of evidence that government preclearance of products based on an assessment of "market need" tends to become a barrier to entry and to reduce competition and raise prices. Consider the evidence in the economics literature assessing the effects of the trucking entry restrictions (Rose 1987; Felton 1978; Owen 1988), of airline entry restrictions (Morrison and Winston 1986; Bailey, Graham, and Kaplan 1985; Ogur, Wagner, and Vita 1988), and of certificate of need regulation for health care facilities (Joskow 1980; Steinwald and Sloan 1981; Noether 1987; Anderson and Kass 1986; Sherman 1988). Those studies indicate that such entry rules often do not serve their stated purpose, but instead end up simply raising consumer prices. I have no objection to price-effectiveness studies, but I would prefer to let the market assess their implications for the market as a whole and for submarkets within it.

Hansen's study on the rising cost consciousness also reinforces one of the worries I keep having about this brave new world we may be forced to enter—that the focus on the costs of health care may lead us to ignore its quality. One of the reassuring features of the current system is that we have a healthy tension on *both* costs and quality. Preferred provider organizations and the health maintenance organizations put a lot of pressure on costs, but the fee-for-service arrangements keep pressure on quality as well. We have counterbalancing forces in the market for medical care. I worry about shifting so completely to the cost-consciousness world that we forget that quality matters, too.

References

Anderson, Keith B., and David I. Kass. *Certificate of Need Regulation of Entry into Home Health Care: A Multiproduct Cost Function Analysis.* Bureau of Economics Staff Report, Federal Trade Commission, 1986.

Bailey, Elizabeth E., David R. Graham, and Daniel P. Kaplan. *Deregulating the Airlines.* Cambridge: MIT Press, 1985.

Benham, Lee, and Alexandra Benham. "Regulating through the Professions: A Perspective on Information Control." *Journal of Law and Economics* 18 (1975): 421–47.

Bond, Ronald S., et al. *Effects of Restrictions on Advertising and Commercial Practices in the Professions: The Case of Optometry.* Staff Report to the Federal Trade Commission, Washington, D.C., September 1980.

Felton, John Richard. "The Costs and Benefits of Motor Truck Regulation." *Quarterly Journal of Economics and Business* 18 (1978): 7–20.

Ippolito, Pauline M., and Alan D. Mathios. "Information, Advertising and Health Choices: A Study of the Cereal Market." *RAND Journal of Economics* 21 (1990): 459–80.

————. "New Food Labeling Regulations and the Flow of Nutrition Information to Consumers." *Journal of Public Policy and Marketing* 12 (1993): 188–205.

Joskow, Paul L. "The Effects of Competition and Regulation on Hospital Bed Supply and the Reservation Quality of the Hospital." *Bell Journal of Economics* 11 (1980): 421–47.

Marvel, Howard. "The Economics of Information and Retail Gasoline Price Behavior." *Journal of Political Economy* 84 (1976): 1033–66.

Morrison, Steven, and Clifford Winston. *The Economics of Airline Deregulation*. Washington, D.C.: Brookings Institution, 1986.

Noether, Monica. *Competition among Hospitals*. Bureau of Economics Staff Report, Federal Trade Commission, 1987.

Ogur, John, Curtis Wagner, and Michael Vita. "The Deregulated Airline Industry: A Review of the Evidence." Economic Issues Paper, Bureau of Economics, Federal Trade Commission, January 1988.

Owen, Diane S. "Deregulation in the Trucking Industry." Economic Issues Paper, Bureau of Economics, Federal Trade Commission, May 1988.

Rose, Nancy L. "Labor Rent-Sharing and Regulation: Evidence from the Trucking Industry." *Journal of Political Economy* 95 (1987): 1146–78.

Sherman, Daniel. *The Effect of State Certificate of Need Laws on Hospital Costs: An Economic Policy Analysis*. Bureau of Economics Staff Report, Federal Trade Commission, 1988.

Steinwald, Bruce, and Frank A. Sloan. "Regulatory Approaches to Hospital Cost Containment: A Synthesis of the Empirical Evidence." In *A New Approach to the Economics of Health Care*, edited by Mancur Olsen. Washington, D.C.: American Enterprise Institute, 1981.

Jeffrey S. McCombs

The market for pharmaceutical products is undergoing a fundamental restructuring, and health care reform will accelerate these changes. We must interpret the studies of Ronald Hansen, John E. Calfee, and J. Howard Beales in light of the emerging market for prescription drugs. Hansen proposes that individual physicians are being replaced as the primary buyers of pharmaceutical products. Managed health care plan administrators, working with their clinical staffs and pharmacy and therapeutics committees, are setting drug use policy for a growing segment of the U.S. population. Previously, managed care organizations concentrated on minimizing the cost of pharmaceuticals. For reasons I shall discuss, however, managed care organizations are becoming more sensitive to the effect of new pharmaceuticals on total health care costs and to the quality of care they provide to their members. Data on the cost-effectiveness of alternative drug therapies are now in demand, and the marketing of pharmaceutical products is adjusting rapidly to those new realities.

Competitive pressures on drug budgets are not new. The Medicare Prospective Payment System for hospitals placed tremendous pressure on those institutions to reduce total costs, including their drug expenditures. In turn, hospitals became aggressive buyers of pharmaceuticals and succeeded in negotiating significant price discounts with drug manufacturers. Hospitals also developed drug treatment protocols to constrain physicians' use of high-cost medications to high-risk patients. Protocols were based, in part, on information from pharmaceutical manufacturers concerning the effectiveness of their products in reducing total hospital costs.

Established managed care organizations have historically faced similar incentives to control their drug budgets and total cost. As long as managed care organizations represented a small proportion of the total pharmaceutical market, drug manufacturers were willing to negotiate discount prices, especially for closed-panel systems such as Kaiser Permanente.

The role of managed care in the health care system has expanded dramatically in the past ten years. The Medicare program began offering a managed care alternative in 1985 (McMillian 1993). Employers facing rapidly increasing health insurance costs have capped their contributions to employee health plans, a step that has made managed care options more attractive. The growth of managed care has made discount pricing a less attractive marketing tool for manufacturers. Recent legislation linking Medicaid prescription prices to the lowest price available on the open market has also heightened this reluctance to discount prices. As a result, drug prices paid by managed care organizations rose significantly and increased the utility of treatment protocols to control use. To support protocol development, managed care organizations have increased their demand for information about cost-effectiveness, especially for patients who are at higher risk for adverse outcomes when using less expensive therapies.

Pharmaceutical manufacturers have responded to these new market realities by better delineating the market niche in which their product can command a premium price. As Professor Hansen points out, research on the cost-effectiveness of pharmaceutical products is expanding rapidly and has become an accepted component of preapproval clinical trial protocols. Such studies often contain data on quality-of-life and productivity outcomes that manufacturers can use to expand their products' market niche.

Manufacturers are also financing the development of "consensus" treatment protocols using expert panels. Those protocols cover broad disease categories and consider a wide range of alternative treatments. Manufacturers market the protocols to the managed care organization and train the organization's physicians on the cost-effective use of all alternative products.

The emerging role of managed care as an informed buyer in the pharmaceutical market has important implications for issues being debated in Washington. First, Congress is concerned about pharmaceutical prices and the return on investment that the pharmaceutical industry enjoys. Under managed competition, the price of drugs should no longer be a national policy issue. Managed care organizations have strong incentives to negotiate on price and develop drug treatment protocols that limit the use of expensive medications to patients for whom the expensive medication is the cost-effective alternative. Drug manufacturers are being forced to price their products competitively or risk a reduction in the types of patients for whom their products are found to be cost-effective.

Unfortunately, while political action by Congress to control drug prices may be ill-advised, Congress may act anyway. Henry Waxman, a House member from Los Angeles, has already raised the specter of linking U.S. drug prices to prices paid in foreign countries (GAO 1992, 110; GAO 1994, 29). Such an approach is similar in structure to Senator David Pryor's linkage of Medicaid prices to the lowest price paid on the open market (GAO 1991, 139; GAO 1993, 43). Any attempt to link U.S. prices to lower prices abroad will have a similar impact: the low price paid in foreign countries will increase and will thus deny patients in developing countries access to newer pharmaceuticals.

A single-payer solution to health care reform has received some support in Washington. This approach would operate much like the Medicare program, under which the government must determine the reasonable price to be paid for services. If past performance is any indication of future success, devising an efficient pricing system for pharmaceuticals is problematic. The Medicare program has struggled unsuccessfully to contain costs since its inception, and the list of failed bureaucratic solutions for controlling use and price are too numerous to detail here. More important, recent attempts at controlling health care prices offer little encouragement that viable bureaucratic solutions are forthcoming.

Medicare's latest attempts to control health care prices, the resource-based, relative-value scale for physicians' fees and the prospective payment system for hospital care, set price through the political process, which introduces a host of new problems (Frech 1991).

Stated simply, pharmaceutical companies will not commit resources to developing new products if they cannot determine the price once new products are approved for marketing.

Alternatively, government could set the price for new drug technologies by using methods developed by the Department of Defense, under which drug manufacturers would be reimbursed for their research and development costs and prices would be set to approximate the marginal cost of production. Unfortunately, as with defense contractors, such an approach would inflate research and development cost, especially if the government is obligated to reimburse manufacturers for all "failed" R&D projects. Manufacturers would have no incentive to control costs or to terminate research projects that are unlikely to produce useful products. A government-run national single-payer program may be reluctant to terminate continuing research projects, just as the Defense Department has historically found it difficult politically to terminate the development of new weapons systems once their cost or future utility has become questionable.

John E. Calfee's study raises the issue of the FDA's role in the use of cost-effectiveness data. Such a role would be a distinct possibility under a single-payer system. Previous respondents to Calfee's proposal have discussed the difficulties and inexactness of the methods used to evaluate cost-effectiveness, including the methods used to estimate quality-adjusted life years. That inherent imprecision may limit the FDA's effectiveness in accurately evaluating the quality of research on cost-effectiveness. Without adequate precision, it would be difficult for the FDA or the single payer to establish treatment protocols that effectively limit the market of specific drugs. Professor Hansen points out that efforts to limit access by using drug treatment protocols would be subject to political second-guessing, especially if the protocol reflected the socioeconomic characteristics of the patient for example, race and age.

The evaluation and application of cost-effectiveness data may best be left to the managed care organization and the pharmaceutical industries as they negotiate the market niche to be filled by the seller's product. Under managed competition, organizations that do not perform such evaluations well will suffer the consequences. The overuse of expensive medications will increase drug budgets and plan premiums. The underuse of such drugs risks increasing health care costs and patient dissatisfaction and decreasing productivity for employer groups.

It is unclear what role data on productivity and quality-of-life outcomes will play in direct negotiations between pharmaceutical manufacturers and managed care organizations. New drugs that improve productivity or quality of life but increase drug budgets may be hard to sell in the managed care arena because of competitiveness in the health insurance market. If drugs affecting quality of life and productivity are to be widely used in the managed care population, the organization must be able to recover its increased costs through higher premiums.

Calfee's study considered the role direct-to-consumer advertising may play in the managed care market. Under certain conditions, a natural alliance may exist between the manufacturer and the managed care organization to expand consumer demand for new drug products with significant quality-of-life and productivity benefits. Such demand translates into increased willingness by consumers and employer groups to pay higher premiums for plans that cover those drugs. It is not inconceivable that the managed care organization and the drug manufacturer, using data on productivity and quality-of-life effects of new medications, may jointly market new drugs to the organization's employer groups and enrollees.

Managed care organizations may also be constrained in their use of innovative medications to prevent or delay the adverse events associated with common chronic illnesses. Consumers frequently change health care plans, often because of changes in residence. This disenrollment pattern limits the return on investment from the aggressive treatment of chronic illnesses and results in the underutilization of those medications from a social perspective. Again, direct-to-consumer advertising could create appropriate consumer demand for health care plans that provide effective long-term therapies for chronic illnesses. Managed care organizations also have an incentive to agree to cover long-term new therapies in recognition that they all recruit enrollees from a common population.

Treatment protocols that reflect the productivity and quality-of-life benefits of alternative therapies may, by definition, use patient characteristics such as employment status, the presence of children in the home, and income as "risk factors" to allocate drug therapies. Managed care plans that make newer drugs more readily available may be attractive to wealthier families or families with children that are willing to pay the required premium differential. The market for health insurance under managed competition will most likely include a wide variety of plans along quality-of-life dimensions, including access to new medications. The public policy issue will be the level of coverage for new medications and other new technologies in the basic plans provided to those segments of the population that cannot afford to pay for premium coverage.

The increased demand for cost-effectiveness data with which to construct drug treatment protocols will have a major impact on the conduct of research and development in the pharmaceutical industry. As Professor Hansen points out, companies are under pressure to include cost-effectiveness measures in phase III clinical trials to have those data for marketing purposes upon approval by the FDA. The treatment protocols used in phase III trials must more closely mimic real-world practice conditions in which the patient is not supervised closely in terms of compliance. A wider array of patients must be included in the phase III trials to develop cost-effectiveness data by risk group with which to document the new product's market niche. Many of the "risk groups" for which the new medication may be cost-effective may be truly high-risk patients: the elderly, patients with multiple confounding diseases, refractory patients, pregnant women, and children. Current phase III protocols exclude those populations. The outcomes of interest for determining cost-effectiveness typically require access to health care utilization and patient survey data. Finally, cost-effectiveness must be measured over much longer periods than clinical markers of treatment success.

All of those factors imply that phase III clinical trials must expand in sample size, duration, and cost. In addition, the sites used for phase III trials must shift to managed care environments in which more real-world protocols can be tested and complete health care use data are available.

J. Howard Beales's study dealt with the impact of marketing on pharmaceutical sales. He used sales data for the second and third indications for selected drugs. While his is an excellent study, its usefulness may be limited as direct marketing to the physician becomes less common. Beales's study does, however, document that second and third indications for older drugs often result in increased sales as new and useful applications for old products are discovered. Unfortunately, the growth of managed care may significantly curb clinical research in this area. Managed care organizations are reluctant to cover experimental uses of pharmaceuticals and may constrain clinicians from prescribing outside established protocols. Restrictions on this avenue of clinical experimentation reduce the likelihood that new indications will be discovered and documented. Equally important, the drug's manufacturer is unlikely to finance the cost of such research, given the limited patent life of the product and the time necessary to conduct the research. The National Institutes of Health may need to fill this void.

Finally, the move to drug treatment protocols based on cost-effectiveness data, the patient's clinical risk factors, and his socioeconomic characteristics will dramatically increase the complexity of prescribing for physicians. Such complexity may create new clinical roles for pharmacists as the "drug experts" within the managed care organization. Outpatient pharmacists may be given gatekeeper authority with regard to protocol adherence and may even assume prescribing duties for routine patients. In summary, all parties in the pharmaceutical market face new challenges as health care reform unfolds.

References

Frech, H. E., III. *Regulating Doctors' Fees*. Washington, D.C.: AEI Press, 1991.

General Accounting Office. *Medicaid: Changes in Drug Prices Paid by HMOs and Hospitals since Enactment of Rebate Provisions*. Washington, D.C.: Government Printing Office, January 1993.

———. *Medicaid: Changes in Drug Prices Paid by VA and DOD since Enactment of Rebate Provisions*. Washington, D.C.: Government Printing Office, September 1991.

———. *Prescription Drugs: Companies Typically Charge More in the United States than in Canada*. Washington, D.C.: Government Printing Office, September 1992.

———. *Prescription Drugs: Companies Typically Charge More in the United States than in the United Kingdom*. Washington, D.C. Governmment Printing Office, January 1994.

McMillian, A. "Trends in Medicare Health Maintenance Organization Enrollment: 1986–93." *Health Care Financing Review* 15 (1993): 135–46.

PART FIVE

The Future of the Pharmaceutical Industry

Commentary

Robert B. Helms

In this concluding part of the volume we shall consider what might lie ahead for the pharmaceutical industry. Predicting the future is easy—anyone can do it. The difficult part is deciding which of the many predictions we would want to believe. Despite the poor reputation of economists for predicting the future, they do not have a monopoly on poor predictions. They face plenty of competition from other social scientists, theologians, political commentators, and stock market analysts. The following are my own thoughts about what public policy developments are likely to have the strongest effects on the future of the industry.

First, consider what we know about the economic behavior of the managers of the individual firms that make up the pharmaceutical industry. The future of the industry will be determined by the investment decisions its managers make, so I think it important to ask what will affect those managers' expectations about future revenues. The research and development process, as the studies in this volume have demonstrated, is characterized by large, upfront costs and by revenues that only start several years after the initial investments. The revenues may be large, but both their amounts and durations are uncertain. Faced with such uncertainty, managers making investment decisions must naturally base them largely on their expectations about future revenue streams. As Henry Grabowski and John Vernon have shown us in chapter 9, we should view this process as a lottery where the large winner is a rare event.

The international nature of the pharmaceutical market also affects the manager's expectations about the revenue he or she may eventually receive from a new product. As Patricia Danzon, Lacy Glenn Thomas, and Henry Grabowski and John Vernon have shown us in this volume, international sales are an important part of the market for almost every company. In international markets pharmaceutical company managers face a variety of pricing possibilities brought on by both the behavior of competitors and the public policies affecting the company's freedom

355

to set its own prices. Compared with most other developed countries, the United States remains both the largest and the most unregulated of the major international markets. Thus, the expected revenue from sales in the United States has a dominant effect on the investment decisions of the typical industry manager.

But sales to other markets are also important, even if they occur under regulatory schemes that substantially restrict the expected revenue. We can better understand this situation by considering the economic theory of multipart pricing.[1] The theory explains how a firm can increase its revenue by charging the highest price that the market or the regulatory authorities will allow in each market.[2] A firm can add to total revenue by selling in a small and price-controlled market as long as the regulated price covers the firm's marginal cost of production and distribution (and as long as those buying at the lower price cannot resell the product for a higher price in another market). But such a strategy can work only if the firm has access to a larger and uncontrolled market like the United States to cover its long-term research and development costs.

While any firm would prefer that all markets were free and unregulated, it can still maintain the intensity of its research effort if it has pricing freedom in a large enough portion of its total market to earn a competitive profit on its investments. In my view, the United States, by not following the regulatory strategies of other countries, has helped to maintain the flow of investment funds into risky pharmaceutical investments at a time when the budget policies of state-run health systems have become increasingly binding. But with the United States playing such a pivotal role in managers' expectations, the adoption of a price-control policy in the United States would have a substantially greater effect on the industry's innovation than the adoption of a similar policy in a smaller country. As we have seen in other industries, when future revenues are both uncertain and delayed, managers' ex-

---

1. This pricing model is also known as price discrimination. For a textbook explanation, see Alchian and Allen (1969, 133–37). For applications of this theory to two health policy issues, see Morrisey (1994) and Berndt (1994).

2. The theory of multipart pricing explains how sellers with some market power and the ability to keep markets separate (prevent reselling) may be able to set different prices to different buyers depending on the intensity (elasticity) of demand by each class of consumer. Substituting the regulatory determination of prices for consumer behavior in some markets is a natural extension of that model, since the effect on the firm of facing different restrictions on its ability to set prices in separate markets is the same.

pectations about future revenue streams play a critical role in decisions about making the initial investment.[3]

In addition to reducing the total amount of investment in R&D, the imposition of price controls in the United States can also change the kinds of products that firms will develop for the market. At any one time, the managers of a pharmaceutical firm will have a portfolio of possible new products that are candidates for additional research and clinical trials. Like any portfolio of future investments, some will appear to be more risky than others. Some will be relatively straightforward in their adoption of known medical knowledge, and others will be only a gleam in a researcher's eye. The decrease in expected revenue that price controls would cause will send a strong signal to managers to pick the less risky potential new products. The investments managers will not make are those that the medical researchers consider to be the longer shots. The eventual effects of such a change in policy will be that the pharmaceutical industry will not produce the information that a higher level of investment would have produced on the riskier class of potential products.[4]

As Heinz Redwood (1993, 79) points out, another effect of price controls will be an increase in expenditures on promotion. When managers face the expected decline in revenue from price controls, we can expect them to try to maintain market share and current cash flow by increasing promotional expenditures on existing products.[5] Redwood reports that promotional expenditures have risen rapidly in France and Italy as a result of price controls.

The losers will be those future patients who would have benefited from the products that managers decided not to research, investigate, and market. One truism about predicting the future is that we have to deal with so many hypotheticals. By necessity, both the future patients and the future benefits are hypothetical. But on the basis of past his-

---

3. For one example of the effects of price controls in markets characterized by high risk and delayed revenues, see Helms (1974).

4. This does not mean that all information has a net positive value. A competitive market with market-determined prices would be expected to produce additional information up to the point where the marginal value is equal to the marginal cost of producing that information. To the extent that regulation reduces the level of market prices, firms will produce a smaller quantity of information with net positive value.

5. As Redwood also points out, the firm may increase R&D expenditures on products that are already in its pipeline to hasten the marketing of existing products. But that is likely to be a transitional effect that will play out as the flow of new potential products declines over time.

tory, we can make two statements about those hypothetical future events that have a high probability of becoming true. First, we know from experience that both the incidence of disease and the expenditure on medical care are strongly related to the patient's age. Second, we know that there was a relatively large increase in birth rates in the United States and most developed countries following World War II. Those two facts allow us to predict with some confidence that there will be a relatively large increase in the demand for medical care as the baby-boom generation continues to age into the next century. In fact, the official actuarial projections for both Social Security and Medicare show large increases in expenditures just after 2010, when the first of the baby-boom generation begins to turn sixty-five (OASDI 1994, 168, table III.A2). If we assume that it takes approximately twenty years from the initial idea for a new pharmaceutical product to the time a firm makes it available to consumers, then the effects of whatever to-day's change in expectations may be having on future supplies will occur at approximately the same time as that increase in the demand for medical care. Price controls today have the ironic potential of reducing the value of some aggregate statistic on current health expenditures but leaving a lot of future pain and suffering that might have been prevented.

In my view, the baby boomers who are now approaching fifty years old should think about the health problems their own aging parents face. Unfortunately, we do not now have the knowledge to help all of them, but we should be able to do more for those problems in the future if the rate of medical research productivity stays anywhere close to its current rate.

There are two aspects of this prediction that are especially difficult for most people to understand. The first is the relationship between the level of investment and the output from medical research. While no one can guarantee that any past trend will continue, there is a strong historical relationship between investments in medical research and the rate of discovery. To help people understand this relationship, it is important for pharmaceutical firms to use their scientific researchers to tell the public about the difficult process of R&D and the potential for new discoveries. Knowledge of how both an R&D infrastructure and competition among firms improve productivity is key to a better understanding of the economic behavior of the pharmaceutical industry. In addition, people need to understand the incentive structure that competitive economic markets create. The case against price controls does not mean that the industry should get special protection from market competition. Both price controls and protection against competition are counterproductive.

358

Economists typically argue against using price controls because they change the incentives of both producers and consumers so that they reduce the potential to produce efficiently what consumers desire and what technology allows. Competitive markets, even if they also put downward pressure on prices, have the opposite effect on a firm's incentives to innovate. By rewarding those who are productive and penalizing those who are unproductive, competitive markets increase the likelihood that firms will find, develop, and market products that will meet consumers' needs. Both price controls and the creation of protected industry cartels lower the probability of achieving the level of efficient innovation that competitive markets foster.

There is little doubt that all health care markets are becoming more economically competitive. The increase in the size of purchasing groups and the development of new data systems present new challenges to the pharmaceutical industry. But this new emphasis on cost-effectiveness does not diminish the potential for pharmaceutical products to compete effectively against other types of medical services or to provide new possibilities to cure diseases or to reduce suffering and pain. Those firms that can successfully develop new products have the potential to capture both profits and market share. But a truly competitive market does not guarantee that result to any one firm. Both history and economic theory tell us that a movement toward government price controls guarantees both inefficiency and a slower rate of scientific progress. The future well-being of consumers requires that we pursue policies to promote competitive markets and resist the temptation of price controls.

References

Alchian, Armen A., and William R. Allen. *Exchange and Production: Theory in Use*. Belmont, Calif.: Wadsworth Publishing Company, 1969.

Berndt, Ernst. *Uniform Pharmaceutical Pricing: An Economic Analysis*. Washington, D.C.: AEI Press, 1994.

Helms, Robert B. *Natural Gas Regulation:An Evaluation of FPC Price Controls*. Washington, D.C.: AEI Press, 1974.

Morrisey, Michael A. *Cost Shifting in Health Care: Separating Evidence from Rhetoric*. Washington, D.C.: AEI Press, 1994.

OASDI Board of Trustees. *Annual Report of the Board of Trustees of the Federal Old Age and Survivors Insurance and Disability Insurance Trust Funds*. Washington, D.C.: Government Printing Office, 1994.

Redwood, Heinz. "New Drugs in the World Market: Incentives and Impediments to Innovation." *American Enterprise* 4 (July/August 1993): 72–80.

Frederic M. Scherer

I have been asked to talk about what the future holds—a task that must be addressed with considerable respect for human fallibility. What does the future hold? It seems to me that very exciting things are happening on the scientific front. We are learning a lot about the biochemical mechanisms of disease. We are learning how to focus on a class of substances that will interact with disease-causing mechanisms. We are learning how to manipulate living organisms and to clone interesting proteins that will act therapeutically. The advances in science are simply breathtaking. Thus, if we do not adopt bad national policy toward the pharmaceutical industry, during the next two decades we shall enjoy another golden age of pharmaceutical discovery.

How might we adopt bad national policy toward that industry? One way is to impose price regulation. I agree with Henry Grabowski that the kind of regulation we are most likely to have will be Willy Sutton regulation—targeting the blockbusters and beating their prices and profits down without worrying about the many other not-so-profitable entities. If we do it that way, it could have disastrous effects, because the *average* profitability of drug R&D will fall sharply. With lower expected profits, there will be less investment in the discovery and testing of new drugs.

Events subsequent to this conference have revealed a decisive rejection of the Clinton health reform task force's recommendations, including its proposal for a form of Willy Sutton regulation. Such initiatives can be considered dead, at least until 1997. But health care costs are likely to continue escalating, and at some time the question of drug price regulation is likely to reappear. After the Willy Sutton approach, the next most likely alternative, which is related to Willy Sutton regulation but more concerned about rates of return on investment for everyone, would be the sort of system used in the United Kingdom. The basic idea, analogous to the way electric utilities have been regulated in the United States, is that each company is given a rate base covering the company's complete array of pharmaceutical sales. Included in the rate base is the value of plant, equipment, and inventories *plus* capitalized investment in research and development. The firm is then allowed a "fair" rate of return on that rate base.

I have simulated that kind of regulation by making assumptions about the distribution of sales, production costs, physical assets, and R&D investments similar to those Henry G. Grabowski and John M. Vernon observed in chapter 9. In brief, I assumed essentially the same log-normal skewed distribution of sales outcomes that they found and

FIGURE C5–1
COMPANY-SIZE IMPLICATIONS OF U.K. RETURN ON ASSETS REGULATION

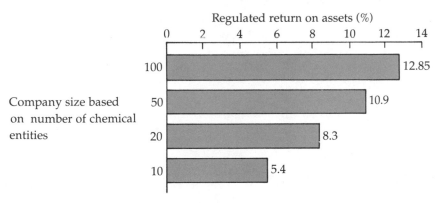

NOTE: Assumes log normal sales distribution and maximum 15 percent return.

used a random number program to create 1,000 simulated new drug product histories. The average return on investment without regulation for this sample of new chemical entities turned out to be 22.3 percent.

Then I cut down the return for each company to 15 percent if it exceeded that presumably generous threshold.[1] I then formed randomized portfolios for companies of different sizes—ranging from 10 to 100 new chemical entities in the company's portfolio in any given year. Figure C5–1 summarizes the result. For the companies marketing 100 new chemical entities, the average return under this regulatory system was 12.85 percent. For those with ten new chemical entities, at the other extreme, the average return was 5.4 percent.

How can this "fair" system of regulation yield such wildly disparate rates of return across company size classes? The reason is the following. A small company, by definition, has very few new chemical entities. If the company is lucky and one of its new drugs is a blockbuster, the regulatory system will tightly constrain the company's return on assets, because the company has few other investments in new chemical entities in its rate base. If the small company is less lucky, the market will constrain its return. So small companies are held back by either the regulatory system or the market.

Big companies, on the other hand, have large portfolios, with a few hits and lots of misses. The many misses increase the company's

---

1. Recall that in chapter 10 Stewart C. Myers and Lakshmi Shyam-Sunder found the average cost of pharmaceutical companies' capital to be 10.5 percent.

rate base, so that the firm can retain more profits or quasi rents from the relatively few big hits. In other words, the large companies have a larger base of assets over which to pool regulatory risk. That is basically how the United Kingdom's system would work, if implemented mechanically according to the procedures our British cousins articulate. Clearly, unless important exceptions were made (as they probably are in the United Kingdom, given the informal way in which the system is implemented), it would work very much to the disadvantage of small companies. Considering America's revealed preference for close adherence to clear-cut and rigid procedural rules, it is doubtful that an analogous U.S. system would be able to compensate for the large-firm bias. That is an important reason for concern.

What else lies in the future? Clearly, there will be substantial changes in the mode of purchasing. The formulary committees of health maintenance organizations are going to play an increasingly important role. There will be more concentration of power on the purchasing side and more playing off one company against another, one chemical entity against another, to win price discounts.

To Ronald Hansen's skeptical observation in chapter 14 about the feasibility of benefit-cost analysis I respond, how can you possibly *not* make benefit-cost comparisons? Somehow or other, the people who decide on formularies must weigh benefits against costs, explicitly or implicitly.

The increased countervailing power strong drug purchasers exert will reduce margins. Alternatively, or concurrently, regulation could reduce margins. If I had my choice, I would let the power of buyers do the job, rather than regulation, because buyers will purchase those drugs that really are therapeutically superior, even if they are sold at high prices. That will generate consistent incentives to search for and to develop new drugs that are therapeutically superior. Under regulation, and especially Willy Sutton regulation, drug R&D incentives are more likely to be skewed.

In the future, safety and efficacy regulation will continue to be important. If the regulatory decision lag that Grabowski and Vernon cite in chapter 9 persists—two-and-a-half years from the filing of a new drug application to actual FDA approval—there is a serious problem. On this score, I have a small quarrel with the Grabowski and Vernon study. They simulate how cutting one year of decision-making time from the two-and-a-half years would affect the stream of discounted benefits minus costs. They find that net discounted quasi rents would be increased by $18 million. Their assumption, however, is that the change affects only the cost side. That is to say, costs are brought one year nearer the year of market introduction, and therefore, the R&D

costs accumulate to a smaller value. It seems to me, however, that quicker approval will also have an effect on benefits. If key patents do not expire in the meantime, the drug developer will have one more year of patent life, and therefore one more year of peak revenues. Re-simulating a model very similar to that of Grabowski and Vernon, but with benefits on both the cost and revenue sides from eliminating one year of FDA decision-making time, I estimate a net gain of $42 million per new chemical entity. If my estimate is anywhere near correct, there must be strenuous efforts to reduce the delays in FDA decision making.

Peter Barton Hutt

The health of our country is directly dependent upon the health of our pharmaceutical industry. Progress against the major diseases and disabilities that continue to afflict us must come, if at all, in the form of new drugs, biologics, and devices designed to treat those problems.

Any rational public policy directed toward enhancing the public health would therefore place a high priority on pharmaceutical research and development. It is quite apparent, however, that this is not occurring. Many politicians have strongly criticized the pharmaceutical industry for excessive prices and profits. The Food and Drug Administration is extremely restrictive and conservative in its review and approval of new pharmaceutical products.

An objective review of current national policy toward the pharmaceutical industry would therefore lead to the conclusion that we are attempting to hinder and even destroy that industry, not to nurture and promote it. Approaching the matter analytically, it appears that our national policy is diametrically opposed to our national health needs.

One can learn a great deal by attempting to design a system that would, in fact, do maximum harm to the pharmaceutical industry. From this, we could then analyze our current policy to determine the true impact of our present approach to this vital industry. The ten easy lessons on how to destroy the U.S. pharmaceutical industry follow.

Lesson 1: Hinder Clinical Investigation of New Drugs

This can be accomplished at all stages of research and development. Unnecessary animal studies can be required before permitting clinical investigation. A lengthy and complex investigational new drug submission can be required before investigation in humans. Meetings to discuss proposed protocols can be made difficult to obtain so that the

363

pharmaceutical industry will have a difficult time knowing what the FDA requires. Clinical holds can be placed on human investigation, for long periods of time, to prevent immediate determinations of clinical utility. Finally, the pharmaceutical industry can be prohibited from charging for drugs used as part of a clinical investigation. That substantially increases the cost of the investigation and reduces the number of products that the manufacturer can investigate. Each one of these, by itself, can constitute a major obstacle to the clinical development of a new drug. Combined, they can drastically reduce the number of new products that the industry could afford to investigate.

Lesson 2: Delay the Approval of New Pharmaceutical Products

Before a pharmaceutical manufacturer can market a new product, the FDA must approve it through a new drug application, a product license application, or a premarket approval application. The FDA's rapid review and approval of products would expedite patients' use of new pharmaceutical products at the lowest possible cost. Accordingly, to inflict harm on the pharmaceutical industry, the FDA can slow down its approval process as much as possible and make it as costly as feasible. FDA reviewers can refuse to meet with company representatives to resolve issues. Individual reviewers can pore over data for months and years on end without coming to a clear resolution. The agency can forward questions to the applicants on a periodic basis in the form of letters and memoranda rather than through telephone calls and face-to-face meetings. If successful in this approach, the FDA can take two to three years to review any application, with the result that the pharmaceutical manufacturer's investment could be in the hundreds of millions of dollars per product. This can drive out all but the largest companies, frighten off new venture capital, and raise to extremely high levels the prices of the few drugs that get through the system.

Lesson 3: Raise the Requirements for an Acceptable Manufacturing Process

Policy makers can impose a regulation that prevents the approval of a new pharmaceutical product until the FDA has certified that the process used to make the product is acceptable. Because the government has a stranglehold on the company at the preapproval stage, the most conservative and demanding requirements can be imposed without any fear that the company can effectively challenge them. The agency can then require the manufacturer to set forth in its application for approval every detail of the manufacturing process. That requirement would lengthen the application, increase time needed for FDA review, and provide a much larger target for FDA disapproval. Once approval is obtained, it is still possible for the agency to conduct periodic inspections to ensure that the manufacturer does not deviate from standards imposed by the individual inspectors. Any such deviation can result in the FDA's shutting down the plant, regardless of whether the deviation bears upon a significant public health concern. Those approaches are certain to reduce the number of companies that can afford to invest in pharmaceutical manufacturing facilities and new products.

Lesson 4: Encourage Generic Competition as Quickly as Possible

Once the cost of discovering and obtaining FDA approval of a new pharmaceutical product is raised to as high a level as possible through the first three lessons, the time within which that investment is recouped can be reduced to as short a period as possible. Policy makers can do this by reducing the patent life from the statutory seventeen years to a much shorter effective patent life because of the long time needed to satisfy FDA requirements. To the extent that patent extension or market exclusivity is granted, it can be less than the actual amount of time it took for the company to develop the product and obtain approval for marketing. This can force the pharmaceutical industry to raise its prices to attempt to recoup the investment in the relatively short period before generic competition begins.

Lesson 5: Impose Additional Taxes

In addition to the extraordinary costs policy makers impose by adopting lessons one through four, they could add a specific tax for every product application to help finance the FDA review and approval process. Such a measure can further help to drive out small entrepreneurs, reduce the number of new pharmaceutical products being researched and developed, and raise the cost of those that make it through the process.

Lesson 6: Hinder Export before U.S. Approval

If a new pharmaceutical product made in the United States could be exported to other countries where it is already approved for marketing, the company would be able to sell the product abroad, finance the U.S. development and regulatory costs, and ultimately reduce the price of the drug to patients upon ultimate FDA approval. By imposing the requirement of obtaining an export license from the FDA, establishing conservative criteria for granting that license, and retaining the threat of license revocation even for minor deviations, policy makers can greatly reduce the possibility of a revenue stream from abroad. Hindering the export of unapproved drugs can force American companies to export their technology, build their manufacturing facilities abroad, and restructure their entire approach to research and development so that they can emphasize foreign marketing before domestic marketing.

Lesson 7: Prohibit Public Education about Unapproved Uses

For any approved pharmaceutical product, there are inevitably unapproved uses that are brought to light through routine use of the product by thousands of physicians on millions of patients throughout the country. The medical literature routinely reports those uses. The FDA can prohibit the companies that market those drugs from providing any form of public education or information relating to such unapproved uses. That restriction can help prevent physicians from obtaining accurate and truthful information about such unapproved uses and inhibit the use of those drugs in preventing and treating disease in patients. Such a policy can limit sales and reduce the profits that manufacturers would otherwise obtain from those products.

Lesson 8: Eliminate Incentives for Industry to Obtain Approval of Unapproved Uses

By maintaining strict requirements for investigation and approval of unapproved uses, providing no patent term extension upon approval of those uses, and allowing no effective form of market exclusivity to permit recoupment of investment, the FDA can effectively persuade the pharmaceutical industry not to undertake the work necessary to investigate and obtain FDA approval of new unapproved uses of approved products. Combined with the prohibition against public education about such uses set forth in lesson seven, this measure can ensure that the sale of those products for appropriate uses is kept to a minimum and that the profitability of the products is reduced.

Lesson 9: Hinder the Use of Efficient New Methods of Manufacture

After the manufacturer has applied for FDA approval of a new product, pharmaceutical firms continually develop new manufacturing methods to increase efficiency, reduce cost, and produce a better product. To make approval of manufacturing changes as difficult and costly as possible, the FDA can require approval of virtually all manufacturing changes, can impede the approval process in accordance with lesson two, and can thus increase the regulatory costs so that they approach the cost savings that the firm would achieve by the new manufacturing procedures. The agency can make the time needed to obtain approval of manufacturing changes so long that, once approval is obtained, the firm has developed further process modifications. Thus, the firm can face continuing requirements to apply for manufacturing changes driven by modern technology. In the alternative, the FDA can force companies engaged in a global market to establish manufacturing facilities abroad that will employ the latest technology and manufacturing facilities in the United States that must continue to use obsolete technology.

Lesson 10: Limit Prices

After exhausting the first nine lessons, all of which are intended to raise costs to the pharmaceutical industry and thus prices to patients, the only thing left for the government to do is to set a limit on prices and thus control the profitability of the industry. The government can do this by establishing mandatory rebates or by adopting any of the mechanisms set forth by the Clinton administration in its proposal for health care reform. To the extent that the government restricts profitability, it will curtail investment and reduce the number of new products developed.

Our current public policy incorporates all ten of those lessons. We are further advanced in some of them than we are in others, but we have not failed to adopt a single one. Rather than encouraging and fostering the development of new products to enhance our public health, the current design of public policy damages the pharmaceutical industry and thus the potential for developing those new products. Unless we change that policy, the prospect for developing important new pharmaceutical products in the future will be far diminished from what it could be.

Claude E. Barfield

I have no claim to special expertise in the pharmaceutical industry, but I shall discuss the developing policy climate regarding industrial policy and trade policy, both of which I think will affect the pharmaceutical industry as well as other industries.

For those of you who are economists, it seems to me that the ad-

367

ministration is trying to put into practical policy the ideas of a young group of economists who came to the fore in the mid-1980s, headed by Paul Krugman and others at MIT, the so-called strategic trade policy advocates. Oversimplifying, these economists argue that there are, under certain circumstances, reasons for the government to intervene in the market, and, in alliance with business, to foster a high-technology, high-wage sector through subsidy on the one hand or protection on the other.

A major theme of mine will be one of Adam Smith's: businessmen do not get together even to have tea without a conspiracy against the public interest. I would argue that if we substituted a gathering of businessmen and government bureaucrats, we would have the same result.

So far, to be fair to the administration, we have not seen a lot of movement in terms of money and resources, but that is because of the budget deficit that Ronald Reagan handed to the Bush and the Clinton administrations. I do, however, see the handwriting on the wall.

Ironically, the handwriting on the wall has caused Paul Krugman to be increasingly acerbic in his comments on where the administration is moving both in industrial or technology policy and in trade policy. The greatest subsidy to technology is the several billion dollars allocated each year for the next couple of years for defense conversion. Under this program, firms that had been receiving federal funding to support research and development when national security was the motivating force will receive federal subsidies to develop commercial technologies. Those firms should instead be forced to produce and market goods and services in the private sector. Past commercial technological successes developed as a result of the incentives of the private enterprise system (Weidenbaum 1994).

A second major subsidy that the Clinton administration announced is $2 billion to the maritime industry, an industry that performed miserably during the Persian Gulf War (Quartel 1991). To be fair, the Office of Management and Budget opposed that subsidy.

Finally, in October 1993, Chrysler, Ford, and General Motors entered into the Partnership for a New Generation of Vehicles with the government to produce automobiles that would be more environmentally friendly for the twenty-first century. The automobile companies immediately turned around and, as a price for their agreement to be dragged into that partnership, began arguing for relaxation of the emissions standards. While there may be very legitimate reasons for the request for reduced emissions standards, the partnership and the subsequent request appear to be a quid pro quo.

Over the next few years the government may sing a siren call to lure a number of industries to join with the administration. But there is a darker side of government, which we have already seen with its view of the pharmaceutical industry: an ill-disguised contempt based on assumptions that managers of pharmaceutical companies are money-grabbing, money-grubbing industrialists.

Another example of the dark side of government is a policy the administration has endorsed relating to its trade priorities: where it will go after other governments in opening markets and where it will defend U.S. industries. The administration's first priority as a trade policy is to require U.S. multinationals to agree that whenever the government goes to bat for them, they will produce their products and keep jobs in the United States. The administration's second priority is to make concessions to foreign multinationals that would also agree to locate their production here. Far down the list of priorities—third in fact—are U.S. multinationals that would not make such a commitment.

If the administration implements its intended policy in any major way, it will have extensive implications not just for the pharmaceutical industry but for a number of our leading, high-technology industries. If the administration makes trade policy on the basis of jobs in the United States on a short-term basis, that is a formula for disaster. If the United States persists in the unilateralism characterized by Section 301 of the Trade Act of 1974, in increased antidumping actions combined with local-content and rules-of-origin regulations and voluntary export restrictions for the Japanese, in more state-sponsored Buy-American programs, and in continued large-scale subsidies, its trading partners are sure to follow suit. In addition, the administration must eschew calls for imposing on its trading partners labor standards and environmental regulations that simply mask protectionism.

Clearly, government policies—tax policy, competition policy, and trade policy, for example—will affect industries. Therefore, the government must be aware that when it puts in place a social policy or an economic policy that it considers a legitimate goal, such a policy can affect competitiveness. What the government must especially consider is whether it is capable of making decisions about which industries, technologies, and projects to support. After a decade of extensive research, the economics profession is no nearer to offering government bureaucracies very strong guidance on which industries to promote and on which policies relating to which industries it should put in place to advance the competitiveness of the United States or of any other nation.

I draw as a final example Laura Tyson's *Who's Bashing Whom?*, a 1992 study of trade conflict in high-technology industries. The book started out to be one in which she promised that at the end the government would have a better analytic foundation for choosing among

369

technologies. Successive drafts were so criticized that the book which emerged was largely about trade policy, not industrial policy. At the beginning of the book's published version, Tyson simply assumed—without proof—that the government can successfully choose among technologies.

With the Clinton administration, the pharmaceutical industry as well as other high-technology industries will be living in an environment with a number of lures and allures. They must be wary of the dangerous trap at the end of the road.

References

Quartel, Rob. "America's Welfare Queen Fleet: The Need for Maritime Policy Reform." *Regulation* 14 (Summer 1991): 58–67.

Tyson, Laura D. *Who's Bashing Whom? Trade Conflict in High-Technology Industries*. Washington, D.C.: Institute for International Economics, 1992.

Weidenbaum, Murray. "A New Technology Policy for the United States?" *Regulation* 16 (4) (1994): 18–28.

Index

*This book was edited by Leigh Tripoli and Cheryl Weissman of the
publications staff of the American Enterprise Institute.
The text was set in Palatino, a typeface designed by the twentieth-century
Swiss designer Hermann Zapf.
The figures were drawn by Hordur Karlsson.
The index was prepared by Shirley Kessel.
Coghill Composition Company of Richmond, Virginia,
set the type, and Data Reproductions Corporation
of Rochester Hills, Michigan, printed and bound the book,
using permanent acid-free paper.*

AEI Press is the publisher for the American Enterprise Institute for Public Pol-
icy Research, 1150 17th Street, N.W., Washington, D.C. 20036; *Christopher C.
DeMuth,* publisher; *Dana Lane,* director; *Ann Petty,* editor; *Leigh Tripoli,* editor;
Cheryl Weissman, editor; *Lisa Roman,* assistant editor (rights and permission).